Jean Chatzky, award-winning journalist and bestselling author, is the financial editor for NBC's *Today*, a contributing editor for *More*, a columnist for the *New York Daily News*, and a contributor to *Oprah*. Her previous books include *Pay It Down!, Make Money, Not Excuses* and *The Difference*. Jean has been recognized as an exceptional journalist. Recently she received the Clarion Award for magazine columns from the Association of Women in Communications, and her radio show received a Gracie Award from American Women in Radio and Television. Jean lives with her family in Westchester, New York.

MONEY
911

JEAN CHATZKY

with Arielle McGowen

MONEY
911

Your Most Pressing Money

Questions Answered,

Your Money Emergencies

Solved

HARPER

NEW YORK • LONDON • TORONTO • SYDNEY

This book is written as a source of information only, and should not be considered a substitute for the advice, decisions, or judgment of the reader's professional advisors.

All efforts have been made to ensure the accuracy of the information contained in this book as of the date published. The author and the publisher expressly disclaim responsibility for any adverse effects arising from the use or application of the information contained herein.

Nothing herein should be construed as an endorsement by NBC of any product or service discussed in this book.

FIRST EDITION

Designed by Kate Nichols

Library of Congress Cataloging-in-Publication Data

Chatzky, Jean Sherman, 1964–
  Money 911: your most pressing money questions answered, your money emergencies solved/Jean Chatzky.—1st ed.
     p. cm.
  Includes index.
  ISBN 978–0–06–179869–6
  1. Finance, Personal. I. Title. II. Title: Money nine-one-one.
  HG179.C5358 2010
  332.024—dc22

                                                                    2009028096

ISBN 978-0-06-179869-6

10 11 12 13 14   WBC/RRD   10 9 8 7 6 5 4 3 2 1

CONTENTS

CHAPTER 1: DEBT ▪ 1–36

CHAPTER 5: BUDGETING AND CUTTING SPENDING ▪ 117–149

CHAPTER 6: CREDIT ▪ 150–171

CHAPTER 7: REAL ESTATE/MORTGAGES ▪ 172–211

MONEY
911

CHAPTER 1

DEBT

1. What is a debt settlement company? How do these companies work? How much do they charge? Should I use one to get rid of my credit card debt?

A: Debt settlement companies work as a middleman between you and your creditor. If all goes well (and that's a big if), you should be able to settle your debts for cents on the dollar. You'll also pay a fee to the debt settlement company, usually either a percentage of the total debt you have or a percentage of the total amount forgiven.

If you'd asked me a few years ago about debt settlement companies, I probably would have told you to avoid them. But things have changed a bit. The Bankruptcy Reform Act of 2005 made it harder for individuals to file bankruptcy, which is always the last resort. Unfortunately, simultaneously consumers racked up so much debt that counseling companies—which are higher up on my list if you need help managing your debt—are sometimes unable to help. So if you fall into this camp, debt settlement may be something to consider.

Here's how it works: The debt settlement company will direct you to stop paying your creditor and instead send the money directly to them each month. The company's goal is to demonstrate to your creditor that you don't have the money to pay up—that's your leverage. After a few months, the company will typically go to the creditor and say, "I'm holding X dollars on behalf of your customer. He doesn't have the money to pay you, so you should take this amount as a settlement or you'll end up with nothing." If the creditor wants to get paid badly enough, it will take the money.

All of this sounds great, but there are negatives. For starters, during the three- to four-month stretch that you're not paying your creditor, your account will accrue late fees and possibly even "over the limit" fees. Both of those fees add to the total debt and to the debt settlement company's fee. Not paying your creditors can do a serious number on your credit score, and having a settlement on your credit history drags it down even further. If you start out in the high 600s, for example, your credit score could be well into the 400s by the time you've gone through debt settlement, especially if you settle more than one account.

And besides: You really don't need to hire a debt settlement company to negotiate with your creditors. Unless you have multiple accounts that you need to negotiate and you think the project is just too big to tackle on your own, you're better off just calling your creditors directly. For what to say, see the script included with the next question.

I Also Need to Know . . .

Q: **How much is working with a debt settlement company likely to cost me?**

A: To be honest, you might have trouble getting a straight-up answer to this question even from the debt settlement company itself, and if you do, that's a reason to walk away. The best companies will charge a percentage, usually about 15%, of the amount of debt that they're able to settle for you. Others may charge 15% of the total debt you have when you enter the program. If the fee is calculated this way, not only are you paying too much but you're also not holding the company accountable to get you the best results.

But if you are able to settle, you'll be getting off rather easy. Debt settlement companies can sometimes get you off the hook for a large percentage of your debt—in many cases, up to 50% will be written off.

Q: **How long will the settlement stay on my credit report?**

A: That you settled a debt instead of paying in full will stay on your credit report for as long as the individual accounts are reported, which is typically seven years from the date that the account was settled. Unlike with bankruptcy, there isn't a separate line on your credit report dedicated to debt settlement, so each account settled will be listed as a charge-off. If a debt has gone into collection, it will be on your report for 7½ years from the date you fell behind with your creditor.

Q: How can I check a debt settlement company's credibility?
A: For starters, make sure that the company is a member of The Association of Settlement Companies (TASC), a trade association that represents debt settlement firms and outlines standards that they agree to meet. The association has a search tool on its Web site that allows you to find a registered member in your area. Once you've pinpointed a few viable choices, ask for an initial consultation. You should also make sure the company has a clean record with the Better Business Bureau (BBB), which you can do at www .bbb.org/us/.

Q: Do I need a lawyer?
A: You don't. If you're filing bankruptcy, you will likely want to hire an attorney. But for debt settlement, a company is sufficient, or as I said, you can often do the legwork on your own.

Four Things You Need to Know About Any Debt Settlement Company

The Fee: It should be based on the amount of debt that the company is able to settle for you.
Red Flag: If the company charges a percentage of your total debt upfront, walk away.

The Return Policy: There should be a money-back guarantee in place of at least 30 days.
Red Flag: If the company doesn't offer a guarantee, find one that does.

The Timeline: No company can promise an end date, but if you have multiple debts, the first one should be settled within a year.

Red Flag: If a company promises a faster return, it may be spinning the truth.

Where Is My Money? Once you send it to the debt settlement company, it should be kept in an FDIC-insured bank account. (The FDIC, or Federal Deposit Insurance Corporation, insures bank deposits, among other duties.)

Red Flag: If the company asks you to hold on to the money or doesn't keep it in an insured account, the company isn't doing its job.

▶ An Example

You have $35,000 in credit card debt that is settled through a debt settlement company. Forty percent of your debt, or $14,000, is forgiven, and you pay $21,000 in full upfront. The debt settlement company charges you 15% of the amount of debt that is forgiven, or $2,100.

- Total paid: $23,100
- Total forgiven: $14,000
- Total saved: $9,000
- Total damage to your credit score: –150 points

2. How do you negotiate with a credit card company? What happens when you settle your debts for less than you owe?

A: I've been seeing this question more with every passing week. You fall a bit behind on a credit card bill, your interest rate soars, your minimum payment rises, and you start falling more and more behind every month. You don't see an end. But you don't want to file bankruptcy either. What you can do—and should do—is negotiate. Here are the steps.

- **Prepare your case.** Why are you in this situation? You need a clear, legitimate excuse for why you're behind, such as a lay-off, divorce, or medical emergency. Be prepared to back up the circumstances with supporting documents. Anything you have to substantiate your story—including proof that you have, for instance, been actively looking for a new job—will help.

- **Call your creditor directly.** In most cases, if you've gotten to this point, you've already received a letter or phone message from your creditor with the name and extension of a representative. If you haven't, you can call the toll-free number on your bill, but keep in mind that the person who answers may not have the power to negotiate a settlement. Ask to speak to someone who is either a supervisor or in the settlement department, if the creditor has one (as many do).
- **Make an offer.** After explaining why you're in trouble, ask the creditor if the company would be willing to accept a smaller amount. Start negotiations at about 30% of the total amount due, with the end goal of paying 50%.
- **Ask the creditor to report to all three major credit bureaus—TransUnion, Experian, and Equifax—that the debt has been paid in full.** Sometimes a creditor is willing to do this as a bargaining point—you give the creditor cash in hand, it gives you a positive listing on your credit report— even though you haven't paid the full amount. Get this agreement in writing.
- **Write the check.** The creditor will want to see the money immediately.

One thing I want to make clear: You never want to hide from your debts. It doesn't work. You'll get much better results by being upfront, answering their calls, and responding to their letters. Delaying the inevitable only digs a deeper hole.

I Also Need to Know . . .

Q: **Does negotiating a settlement hurt my credit score?**
A: It will. Once the settlement is completed, the credit card company will report it to the credit bureaus, which will then make a notation on your credit report that that account was paid by settlement. That's going to signal to future lenders that you left the last guy hanging. That's why, as with bankruptcy, debt settlement is an extreme option, one you shouldn't take lightly. It's not just an easy, cheap way to eliminate debt.

Q: Are there tax liabilities?

A: In many cases, yes. Most people don't know this, but if you settle a debt for less than the amount you owed, you are potentially responsible for taxes on the forgiven debt. Look at it this way: You received goods and services for the full amount of debt, but you're only paying for a portion of it—sometimes less than 50%. Anything more than $600 is generally considered taxable, but the IRS will sometimes waive the tax if you can prove that your assets were less than your liabilities when the debt was settled.

3. Should I consolidate my debts?

A: Rolling all of your debts into a single loan is a good idea—in theory. In fact, it can be a great idea. But before you move forward, you need to be certain of two things: (1) that this consolidation makes sense financially and (2) that it makes sense for you personally.

A consolidation makes sense only if you can lower your overall interest rate. Many people consolidate by taking out a home equity line loan or home equity line of credit (HELOC), refinancing a mortgage, or taking out a personal loan. They then use this cheaper debt to pay off more expensive debt, most frequently credit card loans, but also auto loans, private student loans, or other debt.

You also need to understand that when you consolidate credit card debt into mortgage debt—like a home equity loan or a HELOC—you're taking an unsecured debt and turning it into a secured debt. If you default on an unsecured debt, you won't lose anything (except points on your credit score). When you default on a secured debt, the creditor takes the asset that backs up that debt. When you convert credit card debt to mortgage debt, you are securing that credit card debt with your home. That's a risky proposition.

Personally, can you handle it? In about one-third of credit card consolidations, within a short period of time, the cards come back out of the wallet, and in no time at all, they're charged back up. Then you're in an even worse position, because you have the credit card debt and the consolidation loan to worry about. You're in a hole that's twice as deep—and twice as steep.

If you have even a smidgen of doubt that you'll be able to stay away from racking up additional debt, don't do it. You must be sure—and I mean absolutely positive—that you have the will-power to pay off those credit cards and not use them again. If you are, consolidating at a lower interest rate can help you pay off your debt faster. But if there's even a small chance that you'll spiral back into debt, it's not for you.

THE MATH

If you have $20,000 on a card with an 18% interest rate and you put $300 toward paying it off each month, it will be more than 24 years before you're debt free. If, however, you transfer the debt to a $30,000 HELOC at an interest rate of 5.37%,[*] you'll be able to pay your debt off in a little more than six years.

I Also Need to Know . . .

Q: In this tighter credit market, what sort of a credit score do I need to qualify?

A: Even in the days of the tightest credit in 2008, HELOCs and home equity loans were being made. The interest rate you receive, how-ever, is contingent on your credit score. For example, according to myFICO.com, the consumer Web site of Fair Isaac Corporation, the primary creator of credit scores in the United States, the monthly payments on a 15-year, $50,000 home equity loan vary widely, depending on credit score. As you can see, borrowers with the best credit score pay 28% less each month than borrow-ers with the worst—and $23,940 less over the life of the loan.

---

[*] Bankrate.com: national overnight average on October 19, 2008.

15-YEAR, $50,000 HOME EQUITY LOAN		
FICO SCORE	**APR**	**MONTHLY PAYMENT ($)**
740–850	8.150	482
720–739	8.450	491
700–719	8.950	506
670–699	9.725	529
640–669	11.225	575
620–639	12.475	615

APR = annual percentage rate; FICO score = Fair Isaac Corporation score, or your credit score.
Source: www.myFICO.com, November 24, 2008. Based on national averages.

Q: Do you have any tips for staying out of debt once I've consolidated?

A: I do, and in fact, even if you're sure you have the strength to keep from backsliding, it will help to put some of these safeguards in place:

- **Turn down offers for new cards or credit line increases on your current cards.** Credit's tight, and chances are, you're not getting many offers anyway. But if you do, remember that the less credit you have available, the less trouble you can get into.
- **Take the cards out of your wallet.** A debit card is accepted just about everywhere that credit cards are, and you'll be spending money you have—always a good thing.
- **Pay cash.** For some reason, it's harder for people psychologically to part with their cash than it is to swipe a card. Maybe it's the act of physically seeing the money change hands, or maybe it's because you don't want to break a $20 for a $2 cup of coffee. In fact, the bigger the bill, the less likely you are to spend it. If you want to really save money, spend only cash and carry only fifty-dollar bills.
- **Save for your goals.** Take note of what's coming your way—vacations, the holidays, whatever is going to cost you money—and start saving ahead of time so that you have a stash when the time comes. That way, you won't be caught

off guard and you won't feel guilty, because you'll be spending money that you've allocated for the occasion.

· **Get your friends involved.** Let your shopping buddies know that you're on a tight budget, and they can help you out when your willpower starts to weaken at the mall.

Q: What kind of loan do I want?
A: What you want, in a nutshell, is the loan that is going to give you the best interest rate. Here are the options:

· **Home equity loan:** This is a fixed-rate loan that allows you to take money in a single chunk, and start paying it back right away. You can often find the best deals at credit unions, but you should shop all possible financing sources including big banks, small banks, and online lenders.

· **Home equity line of credit (HELOC):** This is a variable-rate loan, generally tied to the prime rate, meaning that if interest rates go up, your monthly payment likely will too. The line of credit means that you don't have to borrow all the money at once—instead, it's more like an account that allows you to withdraw (and pay back) funds as you need them. You pay interest on only the money you use.

If you can get a HELOC and manage the money wisely, it's not a bad idea to have it in your back pocket in case of an emergency. Shop around for the best interest rates and compare annual fees. Read all the fine print—often HELOCs are advertised with a teaser rate that then jumps after six months or a year.

· **Cash-out refinance:** This loan allows you to refinance your mortgage and simultaneously draw out some of the equity in your home, either a portion of what you've paid back or what has become yours through appreciation (tough, these days). In other words, it's not a second mortgage; rather it replaces your current mortgage, but you still have to absorb the cost of another appraisal and closing. You should go this route only if you've seen a drop in interest rates of at least 0.05% since you last took out your mortgage. And you should ask yourself: How long will I have to live in the house to recoup the cost of the transaction?

Tools

Debt-reduction calculators can help you figure out how long it will take you to get out of debt by factoring your interest rate, balance, and the amount you can afford to pay each month. Two of my favorites:

- www.bankrate.com/brm/calc/creditcardpay.asp
- cgi.money.cnn.com/tools/debtplanner/debtplanner.jsp

Q: **Are there alternatives to a home equity loan or line of credit?**

A: One alternative to consider is a balance transfer—or series of them. Before you look to recast your credit card debt into a different loan altogether, make a series of phone calls to your current credit card companies asking for reductions in your interest rates. If that doesn't work (or doesn't work well enough), start scouting for cheaper credit cards that will allow you to transfer your balance. Ideally, you're looking for a card that caps transfer fees (they're typically 3% of the amount you're moving) at $75 to $100, but these caps are harder to find than they used to be, so you need to do the math to figure out if a transfer is worth it (there are many online calculators to help you, including one at Bankrate .com). One note: Balance transfer offers have been phasing out since the start of the credit crunch, and some experts think they'll soon be gone forever as a result of the CARD Act of 2009, which lays out new rules for credit card issuers. Keep tabs on this, and if you decide transferring will save you money, do it sooner rather than later. This route may not be cheaper than refinancing your debt as some sort of mortgage, but it's definitely lower risk.

4. How do I deal with bill collectors?

A: The first rule of thumb in dealing with debt collectors: Know your rights. We've all heard the horror stories: threats of jail time, calls to employers or neighbors, the nonstop ringing of your phone. But for the most part, it's a bad rap. True, there are a few companies out there that employ these scare tactics, but collection agencies are regulated by laws—both nationally (by the the federal Fair Debt Collection Practices Act) and at the state level.

These laws govern a number of issues. First, they specify

how, when, and where debt collectors may contact you. The Federal Trade Commission (FTC) says that collectors can get in touch by phone, mail, or fax. They can call only between 8 AM and 9 PM. They can contact other people, such as friends, your boss, or relatives, only to find out where you live, what your phone number is, and where you work—not to discuss the debt or the amount of money you owe. They also must honor your request not to call you at work, so if that's a problem, make the request in writing and send it to the collection agency by certified mail with a return reciept.

There are also regulations as to what the collectors are allowed to say. They aren't allowed to threaten you, and if you're told that you'll go to jail or they'll garnish your wages, they are crossing the line. Before they take any legal action against you, they'll need to go to court, a lengthy and expensive process. You should report any inappropriate behavior to the FTC or your state attorney general's office. (For a contact list of attorneys general, go to the National Association of Attorneys General at www.naag .org/attorneys_general.)

If a collection agency contacts you, the first thing you want to do is verify the debt. Doing so not only gives you time to make a plan but also provides you assurance that what they're trying to collect is really a debt you incurred, in the exact amount you owe. Within 30 days of receiving a note or phone call about a debt, write a letter asking for more information about this debt, including how much you owe, to whom, when the debt originated, and what the interest rate is now. The collector should reply with these specifics in writing.

Once you receive this verification and have acknowledged that it is a debt that belongs to you, it's time to negotiate. Debt collectors often pay as little as 5 to 10 cents on the dollar for your bad debts, depending on how recent they are. They don't want to dedicate a lot of time getting the money, and they really don't want to take the matter to court. That means you're in a prime negotiating position. Explain that you want to make good but that you have other expenses to consider as well. Then offer them an amount that works with your budget but is still reasonable for the collector—it's not always going to be the original amount owed. A good place to start is at 50% of the balance for a recent debt and 20% to 25% for a debt older than a few years. Then work up from there.

Once you've reached an agreement, make sure to get it in writing, and as a precaution, don't allow collectors to take the money directly out of your bank account.

I Also Need to Know . . .

Q: **How do I know if I am being contacted by an in-house collector (someone working for my creditor) versus a third-party debt collector? And should I treat them differently?**

A: Collectors have to identify themselves by both their name and the name of the collection company or creditor whom they represent. There are generally three phases to the debt-collection process:

1. For about six months after you fall behind in your payments, you'll be dealing with the creditor's internal collector directly. There's no middleman involved, and because of that, this window is the ideal time to get the debt settled, if you have the money. In fact, your creditor would rather settle with you directly than sell the debt, because you'll likely end up settling for 30 to 50 cents on the dollar, and a collection agency may pay only 5 cents.
2. The original creditor is still owner of the debt, but the creditor will assign it to an outside agency that will try to collect the money from you. If the agency does collect successfully, it will earn a commission from your creditor. Communications may start to get aggressive at this point. While debt collection was in the first stage, the creditor was trying to prevent you from falling behind on your payments. Now it is focused solely on recovering the loss.
3. The third phase starts when the original creditor sells the debt to an outside collection agency. The creditor is no longer involved in the debt, and the agency is now trying to recoup the amount that it paid for the debt, and turn a profit.

The major difference between dealing with your original creditor and dealing with an outside agency is that you need to ask for documentation of the debt from a collection agency in writing. Your creditor, of course, will have at least a few years' worth of statements to prove how much you owe, but in some cases, collection agencies fail to prove their claims or even inflate balances (which is illegal). In general, the sooner you can settle the debt, the better, and that means working with your original creditor from the start.

Q: **I was contacted by a debt-collection law firm. Does that mean I'm going to get sued?**

A: Increasingly, creditors are turning over delinquent debts to debt-collection law firms instead of plain-vanilla bill collectors for this reason: A call or letter from a law firm sounds more official and so is often enough to scare consumers into paying up. But the truth is, whether the creditor takes you to court to get the money owed is still an economic decision based on the amount you're delinquent, the cost of a trial, and whether a win on the creditor's part is likely. Debt-collection law firms must abide by the Fair Debt Collection Practices Act, and in fact, are likely to comply. As attorneys, they stand to lose their ability to practice if they don't. You should treat correspondence from a law firm the same way you would treat that from a collection agency.

Q: **What if my debt is many years old?**

A: You may have heard that paying on old debts is a mistake because it restarts the clock and forces you to pay when you shouldn't have to or when you could have negotiated. But I believe that paying your debts—no matter how old or past due—is always a good idea, from both a moral and a financial standpoint. In general, blemishes stay on your credit report for seven years (and paying the debts won't remove them), but each state has its own statute of limitations to dictate how long a debt collector has in which to sue you for the amount owed. These limitations vary from about 5 to 10 years. The clock starts when the debt first goes past due, so making a payment or negotiating a debt won't turn back time. Just be sure to understand your state's individual policy before you take any action.

Q: **How do I get my credit back on track after a settlement?**

A: Once you've reached an agreement, gotten it in writing, received confirmation that the debt is settled, and reported to the three major credit bureaus, you can start rebuilding your credit. It's a process that takes time. Pay your bills on time every month. Pay down the amount you owe on your credit cards to 10% of your available credit if possible. Don't cancel old cards, because that will reduce the amount of credit available to you, making your debt-to-credit—or utilization—ratio increase. And don't shop around for credit you don't need. Within 18 to 24 months, your credit should start to improve.

THE STATS

- Credit card charge-offs totaled **$22.6 billion in 2007**.
- Debt-collection industry revenues are expected to grow from $16.7 billion in 2006 to **$22.2 billion in 2011**.
- Over the 2006–2016 decade, employment of bill and account collectors is expected to grow by **23%**, which is much faster than the average for all occupations.

5. Which credit cards should I pay off first?

A: That depends what you're trying to accomplish. Are you trying to get out of debt as quickly and cheaply as possible? Or are you trying to boost your credit score as quickly as possible?

If you're trying to get out of debt as fast as you can, paying as little in interest to the credit card issuers, you should pay off the card with the highest interest rate first while paying the minimums on the rest. Once you've retired the debt on that card, move to the card with the second-highest interest rate, and so on. The reason this system works is that the return on your money is equal to the interest rate you're paying. So if you're paying off a 20% card, it's like putting a 20%—guaranteed!—return in your pocket.

The second option is giving the cards with the lowest balances priority. Doing this has three benefits. First, crossing a card off your list is undoubtedly good for your mental health. It feels great and gives you more motivation to tackle the others. Second, it allows you to eliminate any annual fees attached to those cards. And third, if you're looking to boost your credit score to qualify for a mortgage or auto loan in the near term, paying off low-balance cards can give your credit score a boost.

So the answer to your question depends on your end goal. But here's an example so that you can see what the difference looks like in actual dollar terms.

▶ An Example

John has five credit cards. He owes:

- $5,000 at 29.9% with no annual fee
- $1,500 at 24.9% with a $49 annual fee
- $700 at 27.9% with no annual fee
- $600 at 7.9% with a $49 annual fee
- $400 at 11.9% with no annual fee

Total debt: $8,200

Option 1: Pay as much as you can afford on the card with the highest interest rate, while making just the minimums on the others.

Let's say that John can afford to pay $350 a month total. Assuming his minimum monthly payments are calculated as 2.5% of each card's balance, at the onset, $206 of that will go just toward meeting those. He can then start by putting the remaining $144 toward the first card, with the 29.9% interest rate. His end result:

Priority	Original Balance	Total Interest Paid	Months Until Paid Off
Card 1 (29.9% APR)	$5,000	$1,799.15	26
Card 3 (27.9% APR)	$700	$421.52	28
Card 2 (24.9% APR)	$1,500	$861.94	32
Card 5 (11.9% APR)	$400	$94.65	33
Card 4 (7.9% APR)	$600	$89.20	33

APR = annual percentage rate.

Total interest Paid: $3,266.46

Option 2: Pay off the cards with the lowest balances first while making the minimums on the others.

Assuming John still has $350 to throw at his credit card debt each month and that the minimums on the cards are the same, he's still left with $144 extra to go toward the card with the lowest balance, card 5 in the above calculation. Here's how it shakes out:

Priority	Original Balance	Total Interest Paid	Months Until Paid Off
Card 5 (11.9% APR)	$400	$7.43	3
Card 4 (7.9% APR)	$600	$18.54	7
Card 3 (27.9% APR)	$700	$137.72	10
Card 2 (24.9% APR)	$1,500	$422.24	17
Card 1 (29.9% APR)	$5,000	$3,347.19	35

APR = annual percentage rate.

Total interest paid: $3,933.12—a difference of about $666, or a big boost to your savings account.

I Also Need to Know . . .

Q: **What if I can't afford to pay on all of my debts?**
A: You should prioritize, in this order:

- **Necessities.** What do you need to live? Shelter, so you should pay your mortgage or rent. Heat and light, so put the utility bills at the top of your list, along with the car payment if you need the car to get to work. Child support is also a necessity, as are any medical emergencies that come up.
- **The government.** If you don't file your taxes by the due date, you'll be hit with penalties and interest, increasing the amount of your debt. But the IRS will generally work out a payment plan with you if you can't afford to pay upfront. Federal student loans also offer options for you if you can't make ends meet. The key, though, is being upfront about your situation. If you try to avoid Uncle Sam, the IRS can seize

your tax refunds and garnish your wages and even your Social Security benefits.

- **Everything else.** All of your other debts—credit card, department-store debt, the financing for your new television—go on the back burner. You should, of course, make every effort to pay them, but if you can't stretch your money, these are the ones to put on hold.

Q: **What happens if I fall behind on credit card payments?**

A: Your phone will start ringing, and you'll begin to receive letters from your creditors. The mistake a lot of people make is hiding from these communications. If you call and explain the situation—trust me, they have been hearing a lot of this since 2007—they may just help you out by halting the collection process or negotiating the terms with you so you pay less each month. If they won't, and you continue not to pay, then in three to six months, your file will be turned over to a collection agency. For tips on handling bill collectors, see page 10.

6. Is it safe to borrow from people whom you don't know? I have visited Web sites featuring person-to-person lending, where individuals can get loans or give loans to complete strangers.

A: Most of these sites are only a few years old, and I expect to see more competition popping up in the near future. That's not just because it has become harder to borrow money the traditional way, from banks and credit unions, because the credit market is so tight. You need a solid credit score (720) to get some loans these days, and a stellar one (760 and higher) to get the best interest rates.

　　You probably know how the traditional bank lending model works: Someone deposits a chunk of money in a certificate of deposit (CD) at a bank. Let's say it's a one-year term and the interest rate is 4%. The bank then lends that money to someone who needs a loan, charging that person a slightly higher interest rate, maybe 6%, 7%, or 8%. The difference in the interest rates is the bank's profit. If you cut out the bank, forgo the CD, and lend your money to a borrower directly, you can keep the profit for yourself. That's the person-to-person (P2P) lending model. Likewise, if you're the borrower, you'll pay a lower interest rate because the entire sum is going to your lender. Although the facilitator, typically a Web site such as Prosper.com or LendingClub.com, charges fees for both originating the loan and servicing it, there's no middleman to take a cut. (For a look at the fees, see chart on page 20.) It's no surprise that P2P lending is becoming popular.

Is it safe? Well, that depends on the credibility of the Web site. The better sites will do much of the hard work for you, vetting everyone who agrees to make a loan the same way a bank or credit union would. The lender will need to provide a Social Security number and a bank account number to verify identity. The sites also pull the credit reports of potential borrowers and evaluate the risk involved with lending to that person. Most credible sites then assign a rating to each borrower, and it's up to the lender to decide what rating he or she will require. Most sites also collect fees for late payments and report delinquencies to credit bureaus, so there's no getting off the hook—you'll need to adhere to the payment plan laid out for you by the site and your lender, just as you would if you were borrowing from a bank. Otherwise, your credit will suffer.

The downside? You may not be able to borrow the substantial sums of money you could from a bank, at least not from one lender. The typical size of a loan is less than $10,000 (Prosper .com's year-to-date average loan amount as I was writing this was $6,047), so if you wanted to pull together, say, $25,000, you'd need to cobble together three or four loans. Because each loan has to be paid back separately, that can be a bit of an administrative hassle.

Bottom line: P2P lending is safe and quite likely the way of the future as long as you've vetted the site you use, verified that it's secure, read all the fine print, and understand the terms of the loan.

I Also Need to Know . . .

Q: **How do I verify that a P2P company or Web site is legitimate?**
A: First stop: the Better Business Bureau (www.bbb.org/us/). If you visit the organization's Web site, you can input the name of the business and its location, and a report will be generated listing the company's contact information, its BBB rating, and any complaints. Keep in mind that when it comes to complaints, there are always two sides to every story, and the number of customers whom the company handles should be compared with the number of complaints received by the BBB. In other words, if a company counts

millions of people in its customer base (think of the Amazon.
coms of the world), 200 or so complaints shouldn't be a deal-
breaker. If they only have a few thousand customers and the
same amount of griping, however, you might want to think twice.

If I'm satisfied with what the BBB listing turns up, I'll often do
an Internet search just to see what people are saying. Consumers
love to share their experiences online, good and bad. Often, you
can also turn up unbiased, credible newspaper or magazine articles, written by reporters who likely had to vet the company
and spell out both the good and the bad.

After that, whenever money or personal information changes
hands over the Internet, you always want to make sure the site is
secure. The easiest way to do this is by identifying an *https* in the
address bar at the beginning of the Web-site address, instead of
the standard *http*. You should also look for a seal, generally toward
the bottom of the Web page, that signifies that the site is secure. It
often looks like a check mark.

Last—but this is very important—make sure the Web site lists
contact information in the form of a working phone number, and
call it to be sure you can get a real, live person on the line if necessary.

Q: **Is this a good way to borrow money for college?**
A: It certainly can be. A new company launched in 2008 specifically
for this purpose, and it's worth checking out: GreenNote (www
.greennote.com). It focuses on community lending, allowing you to
reach out to people you know, instead of strangers, to help finance
your loan. One thing to keep in mind, though, is that you always
want to max out your federal loan money before you start looking
elsewhere. Federal money, such as a Stafford loan, almost always
comes with a lower interest rate and better repayment terms than
does money from other sources.

If you're still short, then you can turn to P2P sites as an alternative to private student loans or carrying your tuition on a credit
card or home equity loan. There are a few advantages here. Lending standards tend to be a bit more lenient with P2P, so a recent
high school graduate with little or no credit history may not need
a cosigner. P2P loans also tend to carry fixed interest rates. But
you want to make sure that other terms are favorable as well, such
as the repayment period, which may be shorter with a P2P loan.

Q: Do these sites charge fees?
A: They do. Borrowers, in general, will pay more than lenders. Here's a comparison of the major players:

P2P SITE	ELIGIBILITY	LOAN TYPE	BORROWING LIMITS	FEES	LOAN TERMS
Prosper	520 FICO	All	$1,000–$25,000	Borrower pays a 2%–3% closing fee and late/failed payment fees. Lender pays 1% annual servicing fee.	Three years with fixed interest rate. Interest rate is negotiated between borrower and lender. No prepayment penalties.
Lending Club	640 FICO and debt-to-income ratio below 25%, excluding mortgage	All	$1,000–25,000	Borrower pays a processing fee of 0.75%–3%. Lender pays 1% annual servicing fee.	Three years with fixed interest rate. Interest rates range from 7.37% to 19.36%. No prepayment penalties.
Loanio	A credit rating of E, as defined by the company, or a co-borrower	All	$1,000–$25,000	Borrower pays a one-time fee of 2%–3% (minimum $95). Lender pays annual servicing fee of 1%.	Loans are available for 36, 48, or 60 months. Interest rates are negotiated between lenders and borrowers.
GreenNote	Open to everyone	Student	$1,000–total cost of education	Borrower pays one-time fee of 2% (minimum $49). Lender pays 1%.	Currently 6.8% fixed interest rate; six-month grace period after graduation; can defer payments for up to five years while in school; repay over 10 years; no prepayment penalties.

FICO score = Fair Isaac Corporation score, or your credit score; P2P = person-to-person (lending model).

Lender Contact Information

GreenNote
www.greennote.com
1-866-711-5620

Loanio
www.loanio.com
1-800-624-8830

Lending Club
www.lendingclub.com
1-866-754-4094

Prosper.com
www.prosper.com
1-866-615-6319

7. How do I know if I need credit counseling? What type of questions should I ask before signing on?

A: If you've gone over your budget carefully, if you've scraped to-gether every penny, cut out every extra haircut, and started pulling overtime hours, and you still can't make the minimum payments on all of your debt, it's time to go see a credit counseling agency. Putting it off will only make things worse.

The right credit counselor will put you into a debt management plan (sometimes called a DMP) that will help you pay off your debts at lower interest rates. The counselor is essentially negotiat-ing with your creditors to get you a break. How much of a break depends on the creditor, not you or the counselors—credit card companies have a schedule of interest-rate breaks they're willing to give, and they won't veer off that schedule. Late fees and other penalties are generally waived as well, which can be a huge relief and, if you've been delinquent for a long time, a huge savings.

But you're not off the hook completely. In exchange for the reduction in what you owe, you'll need to agree to stop using your credit cards and not to apply for additional credit. Once you do so and your program is set up, you'll no longer make pay-ments to your individual creditors. Instead, you'll make one pay-ment each month (generally by electronic debit) to the counseling agency, which will then distribute your money to creditors. You'll pay both a monthly and an upfront fee to the agency.

So evaluate your financial situation and ask yourself a few questions: Are you taking out cash advances because you don't have money in the bank? Are you using one credit card to pay another? Have you lost track of how much debt you have? Are you worrying about money on a daily basis?

If the answers are yes, you'll likely benefit from credit counseling. But you can't assume that every counseling agency that turns up on an Internet search is legitimate. Narrow your search to a few nearby (I would encourage you to go see a counselor in person rather than working exclusively over the phone) but then make sure that they are not-for-profit, recognized by the BBB (with no history of complaints), and a member of the National Foundation for Credit Counseling or the Independent Association of Certified Credit Counseling Agencies.

Questions to Ask a Credit Counselor (and the Answers You Want to Hear)

Q: What do you do?
A: Evaluate your financial situation to find a solution. Once we do that, the counselor will know whether your finances make you a good match for a DMP or whether you should be able to work through it alone with a bit of guidance. In about one-third of cases, a DMP may be insufficient, and you'll need a bankruptcy attorney.

Red Flag: If the counselor says it will consolidate your debts or set you up with a DMP *without* asking for the specifics of your situation, move on.

Q: How much time will you spend on an initial consultation, and is there a charge?
A: A half hour or more. The initial consultation is always free.

Red Flag: It's impossible to assess your situation in less than a half hour, so if counselors can't commit to that, they won't be very committed to helping you.

Q: What kind of debt do you help with?
A: All kinds. We also have a housing counselor on staff who can help you sort out your mortgage if need be.

Red Flag: Just credit cards. There's no reason to go to a counselor who focuses solely on one area if other areas of your finances—mortgage, auto loan, student loans, medical debts—factor into the problem as well.

Q: **How much will this cost?**
A: Less than $75 upfront, with monthly payments on a sliding scale. You won't pay more than $35 to $50 a month.

Red Flag: More than $75 to start and $50 a month is too much.

I Also Need to Know . . .

Q: **How long does counseling take?**
A: It generally will take three to five years to pay off all your debts and start fresh, depending on how much debt you have going in and how quickly you're able to pay it off.

Q: **Does everyone qualify for credit counseling?**
A: No. If the counselor looks over your finances and concludes that the firm won't be able to get you out of debt in three to five years, you won't be admitted into the program. The level of debt that will push you into this area varies depending on your interest rates and income. If the firm won't take you on, you'll need to look into other options, such as debt settlement (see page 1) or bankruptcy.

Q: **Will credit counseling hurt my credit score?**
A: There are a lot of misconceptions out there, but the truth is, credit counseling won't hurt your credit score in the long run. It could show up on your credit report if you're in a credit counseling program, but when you start the process, your credit is likely already trashed from months of late or missed payments and a high utilization ratio (which means you're using too much of the credit available to you). Throughout the process, you'll be able to bring your numbers up because the service will help you pay on time and lower the amount of debt that you're carrying. In fact, when you emerge from debt, you may do so with a better score.

8. Do you have a script you use when asking credit card companies to lower their interest rates? What is that?

A: Cutting your interest rates can save you a huge amount of money each month, which can then be used to pay your cards down faster. And in good times and in bad, credit card companies are often willing to work with you. One study from U.S. Public Interest Research Group found that 50% of the time, calls asking for a reduction in interest rates were successful.

Recently, however, the advice has changed a bit. When you call to ask for an interest-rate reduction, the representative on the other end of the line is likely to be looking for clues into your financial situation, and reevaluating the risk the company is taking by extending you credit. That means that if you mention financial struggles, or a recent layoff, you might find your call met with an interest rate increase, not reduction. So you want to really stick to my advice and script, because otherwise, you may inadvertently set off the alarms. Here's what I want you to do: Start by laying all your credit cards out in front of you in order of the interest rate (or annual percentage rate [APR]) that you're paying on each, taking note of whether that rate is fixed or variable. Then, gather all of the preapproved cards you've received in the mail lately (admittedly, there aren't as many as there once were, but I've still seen a few in my mailbox), and have a rough idea of your customer history with each card, including how long you've been a member, how much you charge each month or year, how much interest they're earning from your business, and whether you pay on time.

Then pick up the phone and call the toll-free customer number on the back. The script comes in here.
Begin with:

I have [name of card] with you and my interest rate is [X] percent. I received another offer in the mail from [bank's name] for [X] percent, but before I take it, I want to see if you'll lower my interest rate instead.

If the representative says that he or she is not authorized to do that, you say:

Look, you and I both know that if I transfer my balance today, next week your bank is going to send me an offer to come back at an even lower rate. Why don't you just save the bank the cost of that effort by giving me several points today?

If the rep says that's not possible because your card is at a fixed rate, you say:

Actually, that doesn't have anything to do with whether you have the ability to lower my interest rate. A fixed interest rate means only that my rate doesn't vary with fluctuations in the prime rate. In fact, the bank can raise it on my account at any time by just giving me fifteen days' written notice. And the bank can—if it chooses—lower the rate today.

If the rep still says that he or she is not authorized to do that, you say:

I'd like to speak to your supervisor.

Speak to a supervisor and go through the script again. Even if you get a substantial cut in the interest rate from the first person, it's worth it to speak to a supervisor to see if you can do any better. The person on the front line of customer service will be authorized to cut your interest rate by only a preset amount, if at all. The customer service rep may also insist that the supervisor doesn't have the power to cut your rate either, or—if you've already gotten a break—to cut it further. That may not be true, so insist on speaking to the supervisor anyway.

Other tricks:

· **Threaten to close your account.** You don't necessarily want to close your account—in fact, that is generally a bad idea, as it will ding your credit score—but if a bank representative believes you're willing to do so, and you've been a profitable customer, then you stand a better chance of getting what you want.

· **Keep a record of whom you speak to.** If your promised rate cut doesn't come through, you're going to need a paper trail.

· **Transfer your balance.** If you're not successful in reducing your interest rate over the phone, and you have a good credit score, look into transferring your balance. This is harder to do than it has been in the past—balance transfer offers seem to be phasing out—but you may still find an offer in your mailbox, or at Web sites like Bankrate.com and CardWeb.com. Note: An offer to transfer your balance is not an automatic acceptance to give you the card at that interest rate (or at all). Your credit still needs to pass muster. Although it's fine to apply for the card, you shouldn't cancel your old card until you know you've been accepted (if you decide to cancel it at all).

THE MATH

Knocking your interest rate down just a couple of points can have a big impact. How?

Card 1
Balance: $20,000
Interest rate: 18%
Amount you can pay: $500 per month
Payoff time: 5 years
   Total interest paid: $11,000

Card 2
Balance: $20,000
Interest rate: 14%
Amount you can pay: $500 per month
Payoff time: 4½ years
   Total interest paid: $7,000

   Savings: $4,000

I Also Need to Know . . .

Q: **What should I consider before doing a balance transfer?**
A: A few things:

- **The rate.** Transfer offers often come with teaser rates that will then shoot up after a set period—usually 6 to 12 months. If you can't pay off the balance right away, be sure to pay attention to what interest rate the card will jump to after the teaser expires.

· **The fine print.** Balance transfers often incur different interest rates than those for new purchases. Cash advances may have yet a third rate. That's why you need to read every piece of information you receive.

· **The fees.** Most card issuers charge a fee for balance transfers, generally a percentage of the amount you're moving. Sometimes it's capped—up to $100, for example—but more often it's not. Know how much the move will cost you before you sign up.

Q: **Are "preapproved" offers legit?**

A: Sometimes, but as always, you have to read the entire offer, top to bottom and front to back. Get out your magnifying glass if you have to (and you might). The mailing may say you're "preapproved" for a particular card, but the lucrative interest rate in bold print may not be the one you receive. Chances are, the company is using tiered pricing, meaning it offers a range of interest rates depending on your credit history. The advertised rate is generally the lowest of the low, and if you have stellar credit, you just might get it. But if you don't, you'll likely end up with a higher rate.

Q: **What is the Credit CARD Act of 2009?**

A: The Credit CARD Act of 2009—officially named the Credit Card Accountability Responsibility and Disclosure Act of 2009—was signed into law by President Obama in May 2009. The Act provides new consumer protections when it comes to credit cards, most of which go into effect in February of 2010. Here are the big changes:

· Card holders must be notified of an interest rate increase or other significant change to the account at least 45 days in advance.

· Card issuers can no longer change the APR, fees, or finance charges on outstanding credit card balances unless the rate you were given was specified as an introductory rate (lasting only for a specific amount of time), your rate is variable, or your rate was lowered during a short-term hardship arrangement.

- Fees for going over the credit limit are no longer allowed unless you specifically authorized the card company to allow you to make purchases that put you over the limit.
- Card issuers can no longer charge fees for making payments by mail, electronic transfer, or phone unless you need to expedite the payment to make a due date.
- Any payment over the required minimum payment must be applied to the balance with the highest interest rate.
- Floating due dates, which change periodically, are no longer allowed.
- Statements must be mailed to the customer at least 21 days before the due date, and payments received by 5 PM must be credited that day.
- Credit card companies are forbidden from issuing cards to consumers under 21 years old unless they can prove they have the financial ability to repay the debt or they have a cosigner.

Q: Aside from lowering my interest rate, are there other ways to pay off my credit card debt quickly?

A: The best way is paying more than the minimum each month. Paying just the minimum—which is usually 2% to 3% of the total—puts you on a slow road to a zero balance. That's because while you're paying 2% of your balance each month, the bank is charging you 6, 7, 8, even 10 times that much in interest. At that rate, your bill is going up each month, not down.

Just scraping together a few extra dollars a week to put toward your debt can drastically reduce not only the time it takes you to pay it off but also the amount you pay the bank in interest. Look at it this way: Each month, you probably have at least two or three things you buy that you don't need. Most of us have more. I'm talking about everything from a coffee or a sandwich to splurges such as a new pair of shoes or a handful of songs on iTunes. Just taking that money and putting it toward your debt can do a world of good.

▶ An Example

Take a card with a 13% APR and a $4,000 balance. Pay only the minimum each month, and you'll be in debt for the next 13 years and 7 months. You'll also pay more than $2,500 in interest.

On the flip side, if you can add an extra $50 a month to your payments—that's about seven sandwiches, dinner for two, or your coffee bill if you hit Starbucks every morning—you'll shave nearly 11 years off the life of your debt and you'll save almost $2,000 in interest.

Q: Does lowering my interest rate affect my credit score?

A: The decreased interest rate doesn't actually affect your score, because interest rates aren't reflected in your credit report. But the actual act of requesting a lower interest could ding your score slightly. That's because when you ask your company to change your interest rate or balance limit, it's technically considered an application for credit, and in many cases, the company will pull your credit history before making a decision. So you have to weigh your options. If you're a person who rarely shops for credit, one inquiry isn't going to be catastrophic. But if you tend to open new accounts often or you think you might apply for a mortgage or other major loan in the next year or so, you might want to pass on this strategy.

One other suggestion: If you can handle an increased credit limit (meaning you won't use it as an excuse to spend more), you might consider asking for one in conjunction with the interest-rate reduction. That's because an increased credit limit helps your credit score, which might have the effect of evening things out.

9. What is the difference between chapter 13, chapter 11, and chapter 7 bankruptcy? How do I know which one to file?

A: The average consumer considering bankruptcy only needs to choose between chapter 13 and chapter 7. Chapter 11 is primarily for debtors who own a business and want to be able to file bankruptcy without putting that business at risk. Also, filing chapter 11 is expensive—you'll pay a $1,000 filing fee and a $39 miscellaneous administrative fee, not to mention hefty bills for lawyers.

That said, when it comes to putting chapter 13 up against chapter 7, here's what you need to know:

Chapter 7 bankruptcy is a liquidation plan. To file for chapter 7 bankruptcy, your monthly income must be less than or equal to the median income for a household of your size in your state (you can find this on www.census.gov). If it is, you can file for chapter 7, which allows you to liquidate old debts and start from scratch. You'll lose some, but not all, of your property. Each state has laws that allow you to keep certain things, typically part of the equity in your residence, necessary clothing within reason, a few hundred dollars worth of jewelry, and pensions. The charge for chapter 7 is currently $245 for filing fees and about $54 in administrative fees and trustee surcharges.

Chapter 13 bankruptcy is a repayment plan rather than a liquidation plan. It's often called a wage earner's plan because it allows individuals with a regular income to develop a plan to repay all or part of their debts. Basically, you'll propose a repayment plan to make installment payments to your creditors over three to five years. The plan then has to be approved in bankruptcy court, and if it is, you'll be able to reschedule secured debts—such as car loans—and extend them to lower your payments and make them more manageable. Any remaining disposable income must then go toward unsecured debts (credit card or medical bills). In most cases, you don't have to pay these debts off in full, but any extra money you have will need to go toward them.

The charge to file chapter 13 is a $235 filing fee and the standard $39 for administrative costs.

Keep in mind that in most cases, courts will allow you to pay the fees associated with filing for bankruptcy in installments. But you'll also need to take legal fees into consideration, which can range from about $1,200 to $1,400 for chapter 7 and upward of $3,000 for chapter 13.

Finally—and this is important—the Bankruptcy Reform Act of 2005 requires that you go through credit counseling before filing. A good not-for-profit credit counselor (see page 22) will help you figure out if bankruptcy is the best option for you, because it's certainly not something you want to take lightly. It may be that you can use a debt management program (DMP) through the credit counseling service to get back on track without having to file bankruptcy. Over the long term, a DMP will be better for both your credit score and your assets.

THE MATH

How does extending an auto loan (as you may be able to do through chapter 13 bankruptcy) change your monthly payments?

Original auto loan:
Amount: $15,000
Term: 4 years
Interest rate: 6.6%
Monthly payment: $356

Auto loan modified in bankruptcy:
Amount: $15,000
Term: 6 years
Interest rate: 6.6%
Monthly payment: $252

Reduction in monthly payment: $104 a month
Additional interest cost over the life of the loan: $1,100

I Also Need to Know . . .

Q: **How long does it take to redeem my credit after filing for bankruptcy?**

A: Not as long as you think. Bankruptcy is, of course, a big black mark on your credit history, and it will stay on your file for 7½ years. But if you come out of bankruptcy determined to stay on track—and follow through—you'll likely start receiving credit card offers in the mail within about two years. Boost your chances by making your bill payments on time, keeping your debt low, and not shopping around for credit. You also might consider getting a secured card in the interim. A secured card looks just like a credit card, but you have to make an initial deposit that then becomes your credit limit. Most cards will automatically convert to traditional credit cards after about 18 months of good behavior on your part.

Q: **How can I find a good bankruptcy attorney? Do I need one or can I go it alone?**

A: You probably do need one, but do a little research first. About 80% of people who file bankruptcy do it with the help of an attorney, and the reason for this is simple: Bankruptcy laws are complicated, and a misstep can cost you. But before you hire someone, head to the library and read a couple of books on the subject. If your situation is fairly simple—say you qualify for chapter 7 and just have a few credit cards—and you feel comfortable navigating the system on your own, then you have the option to do that. But in most cases, you're going to want an attorney because things can get overwhelming—fast.

To find a bankruptcy lawyer, do so the same way you'd look for a doctor. If you know any people who have filed for bankruptcy, ask them if they used an attorney and whether they'd recommend him or her. If that doesn't work, you can do a search for attorneys in your area through the National Association of Consumer Bankruptcy Attorneys or Nolo.com, or ask your personal lawyer for a referral. Any good lawyer will grant you an initial meeting free of charge, so you can ask any questions you might have and get an idea of the overall cost before you sign on. You do want to make sure that the attorney specializes in bankruptcy, of course.

Resources

Associations

The Association of Credit and Collection Professionals
www.acainternational.org
952-926-6547

This trade association for professional businesses and individuals in the credit and collection industry provides consumers with credit and collection resources, including educational materials, answers to frequently asked questions (FAQs) about debt collection, and explanations of your rights as a consumer.

The Association of Settlement Companies (TASC)
www.tascsite.org
1-888-657-8272

TASC promotes good business practices in the debt settlement industry to protect both consumers and debt settlement companies. Search for TASC-accredited debt settlement companies by name or state.

National Association of Consumer Bankruptcy Attorneys
www.nacba.org

The Web site for this association of consumer bankruptcy attorneys features consumer tips and links to bankruptcy news.

National Association of Consumer Advocates
www.naca.net
202-452-1989
A nationwide organization of attorneys who represent consumers who have been victimized by debt-collection abuse.

National Foundation for Credit Counseling
www.nfcc.org
301-589-5600
The national voice for credit counseling agencies, the foundation is composed of more than 100 member agencies and 900 local offices throughout the United States; search for a member agency, access free debt advice, and more.

The United States Organizations for Bankruptcy Alternatives (USOBA)
www.usoba.org
281-820-0666
USOBA represents the debt-negotiation industry by creating specific agendas for states and advocating fair regulation and protection for consumers. Access answers to FAQ for consumers about settling debts and subscribe to a free monthly newsletter with money-saving tips.

Books

Chapter 13 Bankruptcy: Keep Your Property and Repay Debts Over Time, by Stephen Elias and Robin Leonard (2008).
A well-written, plain-English look at chapter 13 from the folks at Nolo.com.

The Complete Guide to Prosper.com: How to Borrow and Lend Money Online, by Sean Bauer (2008).
A detailed guide on how to use Prosper.com, including tips and resources for the user.

How to Get Credit Counseling, by Quick Easy Guides (2008).
A simple guide with tips and trade secrets for seeking professional help with your credit card debt.

How You Can Profit from Credit Cards: Using Credit to Improve Your Financial Life and Bottom Line, by Curtis E. Arnold (2008).

Insight into how you can benefit from credit card usage and also tips to mitigate your debt and cut back on your cost of credit.

National Consumer Law Center Guide to Surviving Debt, by Deanne Loonin (2008).

A concise, specific guide to managing debt in different stages and situations, which takes current laws and regulations into account to provide consumers with the most up-to-date information on how to handle debt while legally protecting themselves.

Pay It Down! Debt Free on $10 a Day, by Jean Chatzky (2009).

Strategies for finding $10 a day and moving toward financial security.

Stop Debt Collectors, by Gerri Detweiler, Mary Reed, and John Ventura (2008).

A practical guide on how to deal with debt collectors and protect your rights in the process.

You're Nothing but a Number: Why Achieving Great Credit Scores Should be on Your List of Wealth Building Strategies, by John Ulzheimer (2007).

Learn how to build and keep a great credit score; book includes information on the inner workings of the credit card system and companies.

Government Agencies

Federal Trade Commission
www.ftc.gov
1-877-FTC-HELP (1-877-382-4357)

An independent government agency whose mission is to protect consumers and eliminate anticompetitive business practices. On their site you will find information about debt settlement, opportunities to attend workshops, facts about negotiating debt and debt collection (including the complete text of the Fair Debt Collection Practices Act), information on debt consolidation and alternative methods to shrink the size of your debt, several detailed guides with information on how to repay credit card debt, and information on your rights as a consumer regarding credit.

United States bankruptcy courts
www.uscourts.gov/bankruptcycourts.html

This section of the U.S. courts' Web site offers bankruptcy forms, as well as information about how to file and what chapter is best for your situation.

Web sites

American Bankruptcy Institute Consumer Bankruptcy Center
consumer.abiworld.org
703-739-0800

The American Bankruptcy Institute is the nation's largest multidisciplinary, nonpartisan organization dedicated to the researching of and educating others about bankruptcy.

AnnualCreditReport.com
www.annualcreditreport.com

Request a free copy of your credit report once a year from each of the nationwide consumer credit reporting companies.

BankRate.com
www.bankrate.com
561-630-2400

Get news and advice on credit cards, use a credit card repayment calculator, compare interest rates on mortgages and home equity loans nationwide, compare credit card rates, find the best cards for balance transfers, and more.

Credit.com
www.credit.com

Advice and tools for getting out of debt; articles specific to debt settlement; a comparison chart of debt-help products and services; tips on how to negotiate credit card debt; a credit score compass, which navigates you to an estimate of your credit score; advice on credit card balance transfers; and comparisons of cards by criteria such as interest rates and whether they allow balance transfers.

HSH Associates
www.hsh.com
1-800-873-2837

HSH has up-to-date information about interest rates on mortgages, refinances, and home equity loans, so you can find the best deals in your area.

National Consumer Law Center (NCLC)
www.consumerlaw.org
202-452-6252
A national consumer law expert, NCLC works to combat unfair business practices by collection agencies.

Nolo
www.nolo.com
1-800-728-3555
Nolo is a legal information site. It has answers to FAQs and articles about bankruptcy, estate planning, real estate, and other money matters. You can also use the site's attorney search feature to find a lawyer in your area.

CHAPTER 2

MONEY AND LIFE

10. I'd like to hire a financial advisor, but after all the frauds in the news recently, I'm nervous. Can you help?

A: I've always believed that when it comes to your money, someone has to do the work. With so many resources out there for do-it-yourselfers, you may feel well equipped to make decisions and take actions yourself. But if you don't have the time, the confidence, or the inclination, hiring someone is wise. The right financial advisor can get you on track, even back on track. The problem is that there are so many to choose from. A few guidelines:

- **Check credentials.** CFP, CPA, PFS, ChFC . . . the various combinations of letters that signify financial planner certification are more than confusing. Before you start working with anyone, check out his or her credentials with the Certified Financial Planner Board of Standards. (CFP is a very good start.)
- **Know what you're paying for.** These days, there are planners who charge commissions on the investments you buy, those who charge a fee for assets under management, those who charge a fee for drawing up a plan, and those who charge by the hour. There are advantages to each.

  With fee-only planners, you know exactly what you are paying for. Plus, those planners, since they don't sell anything beyond advice, have no financial incentive to recommend one mutual fund or stock rather than another. Planners who charge a percentage of assets under management get paid on the basis of the size of your pie, so they have an incentive I like—they make more when you make more. Planners who charge by the hour are affordable for people who don't want to spend a lot of money (or a lot of time) on a relationship with a financial advisor. If you do most of the work yourself but are interested in having someone look over your finances as a sanity check, this route can be good. (I think of it as short-term therapy).

Finally, there are commission-based planners. There are more of these than any of the other variety. If you want to work with someone in your local area, you may find yourself with a choice among commission-based planners. This selection may be fine. Just make sure you ask how much the relationship will cost you and how high the commissions can be, and then make sure that they are no higher than the average commissions in the chart below.

COMPENSATION MODEL	PERCENTAGE OF ADVISORS	AVERAGE FEES
Fee per hour	19	$175
Percent of assets under management	72	0.7%–1.5%
Fee per plan	27	$361/modular plan, $1,332/comprehensive plan

Source: Financial Planning Association.

- **Get a referral.** Start with friends and colleagues, but if you come up short, plug your ZIP code into the Web sites of respected groups such as the National Association of Personal Financial Advisors (www.napfa.org), Garrett Planning Network (www.garrettplanningnetwork.com), or the Financial Planning Association (www.fpanet.org). You'll get a list of names in your area.
- **Set up a few consultations.** The first meeting with any planner should be free, so if it isn't, cross that name off your list. Meet with as many people as you need to, until you feel that you have a range of options.

Questions to Ask

Q: **How long have you been in the business?**
A: More experience is not always better. Though you should aim for at least five years, make sure that they haven't been around so long that they're behind on the latest products and developments.

Q: **Will I be working directly with you, or will I be meeting with an associate?**
A: If you'll be working with his or her colleague, that's fine as long as you know what the deal is upfront. Ask for an introduction to measure your comfort before you sign on and feel free to ask all your questions—again.

Q: **Do you offer comprehensive planning?**
A: You want a planner who can cover all areas of finance, not just retirement planning or insurance.

Q: **Is your firm registered as an investment advisor?**
A: Federal and state laws require that most advisors be registered with the U.S. Securities and Exchange Commission or your state's regulatory agency.

Q: **Have you ever been cited by a professional or regulatory governing body for disciplinary reasons?**
A: Many have, and they will give you a good reason. Still, financial planning is a popular profession these days. You can easily find a planner without infractions, so I'd move on.

Q: **Can you provide references?**
A: Most will give you the names of satisfied customers. Call them.

Q: **Can you show me a plan you did for someone else?**
A: This will give you the best sense of how the planner will work for you. Be sure that the planner is using realistic calculations for returns at a level of risk with which you're comfortable.

Q: **How will I pay you, and how much will it cost?**
A: Even if you interview only fee-only planners, payment structures will still vary. Some charge a flat fee per plan, while others will charge hourly or by a percentage of the assets managed.

I Also Need to Know . . .

Q: **What financial information does my planner need from me?**
A: Go to the first real meeting with everything the planner will need to be able to put together a comprehensive plan—tax returns, insurance policies, pay stubs, loan, mortgage, credit card and bank statements, brokerage statements, retirement plan statements, and all other investment records. It also helps to make a list in advance of any questions you want to ask while you're there, as it's a bit like the doctor's office in that you always think of a follow-up question on the drive home.

Q: **I'm nervous about my investments, and I haven't heard from my planner in a while. Is that normal?**
A: It certainly isn't good. A good planner with whom you have an ongoing relationship should give you a call when the market is going haywire just to check in and make sure that you're still comfortable with the level of risk that you're taking. But there's no reason why you shouldn't call your planner and ask for a meeting. In fact, you should sit down and go over your plan at least once a year. While there, ask your planner to show you how your portfolio is performing compared with the rest of the market. And if you can't sleep at night, don't hesitate to bring it up. He or she will work with you to tweak your asset allocation and give you less risk and more rest.

One caveat: If you're working with a planner who charges by the hour, he or she can't be expected to call every client when the market takes a hit. It's just not in the job description. Instead, call and see if you can schedule another session.

11. Is it better to lease a car or to buy it? What are the pros and cons of each?

A: The answer here depends on your circumstances. A couple of questions to ask yourself upfront:

- **How long do you plan to keep this car?** Right now you may need a station wagon to pull your weight in the neighborhood carpool, but when your kid turns 16 in a year, the extra room really won't be necessary. In that case, or if you will need this car for only two or three years for any other reason, you should likely lease. But if you anticipate keeping a vehicle for more than 4 or 5 years, then financially speaking, you're better off making the investment and buying.

· **What will the car be used for?** Maybe you just go back and forth to work, or on the occasional road trip, and tend to keep your cars in top shape. Whatever the reason, if you put no more than 12,000 to 15,000 miles on a car per year and you take very, very good care of it, leasing is definitely a good option. But if you log more than 15,000 miles per year or you know that you're a driver who is particularly hard on vehicles, buying is a better option. You'll pay extra for any damages beyond normal wear and tear (and your definition of *normal* may differ from the strict definition imposed by the leasing company) at the end of the lease.

As for the pros and cons of each, they break down simply.

Leasing pros:
· A new car every few years
· No worry about maintenance, as the car is always under warranty
· Potentially lower monthly payments

Leasing cons:
· Extra charges for going over preset mileage limits
· Extra charges for any damage (even minor damage)

Watch Out!

As with any contract, car leases come with a good bit of fine print. You need to read it, but you also need to understand it. Don't hesitate to ask questions, particularly when it comes to vague terms. One phrase you'll see a lot is "excess wear and tear," and its definition varies by lender. Typically car companies won't charge you for damages that are smaller than the size of a credit card; in other words, if you can completely cover that dent on the door with your credit card, you're off the hook. But other lenders, usually banks and credit unions, will nitpick every scratch and water spot, which can add up to hundreds and even thousands of dollars. More often than not, the lease itself won't specify how the company evaluates damages, so you need to ask upfront. Ask the salesperson to show you specific examples of damages that would be considered excessive and that wouldn't, and make sure that the description of each gets added to the lease agreement as an addendum. I'd even go so far as to take pictures and tack those on—it'll be more than worth the effort if you end up facing unfair charges a few years later.

Buying pros:
- Drive as much as you want
- No need to fix damages until—or unless—you want to
- Once it's paid off, you own it and can continue driving it
- A cheaper way to own a car if you keep it for years

Buying cons:
- Monthly payments can be higher than leasing
- Maintenance costs are on you once the warranty is up

I Also Need to Know . . .

Q: What length of lease should I get?
A: Aim for 36 months. Anything longer, and you're likely to start having maintenance issues. The term can be as short as 12 months, but for most people, replacing a car once a year isn't practical or necessary.

Q: What about mileage?
A: Good question, because mileage is one of the most common mistakes when it comes to leases. You'll be allocated a certain number of miles per year, generally 10,000 to 25,000 or more. Low-mileage leases come with low monthly payments, but if you go over the mileage limit, you can end up paying as much as 25 cents a mile. It's not worth it. Even if you drive only 8,000 or 9,000 miles a year, it's best to stick with at least a 12,000-mile lease. There's no point in having a new car if you can't drive it!

Q: **What are drive-off fees?**

A: When you purchase a car, you put money down because you're taking out a loan. When you lease a car, you put down drive-off fees. What's the difference? With a purchase, the more you put down, the better, because you reduce the amount of the loan and thus the interest you pay over time. But when you're leasing, you want to pay no more than $1,000 in drive-off fees. Sure, a higher fee will lower your monthly payment, which looks attractive. But if you get into an accident within the first few months and have to replace the car, and you had put $4,000 down, that money is gone forever.

Q: **Can I negotiate for a lease?**

A: Sure. Once you've figured out the term and mileage of the lease you need, as well as how much you want to pay in drive-off fees, you're ready to deal. The easiest way is to locate a few dealers in your area—maybe three to five—and ask them for a quote on the vehicle you want. Once you have those in hand, you can go back to the best ones and play them off each other: Tell them that you're debating between a few different offers, and see if they can do better or throw in an extra or two (free months are possible). Often salespeople can tinker with the numbers, including the interest rate and the residual value of the car, to make it work. If a dealer can't meet your price needs, move on.

   You may have heard another negotiation tactic, which is to talk down the price of the car—as if you're buying—and then when you have it where you want it, tell the salesperson that you want to lease. This popular advice is a bit outdated: These days, leasing is so common that there are a lot of specials to take advantage of, so this kind of strategy is no longer necessary. Also, one of the first questions you're going to get when you step onto the lot is how you're planning to finance your purchase. You don't want to have to lie.

Q: **How much should my lease payment be?**

A: It's a good idea to figure out how much the monthly payment on your ideal car will be before you walk in the door of the dealership. That way, you know if a price quote is fair and which cars are—sadly—out of range. It's no fun to get your heart set on something you can't afford.

The easiest way to get an idea is to call a few area dealerships and ask for quotes. If they won't give you one over the phone, you can head in or, if that takes up too much time, use this calculator from Bankrate.com: www.bankrate.com/calculators/auto/auto-lease-calculator.aspx.

Q: Should I buy a used car?

A: I have always said that the cheapest way to buy a car is to buy used and then drive it into the ground. That said, the answer to your question depends on the car. There are certain vehicles that are worth buying used. Some cars depreciate rapidly, and if you can pick one up that's a year or two old, you'll save a bundle. In general, American cars fall in this camp. Imports, however, such as Honda and Toyota, hold on to their value, which means you'll pay nearly as much for a relatively recent used car as you would if you were to buy new. In that case, it's sometimes not worth it.

Other things to consider? If you can buy a car that just came off lease, you'll generally get a good deal, but they tend to be hard to find. Corporate cars, if they have less than 50,000 miles on them, are often in great condition. And cars sold under manufacturer-certified used-car programs (often called certified pre-owned, or CPO, programs) are usually great. These programs are gaining in popularity, largely because they turn used-car buying into a new-car buying experience. You get an extended warranty and the peace of mind that the car has been thoroughly checked by the company's mechanics. The downside? You'll pay anywhere from $1,200 to $2,000 more. You can compare programs on Edmunds.com.

One category to stay away from is rental cars. They just aren't taken care of as well as they should be, and there's a good chance they'll come with more trouble than the savings are worth.

Q: Is it worth it to buy the service history?

A: If you buy from a CPO program, the company will hand a service history over for free. But if you're shopping for cars sold by previous owners, you definitely want to spring for a month's subscription to Carfax.com ($39.99/month). Pull each car's service history even before you go look at the car itself, so that you know what to look for and what to ask the seller. Among other things, the report will tell you whether the car has a salvage title, which means it was stolen, flooded, or in a serious accident, and whether the pedometer was rolled back.

THE MATH

How much car can you afford? I advise spending no more than 15% of your net monthly income on transportation, including gas, maintenance, and insurance. Here's how a few loans stack up:

Loan amount ($)	Term (Months)	Interest Rate (%)	Monthly Payment ($)	Total Interest Paid ($)
40,000	48	6.85	955.07	5,843.29
	60	6.59	784.33	7,060.00
30,000	48	6.85	716.30	4,382.47
	60	6.59	588.25	5,295.00
20,000	48	6.85	477.53	2,921.65
	60	6.59	392.17	3,530.00
15,000	48	6.85	358.15	2,191.23
	60	6.59	294.12	2,647.50
10,000	48	6.85	238.77	1,460.82
	60	6.59	196.08	1,756.00

Based on average daily interest rates from Bankrate.com on November 14, 2008.

12. Is it possible to get out of a car lease early?

A: Let me just say upfront that although it is possible—and we will go through the how-tos below—if you can help it, if you can afford to make your payments through the end of the lease, you're better off not getting out of the lease early. It's always going to cost you something extra, either in the form of fees from your dealer or a charge to trade the lease to another driver.

But there are cases in which riding out the lease just isn't possible. Maybe you lost your job and the luxury of an extra car just isn't in your budget anymore. Or you decided to take control of your credit card debt, and getting rid of a massive lease payment would go a long way to digging you out. Whatever the reason, if you find that you're no longer able to afford your lease, you have a few options.

1. **Talk to your dealer.** Explain the situation and see if you can strike a deal that will cost you less than your original payments, preserve your credit, and get you out of your car. Obviously if the amount charged by the dealer is more or equal to the amount remaining on your lease, there's no sense in going this route. But if the dealer is willing to work with you, there may be a way out. It will, however, cost you something, and probably a good bit more than option two.

2. **Swap the lease.** In this scenario, you find someone else to take over your car lease. There are a few companies that specialize in this online. They are the Match.coms of car leases—they'll put you in touch with someone who's looking for a short-term lease, then work with you to make an official transfer of the contract. They do all the dirty work involved in screening applicants to make sure that their credit and income are sufficient to take on the lease. Once the contract is transferred, however, you're not liable for any defaults on their part. It's out of your hands for good. Which sounds perfect, but understand that these services will cost you around $75 to list the car, and then there will be a contract-transfer fee, which varies widely but can be upward of $200. You also may have trouble finding a taker if you're running close to your allotted miles or if your contract's terms aren't competitive. (For specifics on what to look for in a lease, see page 40). And you always want to check with your leasing company first to make sure that this kind of transfer is something it allows and that there aren't any restrictions.

THE MATH

You're in a 36-month lease on a small sports car, paying $355 a month. A year and a half in, you and your mate find out that you have a baby on the way, and that zippy little two-door just isn't practical anymore. You can either return it to the dealer and cough up the remaining balance—$6,390 plus—to get out of the lease or you can trade the lease online. To do so, you'll pay about $230 to the lease-transfer company and an additional $450 to the dealer in transfer fees, for a total of $680.

Savings: $5,710

I Also Need to Know . . .

Q: How do I find a good lease-transfer company?
A: There are only a handful out there, and the best place to start is with an Internet search. You'll easily turn up the biggies: Swapalease .com, LeaseTrader.com, TakeMyPayments.com. Then you'll want to compare prices, making sure you're getting the full picture—most will charge a few different fees, and you don't want to be surprised. You might also compare the number of users on each site, as the more users a site has, the better chance you have of finding a taker for your lease. And just to be on the safe side, always check to make sure that the site lists contact information, including a working telephone number, and check the company's reports with the BBB (www.bbb.org/us/).

Q: What if the leased vehicle I take over breaks down?
A: If it's still under warranty, as many leased vehicles are (eliminating the hassle of handling repairs is one of the primary reasons that people lease), you'll be able to have it repaired under the terms of that agreement. If it's not, you'll be responsible for paying for any service the car needs—the original lease owner is no longer in the picture.

Q: Why can't I just turn in my keys?
A: If you drive the car back to the dealer, hand over the keys, and walk away, you're walking away from a loan; in other words, it will go on your credit report as repossession. And that's not good. Not only will you still owe the balance on the lease—meaning that the lender may come after you via a collection agency—but repossession will also remain on your credit report for seven years and could drag your credit score down by as much as 100 points.

Q: **Is it a good idea to take over someone else's lease, financially speaking?**

A: It depends. Taking over a lease via one of these sites is best if you want the lease for only a short time; otherwise, you're better off heading directly to the dealer. Taking over a lease can be a good way to get a short-term lease at a low cost because you're off the hook when it comes to a down payment, but you want to make sure that (1) there are enough miles left on the lease to meet your needs and (2) the car is in good condition. That means that aside from normal wear and tear, there are no damages. In the end, you're responsible for covering the bill for these, no matter who caused them. Always read the lease agreement before signing.

13. I inherited money. What now?

A: You might be surprised at this answer, but I'm inclined to tell you to do nothing—for six months to a year. Since this money is an inheritance, there's a good chance you're grieving a bit, in which case your emotions may overtake your more rational side. Where finances are concerned, that's not a good thing.

So while you're pondering your next step, stash the funds in a high-interest-rate savings or money market account or CD. (And remember, FDIC limits provide coverage up to $250,000 for each depositor through 2013. If you have inherited more than that, I suggest spreading it around between two or more financial institutions.)

In the meantime, do not make any promises. If you've seen the Nicholas Cage movie *It Could Happen to You*, you know what I'm talking about. In the movie, he promises a waitress half his prize if a lottery ticket proves to be a winner. Needless to say, it does, and his marriage dissolves when he has to pay up. (Not to worry—he got the better gal in the end.)

Once you're ready to start making decisions, seek some counsel. You'll want a financial planner (see question 10 on page 37), and, depending on how much money we're talking about, a lawyer and an accountant might come in handy as well. Talk to these people about how the money fits into your financial picture. I would suggest using it to satisfy needs in the following order:

1. **Emergency funds.** If you don't have an emergency cushion, an inheritance can be an instantaneous way to build one. In a bad economy, even two-income families want a six-month emergency fund to cover fixed expenses in case of a loss of income. Single individuals or one-income families should have a nine-month cushion.

2. **High-interest-rate debts.** In the past, you've probably heard that debt reduction comes first—but not right now. If you use this windfall to pay off credit card debt but you don't have an emergency fund, you're taking a risk that the credit card company will close your card. If that happens, you won't have anything to fall back on in an emergency. So establish that cushion, then use anything left over to pay down high-interest-rate debt. Remember, the interest rate you pay is equal to the return on your money—so if you pay down a 24% credit card bill, it's the equivalent of finding a 24% return on your money.

3. **One small splurge.** A large sum of money that hits at one time often feels like an invitation to spend. You may feel as if you don't *want* to do something with it—you *need* to do something with it. So take a small amount (5% or 10% max) and think about what feels right. What do you want? What would the person who left you the money feel good about? When the answers to those two questions intersect, you'll know what to do.

4. **One big goal.** After you get through the burning-a-hole-in-your-pocket stage, you can think more about longer-term uses for the money. What are your larger goals, and where could the money help you meet them? Are your retirement needs underfunded? How about college for your children? Have you been wanting to start a business on the side? This stage requires consultation with advisors.

Through this process, try to hang on to your old habits. If you were on a budget before, there's no need to toss that budget aside now. Keeping the same money-management routine will not only make your money last longer but will also go a long way toward helping you maintain your friends and your peace of mind.

I Also Need to Know . . .

Q: I didn't particularly get along with the person who left this money to me, and as a result, I'm feeling a lot of guilt. What should I do?

A: Again, you need to take time to sort out your feelings before you do anything. In this case, it might help to bring in a therapist in addition to a financial advisor. You shouldn't feel guilty for accepting an inheritance, but you need to come to that realization yourself, and talking to someone outside of the family can help you do that. Otherwise, you may make a rash decision and blow the money for emotional reasons.

If, after getting some help, you find that you're still shying away from this money, you might consider donating a piece of it to a cause that you support. That way, it will be put to good use and you can get it off your conscience.

Q: Is this inheritance going to hurt my chances of student financial aid?

A: An inheritance increases your assets, but luckily, income is the real factor in determining financial aid. Since an inheritance is basically money in the bank—not money you earned—it's not going to have a huge effect on your financial aid eligibility. According to the federal formula, parental assets are assessed up to a maximum of 5.65%, which means that if you received an inheritance of $100,000, the biggest dent it could put in your student's aid would be $5,650.

That said, if you stash the money in a savings or investment account and draw on the interest or dividends, that portion will be counted as income in the federal formula and could hurt your aid eligibility. You would likely be better off using it to pay off debt, if you have any. As long as the money is out of your hands when you fill out the student aid form (called the Free Application for Federal Student Aid, or FAFSA), you don't have to report it.

Q: My marriage is rocky. Can I protect this money from my spouse?

A: I want to point out that the rules surrounding divorce vary from state to state, so you should check with an attorney licensed where you live. That said, in general, you can protect an inheritance in the event of a split, provided you take the proper precautions.

When you receive the money, you want to put it in an account—brokerage, CD, savings, money market—in your name, and your name only. Don't commingle it with other income, whether yours or your spouse's, and don't use it to purchase something that will be shared between you, like a home. If you do, matters could get messy.

If you do decide to invest the inheritance in something like stocks, do it on your own, without the help or advice of your husband or wife. It sounds far-fetched, but if, for example, he or she recommends a stock to you, you buy it, and make a lot of money, your spouse may lay claim to some of that growth because it was bought based on his or her advice. It's best to leave the potential ex-spouse out of the money—and decisions around it—completely.

One last note: The best way to solve this potential problem is with a postnuptial agreement. This document is like a prenuptial agreement that is drafted after you are already married. Documents like these have become more popular in recent years and can be drawn up by matrimonial or family attorneys.

14. What should I do with my money when interest rates are going up? Or down?

A: It seems as if every time the Federal Reserve System changes the short-term interest rates (the Fed's Open Market Committee gets together eight times a year to weigh in on the fed funds rate, which directly affects the prime rate), Wall Street is a ball of anxiety, and for good reason. Interest rates have a direct impact on bonds and an indirect impact on stocks. They help determine the yield on your savings account and your CDs, and they factor into how much you pay for a mortgage, a home equity loan, and even your credit card debt.

How closely do you need to follow them? That depends. From an investment standpoint, following the Fed and trying to forecast interest rates is like trying to predict where the markets themselves are going to go. You can drive yourself crazy, and if you don't know what you're doing, you might lose a good bit of money.

But, you should know what interest rate movements do to your stock and bond portfolios. Interest rates and bond prices move in opposite directions, so when rates are up, bond prices are down. Stocks, however, are affected because the companies that issue them have to borrow money just as you and I do. When rates go down, that borrowing gets cheaper and so stock prices typically rise. When rates rise, it becomes more expensive for banks to borrow money, which leads to a higher cost of doing business and, in most cases, a decline in the price of stocks.

My advice? When it comes to investing, don't try to chase interest rates. Use these rates to your advantage in other ways:

- **Your mortgage.** When rates are down, monthly payments on adjustable-rate mortgages (ARMs) may be down as well. Fixed-rate mortgages won't be affected, but no matter the kind of mortgage you have, you might want to consider refinancing if your credit score is good. For more on refinancing, see "Should I refinance my mortgage?" on page 184. When rates are up, you may pay more on your ARM. Note: The same goes for many home equity loans and home equity lines of credit.
- **Your credit cards.** If you have a variable rate on your credit card, your monthly payment may go up and down with the Fed's interest-rate changes. However, many cards come with a floor—for example, 10%—and the interest rate can't drop beyond that. And you won't be surprised to hear that rates on credit cards tend to go up a lot faster than they come down.
- **Your CDs and savings accounts.** When interest rates are cut, banks will pay you less on the money you've stashed in savings accounts. When interest rates go up, they'll pay you more. CDs, however, come with rates fixed for the term of the investment, so money you already have in them won't be affected. One strategy often used to lock in those gains while maintaining your ability to get at enough money to keep you liquid is called laddering CDs. For more, turn to the question "What about laddered CDs?" on page 56.

I Also Need to Know . . .

Q: **The interest-rate cuts seem so small. Half a percent, a quarter of a percent—does it really have an impact?**

A: It does seem negligible, but when you're talking about large sums of money, it can have a hefty effect. Here's how it might shake out with an interest-rate cut of 0.5%:

▶ An Example

Your Credit Card

Let's say you have $10,000 on a credit card with an 18% interest rate and a minimum monthly payment of $250. It will take you more than 25 years to pay off your debt, at a cost of $13,370 in interest.

If, however, your interest rate drops to 17.5%, you'll be out of debt after a little more than 24 years and $12,515 in interest—a savings of $855.

Your Mortgage

Your $250,000 fixed-rate, 30-year mortgage is at an interest rate of 7%. You have 25 years remaining. Your monthly payment is $1,663, and by the end of the 30 years, you'll have paid $348,769 in interest.

At an interest rate of 6.5%, your monthly payment would drop to $1,580 and the total interest paid would be $318,862. That's a savings of $83 a month and $29,907 in interest.

Your Savings Account

You have an online-only savings account with an interest rate of 3%. Your balance is $15,000, your six-month emergency cushion. At the end of one year, you would have $15,456.24.

If your interest rate is cut to 2.5%, the interest earned would be reduced by $76.91, bringing your account balance to $15,379.33.

Q: **Why does the Fed change rates in the first place?**

A: It's a way of controlling inflation. When the short-term interest rate is higher, it is more expensive for banks to borrow from the Fed. When it costs more for banks to borrow, it costs more for everyone else to borrow—people like you and me, as well as companies—which means they spend less. When there's less money in the marketplace, inflation is limited.

When interest rates are low, however, it encourages spending because borrowing money is less costly. That's why the Fed continuously cut interest rates in 2008 to stimulate the economy.

15. How do I save for a goal?

A: The first step is coming up with a plan. When you have a goal in mind—say, a vacation or a down payment on a house or even a new pair of shoes—there are a lot of moving parts involved. First, there's the time frame. Does your goal have a concrete deadline? If you're saving for college and your son or daughter is five years old now, you have roughly 13 years to pull the cash together. If, however, you want to plan a big trip to Italy but you're flexible on when your flight leaves, you have a bit more wiggle room and you can put off your trip until you have the cash available to finance it.

Once you know the what and the when, you need to know the how. That's where saving comes in, and it's just a matter of socking that money away. Take a look at your spending and see if you can pinpoint any leaks in your budget. Are you blowing money on $3 cappuccinos five days a week? Do you go out to dinner every Friday night when you could just as easily scale it back to once every two weeks or once a month and pocket the $100 in savings?

If you can give up that cappuccino or a dinner here and there—and trust me, you can—you'll put that money toward your goal. You'll be surprised at how fast the money adds up, especially if you automatically transfer a set amount from checking account to savings account each pay period. It's always smart to take money out of your own hands before you ever get a chance to spend it.

One last thing: If you're the kind of person who starts saving and quickly gets discouraged, try giving yourself a boost at the start. It helps to see a chunk of money in your account, because you'll have the motivation to add to it. Have a yard sale, get rid of your old records on eBay, or volunteer to work a few overtime hours. Deposit that money immediately, and the feeling of seeing that progress might just be enough to keep the momentum going.

THE MATH

How do you get to Italy? Here's one route:

- Pass on that new pair of jeans.
  Savings: $60
- Cut your gym membership and run outside or use exercise DVDs instead
  Savings: $480/year for a $40/month membership
- Carpool to work
  Savings: $600/year in gas and car maintenance
- Plan the week's dinners in advance to reduce waste
  Savings: $10/week, or $520/year

Total: $1,660
Do the same thing again next year: $3,320
Sock it away in a high-interest savings account earning 2.5% in interest: $3,405

I Also Need to Know . . .

Q: **Where should I put the money?**

A: That depends on what the money is for and when you're going to need it.

If the goal is short-term and you need the money within the next three to five years, you're going to want to keep it out of the stock market, where you might lose principal, and put it somewhere where that can't happen. One choice: a high-yielding savings or money market account. (You can find the best rates at Bankrate.com.) Be sure that the account you choose doesn't charge any fees and that you have enough money to deposit to meet the minimum—some require $1,000 or more.

Another option to consider: CDs. They're not as liquid as money market accounts, but the returns can be higher (again, Bankrate .com is a good source of current rates). To get the advertised return on a CD, you agree to lock your money up for a set amount of time. If you need the cash sooner and have to break the CD, you'll pay a fine equal to three or six months' worth of interest, depending on the term, to cash out. There is no maximum penalty, so be sure to read the fine print.

Q: What about laddered CDs?
A: Laddering involves putting your money into a few different CDs with varied dates of maturity. You can then draw on the interest on a regular and consistent basis as each CD matures, and then reinvest the original deposit to keep the cycle going. It's a way for you to have peace of mind, as CDs are FDIC insured, and a predictable stream of income without having to bet on future interest rates.

16. Should I bank online?

A: In a word, yes. I pay all of my bills online, and I love it. It saves me time, it keeps me organized, and it saves money on stamps. It will take you about an hour or so to set up your accounts, get used to the interface, and memorize your passwords, but once you've done so, you're good to go.

The beauty of online banking is that you can schedule certain bills to be paid automatically each month. Things that cost you the same amount month in and month out—your mortgage, your auto loan—are perfectly suited to this feature. Not only is it impossible to forget to pay, but you pay on time, guarding against late fees and damage to your credit score.

For bills that are variable, such as your electricity bill, you just sit down at your computer and type in the amount, and the bank sends off the check or transfers the money for you. No need to go to the post office or stamp envelopes, or fill out and clip the payment form.

Finally, banking online is a great weapon in the fight against identity theft. Research has shown that people who bank online look at their accounts about four times more often than people who bank the old-fashioned way. By simply looking at your account balances, you will notice unauthorized charges, and then you can take action.

THE MATH

The savings that banking online can bring may not sound like much, but it adds up fast, particularly if you've been a victim of late fees. Let's say you pay 10 bills a month, costing you $4.20 in stamps. Over a year, you're looking at $50.20. Add in one late fee—just one—of, say, $17, and that number jumps to $67.20. What if you invested that amount each year at an interest rate of 8% instead?

In 10 years you'd have $1,136.
In 20 years you'd have $3,510.
In 30 years you'd have $8,779.

I Also Need to Know . . .

Q: **Is online banking safe?**

A: It is, particularly if you're worried about identity theft. A lot of people are still wary of banking online because they don't like the idea of their personal information being on the Internet. But keep in mind that banks take extreme measures to keep your information secure, and even after you've logged in, most templates won't display your complete account numbers. Compare that with writing a check, sticking it in an envelope, walking to the end of the driveway, putting it in your mailbox, and raising the red flag. When you do that, you're letting the mail carrier know that there is mail to be picked up, but you're also alerting everyone else in the neighborhood to that, too. Most identity theft still takes place offline, through things such as mail theft, Dumpster diving, and friends and neighbors with access to your home.

That said, you do want to take a few precautions. First, beware of phishing scams, which involve counterfeit e-mails asking for your account information. For more details, see "Signs of a Scam" on page 107 and "National Consumers League's Top Ten Internet Scams" on page 108. You should also access your bank account from only your personal computer at home, not, say, on a laptop in a café, where people could be looking over your shoulder. Be sure to have the appropriate firewalls and security software in place as well.

Q: **How can online banking help me get a grip on my finances?**

A: By monitoring your accounts online, not only do you keep tabs on identity theft, as I just mentioned, but also you always know which checks are outstanding, which deposits have cleared, and where you stand financially—in real time. This watchfulness is helpful for eliminating overdrafts, but it's also a huge factor if you share a joint account, because you and the person you share the account with don't have to keep each other up to date on every little debit.

Online banking can also help you save, believe it or not. One of the major reasons people don't save is because they spend the money before it even makes it into a savings account. But with online banking, you can have a portion of your paycheck transferred into savings immediately, before you're lured into a store to snag that new pair of shoes.

Q: **What about online savings accounts?**

A: These accounts have risen in popularity in the last few years, largely because they offer higher interest rates than traditional savings accounts do. What they don't offer, though, is brick-and-mortar branches. You do all your banking either online or through the mail, although some give you an ATM (automated teller machine) card that you can use to withdraw money in a pinch. To find the best rates on these and other savings accounts, go to Bankrate.com.

17. Which financial papers should I keep? Which should I toss? And on what timetable?

A: All of those bank statements, credit card bills, tax returns, and pay stubs can mean losing your kitchen table under the clutter. Here are the basic rules so you can get rid of some of the unnecessary documents:

Toss immediately:

- Credit card solicitations (shred them, preferably)
- Marketing material included in bank and credit card statements

Toss after a month, or when you reconcile with a bill or bank statement:

- ATM receipts
- Prospectuses and other information about investments you're considering
- Other receipts, assuming you're not planning to return the item and you don't need it for a warranty or rebate

Toss after one year, or when end-of-year consolidated statements come in and you've filed taxes:

- Bank statements
- Brokerage statements
- Cell phone, cable, telephone, and Internet service provider statements (unless you're deducting them for work or home office expenses)
- Credit card bills
- Pay stubs
- Social Security statements
- Utility bills

Toss after seven years, or when no longer needed for taxes:

- Child-care records
- Flexible-spending account documentation
- 401(k) and retirement plan year-end statements
- IRA (individual retirement account) contribution records
- Purchase records for investments
- Records of charitable donations
- Records on houses you've sold
- Tax returns and backup documentation

Keep as long as you own the asset:

- Insurance policies
- Receipts for important purchases (technologic devices, art, antiques, jewelry)

- Receipts for renovations or investments made on your home or property
- Titles
- Warranties

Keep forever, in a safe or safe-deposit box (with a second copy in a safe location off-premises):

- Adoption papers
- Appraisals
- Birth certificates
- Citizenship papers
- Custody agreements
- Deeds
- Divorce papers
- Financial aid documents
- List of credit card numbers, bank and brokerage statements, insurance policies, and toll-free contact information
- List of important contacts, such as your lawyer, accountant, physician, and relatives
- Military records
- Powers of attorney
- Stock certificates
- Wills and living wills

I Also Need to Know . . .

Q: Do I need a shredder?

A: Owning a shredder is a smart idea. Not only will you save space in your trashcan but you'll also protect yourself against identity theft, because a cross-cut shredder makes it virtually impossible for someone to piece your personal information back together. You can pick one up at an office supply store (and many big-box discount stores, too) for less than $100.

Q: How do I organize all of these papers?

A: It's intimidating, I know. I use a system that I call "bills in a box," essentially a file box with a handle. This way, I can take my system with me wherever I want to pay my bills—on the porch in the summer, to my accountant's office, or at the kitchen table. Inside the box, a handful of hanging folders divide my paperwork into these categories:

Taxes
Insurance
Health Care
Banking
Retirement/Brokerage
Credit Cards
Home
Auto
Legal
Estate
To Do
To Be Paid

Then, within each hanging folder, I have manila folders for each subcategory. For example, in "Credit Cards," you might find folders that say "American Express 2009," "MasterCard 2009," "Visa 2009." That way, once I've paid my taxes and closed the books on 2009, I can remove those folders, put them in a file drawer, and replace them with folders for 2010.

Q: **Should I own a safe?**
A: Again, I think a safe is a worthwhile investment. A fireproof safe (you want one that will stand up to fire for at least 90 minutes) can protect your valuable and important documents from damage and theft. At the same time, you have them right in your own home, so you can have immediate access.

But you really don't need to spend a lot of money. Safes can run as much as $1,000, but you can find them for as little as $200 or $300, too. Ideally, you want a standing safe equipped with a re-lock device, and key entry is better than digital. Believe it or not, digital wires can melt in a fire.

Q: **Are the contents of my safe-deposit box protected by the FDIC?**
A: No. When you sign a contract for a safe-deposit box, you want to read it carefully—some banks will make a limited insurance

payment to you if your belongings are damaged or destroyed, but others will not. You can, however, purchase fire and theft insurance to cover these items, typically as part of your home owner's or renter's policy. To do that, you should talk to your insurance company, not your bank.

18. What's the best way to save on airline tickets, hotel rooms, and car rentals?

A: Travel expenses are some of the easiest costs on which to find a deal because prices are generally flexible. Supply and demand varies from day to day, which is why you can often find the same flight priced at $300 one week and $150 the next. Here are some of my favorite tips.

Airlines
- **Sign up for a fare-alert service** like the ones offered by Expedia (www.expedia.com) and FareCompare.com. You can set a maximum price you're willing to pay, and they'll send you a notice when the ticket you need drops below that level.
- **Use a site like Bing Travel** (www.bing.com/travel/), which uses technology that predicts how a ticket will move in price over the next few months. If it says the price will go down, wait to book. If the price is expected to go up, you're better off confirming now.
- **Shop online.** Chances are that you know about the major travel consolidators—Expedia, Orbitz (www.orbitz.com), Price line.com—but did you know that you might be able to get a better fare directly from the carrier itself? Try booking both on a consolidator site and on the airline's Web site and see which offers a bargain.
- **Be flexible about your travel days.** You can sometimes save hundreds of dollars by flying on a Saturday instead of a Friday night, or leaving at 6 AM instead of 10 AM.
- **Pack light.** Several airlines now charge for checked baggage, no matter how much or how little it weighs. If you can fit your stuff into a carry-on, you could save $15. By the same

token, you're likely not going to get a free meal on board, so pack some snacks.

Hotels

· Try a few different approaches and see what nets you the better price. Call the hotel directly, search through a Web site such as Hotels.com, and try to book through the hotel's Web site. Often you'll get the best rates by picking up the phone, but you never know.
· Be flexible about where you're staying. Hotels that tend to book a lot of business travelers might offer great rates on the weekends.
· See if the hotel offers discounts to members of an association you belong to. AAA or AARP members may get up to 10% off at some hotels.
· If you're a regular at a particular hotel, join its loyalty or rewards program, which can net you a free night's stay every once in a while or a percentage off the price of each visit. But just be sure to continue shopping around: Getting a discount doesn't mean that what you're paying is the best price.
· If this trip is for the whole family, find a hotel that offers free meals for children, which could easily save you $100 or more over the course of a week's vacation.

Car Rentals

· Think outside your immediate area. In New York City, for example, car rentals are notoriously expensive. You may pay $100 a day to rent a car in Manhattan, when just through the tunnel in New Jersey, cars are renting for $30 a day. Shop rates at all locations in your area, not just the one that is the closest. The same is often true of off-airport locations.
· Check to see if the credit card you're using—or your own auto insurance policy—offers insurance coverage for rental cars. Most do, free of charge, as long as you decline the coverage offered by the rental company.
· Search the Internet for the name of the car rental company and the phrases *coupon code* or *discount code*. Web sites such as RetailMeNot.com will pop up with a long list of codes. Some work, some don't, but it's definitely worth a shot.

- If you can't get a deal, at least ask for an upgrade. You might be able to switch from economy to a sedan, free of charge.
- Watch the gas gauge. If you don't return your car with enough gas—usually you are required to fill it to the amount it had when you left the lot—you may get charged double the going rate at the pump.

Save on All Three

- If you're flexible about your travel plans—say, you want to go to Mexico but you don't really care when—go during that destination's down season, which means not only flights but also hotels will be less expensive.
- Many travel consolidators such as Orbitz and Expedia can find deals for you if you book your flight, hotel room, and rental car all at once. It's definitely worth it to price each service separately and together.
- Consider buying an Entertainment Book (www.entertain mentbook.com). They retail for about $30 (and often are on sale for half that), but they come with thousands of dollars' worth of savings, including on restaurants, hotels, and attractions. You can buy one for the city you plan to vacation in.
- If you're planning a last-minute trip, use a site such as Last-MinuteTravel.com, which pulls together the remaining airplane seats and hotel rooms at a great price. You can book a rental car as well.

I Also Need to Know . . .

Q: Do I need a travel agent?

A: In many cases these days, you don't. The Internet makes it easy to be your own travel agent, as long as you have the time to do a little searching.

That said, it's important to realize that when you work without an agent, you give up certain benefits, such as hand-holding and insider knowledge. If your travel is complicated and you have a few different legs to your trip, you might want to farm out the research to a travel agent, as he or she will do all the work for you. All you have to do is tell that person where you want to go and when. And, of course, show up.

Travel agents also sometimes have access to deals or discounts that you may not find online, because they may have pull with the major airlines and hotel chains. But you need to weigh that savings against the cost of hiring the agent. In the past, travel agents worked on commission from air carriers, but most major airlines have phased that out. Now, 93% of agents charge service fees. Typically, you'll pay a fee for airline-related services, and you may pay extra for trip research, car rental, and hotel reservations. The average charge to issue an airline ticket is $36.76, according to the American Society of Travel Agents. Keep in mind that that charge is per ticket, so if you're traveling with family, multiply that accordingly. If you find you'll simply break even, I'd work with an agent to have someone on your side.

19. Should I borrow money from a family member or a friend? How should I go about doing so?

A: The trouble with borrowing from family or friends is that it so often ends badly. It's awkward, and so both the borrower and the lender avoid the sticky conversations about when and how the money will be paid back, whether interest will be involved, and what will happen if the borrower falls behind. Then, when these issues come up, as they do frequently, you're often unclear about each other's expectations, and the relationship suffers. Not good.

That's why I'd avoid borrowing from friends and family, if you can. There are other options out there (see details about a newer form of Internet-based lending called P2P, short for *person-to-person*, on page 17). But if you have an emergency (and I'm talking about the kind that involves something like a health crisis, not a new pair of shoes) and don't have other borrowing options, and a friend or relative is willing to step in and help you out, try to follow these guidelines:

1. **Put the terms in writing.** You will be best served if you think of this transaction in business terms rather than in terms of your relationship. Sit down and ink the terms of

the arrangement. How much are you borrowing? When will you begin paying it back? How much will you pay back each month? When will you be finished paying back the loan? Will interest be involved? What will happen if you cannot make a payment? Will either of you be discussing this arrangement with anyone else in your circle of friends or within your greater family? It sounds formal to write it all down, but doing so helps eliminate misunderstandings that might come up.

2. **Discuss how the money will be used.** People who agree to lend you money often have an agenda—they want you to go to college, for example, so they agree to help you out until you graduate. If you say you'll use the money in a certain way, it is important that you follow through.

3. **Plan for the worst.** It helps to talk about what will happen if, on the off chance, you cannot pay when you say you will. How will your friend or relative feel? Will that make it impossible for the two of you to continue your relationship? You need to be open about the emotional side of your arrangement.

There is also one relatively new company that may be able to step in and help. Virgin Money (www.virginmoney.com)—yep, *that* Virgin, from Richard Branson—will draw up a contract, process the loan payments by direct debit and direct deposit, send reminder e-mails, and even send statements. There is a fee, of course—the basic package for a standard loan costs $99—but you may find that having a third-party intermediary takes a little bit of the emotional baggage out of the transaction. The company also reports to the major credit bureaus, which means that lending through them is a good way for borrowers to improve their credit score if they manage loan repayments correctly.

THE STATS

- **30%** of first-time home buyers borrow money from their parents
- **50%** of entrepreneurs borrow from friends or relatives

- **19%** of students finance all or part of their education by borrowing from friends or relatives
- The annual volume of loans between friends and family members is **$89 billion**.

I Also Need to Know . . .

Q: Should I *lend* money to a family member or friend?

A: You first need to look at your own financial situation and where you would get the money. Can you afford it? If you can do it without raiding your own retirement, college funds, and so on—*and* have the desire to help—it is something to consider. Before you do it, though, ask yourself some of the questions above in reverse. What happens if the person doesn't pay back the money on time? What happens if the money is not repaid at all? Will it harm the relationship irreparably?

If the answer is yes, do one of two things: Make a gift rather than a loan. Or decline the loan and volunteer to help your friend or relative find the money from another source. In other words, offer to help with information and emotional support rather than actual money.

20. What's the appropriate amount to tip?

A: In restaurants, the general rule is to tip 20%, which is up from the standard 15% of the 1990s. Customers have slowly caught on that servers earn far less than minimum wage (often little more than $2 an hour). They rely on tips to pick up the slack. You can tip a bartender slightly less—closer to 15%.

In terms of tipping for other services, 15% is the standard rule when it comes to the person who cuts or colors your hair, does your nails, or polishes your shoes (with a $2 minimum tip for these services). You can tip a taxi driver 15% of the total fare as well.

Finally, if you want to give an end-of-the-year or holiday tip to someone whom you don't steadily tip all year—the babysitter, for example—you can give the value of a few instances of the person's services instead of working out a percentage. So a babysitter might get two nights' pay, and a cleaning person should receive about a week's pay.

See the chart below for a few other rules. One thing to remember: You're never expected to tip the owner of a company. So if, for example, your hairdresser owns the salon, she doesn't expect a tip. You should still tip the person who shampoos your hair, though. Likewise, if you have an event catered, you don't tip the caterer herself if she owns the service, but you'll tip the waitstaff if the tip isn't already included in the cost of your contract.

SERVICE	STANDARD TIP
Skycap	$1 per bag
Bellhop	$2 for the first bag; $1 for each additional bag
Hairdresser	15%, plus $1 to $2 for the shampoo person
Furniture or appliance delivery person	$10 a person; more if the item is particularly heavy
Food delivery	15%–20%
Door attendant	$25–$100 as a holiday gift
Personal trainer	$50 as a holiday gift
Newspaper delivery person	$15 as a holiday gift
Movers	$20–$50 a person
Valet parking	$1
Coatroom attendant	$1 per coat
Dog groomer	15%
Dog walker	1 week's salary as a holiday gift or a few dollars for each walk

Source: www.tipping.org/.

I Also Need to Know . . .

Q: **At a restaurant, do I tip on tax and alcohol?**

A: You always tip on the pretax amount. But when it comes to alcohol, tipping gets a bit trickier. Most people tend to tip on the entire bill, including wine and other drinks, and I think that that's the way to go in general. But if you order an expensive bottle of wine—more than $100—you can tip a flat amount per bottle ($20 is plenty).

Q: **Should my tip reflect the level of service I received?**
A: I tend to think that unless the service was atrocious, it shouldn't.
Let me explain why: In many restaurants, tips are pooled together
and then distributed among the busboy, the bartender, and the
waitstaff. So if you tip poorly, you're affecting everyone, not just
the server who screwed up your order. Plus, if the food is im-
properly cooked or slow, it's often the kitchen's fault, so you may
be misdirecting your response.

   You're better off speaking up instead: Ask to talk to a manager,
and then explain what went wrong. That way, the restaurant can
learn from the experience, and if you decide to return, you may
get especially good care.

Q: **Is there anyone that I should never tip?**
A: You don't want to give money to your children's teachers, or to
your doctor or accountant. (I even feel funny giving money to the
people who drive the school bus, although I know people who
disagree with me.) In that case, you can give a nice holiday gift
or perhaps a box of chocolate or your famous chocolate chip
cookies.

   There are also employer-based limits in some cases—for
instance, your mail carrier. As a government employee, mail carriers are not allowed to accept cash or gifts valued at more than $20.
So you're welcome to give a small gift—maybe those cookies—but
no money. Many other delivery companies have regulations in
place as well, so research those before you give or just opt to give
cookies all around.

21. What's the etiquette when splitting an uneven check?

A: We've all been in this situation: You're out with a group of friends,
and they're drinking and you're not. Or they all order the filet
mignon and you opt for a salad. Either way, the check lands on
the table and someone suggests that splitting it evenly will be the
easiest way to go.

   But that means you're paying $20 for a few bottles of wine or
a steak that you didn't even taste. Paying for more than you ordered can leave you feeling bitter; speaking up can be embarrass-
ing. So what do you do?

The best way to approach a situation like this is to preempt it by either asking for a separate check at the beginning of the meal or telling your friends beforehand that you're only going to have something light, or that you're not going to be drinking, so you'd rather pay just your share.

But things happen—you forget to speak up at the start or you decide you don't want any wine after the bottle is ordered. In that case, it's okay to speak up when the check comes and say something like "Let's just adjust the bill, if we could, to account for my not drinking any alcohol tonight." That way, you're politely letting everyone know that you're just going to cover your share, and they can split the rest if they'd like. Chances are, no one will protest—just don't forget to add tax and tip. And remember that if the difference is only a few dollars, it's easier to skip the awkwardness for everyone.

One final note: This situation is a two-way street. If you're out with friends, and you notice that one person spent considerably less than the others, don't suggest splitting the bill evenly. It puts that person in an awkward position, and it's just not fair. The polite thing to do is recognize that they should pay less, so they don't have to navigate the awkwardness of speaking up. It's easier on everyone.

I Also Need to Know . . .

Q: My wife and I often go out to dinner with another couple and their teenage son. When the bill comes, we split it in half, but that leaves us paying for part of their son's dinner. Is there an easier way?

A: You shouldn't get stuck paying for your friend's son's dinner if you don't want to be, so go ahead and speak up in this situation. Next time you're out, simply pick up the check when it comes and divide the total, including tax and tip, by five. That way, they can pay three-fifths of the bill and you and your wife can pay your share, two-fifths. Restaurant servers are used to these kind of splits, and they'll happily allow you to put one amount on one card and another amount on the second. For instance, if the total is $100, your friends will pay $60 and you'll pay $40.

Of course, this math assumes that the teenager is eating and drinking as much as the rest of you, which may or may not be the case. (I know some teenagers who eat considerably more than some adults.) In that instance, you might just ask for separate checks at the start, or subtract his meal from the total, divide that by two, and then tack his meal on to their ticket. That gets a bit complicated, though, so if you can, just get two checks and enjoy the meal.

Q: **Who should pay on a date?**

A: The general rule here is that the person who does the asking picks up the tab, male or female. If a woman asks a man on a date, she'll foot the bill, and vice versa. If you don't feel comfortable with this scenario—you'd rather pay, or you'd rather go dutch—just say so upfront. A simple "I'd like this to be my treat tonight" or "If you don't mind, I think I'll pay my own way" will be just fine. Personally, I'm a fan of "I'll get this one; you can get the next one." Not only is it somehow nicer but it's also optimistic in assuming that there will be the next time.

Q: **How long is too long to haggle over the bill? My mother always insists on paying, and I'd rather she not. But I don't want an extended argument.**

A: Fighting over the bill is awkward for everyone involved, including the server, who often has to act as a mediator. Again, it's better to discuss it upfront. But if you foresee a problem, the best fix is to excuse yourself toward the end of the meal and give your credit card directly to your server. Ask that the server run it, add the 20% tip, and tell him that you'll sign it on the way out. This eliminates any arguing and allows you to focus on the person that you're spending time with, instead of on who is footing the bill. As for your mother, consider that it may make her feel good to pay and that you might want to allow that once in a while.

22. Should I use my debit or credit card for everyday purchases?

A: There are pros and cons to using either. Let's break it down.

Debit Cards

Pros:
- **You're spending your own money,** which means you're forced to live within your means. You don't have to worry about paying interest.
- **Frugality.** People tend to spend less when using a debit card than when using a credit card. (The same, by the way, goes for cash: If you use cash, you'll spend less than you would with a debit card. And if you keep large bills in your wallet, you'll spend even less.)
- **No late fees.** You'll have no bills to pay, which means no late fees.

Cons:
- **Fewer perks.** Limited, if any, rewards programs.
- **Overdraft fees can add up.** Indeed, they add up fast if you don't keep an eye on your account balance. These days, some banks still allow you to use the card, don't tell you that you're overdrawing, then hit you with a $35 fee for overdrawing your account. (Opt out of overdraft protection if you can.)
- **Administrative Hassles.** If someone steals your card, you likely won't be liable for the purchases they make, but you'll have to jump through a few administrative hoops to get your money back, which may leave you in a bind for a few days or even a week.
- **Account blocking.** If you go to a hotel, for example, they'll generally put a hold on a certain amount of money just in case. Gas stations often do this as well. This trigger could cause you to overdraw.

Credit Cards

Pros:
- **Track record.** They help you build up a credit history so that you can take out additional loans when the time comes.
- **Rewards.** You can get a card with almost any perk, from frequent-flyer miles to cash back to dollars toward a car. But keep in mind that studies have shown that consumers tend to spend more on rewards cards. And rewards cards generally

have higher annual fees and interest rates than plain-vanilla cards do.

· **Consumer protection.** If you're legitimately dissatisfied with a purchase or service, and you paid by credit card, your issuer will often stand behind you and you can withhold payment.

· **Zero liability.** More protection in the event of theft and fraud, because your money isn't being spent. You don't have to worry about not having access to your funds while the bank sorts things out.

Cons:

· **Interest.** This point is a biggie. If you don't pay your balance off every month, you'll pay for it. If you have a $2,000 balance on a card charging 18% interest and you only pay the minimum each month, you'll be in debt for 18 years and end up paying $2,615 in interest alone.

· **Late fees.** If you don't make your payment on time—and in the world of credit cards, that actually means early—you'll pay a hefty fee and damage your credit score.

· **Temptation.** Consumers spend more on credit cards than they do using debit cards or cash. Using credit cards doesn't feel like using "real" money.

So what's the answer? That depends on your end goal. If you're looking to build a credit history—which you need if you want a mortgage, car loan, or any other kind of credit—you have to have a credit card, and you have to use it. That's not an invitation to spend more than you make. Rather, you should use the card for purchases for amounts that you know you can afford to pay off each and every month.

You should have at least one credit card. But for everyday purchases, I'd stick to a debit card, particularly if you don't trust yourself to spend within your means on a credit card. If you want to cash in on rewards, it's okay to use a credit card, but pay it off in full each month.

I Also Need to Know . . .

Q: I can often choose to run my debit card as a credit card in stores. What's the difference?

A: Although this might seem like one and the same to you—either way, the money gets pulled out of your checking account—it's not. When the retailer processes your payment as a debit card purchase, you have to enter your PIN (personal identification number). Some identity-theft experts think that this system is more secure. After all, it's easier to forge a signature than figure out a PIN. Not only that, but running your card as a debit is cheaper for the retailer. Banks charge retailers hefty fees for processing credit card purchases.

One other difference: When you use your card as a debit card, you'll notice that the money is immediately pulled from your account. When you run it as a credit, it sometimes takes a day or two to process. My advice? If you're using a debit card, process the payment as a debit. The one exception is if your bank charges you a fee for in-store PIN transactions. This practice is rare these days, but it's worth a call to your bank just to double-check.

THE STATS

- **78%:** The percentage of American households—about 91.1 million—that had one or more credit cards at the end of 2008, compared with 90.4 million in 2007 (Nielsen)
- **$10,679:** The average outstanding credit card debt for households that have a credit card at the end of 2008 (Nielsen)
- **2006:** The first year that debit card spending topped $1 trillion for the first time. The total number of transactions outnumbered those on credit cards by more than 2 billion.

Resources

Associations

The American Bar Association
www.abanet.org
1-800-285-2221
Visit the ABA's Division for Public Education for information on buying, selling, or leasing a vehicle.

The Financial Planning Association
www.fpanet.org
1-800-322-4237
Access tips, tools, articles, and additional information about financial planning, as well as a tool for searching for a certified financial planner.

National Association of Certified Credit Counselors
www.naccc.us
321-725-3497
A nonprofit credentialing body that oversees the education and certification requirements of its members; includes links to helpful information on credit reports, scoring, and financial literacy.

National Association of Personal Financial Advisors (NAPFA)
www.napfa.org
847-483-5400
Search for a fee-only comprehensive financial planning professional.

National Child Support Enforcement Association (NCSEA)
www.ncsea.org
240-595-6600
A voice for the child-support community, NCSEA offers access to public policy, research, and legislative updates.

Books

Consumer Reports Used Car Buying Guide 2009
Consumer Report's 2009 reviews of used vehicles.

Consumer Reports New Car Buying Guide 2009
Consumer Report's 2009 reviews of new vehicles.

The Complete Divorce Handbook, by Brette McWhorter Sember (2009)
Retired divorce attorney Brette McWhorter Sember answers hundreds of divorce questions from all aspects in simple terms.

Don't Get Taken Every Time: The Ultimate Guide to Buying or Leasing a Car, in the Showroom or on the Internet, by Remar Sutton (2007)
A guide to buying or leasing a new or used car; includes step-by-step strategies and tips and tricks to protect yourself from dealer scams.

Easy Money: How to Simplify Your Finances and Get What You Want Out of Life, by Liz Pulliam Weston (2007)

A guide to help you take control of your finances and attain financial security; includes checklists, charts, and tables to help get you organized.

Follow the Fed to Investment Success: The Effortless Strategy to Beating Wall Street, by Douglas S. Roberts (2008)

Roberts explains the idea that there is direct connection between stock market performance and the actions of the Federal Reserve Bank.

The Lies about Money: Why You Need to Own the Portfolio of the Future, by Ric Edelman (2008)

A simple and fun explanation of seemingly complex financial concepts; includes a guide to help you build an investment portfolio.

Sudden Money: Managing a Financial Windfall, by Susan Bradley and Mary Martin (2000)

Advice from Susan Bradley, founder of the Sudden Money Institute, on how to manage a sudden influx of money.

Who's Sitting on Your Nest Egg? by Robin Davis, CFP (2007)

A guide to finding a reliable, competent financial advisor.

Essential Manners for Men: What to Do, When to Do It, and Why, by Peter Post (2003)

Etiquette tips for men on everything from weddings to Power-Point presentations.

Isn't It Their *Turn to Pick Up the Check? Dealing with All of the Trickiest Money Problems Between Family and Friends—from Serial Borrowers to Serious Cheapskates*, by Jeanne Fleming and Leonard Schwarz (2008)

Advice on financial etiquette and fiscal ethics.

Government Organizations

The Federal Reserve
www.federalreserve.gov

Financial information bank accounts, credit, identity theft, leasing, mortgages, personal finance, and recent financial news.

Federal Trade Commission
www.ftc.gov
1-877-FTC-HELP (1-877-382-4357)
   Information about credit counseling and debtor education.

MyMoney.gov
www.mymoney.gov
   The U.S. government's Web site dedicated to educating Americans on financial basics; includes a section devoted to financial planning.

Office of Child Support Enforcement
www.acf.hhs.gov/programs/cse/
202-401-9373
   Links to contact information and Web sites of individual states' child-support agencies, a glossary of child-support terms, a child-support enforcement handbook, child-support report newsletters, and more.

United States Department of Justice
www.usdoj.gov
202-514-4100
   A list of approved credit counseling agencies, facts for consumers, FAQs about credit counseling.

Web sites

All Law Child Support Calculators
www.alllaw.com/calculators/childsupport/
   Access a child-support calculator for your state to estimate how much child support will cost you.

American College of Trust and Estate Counsel
www.actec.org
310-398-1888
   A national organization of approximately 2,600 lawyers; public resources with information pertaining to inheritances.

Bankrate.com
www.bankrate.com
561-630-2400
   The Web's leader in financial rate information providing free rate information on more than 300 financial products, including money

market accounts, checking and savings accounts, CDs, credit cards, and more. The auto section allows you to compare local auto loan rates, rates for new and used vehicles, and auto refinance rates; and several calculators, including a buy-versus-lease calculator.

Better Business Bureau
www.bbb.org/us/
703-276-0100

Search for BBB-accredited businesses, including counseling agencies and lease transfer companies.

Carfax.com
www.carfax.com

For a fee (one report costs $29.99; multiple reports can be purchased at a discount), CARFAX will search its nationwide database to provide you with a detailed vehicle history report; there are also several free reports, including a Recall Check, Record Check, Lemon Check, and a Problem Car Check.

Certified Financial Planner Board of Standards
www.cfp.net
1-800-487-1497

Learn about financial planning and search for a certified financial planner.

Credit.com
www.credit.com

Information on how to find a quality credit counselor.

Edmunds.com
www.edmunds.com

Advice on all aspects of leasing, including information on how to get out of a lease.

Garrett Planning Network
www.garrettplanningnetwork.com
1-866-260-8400

An international network of independent financial advisors and planners who offer hourly, as-needed financial planning and advice.

Inheritance Project
www.inheritance-project.com

Explores both the emotional and social impact of inheriting money and offers networking opportunities and educational resources for heirs and their professional advisors.

Investopedia.com
www.investopedia.com

A wealth of investment information; includes a dictionary of financial terms, recent news, free investing tutorials, answers to FAQs, and financial calculators.

LeaseGuide.com
www.leaseguide.com

Everything you need to know about leasing, including information on getting out of your lease early, lease payment tables, a lease deal evaluator, a leasing worksheet, and a lease calculator.

Martindale-Hubbell Law Directory
www.martindale.com
1-800-526-4902, ext. 8001

Locate a lawyer in your area and search the profiles of more than one million legal professionals worldwide.

National Foundation for Credit Counseling
www.nfcc.org
1-800-388-2227

Find a foundation member agency near you for debt advice.

Nolo
www.nolo.com
1-800-728-3555

Visit Nolo's section on divorce and child custody for answers to FAQs about child support.

Sudden Money Institute
www.suddenmoney.com
1-888-838-9446

Find a well-established financial planner in this national network of advisors, including financial planners, wealth coaches, psychologists, attorneys, and philanthropy experts.

Virgin Money
www.virginmoney.com
1-800-805-2472

For a fee (fees start at $99), Virgin Money will assist in lending money to or from a friend or family member.

Emily Post Institute
www.emilypost.com
Etiquette advice and answers to manners questions.

Original Tipping Page
www.tipping.org
Information on all aspects of tipping; features a tip calculator, advice, and a forum.

CHAPTER 3

PROTECTING YOUR FAMILY

23. How do I go about naming guardians for my children?

A: You'll name guardians for minor children as part of your will (to read more about how to create a will, turn to page 83). Your lawyer will help you with the legal language, but it's your job to select the person or people you'd like to care for your children, if something should happen to you.

Tough stuff, I know. So difficult, in fact, that it stops many parents from getting a will in the first place, but that's a huge mistake. If you don't name guardians, the decision will be passed on to a court in most cases. It can turn into a long and drawn-out legal battle, one that comes for your children at the worst possible time in their lives. You owe them a will. And you owe them a choice. (And even if you think no one is perfect, picking the best of your not-so-perfect options is the right thing to do.)

The easiest way to start the process is by making a short list of people to consider. Remember that guardians have two jobs: One is to make the basic decisions for the child, decisions that you would be making if you were alive, and the other is to manage any money left to the child. You can separate these responsibilities, if you'd prefer, and have a guardian of the child and a guardian of the estate, but in most cases it's easier to have one person handle it all.

I also recommend naming one person instead of a couple, for a simple reason: If you name a couple (say, your brother and your sister-in-law) and they get divorced, who gets custody of your children is undecided. That's fine, if you're happy with either of them raising your kids. But if your intention was for your brother to be guardian and you have named his wife as well, you're running a risk.

Once you make your short list, ask yourself the following questions. By the time you get to the end, you should have your answer. And note that one of the other reasons that many people avoid this process is having to tell the people *not* chosen. Those are not conversations you have to have. As long as you and the person you have selected are on the same page, you do not have to discuss your will with anyone else.

SIX QUESTIONS TO ASK YOURSELF ABOUT A POTENTIAL GUARDIAN

1. Does this person have the time to take care of my children?
2. Does he or she share my values?
3. Is this person young enough and in good enough health to take on this challenging and lengthy task?
4. Is the person's geographic location desirable, or would the person or my children be required to move?
5. Does he or she have the resources necessary, or will I be leaving enough in life insurance and other resources so that's not an issue?
6. Is he or she willing to do it?

I Also Need to Know . . .

Q: **I have two brothers and want to name one as the guardian of my children. How do I explain this decision to the other?**

A: It's tricky, particularly if there aren't practical reasons for picking one over the other. It's easy to explain to Sam that you picked Joe because he lives in your town whereas Sam lives across the country, but it's harder to say that you think Joe would be a better father for your children. You don't have to bring this up at all if he doesn't, but if he asks, I think your best bet is to sit down and communicate with your brothers directly. Be honest and open about why you made the decision, without insulting him or his lifestyle. Talk about his concerns. You'll defuse tension by addressing the issue upfront rather than trying to hide it.

You should also consider that maybe you won't have to explain yourself at all—there's always a chance that your brother will be relieved to not have the responsibility. It's a lot to take on, and some people just aren't up for it. Everyone should keep this top of mind when asking someone to be a guardian, because if that person says no, it isn't a personal insult. It's the responsible response, because you wouldn't want anyone taking on this important role who is unprepared.

But note: As I said above, if you cannot bring yourself to have this conversation with Joe, the brother you haven't chosen, don't let that get in the way of selecting the brother you do want and putting it in writing. This piece of paper should get old and wrinkled without it ever becoming an issue, but just in case, the biggest mistake you can make is not taking action.

Q: I'm divorced and have custody of my children. Will the guardian I name take precedence over their father if something happens to me?

A: No. The other spouse gets the children if he or she is still alive, even if you're divorced and you have full custody. But that's not to say you shouldn't still name a guardian, because if for some reason your ex-husband doesn't want to take responsibility for them—or a court determines that he's unfit to do so—the person you've selected comes into play.

24. How do I write a will?

A: Creating a will doesn't have to be complicated, or expensive. The cost depends on how complicated the will is, which, of course, depends on the complexity of your family life and your financial situation. But a will is important. It is the only document that allows you to name guardians for minor children. And if you die without one, the rules of your state govern what happens to your belongings and your children.

If your situation is simple—maybe you're married with a few children and want to set it up so that everything you own goes to a spouse if he or she survives you, and to your children in equal shares otherwise—you can make a will yourself. Although wills written on napkins have been known to hold up in court, I wouldn't recommend handling yours that way. Instead, if you want a low-cost solution, use a Web site such as LegalZoom.com for the framework. If you go this route and you're willing to spend a little more money, hire an attorney to give your document a once-over before you sign it to make sure you have done everything correctly.

As things get a bit more complicated—as you add to your family or your assets—it pays to see an estate-planning attorney who can draw up a basic estate plan for around $1,000. He or she will ask you what assets you own, and what you'd like to happen to them after you pass away. It helps to make a list beforehand so that you can take stock of the important things and where you'd like them to end up. The attorney will then be able to incorporate the legal language.

I Also Need to Know . . .

Q: Is there anything that's not covered by a will?

A: There are a few things that will be passed in a certain way no matter what your will says. Property owned jointly will go to whoever remains on the deed as a tenant if one party passes away. So, for instance, if you own a home with your mate, the surviving mate will take ownership of the home.

Pay close attention to anything that has a beneficiary designation, including life insurance policies and retirement accounts. These all require you to name a beneficiary of the money should it need to be passed on, and that designation takes precedence over a will. That's why it is important to keep these up to date throughout all major life events.

Q: How do I find a lawyer to help with my will?

A: You need an estate-planning attorney, someone who specializes in putting together the whole package: the will, the health-care proxy, the living will, the durable power of attorney for finances (see the next question for information on these documents and why they're so important). I'd start by asking friends and family if they've worked with someone they can recommend, and if that doesn't work, you can do a search through your local bar association or at FindLaw (www.findlaw.com). Set up initial consultations to make sure you're comfortable working with the person you choose and with his or her fee. If you need to make changes to the plan in the future (and it's likely you will), you can streamline the process by going back to the same attorney.

Q: **What are a health-care proxy, living will, and durable power of attorney? Do I need those documents as well?**

A: Most people should have the whole package:

- A **living will** is a document that tells a doctor or hospital what action you want taken in a dire situation. It answers the question "Do you want life support?" This document should accompany a basic estate plan, but you can also draw one up using a form offered on many Web sites. To find a form, check with your state's bar association. All you have to do is fill out the form and sign it, no lawyer necessary. If you split time between two states, though, it's a good idea to fill out the forms for both states.

- A **health-care proxy** gives a person you choose the authority to make medical decisions on your behalf. Many medical problems have gray areas, so this person could be critical. A doctor may rely on this person's decision over what your living will dictates. Your lawyer can draw up the document, you can pull one from the Internet (the Web site of your state chapter of the American Bar Association chapter may have one available for print, or you can try a site such as www.nupplegal.com [NUPP Legal]), or you can pull a plain-English living will and health-care proxy combo document called "Five Wishes" from Aging with Dignity (www.agingwithdignity.org). It asks you questions, you answer them, and the job is done. The downside: It is effective in only 20 states, so check to be sure that yours is one of them.

- A **durable power of attorney** for finances allows another person to make financial decisions for you, including writing checks and conducting transactions with your accounts, if and when you're unable to make them. This document is another important part of your estate-planning package.

Q: **Who should I name as my health-care proxy? As my durable power of attorney for finances?**

A: The same person, or two different people, can fulfill these roles. If you're married, you'll probably name your spouse for both of these roles. If you're not, you can name an adult child, a sibling, a parent, or a friend who you trust to carry out your wishes. It's wise to name a backup as well, just in case. Ask yourself not only who you might trust in this situation, but whether this person has the fortitude to stand up to other members of your family and the medical establishment if necessary. Then check with the person to make sure he or she is willing to do it.

Should the durable power of attorney for finances need to be invoked, it could turn into an ongoing role that requires considerable work on this person's part, so keep that in mind. You want to make sure the person you name is up to the challenge and has the time available. If you can't find someone, you can give the power to an accountant or other financial professional whom you trust, but keep in mind that your accounts will be billed accordingly.

25. How often do I need to update my will?

A: Every three years or after certain major life changes, including:

- Marriage or divorce
- Death of an heir or beneficiary
- Birth of a child
- Purchase or sale of a business
- When a guardian, executor, or trustee dies or is no longer able to serve
- When your children are no longer minors
- Your preferences have changed (in other words, you wanted to leave a chunk of money to someone but you've since changed your mind)
- Major changes in the value of your estate

Because of that last item on the list, I review my will once every three years with the attorney who drafted it, no matter what. Chances are, you will see significant changes in the value of your net worth every few years, and going through your will—as well as your entire estate plan—to make sure everything is up to date is a smart idea. If you want to make changes, you've already involved the lawyer in the process. If there was no law-yer and you used software or drafted your will online, you can use the same tools to draft an update.

One other thing to note: When you make changes to your will, be sure to review the beneficiary designations on life insur-ance and retirement accounts as well. These designations over-ride your will.

I Also Need to Know . . .

Q: **After I update a will, what do I do with the old documents?**

A: The last thing you want is for an old will (or two) to confuse the executor of your estate. In your new will, you'll revoke the old document by including a sentence that indicates the new docu-ment overrules anything in prior documents (the legal language is usually "I revoke all previous wills"). Then you want to destroy all copies of your old will, by shredding it, burning it, or writing "I revoke this will" on each page, along with your signature.

Q: **What happens if I move?**

A: If you move within the same state, you're fine, but if you move to another state, you will want to have an estate-planning attorney look over your will to make sure it fits in with the new state's laws. In Florida, for example, the will's executor must be either a rela-tive, spouse, parent, or child of the will's owner or a legal resident of the state. That means that if you moved from New York and your will's executor is your longtime friend in New York, you'll need to name a new executor.

You should also update your durable power of attorney for fi-nances, your living will, and your health-care proxy (for more on these, turn to page 85) because forms differ from state to state. Hospitals and doctors may be more comfortable with one that they're used to seeing. Or worse, the form you used previously may not be legally recognized in your new state.

Q: **What is probate?**

A: When someone dies, his or her will goes to probate court, which must verify that the document is authentic and must dole out the property as the will dictates.

Probate is often talked about as a long, drawn-out, expensive process for the heirs, and it can be, if you don't have a will. Without a will to direct it, the court must divide the property as it sees fit, which can be time consuming and challenging. As long as you have a will, however, most states have streamlined procedures, limiting the time your heirs spend in court.

And as long as your will has been drafted correctly, probate is relatively painless. There are two states—Florida and California—where the process tends to be more expensive and lengthy no matter what. (For that reason, the living trust business, which helps avoid probate, booms in those states. See the next question, "Should I leave money to my children?", below). But in general, probate isn't something you should fear.

26. Should I leave money to my children?

A: Investor and businessman Warren Buffett once said that he wants to leave his children enough money so that they can do anything, but not so much that they can do nothing. I agree with that philosophy. These days, an inheritance of any scope is a huge gift—it might allow your children and their children to avoid student debt, buy that first house, or start a business. But leaving children so much money that it eliminates their drive to work, to accomplish things on their own, can be a huge mistake.

Once you've come up with a philosophy—and a number—of your own, you must ask another question: How, exactly, should I go about making that bequest?

Whether your children are minors or are up to 25 or 30 years old, I would suggest not leaving their inheritance in your will. Instead, I would set up a trust. If you leave minors a lump sum of money in a will, they will be assigned a guardian (typically a relative or close family friend) to manage that money until they turn 18. Once they're of age, the money becomes theirs, and they can spend or save it as they please. I don't know about you, but when I was 18, I was not capable of handling large amounts of money.

A trust, however, allows you to leave that money with conditions. You can lay ground rules and dole out the money in chunks over a period of time to keep your kids from using it all immediately. Often, children receive one-third at age 25, another third at age 30, and the final third at age 35, but you can establish any schedule you like. This way, you're protecting your money, and if they act rashly in their twenties, at least they're out only a portion of their inheritance instead of the whole shebang. By the time they're allowed access to the next increment, hopefully they've learned a valuable lesson.

To set up a trust, you need to talk to an estate-planning attorney. You'll tell him or her whom you want to benefit from the money or property and under what conditions they'll receive the assets. Then the trust will function like a bank account, and you'll have to name a trustee responsible for doling out the money as you've described, as well as a successor trustee who can step in if the first one is unable to do the job.

If, however, your kids are older, and you don't want any conditions tied to the inheritance, you can leave them money directly through a will. For more on writing your will, see "How do I write a will?" on page 83.

I Also Need to Know . . .

Q: Should I have a testamentary trust or a living trust?

A: Let's sort out the differences first: A testamentary trust is created after you die. It is established within your will, and is irrevocable, for obvious reasons: When it takes effect, you are no longer around to make amendments. A living trust is created while you're alive, hence the name. A living trust can be revocable or irrevocable.

If you have a testamentary trust, there will be annual court hearings regarding the property within it. It will be public, and the court fees make it more expensive. A living trust, however, is a private document and allows your trustee to avoid those court fees and hearings.

There is only one reason why you would choose a testamentary trust over a living trust: A testamentary trust allows you to pass money on to your surviving partner without affecting his or her eligibility for Medicaid.

Now, as for whether you should have either one: We've already talked about one situation that requires a trust—if you're leaving money to minor children. The other reason is that trusts allow you to avoid probate. But unless you live in California or Florida, where probate is a lengthy and expensive process, that isn't reason enough on its own to establish a trust. Fees for establishing and maintaining trusts can be expensive in their own right—$1,500 plus.

Q: How much should I leave?

A: This decision is personal, but I'd encourage you to talk to your children about what they can expect. This is particularly important if, for whatever reason, you decide to dole out unequal amounts to your children. You could have legitimate reasons for doing this—say one child is more than financially comfortable after a business success and the other is still struggling along—but you should be open and honest with all of your children about the thoughts behind your decision. Otherwise, you risk compromising their relationships with each other when you are gone.

Q: Any recommendations for conditions I should write into the trust?

A: Exercise at least some caution, even if your children have been socking away their pennies since they were five. Getting a big chunk of money can be overwhelming to even the most financially savvy person, and when you add grief to the mix, bad decisions often result. And since presumably you're setting this up when your children are young, you don't know how they'll manage their money as grown-ups.

Consider splitting the money up, allowing the trustee to dole out portions of it every 5 or 10 years.

▶ An Example

You have three children, ages 6, 8, and 11. You want to leave them each $400,000 in a trust. You could break the money into quarters:

- $100,000 at age 18
- $100,000 at age 25
- $100,000 at age 30
- $100,000 at age 35

Or you could give up a little at first and then the rest when they've matured a bit:

- $100,000 at age 18
- $300,000 at age 30

Or you could hold the money until they hit age 40, with provisions for withdrawals in certain circumstances:

- First car
- College
- Grad school
- Wedding
- Down payment on a home
- Launch of a business

Q: **Who should I name as a trustee?**

A: Someone who shares your values, has good judgment, and knows you well enough to mimic what you would do if you were still around. The trustee doesn't have to be a person who knows about money or law (although both skills would be a bonus), but you should be confident that this person will make the right decisions under pressure. You can also pay a bank or institution to serve as a trustee. This choice is not as ideal, though, because while a bank will be skilled at managing the money in the account, it will not exercise discretion in the same way that someone who knows you well would when it comes to decisions about how the money should be spent.

27. How do you secure the financial future for a child with special needs?

A: This scenario is complicated—one that many parents face these days. If you leave money or assets to your child directly through a will, when he turns 18 that money will be counted against him when it comes to determining his eligibility for government programs such as Medicaid and Supplemental Security Income (SSI). For most people these programs are vital for long-term support.

These programs work in the following ways: Medicaid and SSI are federal programs, but states regulate and administer the benefits. The rules vary by state, but most states require your child—at age 18—to have assets of less than $2,000, not including a home or car, to qualify for care programs.

That is not a lot of money, particularly if you are considering leaving an inheritance to your child. Enter the "special-needs trust."

A special-needs trust is a special trust account that the tax code allows you to create for your child. You can fund it with any assets you'd like to pass on to him or her, including real estate and paper investments such as stocks or bonds. But because this account is managed and the proceeds are used for your child's needs, rather than being owned by and managed by your child for his or her own wants and needs, anything in this trust is not counted against your son or daughter for Medicaid or SSI purposes.

If you have a special-needs child, you want to establish a special-needs trust sooner rather than later. Why? Because it must be in place to receive your assets in the awful case that something happens to you and your spouse. The good news is that the process is simple, provided you have some help from an estate-planning attorney. You will need to appoint a trustee to manage the account in the event that you and your spouse are no longer around. Your best bet is finding a planner or estate-planning attorney who specializes in these trusts. You can locate one through either the Special Needs Alliance (www.specialneedsalliance.com) or the Academy of Special Needs Planners. The financial firm Met-Life also has a division dedicated to special-needs planning.

I Also Need to Know . . .

Q: How do I pick a trustee?

A: This decision is crucial when setting up the trust, and you want to think seriously before you appoint anyone. Obviously, you want someone you can trust, but you also want to choose a person who has a connection with your son or daughter, whether that's a relative or a close family friend. The trustee should also have the time to devote to managing the trust, and he or she should be responsible with money. You're handing off a blank checkbook, and this person is responsible for making the money last throughout your child's life, while also following the federal restrictions, which dictate that the money can only be used to benefit your child as a supplement to state and federal benefits. In addition to picking a trustee, you should select a successor trustee—a second choice—in case the original trustee is unwilling or unable to serve.

Your other option, if you can't find a suitable trustee within your circle of family and friends, is to hire one. To do that, you probably need at least a quarter of a million dollars in the account, but professional trustees have done this work before and are familiar with all of the complexities of these kinds of accounts.

Q: My parents and other relatives like to give my son money for his birthday and other holidays. Does this count against him?

A: If your child is 18 or older, it will count against him, because that's the age that his own income and assets will play into his Medicaid eligibility. To work around this limitation, you can politely ask that all gifts be in the form of a check made out to his special-needs trust.

Q: Can I use life insurance to fund a special-needs trust?

A: Yes, in fact upward of 90% of these trusts are funded by life insurance settlements. Survivorship life insurance, which allows you and your spouse to buy coverage under one policy that doesn't pay out until the second spouse dies (it's cheaper than a policy written on a single life), can cover costs such as estate taxes. It can also be a great way for grandparents to pass money along for your child's future. They will just have to designate the trust as the beneficiary. Keep in mind that this option works only if you have enough money not only to support yourself after the death of a spouse without the help of life insurance benefits but also to continue paying the premiums on the policy until you yourself pass away.

Q: Is my child taxed on the trust funds?

A: Yes, but there are special income tax rates for money in trusts. They've fluctuated over the years, but in general, they tend to be similar to personal income tax rates. The trustee will be responsible for filing a tax return each year.

Resources

Associations

Academy of Special Needs Planners
www.specialneedsplanners.com
1-866-296-5509

Information on financial planning for families with special-needs members; access to a network of attorneys who focus on special-needs planning.

American Bar Association (ABA)
www.abanet.org
1-800-285-2221

An introduction to wills from the ABA, information on and answers to estate-planning FAQs, and a glossary of estate-planning terms.

American College of Trust and Estate Counsel (ACTEC)
www.actec.org
310-398-1888

A nonprofit association of trust and estate counselors; find an ACTEC fellow, browse public resources, governmental resources, and trust and estate blogs.

Special Needs Alliance (SNA)
www.specialneedsalliance.com
1-877-572-8472

A national nonprofit organization; search the network of SNA attorneys across the United States and browse literature on financial planning for families with special-needs members.

Books

8 Ways to Avoid Probate, by Mary Randolph (2008)

Effective methods to help you skip the probate process; includes the latest estate and gift tax rules and updated 50-state tables on simplified probate.

60-Minute Estate Planner: Fast and Easy Plans for Saving Taxes, Avoiding Probate, and Maximizing Inheritance, by Sandy F. Kraemer (2006)

Contains estate-planning basics and includes helpful tools such as sample forms and worksheets to help you plan.

The AARP Crash Course in Estate Planning: The Essential Guide to Wills, Trusts and Your Personal Legacy, by Michael Palermo (2008)
Covers every aspect of planning an estate or a will.

Be Prepared: The Complete Financial, Legal, and Practical Guide to Living with Cancer, HIV, and other Life-Challenging Conditions, by David S. Landay (2000)
Medical, financial, and legal advice on how to face some of life's toughest issues.

Estate Planning Basics, by Denis Clifford (2007)
A basic overview of the estate-planning process.

Kiplinger's Estate Planning: The Complete Guide to Wills, Trusts, and Maximizing Your Legacy, by John Ventura (2008)
Detailed information on wills, trusts, and estates.

Special Needs Trusts: Protect Your Child's Financial Future, by Stephen Elias (2007)
A guide to how to leave money to a loved one who is disabled or has special needs without interfering with government benefits.

The Special Needs Planning Guide: How to Prepare for Every Stage in Your Child's Life, by John W. Nadworny and Cynthia R. Haddad (2007)
A book by financial planning experts with special-needs family members; includes advice on the financial, legal, governmental, and emotional aspects of financial planning for someone with special needs.

Wills, Probate, and Inheritance Tax for Dummies, by Julian Knight (2008)
How to plan and write your will, minimize the stress of probate, and more.

Government Resources

Centers for Medicare and Medicaid Services
www.cms.hhs.gov
1-800-633-4227
Detailed information on Medicaid and Medicare, including information on initiatives, coverage, and how to protect yourself from fraud.

Web sites

AARP
www.aarp.org/families/end_life/
1-888-687-2277

An estate-planning guide, explanations of commonly used terms in the estate-planning process.

Aging with Dignity
www.agingwithdignity.org
1-888-594-7437

Educational resources and access to the "Five Wishes" legal document that helps you to express how you would like to be treated if you are ill and unable to communicate your wants and needs.

FindLaw
www.findlaw.com

Visit the organization's Estate Planning Center to find an estate-planning lawyer, access legal forms, post an estate-planning question for lawyers to answer, browse a legal glossary, read estate-planning tips and more.

LegalZoom.com
www.legalzoom.com
1-800-773-0888

Guides on specific legal topics, answers to FAQs, a glossary of legal terms; create legal documents from home and have them sent to you directly.

MetDESK (of MetLife)
www.metlife.com/desk
1-877-638-3375

Free information for families with special-needs children; includes a special-needs calculator, a special-needs planning quiz, newsletters, and more.

Nolo.com
www.nolo.com
1-800-728-3555

Information on selecting a guardian for your children, wills, estates, and probates; search for an estate-planning lawyer.

Special Needs Planning
www.specialneedsplanning.com

Special-needs financial planners John Nadworny and Cynthia Haddad's site featuring information on special-needs planning, special-needs news and articles, answers to FAQ, a glossary of terms, and links to resources for specific types of disabilities.

Survivorship A–Z
www.survivorshipatoz.org

Practical, financial, and legal information for anyone facing a challenging medical situation.

CHAPTER 4

IDENTITY THEFT AND SCAMS

28. Could my child be a victim of identity theft?

A: Yes. One of the fastest growing areas of identity theft today is child identity theft—1 in 10 children today have their identities used or abused in some way—so it's important to know how to protect your children.

You might wonder how thieves get their hands on this information—after all, young children don't generally shop online or use e-mail the way adults do. But you have to remember that things—like a child's Social Security card or Social Security number—can be stolen. In addition, about one-third of identity theft is perpetrated by friends or family.

As for checking your child's credit, you need to write a letter to the three credit bureaus and ask them if there is a file with your child's Social Security number on it. (You can find the contact information for all three among the resources at the end of this chapter.) You may be asked to include copies of your child's birth certificate or other information that confirms his or her identity. If you find out that there is a report under that number, you need to inform the bureaus that it is a fraudulent file. You should do this in writing, and keep a paper trail. They should automatically add a fraud alert to the file, but you should double-check to make sure that they do.

Then, head to your local Social Security Administration (SSA) office. As a parent, you have a right to ask if anyone is working under your child's Social Security number. If the answer is yes, you should have them issue a new number for your child. You should also file a police report at this point, if you haven't already.

Once a new Social Security number is issued to your child, he or she has a clean slate. He or she can start fresh, and the credit reporting bureaus will shut the other number down, if it was active, so that it cannot be used fraudulently.

One last thing to note: If you can, it's a good idea to start this process by the time the child is 16, because at that point, he or she is close to looking at colleges and if private loans are needed, the student's credit comes into play. It can take up to two years for the process to be completed.

SIGNS YOUR CHILD MAY BE A VICTIM

- Preapproved credit applications sent to your child
- Bills or bank statements mailed to your child's name for accounts that aren't his or hers
- Calls or letters from debt collectors
- Denial of a driver's license, as this could mean that another person already has a license under that Social Security number

I Also Need to Know . . .

Q: **Should I invest in credit monitoring for my children?**

A: You can do the work of a credit monitoring service on your own and save yourself the cash. If you think your child is vulnerable to identity theft, you should request his or her credit report a few times a year from each credit bureau. Keep in mind, though, that children aren't eligible for the free reports provided by AnnualCreditReport.com; instead, you must contact each bureau directly to request copies of the report. If there isn't one (and that's the hope), you won't have to pay anything.

29. How do I protect my identity? What should I do if my identity has been stolen?

A: It's difficult to shield your identity from thieves completely. I don't want to give you a false sense of security, because no matter what you do, you're always vulnerable. That's one of the first things that the FTC tells people when asked this question.

That said, there are steps you can take to limit your exposure to identity theft, and luckily, most of them are fairly easy and cheap, if not altogether free. Here's a run-through:

1. **Maintain control over your information.** Shred documents before you put them in the trash. You can get a good cross-cut shredder at an office supply store for less than $50, and it's worth it. What should you shred? Preapproved credit card offers, convenience or balance transfer checks from your credit card company, and any other mail or documents with account or credit card numbers, or other personal information. When in doubt, shred it.

2. **Don't respond to online or phone solicitations for your personal data.** A caller or someone e-mailing may ask for your Social Security number, bank account information, or other personal details. This practice is called phishing, and it's a popular form of identity theft. The thief will design an e-mail—and often an e-mail address—that mimics one from a bank, credit card company, or a business like PayPal or the UPS. It will direct you to a fake Web site, also designed after whatever company the bank is mimicking, that asks you to input sensitive account information or personal details such as your Social Security number. Once you do, the thief has your information. A good general rule of thumb: No bank, lender, or store will send you an e-mail or even call you asking for personal information. Don't fall for it. When in doubt, pick up the phone and call the company to verify the e-mail or call's authenticity. For more on this issue, turn to the question "How do I know if I'm being 'phished'?" on page 109.

3. **Install a firewall on your computer.** If you're like me, you use a DSL or cable modem that leaves you connected to the Internet at all times. Great for convenience; not so great for security. Without some kind of protection, thieves can plant a program or virus into your machine and access the information on your hard drive. To stop this from happening, you need to install a firewall, which functions like

a lock would on your home, and antispam and antivirus software. Be sure to keep them updated as well. Norton and McAfee are two well-known brands.

4. **Be selective about what you carry in your wallet and handbag.** A good general rule is only to carry what you need to have with you. If you have a few credit cards, limit it to one on a daily basis. Leave the Social Security card at home. Don't keep your bank account numbers and passwords in your wallet. And take a general inventory of what is in there, so if the wallet is lost or stolen, you'll know what is missing.

5. **Keep on top of your credit report.** You're entitled to a free credit report once a year from each of the three major credit-reporting agencies, which means you can, and should, pull one every four months from AnnualCreditReport.com. Once you have it in your hands, look it over and make sure that you recognize all the accounts and that your personal information is accurate.

If you do fall victim to identity theft, the first thing you want to do is put a fraud alert on your credit file. You can do this by contacting one of the three credit reporting agencies: Experian, Equifax, or TransUnion. They are required by law to contact the other two. The fraud flag signals to creditors that they need to take additional steps to confirm the identification of anyone who applies for credit in your name.

Next, you want to contact the creditors where the fraudulent accounts were opened, whether that's a credit card (in most cases, it is), a bank, or a retailer. Ask that the accounts be closed, and follow up in writing via certified mail.

After you've done that, head to your local police department and file a police report. This step is important, because having a copy of the police report will help legitimize your claims. You should also file a complaint with the FTC, which collects complaints and makes them available to police departments so that they can connect the dots and catch repeat offenders. Print the complaint form. Along with the police report, the FTC complaint form can be used to dispute illegitimate accounts and make debt collectors stop collecting on fraudulent debts.

Throughout the whole process, you want to be sure to keep a record of the complaints you've filed, letters you've sent to the credit bureaus, and any other correspondence related to the identity theft. That way you have backup should you ever need it.

I Also Need to Know . . .

Q: I heard that fraud alerts only last for a few months. Is that true?

A: It is. Fraud alerts last for 90 days, unless you've been the victim of identity theft. Essentially, anyone can put what's called an initial fraud alert on his or her credit report. You can do it if you've been a victim, if you lost your wallet and want to take precautions before it's too late, or even if you just like the idea of creditors double-checking before they grant credit in your name.

In the last two cases, though, you'll need to make a note on your calendar to renew the alert if you want it to continue past 90 days. In the first case, because you've been a victim, you can produce a police report or an identity theft report filed with the FTC that entitles you to request a seven-year fraud alert, so you don't have to worry about it expiring if you forget to renew it. With this extended alert, creditors must contact you, or meet you in person, before they issue you credit. An initial fraud alert only requires them to use "reasonable policies and procedures" to verify your identity before issuing credit in your name.

One other thing to note: To place a fraud flag on your report, or to have one removed, you'll be asked for your name, address, Social Security number, and other personal information. That's okay, so long as you placed the call to the credit bureau. If someone calls you, however, never give out that information.

Q: How will a creditor contact me if I have an extended fraud flag?

A: It's important to keep the information on your credit report up to date—the creditor will most likely contact you by phone. Keep in mind that having an alert on your account may slow down the process of obtaining credit, but in most cases, it's worth it. Speed things up a little by providing your cell phone number in your alert. That way, the creditor can contact you wherever you are.

Q: **What about the cards I already have?**

A: A fraud alert doesn't do much for the cards you already have in your wallet, or your open credit lines, because it only stops a thief from obtaining new forms of credit in your name. The best way to keep tabs on the credit you already have is by checking your accounts regularly, pulling your free credit report three times a year from annualcreditreport.com, and following the steps above to avoid identity theft in the first place.

Q: **I've heard of something called a credit freeze—is that the same thing as a fraud alert?**

A: No. A credit freeze blocks creditors from gaining access to your report at all. Like the name implies, you're putting your information in a block of ice, making it unlikely that a thief will be able to open new accounts in your name. Credit freezes are regulated by state law. In some states, anyone can implement a freeze; in others, you have to be a victim. Some states may also charge a fee for putting a freeze on your account if you're not a victim, generally about $10 for each credit-reporting bureau (you need to freeze your report at all three; otherwise, there's no point).

In case you need to lift the freeze—say you want to apply for a mortgage—you'll be given a PIN from each credit-reporting agency. Keep in mind that you'll likely pay a fee and that most states give the bureaus three days to lift the freeze, meaning that it will be difficult, if not impossible, to receive quick credit.

THE STATS

- In 2007 alone, the FTC received more than **800,000** consumer fraud and identity-theft complaints. Consumers reported losses from fraud of more than **$1.2 billion**.
- Every minute, **28 people** become a new victim of identity theft (Gartner).
- Identity theft cost U.S. businesses and consumers **$56.6 billion** in 2005 (Javelin).
- Victims spend an average of **330 hours** in 2004 recovering from this crime (ID Theft Resource Center).

Resources

Equifax

Equifax Fraud Division
P.O. Box 105069
Atlanta, GA 30348
www.equifax.com
1-800-525-6285

To Place a Fraud Alert

By mail:
Equifax Information Services LLC
P.O. Box 105069
Atlanta, GA 30348–5069
Online:
www.fraudalerts.equifax.com
By phone:
1-800-525-6285

To Add a Security Freeze

By mail:
To submit your security freeze request via mail, submit the following personal ID information:

1. Name, including any suffix (e.g., *Jr.*, *Sr.*)
2. Address
3. Social Security number
4. Date of birth

The charges for a security freeze request on your Equifax credit file vary by state. Visit www.equifax.com and select the Customer Service tab to find a list of fees by state.

If submitting a request by mail, include payment by check, money order, or major credit card for the appropriate fees. For Visa, Master-Card, Discover, or American Express payment, include the following:

1. Name of the cardholder, as it appears on the card
2. Card number
3. Card expiration date

If you are an identity-theft victim and are requesting a security freeze, you must also include a copy of a police report, identity-theft report, or other government law-enforcement agency report, such as a Department of Motor Vehicles report.

Send your request information via certified mail to the address below.

Equifax Security Freeze
P.O. Box 105788
Atlanta, GA 30348

Online:
www.freeze.equifax.com
By phone:
1-800-685-1111

Experian (formerly TRW)

Experian Consumer Assistance, Security Alerts
P.O. Box 9532
Allen, TX 75013
www.experian.com
1-888-397-3742

To Place a Fraud Alert

By mail:
Experian Consumer Assistance, Security Alerts
P.O. Box 9532
Allen, TX 75013
Online:
www.experian.com
By phone:
1-888-397-3742

To Add a Security Freeze

By mail:
Placement information is available by calling 1-888-397-3742
Online:
www.experian.com
By phone:
1-888-397-3742

Trans Union

P.O. Box 6790
Fullerton, CA 92834
www.transunion.com
1-800-680-7289

To Place a Fraud Alert:

By mail:
P.O. Box 6790
Fullerton, CA 92634
Online:
www.transunion.com
By phone:
1-800-680-7289
By e-mail:
fvad@transunion.com

To Add a Security Freeze:

By mail:
   Written requests to add a security freeze must include your name, address, and Social Security number along with the applicable fee, if any. You may pay by check, money order, or credit card. You must include proof of your current residence, such as a copy of a state-issued identification card or driver's license. Requests can be mailed to
   TransUnion, Fraud Victim Assistance Department:*
   P.O. Box 6790
   Fullerton, CA 92834
If you prefer, you may make your request via overnight mail to
   TransUnion, Fraud Victim Assistance Department
   1561 E. Orangethorpe Ave.·
   Fullerton, CA 92831

* Note: If you are a victim of identity theft and can provide TransUnion with a copy of a valid identity theft report, a Department of Motor Vehicles investigation report, or similar proof that you have been a victim of ID theft, you will not be charged a fee for the security freeze services. If you are a resident of North Dakota, you may fax your request with your identity theft document(s) to 714-525-0668.

Online:
www.transunion.com
By phone:
1-888-909-8872

30. Am I being scammed?

A: Perhaps you've received an e-mail from someone overseas, explaining that they need to move money to a U.S. bank and they'll reward you for helping them do so. Or from someone telling you that you won a lottery, and they need your bank account information to deposit the money. Or perhaps it's tax time and you receive an e-mail from the IRS asking for clarification of your Social Security number or other personal information. You're ready to do exactly as you've been asked—but something, some inkling, stops you short. Listen to it.

If something in your gut is telling you a situation is off, not right, a little bit strange, and you are being asked for money or information, don't comply, at least not immediately. Figure out a way to end the interaction and do a little homework. These are the signs of a scam. Any one of them should be enough to raise your hackles.

Signs of a Scam

- A promise that you can very easily win, earn, or borrow money
- A charge for entering a contest or sweepstakes or to claim a prize they say you've already won
- A refusal to provide written information as backup
- A refusal to give you contact information
- A request for your bank account information, credit card number, passwords, Social Security number, or other personal details
- Pressure to act quickly or persistent phone calls or e-mails
- An e-mail or call requesting personal information that the company should have on file

It's also helpful to know which scams occur most frequently. Scams tend to be viral—when one catches on, it can go for years before running its course. Here's a list of the most common scams being perpetrated today.

National Consumers League's Top Ten Internet Scams

1. **Fake check scams.** Consumers are paid for work or items sold with fake checks written for more than the amount due; they are then asked to wire the extra money back. Average loss: $3,310.87.
2. **General merchandise.** Sale of goods never delivered or misrepresented. Average loss: $1,136.84.
3. **Auctions.** Goods never received or misrepresented. Average loss: $1,371.08.
4. **Nigerian money offers.** False promises of riches if consumers pay to transfer money to their bank accounts. Average loss: $4,043.14.
5. **Lotteries/lottery clubs.** These charge consumers to claim lottery winnings or get help winning foreign lotteries. Average loss: $998.43.
6. **Advance fee loans.** Promise of a loan, even with bad credit, for an upfront fee. Average loss: $1,310.77.
7. **Prizes/sweepstakes.** These request a payment to claim prizes, which never come. Average loss: $1,181.58.
8. **Phishing.** E-mails pretending to be from a well-known source asking to confirm personal information. Average loss: $220.47.
9. **Friendship/sweetheart swindles.** These start an online relationship, then convince the victim to send money. Average loss: $3,038.31.
10. **Internet access services.** Cost of Internet or other services misrepresented or services never provided. Average loss: $896.99.

Bottom line: Don't give out your personal information over the phone, via the Internet, or even by mail unless you've initiated the contact yourself and you know exactly to whom you're talking or corresponding. You can always check the Web site and e-mail addresses by putting them in your browser or doing an Internet search, and many companies will have information on their Web sites if they have been used as part of a scam.

I Also Need to Know . . .

Q: How do I know if I'm being "phished"?

A: Phishing is when someone uses a fake e-mail to draw consumers to counterfeit Web sites as a way to collect personal information such as bank account numbers, passwords, user names, credit card information, and Social Security numbers. You might, for example, get an e-mail from your "bank." Maybe it has your bank's logo, the e-mail address it was sent from has your bank's name in it, and it is written in a style that mimics other e-mails you've received from the bank in the past. It tells you that you need to update or confirm your account and provides a link to do so. When you click on the link, you're directed to a landing page that looks like the one you've seen every time you go check your account balance.

It's a scam. No bank would ever ask you to provide sensitive information by sending you an e-mail or calling you on the phone. For that matter, neither would legitimate social networking sites, or eBay, or PayPal, or Yahoo!, or Amazon.com, or computer companies such as Dell, all of which have been used by identity thieves to phish information from consumers.

If you receive an e-mail like this, and you're worried it might be legitimate—say it's from your credit card company telling you that you need to update your account or your recent payment won't be applied—pick up the phone and call the company directly. Use a number you find by typing their Web address into your search bar, not a number that was included in the e-mail sent to you or is listed on the page linked to the e-mail.

If you received a call for information, not an e-mail, hang up, then dial the company directly and ask if the call was legitimate.

Q: What do I do if I have been scammed?

A: As soon as you realize you may have fallen for a scam, you should close any possibly affected accounts and let your bank or lender know that you've been a victim of fraud. At the same time, contact both your local police department and the FTC to file a report, change the passwords on any online accounts that may have been affected, and place fraud alerts or freezes on your credit reports (to read more about these, see page 103). Get a copy of your credit report—always free to victims of ID theft—and look it over for new and unfamiliar inquiries and charges.

Create a paper trail every step of the way, noting phone calls you make to your lenders and any letters you send. Save a copy of your police report and the complaint you file with the FTC.

Q: How do I keep my e-mail address out of the hands of thieves?
A: Have three e-mail accounts—one for business, one for personal use, and one that you use for things that might generate a lot of spam or when you don't know who is on the other end of the transaction. That way, you can give your two primary e-mail addresses to friends, coworkers, and relatives only and use the other address when you're shopping online or signing up for offers that might send your e-mail address into the hands of spammers or scammers.

Q: How do I choose a good password?
A: In about one-third of identity-theft cases, the thief is a friend or family member of the victim, which means using your dog's name or your birthday or anniversary isn't a good idea. In fact, in the age of MySpace and Facebook, those kinds of passwords may not even be strong enough to keep strangers out. So much information is out there where anyone can see it.

When you're choosing a password, you want to consider three things:

- **Length:** The longer it is, the harder it is to crack. Aim for at least eight characters, but the more, the better.
- **Variety:** Numbers, symbols, letters, spaces—mix it up whenever possible, and make use of everything on your keyboard, not just the most common forms of punctuation.
- **Staying power:** A password doesn't do you any good if you can't remember it, so choose something that will stick with you.

Remember not to use the same password for every account. If you do, a thief will be able to crack into your credit card, e-mail, and bank account in one swipe—and don't carry your passwords around with you. There's nothing wrong with writing them down, but leave them out of your wallet and away from your computer in a safe place.

THE STATS

- In 2004, $137 million was lost in phishing attacks. In 2006, that number jumped to **$2.8 billion** (Gartner, an IT research company).
- The number of U.S. adults who received a phishing e-mail doubled between 2004 and 2006, jumping from 57 million to **109 million** (Gartner).

31. Is there a way to get rid of junk mail?

A: There isn't a way to stop junk mail completely, but you can reduce it dramatically. Here's what I want you to do.

1. Go to the Direct Marketing Association's Mail Preference Service at www.dmachoice.org. There, you can opt out of unsolicited mail for about five years. It will cost you $1 to register, and only mail from companies that use the DMA's Mail Preference Service will be stopped. (DMAchoice represents about 80% of the total volume of marketing mail in the United States.)

2. Pick up the phone and call 888-5-OPTOUT or go on the Web to www.optoutprescreen.com. This will get rid of a different kind of junk mail—preapproved credit card offers. Both the hotline and the Web site are a joint venture of the four credit bureaus—Equifax, Experian, Innovis, and TransUnion. (You may not have heard of Innovis, because it isn't a big player in the consumer space. The company's main focus is providing your credit history to lenders so that they can determine whether you qualify for the preapproved offers that end up in your mailbox.) Again, you'll be able to opt out of offers for five years. Note, when you use this service, you'll be asked

for your Social Security number. I know that if you're following my ID theft-protection advice, you'll be reluctant to provide it, but in this case you have to, so make an exception. Getting rid of these solicitations is taking another step to protect yourself against identity theft. Why? Because there will be less ammunition for unsavory types to swipe and then attempt to open a card account in your name.

3. If the five-year time frame isn't enough for you, and you want to opt out of credit card offers permanently, you need to supplement your online or phone registration by mailing in a signed Permanent Opt Out Election Form, which can be printed optoutprescreen.com.

THE STATS

- More than **100 billion pieces** of junk mail are delivered each year—more than 800 per household.
- Junk mail accounts for **one-third** of all mail delivered in the world, and **44%** of it goes to the landfill unopened.
- We each spend **eight months** of our lives dealing with junk mail.
- There were **1.34 billion** credit card offers mailed during the third quarter of 2008 alone.

I Also Need to Know . . .

Q: How do I get rid of telemarketers and spam?

A: To get through a dinner uninterrupted, you need to add your name to the U.S. government's National Do Not Call Registry. It's free—you just go to www.donotcall.gov or call 888-382-1222 from the phone number you want to register. You should notice a decrease in calls within about 31 days after signing up, and your number will remain on the registry until you disconnect or remove it.

As for your e-mail, some of that spam will never go away. But you can opt out of those that come from the Direct Marketing Association's affiliates by going to their E-mail Preference Service at www.ims-dm.com/cgi/optoutemps.php. It works in much the same way as the mail service.

Credit Bureau Mailing Addresses

Equifax
Options
P.O. Box 740123
Atlanta, GA 30374–0123

Experian
901 West Bond
Lincoln, NE 68521
Attn: Consumer Services Department

Innovis Consumer Assistance
P.O. Box 725
Columbus, OH 43216–0725

TransUnion
Name Removal Option
P.O. Box 505
Woodlyn, PA 19094

Resources

Associations

Anti-Phishing Working Group
www.antiphishing.org
An industry association whose aim is to eliminate identity theft and fraud via phishing, it features a forum for people to discuss phishing issues, a place to report phishing, current news, and guides to help consumers recognize phishing.

Books

Scam-Proof Your Life: 377 Smart Ways to Protect You & Your Family from Ripoffs, Bogus Deals & Other Consumer Headaches (AARP), by Sid Kirchheimer (2007)
Interviews with nearly 100 former scammers provide advice on how to protect yourself from various types of scams.

Stealing Your Life: The Ultimate Identity Theft Prevention Plan, by Frank W. Abagnale (2008)

Learn how to protect yourself from identity theft with advice from counterfeiting expert Frank Abagnale; includes case histories, a 20-step prevention plan, tips, and instructions on how to do such things as file a police report and contact the FTC.

The Wall Street Journal Complete Identity Theft Guidebook: How to Protect Yourself from the Most Pervasive Crime in America, by Terri Cullen (2007)

Detailed information on identity theft and how you can protect yourself; also includes sample letters, forms, and other tools to help victims of identity theft recover.

Government Resources

Federal Trade Commission
www.ftc.gov/idtheft
1-877-438-4338

The FTC's identity-theft site, with information for both businesses and consumers, a place to file a complaint with the FTC as well as a place to report identity theft, and resources such as data, reports, and laws pertaining to identity theft.

National Do Not Call Registry
www.donotcall.gov
1-888-382-1222

Register your phone number to decrease the amount of telemarketing calls you receive.

OnGuardOnline
www.onguardonline.gov

Tips from the U.S. federal government and technology industry to help protect you against Internet scams; explore information on various aspects of identity theft, learn from interactive quizzes, and watch videos about online safety.

United States Department of Justice
www.usdoj.gov
202-514-2000

Visit the fraud section of this site for information on identity theft, details on how you can protect yourself, answers to FAQs, and more.

United States Post Office
www.usps.com
1-800-275-8777

Get your questions regarding mail delivery answered via the Web or phone.

Web Sites

Carnegie Mellon's The PhishGuru
www.phishguru.org

An e-mail-based antiphishing training system that teaches you how to distinguish legitimate e-mails from phishing scams.

Consumer Fraud Reporting
www.consumerfraudreporting.org

A free online service with thousands of actual examples of scam letters, e-mails, faxes, and transcripts of phone conversations to help you recognize scams.

OptOutPrescreen.com
www.optoutprescreen.com
1-888-567-8688

A joint venture among the consumer credit reporting companies that allows you to opt out of receiving offers for credit or insurance.

Direct Marketing Association (DMA) Mail Preference Service
www.dmachoice.org
212-768-7277, ext. 1500

For $1 you can opt out of unsolicited mail from companies that use the DMA's Mail Preference Service; you can also register for eMPS, which allows you to remove your e-mail address from national lists.

Fraud.org
www.fraud.org

The National Consumers League's Fraud Center site with information on various types of fraud and scams, links for stopping unwanted sales and marketing calls, and an online complaint form for reporting suspicious activity.

Identity Theft Resource Center
www.idtheftcenter.org
858-693-7935

A nonprofit organization dedicated to educating consumers and victims on identity theft; features tips, guides, answers to FAQs, a reference library, and more.

Privacy Rights Clearinghouse
www.privacyrights.org
619-298-3396

A nonprofit consumer organization whose aim is teaching people how to protect their personal privacy; offers identity-theft fact sheets, identity-theft quizzes, and more.

CHAPTER 5

BUDGETING AND CUTTING SPENDING

32. How do I set up a monthly budget?

A: Setting up a budget is a matter of figuring out where you are, and where you want to be. And to do that, you need to answer two questions:

1. **How much are you bringing in each month?** This amount includes your take-home pay and any other sources of income—maybe you run a small business on the side or you sell on eBay or you own rental properties. Add it all up. If it varies from month to month, find an average for the last year, assuming your income didn't decline recently.
2. **How much goes out each month—and where is it going?** This amount tends to be the sticking point for most people. They just don't know how much they spend each month, and if they do, they don't know what they spend it on. Getting the answer to this question is paramount to your financial success, because if you don't know where your money is going, you're going to have a hard time staying out of debt, and you're going to have an even harder time saving.

You need to look back over the last month or two of your bank and credit card statements to see what you have been spending your money on, then track your spending for the next month. (Note: If that corresponds with a period when your spending was out of the ordinary—the holidays, for example—be sure to keep that in mind and make adjustments as needed.) Every time you take your wallet out, whether it's for $2 or $50, write it down. If what you find surprises you—$100 to lunches out, $30 to ATM fees—then you know where you need to make changes.

Now you can start building a budget. As a general rule, I like to follow this breakdown:

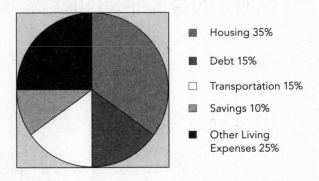

- ▪ Housing 35%
- ▪ Debt 15%
- ☐ Transportation 15%
- ▪ Savings 10%
- ▪ Other Living Expenses 25%

What falls in each category:

- **Housing** includes your mortgage or rent, maintenance, taxes, utilities, and insurance. In other words, the cost of the place you're living and the cost to actually live there.
- **Debt** includes student loans, credit cards, personal loans, and any other debt you're carrying above and beyond your mortgage or auto loan.
- **Transportation** includes your car payments, gas, insurance, repairs, parking and tolls, and train or bus tickets.
- **Savings** includes all the money you're putting away for your emergency cushion, retirement, college, and other goals.
- **Other Living Expenses** includes everything else: health care, groceries, eating out, vacations, entertainment, clothing, gifts, and all the other items you spend your money on every day.

There are some expenses that are locked in—you can't change them. Examples of this category might be your car payment, your mortgage, your credit card payments. But other expenses—primarily those that fall under living—are a bit more flexible. So if your living expenses are taking up 30% of your budget and that extra 5% is coming from money that should go toward savings, you need to cut back. And because you tracked your spending for a month, you know where to start.

I Also Need to Know . . .

Q: **Do you have a recommendation for a program that can help me keep organized?**

A: These days, it's easy to find some help. Free online budgeting Web sites pop up all the time. These sites will pull your account information together, allow you to set spending limits in each category, and alert you when you've gone over. They will also code your purchases, so at a glance you can tell how much you spent dining out, at the grocery store, or on clothes in a single month. There are a handful of good ones, including Wesabe (www.wesabe.com) and Mint (www.mint.com).

Q: **What if I don't have any credit card or student loan debt? Where do I put that 15%?**

A: Ideally, you'd put it toward savings or toward an investment that will generate more income. But it's okay if you put the bulk into savings and use a small portion to treat yourself every once in a while to a vacation or something else you think is worth the money. There is such a thing as saving too much—although to be clear, few people have this problem—but you don't want to look back and regret being unnecessarily frugal.

33. I am hiding financial secrets from my spouse—in particular, my uncontrollable spending. How do I stop?

A: There are two parts to this question. First, there's the issue of your hiding this habit from your spouse. Second, your spending could be out of control. Let's deal with them one at a time, the secret and then the spending.

The secret: When you spend and hide it, not only are you being unfair to your mate, you're being unfair to yourself. You need to fess up, but not necessarily right away. I want you to picture yourself telling your spouse about your problem. How does he or she react? Of course your mate is likely to get angry at first, but overall, what is your mate's response? Support? A desire to help you stop? Or does your mate react in a way that is going to cause the same kind of friction—and emotional emptiness—that started you down this spending cycle in the first place?

If you think your partner will be supportive, then I want you to talk to him or her within the next three days. Pick a good time (that's the reason for the three-day time frame, to give you enough room to maneuver), a time when your partner is relaxed and not overly stressed out, and talk about what's been going on. Be prepared for the conversation with facts about how much you're spending, what you've already done to cut back, if anything, and what you plan to do about it for the future. And if you have no plans, if you're at a complete loss as far as how to stop, say so. Explain that you need your partner's help.

If, however, you have some reason to believe your partner will not be supportive and that fessing up while you're in the throes of the problem is likely to exacerbate the problem, you need to take steps to get a handle on it yourself first. Talk to someone else, whether it's a best friend, a relative, or a therapist. Join a support group like Debtor's Anonymous. Follow the steps I've outlined on page 137 in response to the question "How do I cut back on my shopping habit?" Then, once you feel like you have a bit more control over the situation—and you've established healthier ways of dealing with a possible blowup, aside from shopping, such as exercise—sit down with your partner and explain the situation, outlining the steps you've already taken to stop and what your partner can do to help you from here on out. That way, if your partner blows up, you'll have the tools you need in your arsenal.

It's important to understand, no matter when you come clean, you're going to have to dig yourself out of this shopping addiction. And it will help to have your mate (or if that's not possible, someone else close to you) aware of the situation, so that that person can help you hold yourself accountable for your actions.

I Also Need to Know . . .

Q: If my partner and I have separate bank accounts, why do I have to explain myself for the things I buy? It's my money.

A: You don't. Part of the beauty of using a three-pot banking system in a relationship—where you each have separate accounts and then a joint account for shared expenses—is that you have the ability to buy things without checking with your partner for permission. We all need to be able to pick up a cup of coffee or buy a new pair of shoes once in a while.

The exception is that the *don't ask, don't tell* system only works if you're not an excessive shopper (about 15% of the population) or worse, a compulsive shopper (about 2% of the population). It works if you can go into a store, stick to your budget, and buy something that you need rather than something you've agreed (with your spouse) not to buy. It works if you are living within your means. But if your shopping is out of control, if you're hiding bags under your bed, if you're lying about whether a blouse is new or where you got those shoes your mate hasn't seen before, you have a problem. Don't kid yourself. Your spouse's finances are on the line, too. Seek help.

THE STATS

- A 2005 *Money* magazine study found that **71%** of women and men with incomes above $50,000 had money secrets.
- In a 2007 survey, **one-third** of the respondents admitted to lying to their partner about money.
- **Four out of five** people say they hide purchases from the one they love.

34. Can you negotiate prices in stores?

A: It certainly doesn't hurt to try. It's always worth asking for a little extra something, if it's not a lower price outright then free delivery, price matching (when a store matches a lower price offered by a competitor), or an extended warranty.

How you go about it, though, matters. First, you'll want to time it right. You're more likely to get a deal in the morning on a weekday, because store sales are slower then and the salesperson will have more time to talk to you.

Then put on your happy face. You're not going to get any favors by being rude. Try to develop a rapport with the salesperson.

Ask her how she's doing, joke around, anything you can do to get a conversation flowing. When the time is right—usually after you're quoted a price—ask if she can do better.

Don't show too much excitement. You want the salesperson to think—indeed, believe—you're willing to walk out if you don't get the price you want. If the salesperson says he's not authorized to negotiate, ask to speak to a manager and see if that person will work with you. If you still can't get the store to budge on price, try to get an extra, such as an extended warranty, thrown in gratis.

If you know what you're looking for beforehand, you should also do some research upfront so you know how much that particular product sells for on the low end. Just type the name of the item—say, a television—into a comparison-shopping site (Biz Rate.com and PriceGrabber.com are good ones) and see what pops up. Once armed with that information (you should bring a printout or advertisement as evidence), you can ask if the store will match the lower price. Often it will.

I Also Need to Know . . .

Q: I am too embarrassed to haggle with a salesperson. Is there any other way to go about it?

A: Rather than asking for a deal, ask about promotions or sales in the near future. If there's one right around the corner, the salesperson may offer to give you the discounted price right now, or he may hold the item for you until it goes on sale. At the very least, you'll know when to come back.

Other ideas? If a piece of clothing seems slightly damaged (maybe missing a button that is easily replaced) retailers can, and usually will, knock 10% to 15% off. You can also ask for open boxes at electronics stores, which means an item has been returned but has been inspected to make sure that it's in working order. Usually you can get about 15% off, but keep in mind that it may be a final sale. And finally, my favorite way to get a discount without haggling is by searching online for the store name and the words *coupon code* or *promotion code*. There are tons of Web sites out there that aggregate discount codes from all different kinds of retailers so that everyone can take advantage. (I like RetailMeNot.com and couponcabin.com.) Some are good for online purchases, but others can be printed and used in the store.

Q: **What about services? Can I negotiate with the person who mows my lawn or walks my dog?**

A: Sure. You probably want to do it when you first hire this person, and not when they've been working for you for a few years. At that point, they're probably looking to raise their prices a bit, not lower them.

When you're looking for any service company, do enough homework to understand what the going rates are in your area, so that you can tell when the prices you're quoted are good. Then pick the most reasonable prices—but remember, you get what you pay for—and ask if they can do better. Often if you use that service a lot, they'll throw in a freebie: Maybe the dog walker will give you a free walk once a month, or the lawn care company will offer you a 10% discount if you commit to their services for the entire summer. Again, you want to be polite when asking for any extras, because if you're not pleasant to work for, they aren't going to try hard to earn your business. And, if you'd like to use someone's services but his or her prices are out of reach—say so. Sometimes that's all it takes to get them to negotiate against themselves.

THE STATS

- **72.4%** of shoppers have tried negotiating at a retail store in the past three to four months, according to a survey by America's Research Group in March 2009. Ten years earlier, only 32% of the shoppers surveyed said they were comfortable haggling over prices.
- **94%** of shoppers said they successfully haggled on the price of furniture at least once in the past three years (*Consumer Reports,* November 2007). Percentage of people who have negotiated for

  - Floor and demo models, **65%**
  - Furniture, **49%**
  - Large and small appliances, **39%**
  - Jewelry, **38%**
  - Home electronics, **35%**

35. How can I save money on groceries?

A: Don't be afraid to buy generic. Many of the less-expensive brands at the bottom of the shelf are manufactured by the same companies that make the brand name products. Companies are understandably reluctant to acknowledge this, but *Consumer Reports* published a report in 2005 of a study that found that big names such as Reynolds Wrap, Bausch & Lomb, and Birds Eye Foods also make store-brand versions of their products. In these cases, what you're getting is virtually the same product in a not-so-flashy wrapper. Other tips:

- **Go frozen.** Fruits and vegetables are flash-frozen at the peak of freshness, so you can get them out of season for less in the freezer aisle. Once defrosted, they taste great and are much cheaper than fresh.
- **Limit your shopping trips.** Every time you go into the grocery store, you're bombarded with opportunities to buy on impulse. Chances are, you will walk out with one or two things not on your list. Instead, make one big trip for the whole week.
- **Shop health-food stores.** They tend to have bulk food sections, where you can buy things such as cereal, dry beans, and dry fruit by weight at a big savings. If you need other items in bulk, such as toilet paper and packaged snacks, consider a membership in a club such as Costco or Sam's Club. You'll pay about $40 a year for membership, but it can be worth it if you shop often enough.
- **Stock up.** If the store is having a big sale on nonperishable items such as canned goods, grains, or toilet paper and you know you'll use them eventually, buy now and put them in your pantry or basement.
- **Remember that convenience costs.** You can buy a single-serving can of vegetable soup for $2 or ingredients to cook up a potful of soup that will last you a week for a few more bucks. If you have the time, you're always better off forgoing convenience items—those 100-calorie packs, for instance, are pricey—and doing the packaging yourself.
- **Compare apples with apples.** Make sure to look at the unit price, which will tell you the cost by weight. It might make sense to pay $1 more if you're getting more servings.

· **Clip coupons.** Spending a few minutes with the store and Sunday circulars—without a great deal of effort—saves the average family about $5 to $10 a week, according to the Promotions Marketing Association. That's $250 to $500 a year.

I Also Need to Know . . .

Q: **Is buying organic worth it?**

A: It depends on the item. Personally, I'd love to buy everything organic, because I know it's better for the environment and likely my health. But in reality, it's just not affordable when, say, an organic avocado can be more than twice the price of one grown conventionally. The one organic item I buy consistently is milk—the shelf life of organic milk is much longer than nonorganic, and we don't drink all that much of it in my house. Organic prevents me from throwing milk away. Then I often refer to this list, put together by the Environmental Working Group. It shows both ends of the spectrum—the 12 foods that tend to have the highest levels of pesticides, and the 12 with the lowest. This way, you can prioritize and put your organic dollars where they count most:

MOST CONTAMINATED	LEAST CONTAMINATED
Peaches	Onions
Apples	Avocado
Sweet bell peppers	Sweet corn (frozen)
Celery	Pineapples
Nectarines	Mangos
Strawberries	Asparagus
Cherries	Sweet peas (frozen)
Pears	Kiwi
Grapes (imported)	Bananas
Spinach	Cabbage
Lettuce	Broccoli
Potatoes	Papaya

Another strategy for stretching your dollar is buying local. Often, if you find a farmer's market in your area, the fruits, vegetables, bread, and meats sold there will be cheaper because you're buying direct from the producer and the items don't have to travel as far to get to your table. They may be organic as well.

Q: Where's the best place to find coupons?

A: Your Sunday supplement is still a gold mine when it comes to finding deals—about 80% of grocery store coupons come from those pages. That said, the Internet makes it easy to find even more coupons. If you have a specific store or item in mind, you can search for a coupon by typing the name of the merchant and the word *coupon* into a search engine such as Google. I often do so and routinely come up with discounts like free shipping or 10% off. There are also Web sites that give consumers the opportunity to post coupon codes for others to use. RetailMeNot.com, Coupons .com, CouponMom.com, and SmartSource.com are among the most reliable. If you try the code and if it works for you, report back and let other users know; if it doesn't, you should report that too.

Finally, there's a new form of electronic couponing that will load coupons directly onto many store loyalty cards. It's provided by Shortcuts.com, a division of AOL. The site allows you to register your loyalty card and sort through thousands of coupons. You don't have to print them out, because they'll automatically register once you swipe your loyalty card at the checkout. Unfortunately, right now this program is only available at the Kroger grocery-store chain and its affiliates. We hope it goes national soon!

Q: Are those loyalty cards really worth all the junk mail I receive?

A: Yes. These days, grocery stores can track your purchases and then filter deals that are relevant your way. So if you tend to buy a lot of dog food, you might get coupons for your brand in your mailbox. Note: To get these mailings, you have to give the store your correct address when you sign up for the loyalty card.

Q: I've heard that grocery stores take competitors' coupons. Is that true?

A: Some do. Price-matching, as it's called, means that if a product is on sale at a competitor's store, your local store will sell it to you for the same price. You have to be proactive, though. Bring proof of the item's price at the other store (a circular will do the job) and show it to a manager, then ask for the discount. Most are authorized to give it to you. This strategy extends outside the grocery store—some big-box retailers have similar policies.

36. How do I create a budget for my daughter (or son) who is going off to college?

A: This budget has to be a joint effort between you and your child. Not to do it that way is a mistake. Why? She needs to buy in and agree upfront—and you need to communicate so that you can modify the plan if expenses on campus turn out to exceed your expectations.

That said, the most important piece of advice I think I can give you is to be flexible. This is her freshman year. She doesn't know what to expect. You don't know what to expect. And so setting a strict limit on how much she can spend on groceries or laundry just isn't feasible in most cases.

You can, however, set a reasonable limit on how much she can spend total, and to do that, you have to figure out how much money she has. Will you be contributing? Start with the amount you can afford to give her, and then add in any scholarship or grant money she will be receiving in excess of tuition, supplies, and room and board. Include any savings she's accumulated over the summer, as well as any earnings she can expect to receive from a part-time job, if she'll have one. That gives you the framework for your budget.

Then you need to get a sense of fixed expenses, such as car insurance and rent if she's living off campus (others, such as on-campus housing, tuition, and books, should be taken care of beforehand out of the money you've saved for college, loans, or the financial aid and scholarships she's earned). Once you have those, it's time to tackle flexible expenses—clothing, food outside the meal plan, phone, transportation. This calculation can be tricky, but I'd start by calling the school's financial aid office or by looking at the section for incoming students on the school's Web site, which can often give you a sample budget or, at the least, a list of common expenses.

SAMPLE SEMESTER BUDGET	
EXPENSE TYPE	**AMOUNT**
INCOME	
Parent contribution	$500
Work	$2,000
Financial aid/scholarships after tuition	$500
Total	$3,000
FIXED EXPENSES	
Rent, if applicable	$0
Car insurance/payment	$1,350/semester
Cell phone	$180/semester
Total	$1,530
Amount remaining	$1,470
FLEXIBLE EXPENSES	
Groceries, in excess of meal plan	$250
Eating out	$250
Gas	$300
Entertainment	$400
Clothing, miscellaneous	$150
Total	$1,250
WIGGLE ROOM/SAVINGS	$120

Once you have your number, you want to break it down into months, so that she knows how much she has to spend each month. And then, if she's more comfortable, from months into weeks. You do it this way because it will be easier for her to keep tabs on her money. If she gets ahead of herself and overspends, she can make adjustments or cut back for the remainder of that month or week and be back on track when it's time to flip the calendar page. I'd suggest keeping the bulk of the money in her savings account—where it will earn a little interest—and showing her how to set up automatic deposits into her checking each month, similar to a paycheck. Try to encourage her to make one—not more than one—trip to the ATM each week, with the goal of making the money last.

SAMPLE MONTHLY BUDGET	
EXPENSE TYPE	**AMOUNT**
INCOME	$666/month (4½ months per semester)
FIXED EXPENSES	
Rent, if applicable	$0
Car insurance/payment	$300
Cell phone	$40
Total	$340
Amount remaining	$326
FLEXIBLE EXPENSES	
Groceries, in excess of meal plan	$50
Eating out	$50
Gas	$65
Entertainment	$90
Clothing, miscellaneous	$35
Total	$290
WIGGLE ROOM/SAVINGS	$36

| SAMPLE WEEKLY BUDGET ||
EXPENSE TYPE	AMOUNT
INCOME	$167
FIXED EXPENSES	
Rent, if applicable	$0
Car insurance/payment	$75
Cell phone	$10
Total	$85
Amount remaining	$82
FLEXIBLE EXPENSES	
Groceries, in excess of meal plan	$15
Eating out	$15
Gas	$20
Entertainment	$20
Clothing, miscellaneous	$10
Total	$80

One final note: If she dips into that savings account and blows her budget midsemester, it's important not to bail her out. If you do, I can guarantee you that the same thing will happen the next semester (and the one after that). Instead, help her along the way by going over the budget with her on a monthly basis so that she stays on track.

► An Example

Expenses will vary by school, by student, by location. But here's a general budgeting worksheet to get you and your student started:

Income

Add up the amount your student expects to receive this semester from each source, then divide the total by the number of months in the semester:

Scholarships, grants, or loans	$_____
Part-time job or work-study earnings	$_____
Parental contributions	$_____
Additional money (from savings, etc.)	$_____
Total per semester	$_____
Total per month	$_____

Fixed Expenses

Add up the fixed expenses your student will be responsible for on a monthly basis:

Car insurance	$_____
Car payment	$_____
Rent and utilities	$_____
Cell phone	$_____
Other	$_____
Total per month	$_____

Subtract monthly fixed expenses, $_____, from monthly income, $_____, to get the amount that is left for variable expenses: $_____.

Variable Expenses

Divide the amount from above into the following categories. You may have to make a few hard decisions to stretch the dollars. Does your student need a $100 allowance for groceries if he or she has an unlimited meal plan? Keep in mind that this area is flexible.

Laundry	$_____
Groceries	$_____

Entertainment (includes dining out)	$_____
Gas and car maintenance	$_____
Other living expenses	
(clothing, room decorations, etc.)	$_____
Total per month	$_____

The total of fixed and variable expenses should now be equal to—or, in the best-case scenario—less than income. If it's not, go back over everything with a fine-tooth comb and figure out where she can either cut back or bring in more money.

Watch Out for These!

- **ATM fees**, which can add up fast and blow a hole in your daughter's budget. On average, it costs more than $3 to use an ATM that doesn't belong to your bank, according to Bankrate.com's 2008 checking study. Just two out-of-network transactions a week will cost $24 a month. That's a lot of laundry.
- **Overdraft charges from the bank**, which often cost $35. Many checking accounts come with a built-in protection that allows you to keep spending, even if the money runs dry. Each additional swipe of the debit card will incur another charge. Opt out of overdraft protection if you can.
- **Over-the-limit charges on cell phone plans** often run 50 cents a minute and 15 cents a text message. Advise your daughter to keep costs down by tracking her usage on her carrier's Web site. Also, the first time she does go over the limit, have her call the carrier herself and see if she can work out a deal.
- **Parking tickets.** Most colleges have strict rules about where students can and can't park. Freshmen, in particular, tend to get the worst spaces (and at some schools aren't allowed cars at all), and parking illegally could cost anywhere from $10 to $50. If she gets towed, add another $80 to $150 to that.

I Also Need to Know . . .

Q: Should my child have a credit card at college?

A: I think it's important to have a lifeline in case of emergencies, and if your child doesn't have adequate savings (and many college students don't), a credit card can function as a backup plan, provided it is used as such. The new CARD Act of 2009 has tightened the rules here, though, and anyone under age 21 must either have a cosigner or be able to prove that they have the income to support the card's payments.

Should you cosign? A better option is to add your child to your own card as an authorized user. That way, she'll be able to build up a credit history and carry a card in her wallet, but the bills will come to you so you can monitor spending and make sure payments get in on time.

Even so, you can't just hand her a piece of plastic and expect her to know how to use it. You need to talk to her about not only how and when the credit card should be used (sparingly) but also about how it shouldn't be used. She needs to know about credit scores, and the ways that abusing that credit card will damage hers. (You can have her read both the Debt and Credit sections of this book, particularly the question "What's a good credit score? How can I improve mine?" on page 161.) You should also explain how interest works, and how much she'll pay if she uses the card for a nonemergency (pizza, a new pair of shoes) and doesn't pay it off right away.

If you do decide to cosign, keep in mind that while the card company does set the credit limit, you can always reduce it, something that people often don't realize. So if you want your child to have room for emergencies but not for racking up thousands of dollars in debt, set a limit on the card of $500 or so.

THE STATS

- **26%:** The percentage of teenagers who said they understood credit card interest and fees, when asked in a 2007 Charles Schwab survey.
- **$2,864:** The average amount of credit card debt college students are carrying by the time they reach their senior year, according to Nellie Mae.

- **30%:** The percentage of their monthly income that 18- to 24-year-olds spend on debt repayment, according to the book *Generation Broke: The Growth of Debt Among Young Americans.*

---

37. How do I find the most budget-friendly cell phone plan? What about for text messaging?

A: By figuring out what you need in a plan. Pull out your bills from the past few months and answer these questions:
1. What services do you have now?
2. How many minutes are you buying? How many are you using?
3. Do you pay extra for voice mail, caller ID, call forwarding, or call waiting? Do you use these services?
4. How many text messages are you paying for? How many are you using?
5. Are you buying services for other people, including your children, partner, or other family members?

The answers to these questions should give you a general idea of your usage. You'll be able to see if you're paying for minutes or text messaging that you don't use, or if you're paying up to seven times as much (yes, you read that correctly!) for additional minutes and text messages that aren't included in your plan.

Now it's time to go shopping. Chances are, you are one of the following consumer types. Find your type, then follow the corresponding advice. And if you see yourself in more than one category—or you like what you see all around—go ahead and mix and match.

- **Family planner:** Your decision would be a snap if you only had to buy for yourself. But you have two teenagers and a mate to consider.

   Plan of attack: Have your children come up with a ballpark estimate of how many text messages they send and receive per month, as well as the number of daytime minutes they use. You should do the same for you and your spouse. Then add it all up and buy a family plan that allows you to purchase a bundle of minutes and text messages that you can share. You can typically get 1,500 text messages for about $15, but if you don't have a plan, it could cost you 20 cents a text, or $300 per month. (Use the calculator at MyRatePlan.com to figure out if you have the right messaging plan: www.myrateplan.com/text_messaging/.) Same goes for minutes—and if together, your family members come close to reaching the amount of minutes offered in the biggest plan, play it safe and opt for an unlimited plan.

• **On your own:** You're single, so you need to shop only for yourself.

    Plan of attack: You can shop for the precise services you want, without worrying about anyone else's usage. Go through the points discussed for the "family planner" to figure out what you need. Then add 20% to the number of minutes you think you need, just to be on the safe side. If you don't want text messaging or Web service on your phone, don't get pressured into buying it.

• **Sporadic talker:** You use a ton of minutes one month and hardly any the next. Sometimes you prefer the convenience of texting, but other times you'd rather chat over the phone. In other words, it's hard to figure out an average usage.

    Plan of attack: Whatever you do, you don't want to underbuy. You may think you're saving money, but if you go even 20 minutes over, you could end up paying 45 cents a minute, or $9 per month. Often, that's enough to bump up to the next plan level and save you the headache. Purchase enough minutes to accommodate your heavier months, and keep track of your usage online so you don't go over. Alternate approaches: Purchase a plan that recognizes rollover minutes, so if you don't use all of your allotted minutes one month, they'll be available the next when you may need them. Or start keeping tabs on your minutes once a day or so (your provider can tell you how to track them). If you can see that you're going to go over, call your provider and swap to the plan with the next-higher number of minutes for this month only—they'll allow that—and then swap back.

• **Old-fashioned:** You don't even want a cell phone, but you have one for emergencies. You use it rarely.

Plan of attack: You need to be sure you're not over-buying. If you're not using voice mail, call forwarding, or text messaging, don't pay for them. (Often, voice mail and call forwarding are included, but it doesn't hurt to ask.) Opt for a basic package.

Once you've decided on a carrier and plan, there may be other ways to save. Ask if your employer will pick up any of the tab—if you use it for work, the company may do so—and see if the provider itself offers a discount to employees at the company you work for, which is more common than you'd think. If you happen to go over your minutes, call your provider to see if you can get a free waiver (many will give you that mulligan once a year). And remember that you're agreeing to a contract that will charge you a fee—generally $200—if you want to get out, so look it over carefully before you sign.

I Also Need to Know . . .

Q: **Any tips for saving on the phone itself?**

A: A lot of carriers offer phones for free when you sign a two-year contract, so start there. If you're offered a two-for-one option, take it. Put the second phone in a drawer and know that if you lose one or break one, you're covered. If you need something more advanced than the free option, you might save money by purchasing it from an authorized retailer, instead of buying it from the wireless service provider itself. I've also had good luck buying phones from highly rated sellers on eBay—they are sometimes less expensive than you'd find in stores.

One final note: Unless you're dealing with a child or teenager (or know you yourself tend to lose things), skip insurance coverage for cell phone loss. It will add about $5 to your monthly bill, and you'll have to pay a pretty steep deductible (sometimes up to $100) before the coverage even kicks in. You also may find that the replacement phone isn't the same—or as good—as the one you lost.

Q: **What about pay-as-you-go phones?**

A: Pay-as-you-go phones are gaining popularity, mostly because they eliminate unexpected charges, and they often come without a contract, so you can switch carriers at any time. Other perks? You have total control over how many minutes are used, and you can't go over. You buy minutes in advance with a prepaid card, online, or by phone. Once those minutes are up, you either have to stop talking or buy more minutes.

The downside is that minutes are nearly always more expensive than standard cell phone plans, and you often won't get free nights and weekends. You also have to be careful because some pay-as-you-go cards expire—which means you'll lose any unused minutes—if you don't refill them by a certain date. Finally, you may be charged an extra flat fee (generally $1) on the days you use your phone.

Bottom line? Pay-as-you-go can be a helpful budgeting tool if you—or your teenager—tend to go over your allotted minutes on a regular basis. But this kind of plan takes a bit more hands-on work as you'll need to keep track of your minutes and card expiration dates.

38. How do I cut back on my shopping habit?

A: First, you need to get to the root of the problem and ask yourself why, exactly, you're shopping. Sometimes we buy things because we need them—food, heat, new sneakers to replace the ones your 13-year-old has outgrown . . . again. Sometimes we buy things we want. That's okay too, as long as we have thought about what we're doing and where the money is going to come from. But sometimes we shop for a whole host of other reasons.

Over the years, I've compiled a list of 12 reasons we shop—other than need or conscious want. The first step to getting a grip on any unwanted habit is to try to figure out why you're doing it. So look at this list and see if any of these reasons resonate with you.

THE TWELVE REASONS YOU SHOP

1. **You're feeling blue.** The term *retail therapy* isn't just a joke. Research has shown that shopping causes a rush of dopamine to your brain, which makes you feel happy in the short term.
2. **You want to feel powerful.** Having the cash or plastic in your hand to make a purchase makes you feel in control, particularly when salespeople are bending over backward to help you.

3. **You want to be someone else.** Often people shop because they believe that a purchase will, in fact, make their lives significantly better. Those jeans will make you look and feel like you're in college again, for instance, or that gigantic HDTV will make all your friends jealous.

4. **You just don't want to be you.** You want to escape your own reality, and a trip to the mall does the trick.

5. **You deserve it.** This is the mother of all reasons, in my experience. You've had a long, hard day at work—or at home with the kids—and you're tired, stressed, and overwhelmed. You want to reward yourself for your hard work.

6. **You're socializing.** For women in particular, shopping is a day out with the girls, and getting the full experience means coming home with a purchase. If your friends are buying, you want to buy, too.

7. **You're making a point that no one can tell you what to do.** You have a fight with your spouse, and you hit the mall in retaliation to send a message that he or she can't control you.

8. **You need a friend.** The rest of your world may be upside down: There are layoffs coming down the pipeline at work, your teenager doesn't want anything to do with you, and your partner is in a mood. But the salespeople at the mall are your best friends.

9. **You're on autopilot.** You may not remember how to do anything else, you've been shopping for so long. You stop at the mall every week on the way home from work just because that's the routine.

10. **You don't want to die.** When you buy something that you're going to use, wear, or drive, you do it with the expectation that you'll be around for a while to use, wear, or drive it.

11. **You acted on impulse.** These purchases happen in the blink of an eye. You go into the store looking for something in particular—maybe even something you need—and you buy something else because it's appealing.

12. **You just can't help it.**

If you regularly find yourself in one or more of these situations, you're already on the right track. In most cases, knowing the why behind your shopping is the first step toward eliminating the habit. You can find other ways to assuage those feelings. For example:

- If the rush from hitting the mall pulls you out of a bad mood, go for a run or to the gym instead. Doing something physical will improve your emotional situation.
- You want to feel powerful? Read a book that broadens your understanding of a subject that interests you.
- If you want to be someone else, pretend your bedroom is a dressing room and try on the clothes you already have—chances are, you'll find a shirt or a skirt you'd forgotten all about.
- If you want to reward yourself for a long day, take a bubble bath or go on a long walk with your iPod.
- Instead of shopping with your friends, have them over for dinner. And ask them all to bring a dish.
- If you shop because you need a friend, put one on speed dial. A real one, I mean. Ask one of your friends or even a relative if you can call when you feel the urge to shop.

If you've found other outlets to replace shopping, and you still find yourself drawn to the mall, there are a few more ways you can help yourself:

- **Reduce your exposure to advertising.** Get yourself off mailing lists for catalogs by calling the retailer directly, or using a service like Catalog Choice (www.catalogchoice .org). Unsubscribe from retailer e-mail lists. Use your DVR, if you have one, to fast-forward past commercials, or at the very least, mute them.
- **Break the habit.** If you hop on the computer to shop at the same time each night or drive by the mall on your way home and inevitably pull into the parking lot, you have to make a change. Find something else to do after dinner, like knitting or playing board games with your children, and change your route home from work. Even if it adds a few bucks to your gas bill, you'll come out on top.
- **Carry a diary.** Write down everything you buy, including how you're feeling and what your rationale was for making a purchase.
- **Go back the next day.** The vast majority of retailers will let you put an item on hold for the night or even a few days.

If you wake up in the morning still thinking about it, you can always go back. But chances are, you'll be over it.

· **Make returns.** Save every single receipt. Not only is it good for keeping track of how and where you've spent your money, it also gives you an out if you change your mind.

· **Run the numbers.** There are countless online calculators that can show you what a $200 shopping spree will cost you if you let it ride on a credit card for a few months. Likewise, they can also help you see what that money could turn into if invested.

THE MATH

Let's see what your shopping sprees are costing you.

In Interest (Assumes a Card with an 18% Interest Rate)

Purchase: coat, $370
Time until paid off with minimum payments: four years, six months
Interest paid: $161.57
  Total cost: $531.57

Purchase: HDTV, $1,800
Time until paid off with minimum payments: 11 years, 6 months
Interest paid: $1,811.04 (*more* than the value of the television!)
  Total cost: $3,611.04

In Your Retirement Savings

Invest the money at 8% in a tax-deferred account such as an IRA or 401(k) and watch it grow.

Purchase: shoes, $130
Savings in 10 years: $288
Savings in 20 years: $640
Savings in 30 years: $1,421

Purchase: coat, $370
Savings in 10 years: $821
Savings in 20 years: $1,822
Savings in 30 years: $4,046

Purchase: HDTV, $1800
Savings in 10 years: $3,995
Savings in 20 years: $8,868
Savings in 30 years: $19,684

I Also Need to Know . . .

Q: I've heard you can be addicted to shopping. How do I know if I am?

A: About 2% to 5% of people are compulsive, addicted shoppers.

The people in this group have shopping patterns that are drastically different from those of a normal shopper. Their mood goes way up at the point of purchase and way down after, which drives them to shop again. They shop more often than they'd like to, and feel like they can't stop. They're likely trying to fill a void with whatever they're buying, when in reality, the void is only getting deeper.

Compulsive shopping is tricky because unlike many other addictions, it's easy to mask. Shopping is more than socially acceptable; in many cases, it's a social engagement. But that doesn't mean you don't need help if you find yourself answering yes to these questions. There are professionals who can work with you to overcome the addiction. Consult the resources at the end of this chapter to get started.

Are you a compulsive shopper? Ask yourself these questions to find out:

1. Do you have racks of clothes or other items in your closet that you've never worn or used?
2. Do you routinely lie to your spouse or partner about how much an item cost, or pay with half credit, half cash to hide the damage?
3. Do you feel your heart racing as you head to the checkout?

4. Do you feel disappointed, guilty, or angry with yourself for spending money after most shopping trips?
5. Do you hide your purchase or receipts?
6. Do you crave shopping?

39. How can I cut my utility bill?

A: There are so many ways to shrink the amount you pay each month for things such as heat, water, and electricity. In fact, I think the utility bill should one of the first places to look when you're trying to open up some wiggle room in your budget. Let's break it down:

Heat:
- **The absolute easiest way to lower this bill is by lowering your thermostat.** According to the U.S. Department of Energy, for every degree you turn down the thermostat, you'll shave about 1% off your bill. Take it a step further and invest in a programmable thermostat (not expensive, only about $20), which you can set to keep the heat or air conditioner down when you're not home and while you're sleeping and bump it up when you are. You'll save money without even thinking about it.
- **Ask your utility company to conduct an energy audit on your home.** Many offer this service to customers for free, or at a steep discount, but if yours doesn't, you can find a professional auditor through the Residential Energy Services Network (www.natresnet.org). An auditor will go through your home and pinpoint areas where you're bleeding energy—and money—unnecessarily. That way, you can seal up leaks with caulk or cover drafty windows with plastic. You can buy a case of caulk (12 bottles), for less than $20. Weatherizing your entire house can save you up to 25% on your heating bill.
- **Use Mother Nature wisely.** In the winter, open your curtains so the heat from the sun can warm your home naturally. In the summer, keep them closed to keep out unnecessary heat.
- **Have your heating system serviced annually.** The heating and cooling contractor will check your thermostat settings,

tighten electrical connections, lubricate moving parts, and inspect, clean, or change the air filters in your furnace or heat pump. You can expect to pay about $100 for the visit, but your system will run more efficiently, saving you money overall.

· **Keep the flue in your fireplace closed when you're not using it**; otherwise, warm air from your heater will go right outside.

Air conditioning:
· **Again, look to your thermostat, but this time, raise it a few notches.** You'll hardly notice.
· **Switch to high-efficiency models.** You could reduce your energy use by 20% to 50%, which means you'll see a noticeable reduction in your electricity bill as well. Compare the cost of a new unit—which will run $200 and up, depending on the size—with how much you'll shave off your electric bill each month.
· **Keep filters serviced.** They should be cleaned, if they are reusable, or replaced, if they're not, every two months. Next time, buy a model with reusable filters to reduce waste as well. Replacement filters are about $5 to $25, depending on the model.
· **Take out window air conditioners in the winter to reduce drafts and your heating bill.**

Water:
· **Turn down your water heater temperature by a few degrees.** Just like your home heating, if you turn down your water heater, you'll save as much as 4% of your bill for every 10 degrees. Don't worry about a cold shower: 120 degrees is the magic number that will save you money and keep you warm. Most water heaters come preset at 140.
· **Use low-flow attachments.** If you have an older showerhead, it may be adding to your water bill. You can purchase a new, low-flow one for less than $20 and save more than 25% in water. Do the same for the aerator on your faucet.
· **Use an energy-efficient dishwasher.** It seems like going at it by hand would save more water, but that's not the case, particularly if you wash dishes a few times a day and let the

water run throughout. You can spot an efficient dishwasher by its Energy Star label. Dishwashers are expensive, and it doesn't pay to buy a new one if you don't need it. But when that old one bites the dust, don't consider anything that isn't Energy Star approved.

· **Fix dripping faucets or running toilets.** Not only are they annoying but they waste tons of good water and bump up your bill. You could easily waste more than 20 gallons a day this way, adding $5 to $10 to your monthly bill.

Electricity:

· **Use daylight when you can (open those curtains!) and energy-efficient compact fluorescent lightbulbs (CFLs) when you can't.** They're a bit more expensive, but they last about 10,000 hours, compared with the 2,000-hour life span of the standard bulb. Replacing 10 incandescent bulbs in your home with CFLs will save you $44 a year and $398 over the lifetime of your new bulbs.

· **Unplug.** Group your appliances and electronics onto power strips—your television, DVR, DVD player, and game console can share one, for instance—and pull the plug when you're not using them. People often don't realize that these appliances draw electricity whether they're on or not. Do the same for computer accessories, your microwave and toaster, and your cell phone and MP3 chargers. Leaving these plugged in all the time can add up to 4% to your monthly bill.

· **Turn off your computer's monitor** if you're going to leave it inactive for more than 20 minutes, and turn off the entire machine if it will be inactive for more than two hours.

I Also Need to Know . . .

Q: What should I look for in a new appliance?

A: Look for two labels. One, called the EnergyGuide, is required by the FTC on nearly all home appliances, with the exception of stoves and ovens. This label will show you the approximate energy consumption, as well as a comparison to the energy efficiency of other models. It will also likely give you an estimate of how much it will cost to run the appliance on a yearly basis. This information is important, because if a less-expensive model takes more energy to run, you may be better off going with a higher-priced one that will save you money on a monthly basis.

The second label to look for is the Energy Star logo. The U.S. Department of Energy has strict guidelines for products with this label, and they must meet certain criteria. That they do so will reduce your energy costs—sometimes up to 20%—compared with buying an appliance that isn't Energy Star approved.

Aside from that, I like to read reviews of products in publications such as *Consumer Reports* and ask around among my friends and family members. A dishwasher or refrigerator is a hefty purchase, and often you can save more over the long haul by paying a bit more upfront and avoiding maintenance costs later.

THE MATH

Want to estimate how much an appliance will cost you in energy before you buy? Use this formula, from the U.S. Department of Energy:

(wattage × hours used per day × days/year) ÷ 1,000
= daily kilowatt-hour consumption (kWh)

kWh × your local facility's rate per hour of kWh = cost per year

Let's say you need a new dishwasher. The wattage of the model you're looking at is 2,000 (you can find wattage of most appliances on the bottom or back of the machine, or use the following chart). You typically do one load a day, and it runs for about an hour. Your electric company charges 11.94 cents per kWh (kilowatt-hour), which is the U.S. average.

$$2,000 \times 1 \times 365 = 730,000$$

$$730,000 \div 1,000 = 730\,kWh$$

$$730\,kWh \times 11.94 \ cents/kWh = \$87.16/year$$

Typical Wattage of Popular Household Appliances	
Appliance	Wattage
Coffee maker	900–1,200
Clothes dryer	1,800–5,000
Dishwasher	1,200–2,000
Ceiling fan	65–175
Hair dryer	1,200–1,875
Microwave	750–1,100
Laptop computer	50
Flat screen television	120
Toaster oven	1225
DVD player	20–25
Vacuum cleaner	1,000–1,440
Water heater	4,500–5,500
Stereo	70–400
Clothes iron	1,000–1,800

Source: U.S. Department of Energy.

Q: **My dishwasher broke. Should I repair or replace it?**

A: This is always a tough call, but as with so many things, it all comes down to cost. According to the Good Housekeeping Research Institute, which tests and evaluates hundreds of household products, you should go by this general rule: If your estimated cost of repair is more than 40% to 50% of the cost of a new appliance—including delivery, installation, and taxes—you should buy a new one. I'd add that if we're talking about an old model that tends to be a real energy drain, I might go ahead and buy a new one even if the cost is a little higher.

THE STATS

- **56%:** The percentage of energy use in the typical U.S. home that can be attributed to heating and cooling.
- **$550:** The amount of money an Energy Star–qualified clothes

washer can save you in operating costs over its lifetime, compared with a regular washer.

Resources

Associations

American Association for Marriage and Family Therapy
www.aamft.org
703-838-9808

Locate a therapist near you, plus find answers to FAQs on marriage and family therapy.

Books

To Buy or Not to Buy: Why We Overshop and How to Stop, by April Benson (2008)

Helps shoppers to identify their problem and provides approaches for recovery; includes patient stories, strategies, exercises, and advice on financial planning.

The Financially Intelligent Parent: 8 Steps to Raising Successful, Generous, Responsible Children, by Eileen Gallo and Jon Gallo (2005)

Tips on how parents can raise financially responsible children.

Good Deals & Smart Steals: How to Save Money on Everything, by the editors of *Good Housekeeping* (2008)

Cut back on spending with money-saving tips from *Good Housekeeping*.

Greatest Secrets of the Coupon Mom, by Stephenie Nelson (2005)

Stephanie Nelson, the Coupon Mom, teaches you how to put her grocery-shopping secrets into practice.

Overcoming Overspending: A Winning Plan for Spenders and Their Partners, by Olivia Mellan (2004)

A self-help book for couples where one or both partners suffer from an addiction to spending.

Reader's Digest Amazing Insider Secrets: 1,703 Money-Saving Tips, by Jeff Bredenberg (2008)

Tips on how to save money on food, health care, travel, and much more.

Shop Smart, Save More, by Teri Gault with Sheryl Berk (2008)

Teri Gault, founder of the Grocery Game, teaches readers how to save at the supermarket; offers organizing, cooking, and storing tips; and even gives advice on how to get the whole family to help in the process.

Web sites

Addicted.com
www.addicted.com
1-877-233-4283

Addiction-recovery resources and tools for addicts, family members, and friends; includes self-tests and a tool to search for help near you.

Coupons.com
www.coupons.com

Print and clip more than 100 grocery coupons per week.

CouponMom.com
www.couponmom.com

Gives you free access to printable coupons, finds grocery deals by state, lets you sign up for alerts and access Coupon Mom's free e-books, which include tips on how to save at the supermarket.

Debtors Anonymous
www.debtorsanonymous.org
1-800-421-2383

Information, resources, and help for compulsive debtors.

Jump$tart Coalition for Personal Financial Literacy
www.jumpstartcoalition.org
1-888-453-3822

A national coalition of organizations committed to improving the financial education of youth from kindergarteners through college students; their site features free educational resources.

Grocery Game
www.thegrocerygame.com

Sign up for the Grocery Game and get a weekly list of the lowest-priced items at your local supermarket that, when matched with manufacturers' coupons and weekly specials, are available to you at a discount, sometimes even for free.

Mint.com
www.mint.com

A free online money-management program; see where your money is going, check on how your investments are doing, and set up a budget. You can also set up your account to alert you via e-mail or SMS text when there has been a change to your finances.

Shopaholics Anonymous
www.shopaholicsanonymous.org
248-358-8508

Information on compulsive shopping, its causes, and behaviors, along with a compulsive-shopping checklist.

Shortcuts
www.shortcuts.com

Register for Shortcuts and get coupons automatically sent to your supermarket's store loyalty card.

Smart Source
www.smartsource.com

Printable coupons, online deals, local grocery deals, and access to grocery circulars.

Stopping Overshopping
www.stoppingovershopping.com

Dr. April Benson's Web site with information for overshoppers; includes explanations about overshopping and why people overshop, information about treatment, and a resource center for overshoppers and their families.

Young Americans Center for Financial Education
www.yacenter.org

Home to the Young Americans Bank, the Young Americans Center for Financial Education oversees many nonprofit programs geared toward teaching young people ages 21 and younger about financial issues. On their site, you will find financial tips, links to their nonprofit programs, and more.

CHAPTER 6

CREDIT

40. When should I cancel a credit card?

A: The answer to this question depends on why you're asking. If you're just uncomfortable with the number of cards in your wallet, or you paid off a few and no longer have a use for them, then you don't want to cancel them. Why? Because canceling credit cards hurts your credit score in two ways. First, it reduces the amount of credit you have available. That increases your debt-to-credit ratio (also called your utilization ratio), which accounts for about one-third of your credit score. Not good. Second, creditors want to see that you've been able to maintain long relationships with your lenders. If any of those cards you're thinking about canceling are the ones you've had longer than the others in your wallet, you'll especially want to think twice.

So if you no longer want a card, the best option is to shred it without closing the account. That way, it'll still show up on your credit report, but you won't have it around to tempt you. This strategy works in almost all cases, except if you know the card number by heart, because then you can still do damage online. If you think that you won't be able to control yourself, call the card company and report your card lost. When you receive the replacement card with the new number, do not memorize it.

If that advice doesn't work for you—if you want to unburden yourself of your plastic or if a check of your credit score shows that one of the things dragging it down is an excess of available, unused credit, you should cancel cards. Do it in a methodical way.

Cancel one card. Pay down debt on your other cards to bring your utilization ratio back in line (you're best off using only 10% to 30% of your available credit). Then cancel another card. And if you're planning to hunt for a mortgage or other major loan in the next year, wait to cancel until after the papers are signed.

When choosing which cards to cancel, if you have a choice, you want to cancel the ones with the lowest credit limits that you've had the least amount of time. If any of your cards have annual fees, put those on the to-be-canceled list as well.

I Also Need to Know . . .

Q: **How many credit cards are too many?**
A: I tend to think that two is a good number. You want one with a low interest rate, because if you need it in an emergency and can't pay off the balance within the grace period, at least you won't be up against a 20% finance charge. For your second card, aim for one that offers some kind of reward that you'll use, whether that's cash back, frequent-flyer miles, or hotel points. You can use this card for everyday purchases that you'll always pay off at the end of each month, because rewards cards tend to have higher interest rates.

Q: **What's considered a good APR?**
A: Your credit card's APR—annual percentage rate—is the amount you'll pay in interest on the money you borrow and don't pay back within the grace period given by the credit card company, which is generally 20 to 30 days. In general, anything below about 14% is pretty good, but the rate your card charges is going to be based on a wide range of factors, including your credit score, what kind of card it is, whether the rate is fixed or variable, and how long you've been a customer. The better your credit score is, the lower your interest rate tends to be. Also, rewards cards generally charge more than standard cards, because you're getting something back. And store cards are also known for heftier interest rates that often overshadow any discounts you receive for signing up.

To make matters even more complicated, a single card can have a few different APRs.

- **Purchase APR.** This is the standard interest rate, and the one that you should be most concerned about. It will be applied to the things you buy with the card.
- **Cash-advance APR.** Believe it or not, you can use your credit card to withdraw cash—a loan of sorts. Unfortunately, it comes with a high interest rate and no grace period, which means this kind of loan is for serious emergencies only.
- **Balance-transfer APR.** Often a separate rate is applied to balances that are transferred from another card. There is usually a teaser rate involved—0% for six months—and then the interest rate on the transferred debt will jump, often higher than the purchase APR.
- **Penalty APR.** Your interest rate may increase if you're late or delinquent in your payments. Under the Credit CARD Act of 2009, it must revert back to the original rate after six consecutive months of on-time payments.
- **Introductory APR.** These are the offers you see in your mailbox that boast 0% APR for six months or even a year. While you may get that rate—often it's reserved for borrowers with pristine credit—the APR will jump after the introductory period, so it's important to find out what your new rate will be if you don't plan on paying off the balance in time.

There are also fixed-rate and variable-rate cards. Cards that carry a fixed APR generally hold the interest rate steady, although it can still change if the company provides you with 45 days written notice. (Thankfully, credit card reforms provide that the rate at which you incur a debt will be the rate at which you are allowed to pay them off.) Variable-rate cards will carry interest rates that fluctuate on the basis of the prime or Treasury bill rate.

Before you sign up for a credit card, be sure to read and understand the terms and conditions (the fine print). Compare a few different cards to make sure you're getting a good deal, and if the rate on your current card seems high, give the company a call and ask the company to lower it. Companies often will. For more on that, see my script on page 24.

41. Should I cosign a loan for my child, significant other, or any-one else?

A: When you cosign on a loan, you're putting your credit on the line, plain and simple. If the person you're signing for makes any of the mistakes that damage a credit score—paying late, missing payments, defaulting—it is going on your file as a big black mark. Your credit score will be dragged through the mud right along with theirs. You're both liable for the loan.

Worse yet, if this person loses contact with you, you're in trouble. Let's say you cosign a loan for a boyfriend, and you go through a messy breakup. You don't hear from him for a few years, and when you go to get a mortgage, your credit score is 100 or 200 points lower than you thought it was. Why? He hasn't been making the payments on that auto loan. And you don't know it because typically the creditor doesn't send notices to your home. They send them to the address of the person responsible for making the payments.

This scenario shows up in my e-mail inbox all too often.

Other cons of cosigning? In some states, creditors can collect the unpaid debt from you without first trying to collect from the borrower, which means that in addition to a bruised credit score, you could be stuck with the balance—as well as the late fees and collection costs. According to the FTC, studies have shown that when cosigned loans go into default, three out of four cosigners end up paying on the loan.

Even if the person you signed for is spot on with his payments, having this loan on your credit file will increase the amount of your outstanding debt, which means your utilization ratio—the amount of debt you're carrying versus the amount you have available to you—will take a hit. If you need a loan of your own, you may be turned down because you're already borrowing too much money.

That said, the CARD act makes it impossible for a child under 21 (say, a college student) who doesn't have the income to support a credit card on his or her own to get a card without a co-signer. If you want your child to have a card at college, you're either going to have to move quickly before the law takes effect (February 2010). Add him or her as an authorized user on your own card or cosign and monitor carefully. Signing up for online bill receipt payment allows you to do this more easily than waiting for paper copies to arrive in the mail because you can track spending in real time, not just once every 30 days.

For anyone other than a child in school, and anything other than a credit card, remember, when you cosign for anything, you're taking a risk on someone who isn't able to get a loan on his own. That means he either doesn't have a lot of experience with credit, so he doesn't have a credit history, or he has screwed up a few times in the past. Either way, it's not a great gamble.

I Also Need to Know . . .

Q: Are there any alternatives to cosigning?

A: Your best option may be to help the borrower find the money he needs. Maybe you can help him get a second job or show him how to sell things on the Internet. If it's a small amount, and you can afford to lend it, you can do that. I suggest enlisting the help of a company like Virgin Money, though, to manage the loan and make sure you're repaid (for more on this, see "Should I borrow money from a family member or friend?" on page 65).

If you're dead set on cosigning, though—say your son or daughter needs a private loan for college—at least go about it the right way. For starters, always make sure that you can afford to pay the loan back on your own, just in case it comes to that. If something goes wrong, you need to be able to take over the payments without turning your own financial world upside down.

Then, maintain control of the payment stream. Have the person pay you each month, and then you pay the lender directly, so that you know that the checks are going out, and that they're going out on time. And be sure to have copies of all of the loan papers, either from the borrower or from the lender itself. You may need these if something goes wrong.

Q: If I agree to cosign, and then I change my mind, can I be removed from the loan?

A: No. Once you sign, you're in for the duration of the loan. If the borrower pays on time for a while, however, his or her credit may improve over time. Have that person check periodically, and if it does, suggest the loan be refinanced without your involvement.

Q: **What about cosigning on an apartment or house lease?**

A: It's the same situation, although in most cases, there's less money involved if the borrower defaults—you may be liable only for the remaining months on the lease, as opposed to the tens of thousands of dollars that could remain on an auto or other loan. But you are still putting your credit on the line, and if the tenant misses payments or gets evicted, most landlords will report that to the credit bureaus. The same rules apply: Have the person renting the apartment pay you, and then write the checks to the landlord yourself. Be sure you have enough money to cover the balance if things go wrong.

42. How can I get my credit report and credit score—for free?

A: Getting your credit report for free is easy. Several years ago, the three major credit bureaus came together to create and host a Web site, AnnualCreditReport.com, that allows you to pull one copy of your credit report from each bureau every single year. That's three free copies total within a one-year span, and I suggest spreading them out throughout the year. Pulling one every four months means that you can stay on top of your file and spot any suspicious or inaccurate activity quickly.

Unfortunately, *free*, when it comes to your credit score, is a more complicated word. The information collected by each of the three major bureaus is used by a company called Fair Isaac Corporation to calculate your FICO, or credit score. That means that you have three FICO scores (you also have others; more on that momentarily), although the numbers should be relatively similar. You can buy one score from myFICO.com for about $16, or all three for about $48. It is worth buying one six months to a year before you apply for any sort of financing (a mortgage or a car loan).

I can see you scratching your head. You listen to the radio. You see those commercials on television—such as the funny one with the guy now working in some fast-food seafood joint because he didn't go to www.freecreditreport.com and get his score. Doesn't that mean you *can* get your score for free? Not exactly.

When you order a "free" credit report from that particular site, you have to sign up for a credit-monitoring service called Triple

Advantage. If you don't cancel your membership within the next seven days—the "trial period"—you'll be billed $14.95 a month until you do cancel. So can you get one for free? Yes, but only if you get it and then cancel practically immediately.

There is another loophole that I've found courtesy of the Web site www.credit.com. You can get a free score from that site, which uses TransUnion data. The tool then converts your data to a letter grade, which is calibrated to all of the consumer scoring methods, including FICO and VantageScore. That way you'll know where you stand across the board. The catch? Once you have your score, you'll be presented with a range of credit offers. All you have to do is ignore them if you're not in the market for a mortgage or auto loan.

I Also Need to Know . . .

Q: How do I read my credit report?

A: Start with your personal data. Are there any mistakes? You're looking for red flags, such as names you've never gone by, addresses you've never occupied, or errors in your Social Security number's digits. If all of that information is correct, move on to your accounts. Make sure that they are all ones that you're aware of, and that the information is accurate right down to the credit limit, account status, balance, and payment history. If you have any negative information on your report, you need to check the accuracy of that too. Make sure that if you've declared bankruptcy, all debts included in your filing are noted on your report, and if you've settled debts, they should be listed as such.

Finally, you want to look at your inquiries. Every time you apply for credit, whether it's a new credit card, an increase in your credit limit, or a loan, the lender takes a peek into your credit file. Make sure that the inquiries listed on your report are ones that you are aware of—in other words, you applied for that loan or credit card, and no one was trying to apply in your name without your knowing.

If you find an error, it's up to you to dispute it. If it's just a simple mistake—such as an address that needs updating—you can contact the creditor and ask to have it fixed. The creditor will send an update to each credit bureau, so follow up to make sure it does so. If your creditor is unable to make the correction, you will have to dispute it with the credit bureaus by sending a notice to each one. All three bureaus allow you to dispute information online, but where you can, you should also send a written letter. List all mistakes with a description of why the information is inaccurate and how it should be updated. Include any backup information, such as your account records, for proof, as well as your phone number and Social Security number. Give the bureau 30 days to investigate. If you don't hear back (you should receive a letter detailing what was updated on your credit report, or an e-mail if you submitted your dispute online), follow up and keep a paper trail.

Q: **Which credit score should I buy?**
A: Your scores, as I said, should be in the same ballpark. A lender is going to pull only one score, with the exception of mortgage lenders, which pull all three and take the middle one. That means that if you're applying for something such as an auto loan, it's a good idea to ask the lender which credit bureau they rely on, so that you can pull the same score and know where you stand before heading in. If the lender won't give up the information—most will—there are a few geographical rules of thumb: In the Southeast, most lenders will use Equifax; on the West Coast, most will use Experian; and in the Northeast, lenders tend to rely on TransUnion. If you're applying for a mortgage, go ahead and pull a package of all three FICO scores.

You may have heard of another score, called the VantageScore. This new score was created by the three credit bureaus as a competitor to FICO. The numbers in a VantageScore don't track the numbers in a FICO score—they're higher—so they may confuse you. It's tempting to buy this score because the price tag is lower. Don't. The VantageScore is an irrelevant model at this point. It hasn't caught on with many lenders, and as long as they are still using FICO, you want to also.

Q: **I found another Web site that offers free credit reports. Is it just as good as AnnualCreditReport.com?**
A: There are more than a few copycat Web sites that boast free credit reports, but there is always a catch. Many ask you to input your credit card information immediately. If they do, you're in the wrong place. Generally you're signing up for some sort of

credit-monitoring service or other program, which will then charge you a monthly fee. That's not to say that these services are useless, but you should know what you're paying for and why before you click Submit.

Q: What is credit monitoring, and who needs it?

A: Credit monitoring is basically paying a company to keep an eye on your credit file at all times. There's a large crop of services out there, including one from each credit bureau. It's up to you to weigh the costs of the service—generally a monthly fee of $10 to $15—and determine whether you need it and if you can afford it. Good services will monitor all three credit bureaus and tell you in real time when credit is requested in your name. That way, you can stop a crime before it occurs. If, for instance, someone walks into an electronics store and attempts to apply for credit to buy a new HDTV in your name, as soon as the store attempts to look in your file and approve the application, you'll get a text message or phone call as an alert.

On the downside, these services don't do much for accounts you already have, so if you lose your wallet, a thief will still be able to go on a shopping spree with your credit card. Bottom line: You may be able to do just as well monitoring your credit on your own by pulling your free reports at regular intervals each year, but if having a service in place makes you feel more secure— particularly if you've already been a victim of identity theft—it's probably an investment worth making. With or without monitoring, you should continue to take all precautions to protect your identity. For more on this topic, see "How do I protect my identity? What should I do if my identity has been stolen?" on page 99.

43. Are the 0% credit card offers I get in the mail legitimate? Should I transfer my existing debt onto one of these cards?

A: They are legitimate, sure. But that doesn't mean there aren't a few catches. First of all, the 0% interest rate doesn't last forever; in fact, in most cases, your rate will jump in six months to a year. This rate is what you call a teaser. Second, although it says 0% in the solicitation, the interest rate you receive if you apply for the card may be much, much higher. That's because the 0% is re-served for people with stellar credit. You still have to apply and be approved.

So if you receive one of these offers, what should you do?

1. **Read the fine print.** All of it. You need to know how long the teaser rate is going to last in order to figure out how much higher-interest-rate debt you'll likely be able to elimi-nate in that time. This is the only way to figure out if this particular 0% offer is the one for you.

2. **Look for fees.** Balance transfers typically have them. The charges vary by card, but you'll generally pay about 3% of the balance. Look for a cap on that amount. Ideally you should pay no more than $75 to $100 for the transfer no matter how much debt you're moving. If the details of the deal aren't apparent, call the toll-free number on the solici-tation and ask any remaining questions you have.

3. **Consider your credit score.** A lot of people consider transferring their debt from card to card to card a good, money-saving move. In other words, your first teaser rate expires, so you move the money to another one, and again and again and again. This strategy is a good way to pay off your debt at a low or no rate of interest, but you're doing damage to your credit score, particularly if you close each card after moving the money off it. Each time you apply for a credit card, you are allowing that lender to look at your credit file, which dings your score. Canceling a card is an-other hit, so be careful about the number of times you em-ploy this tactic.

I Also Need to Know . . .

Q: I was approved for a card at an introductory rate of 0%, but after I transferred my balance, I was charged interest. Is this a scam?

A: No, it's not—cards often charge a few different interest rates, in fact. There may be one for balance transfers, one for purchases, and a third for cash advances. Unless the card you applied for advertised that 0% interest rate on balance transfers—and even then, you should read the offer cover to cover to make sure you're clear—you may have overlooked that the advertised rate applies to new purchases only.

There are still a few cards out there that will give you an introductory 0% rate on new purchases and balance transfers, despite the changing credit market and the Credit CARD Act of 2009, so there's no reason to settle for less. CardRatings.com maintains a list of the best offers.

Q: I used to get five or six 0% credit card offers a week; now it's more like one every two weeks. Is this a sign that my credit score has dropped?

A: It could be, but it's more likely a sign of the larger economy. Card issuers have cut back on the number of offers they're sending out to consumers. They're being more and more careful about who they're lending to and how much they're offering. So while at one point a credit score in the high 600s would have had lots of credit card offers hitting your mailbox, these days, you really need 720 or above to get the bulk of them, and 760 or above to get the best interest rates.

That said, if you haven't pulled your free credit report in a while, you should go ahead and do so just to make sure everything is still in order. You can pull one report a year from each of the three credit bureaus for free at AnnualCreditReport.com.

THE STATS

- **14%:** The drop in credit card solicitations during the second quarter of 2008.
- **Nearly 70%** of financial institutions say they have cut back on credit card solicitations, according to a 2008 study by Javelin, a provider of financial services research.
- **6 in 10:** The number of financial institutions limiting the amount of credit offered to customers.
- **1.34 billion:** Total credit card offers in the third quarter of 2008—a huge drop from the more than 2 billion tracked quarterly in 2005 and 2006.

44. What's a good credit score? How can I improve mine?

A: After the credit crunch of 2007–2009, the bar raised for credit scores. What is considered a good score tends to vary according to each lender's standards, but there are some general ranges you can use to evaluate your position.

First of all, scores—and here we are taking about FICO scores, those generated by Fair Isaac Corporation and that are used for the vast majority of lending decisions in the United States—range from 300 to 850, and you want to strive for the higher end of that spectrum. Here's the breakdown:

- **Very good: 760+.** You'll easily qualify for the best interest rates.
- **Good: 700–760.** You'll be viewed by lenders as a low credit risk. You may not get the best interest rates out there, but the rates you're offered will still be competitive.
- **Fair: 650–700.** Lenders will consider you a moderate credit risk, and you might struggle a bit to find an affordable loan.
- **Bad: 600–650.** You're in high-credit-risk territory and likely won't be approved for loans or credit cards at competitive rates.
- **Very bad: below 600.** Lenders and insurance companies are likely to turn down your applications for credit, and if you happen to be approved, you'll pay high interest rates or premiums.

If you're not satisfied with the category your score falls into—and there's always room for improvement—there are a few ways to give it a boost:

- **Pull your credit reports.** The three major credit scoring bureaus, TransUnion, Equifax, and Experian, will each allow you one free copy of your report a year. You can get yours (and I suggest spreading them out by pulling one every four months) on AnnualCreditReport.com. For more on this site, including what to look for in your file and how to dispute errors, turn to page 157.
- **Pay your bills on time.** Yes, one day late is still considered late.
- **Don't run up your cards.** You want to aim to use just 10% of the total credit available to you.

- **Hang on to old cards.** Your credit score benefits from long relationships with lenders, so cut them up but don't cancel them if you can help it.
- **Stop shopping for new credit.** Every time you apply for a new card or loan, the lender takes a peek at your credit history, which dings your score.
- **Spread your debts around.** The mix of credit you have in your file—mortgages, student loans, auto loans, credit cards—shows that you can juggle debt from multiple sources.

THE MATH

How does your credit score affect your wallet? See for yourself.

Interest rates and monthly payments on a $300,000, 30-year, fixed-rate mortgage, broken down by credit score:

FICO Score	APR	Monthly Payment ($)
760–850	5.675	1,736
700–759	5.897	1,779
660–699	6.181	1,834
620–659	6.991	1,994
580–619	9.024	2,419
500–579	10.310	2,702

APR = annual percentage rate; FICO score = Fair Isaac Corporation score, or your credit score.
Source: myFICO.com, November 24, 2008. Based on national averages.

On a 36-month, $20,000 auto loan:

FICO Score	APR	Monthly Payment ($)
760–850	6.686	615
690–719	8.229	629
660–689	9.451	640
620–659	12.087	665

(continued)

FICO Score	APR	Monthly Payment ($)
590–619	15.270	696
500–589	16.285	706

APR = annual percentage rate; FICO score = Fair Isaac Corporation score, or your credit score.
Source: www.myFICO.com, November 24, 2008. Based on national averages.

On a 15-year, $50,000 home equity loan:

FICO Score	APR	Monthly Payment ($)
740–850	8.150	482
720–739	8.450	491
700–719	8.950	506
670–699	9.725	529
640–669	11.225	575
620–639	12.475	615

APR = annual percentage rate; FICO score = Fair Isaac Corporation score, or your credit score.
Source: www.myFICO.com, November 24, 2008. Based on national averages.

I Also Need to Know . . .

Q: How is my score calculated?

A company called Fair Isaac does most of the legwork in calculating your score on the basis of information reported to the three credit bureaus by your lenders. Here's how it all breaks down:

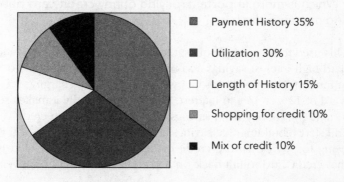

- Payment History 35%
- Utilization 30%
- Length of History 15%
- Shopping for credit 10%
- Mix of credit 10%

- **35%** is based on your payment history and whether you pay on time.
- **30%** is the amount you owe compared to the credit you have available, or utilization. Credit card debt is going to drag your score down more than installment debt such as mortgages, auto, and student loans will.
- **15%** is made up of the length of your credit history, with longer relationships with creditors always viewed as better.
- **10%** is how often you shop for credit and open new accounts.
- **The remaining 10%** is based on the kind of credit you have. A mix of cards and loans is best.

Q: **What if I have no credit at all?**
A: You might think a blank slate is good, but having no credit at all means there is no way for lenders to evaluate you, putting you in the high-risk category by default. But no credit is better than bad credit, because you still have a shot at being approved for new accounts. Once you have your first credit card (and if you have trouble getting a traditional one, apply for a secured card where you deposit money with the issuing bank as collateral), you can build up your credit history by keeping those accounts open, paying on time, and using your card on a regular basis. That's not to say you should buy things you can't afford, but swiping it a few times a month for things you'll easily be able to cover by the time the bill comes is a good idea. After a few months, the lender should show up in your credit file and you'll be on your way to building a history. For a list of secured credit cards, go to www.cardweb.com.

45. Which is more important, paying off my credit card debt or having money in the bank?

A: This used to be a simple question with a simple answer: On a standard high-interest savings account, you're likely earning 3% or less in interest. Your credit card, however, is probably charging you upward of 12% or 13% in interest. That's why typically it makes sense to take the money from savings, use it to pay off the credit cards, and start rebuilding that savings account with the money you were using to pay down the credit cards. In the meantime, you have that credit card to fall back on if you do run into an emergency.

Unfortunately, "typically" was yesterday's advice. After the credit crisis began—and card issuers started cutting lines of credit and canceling inactive accounts altogether—there was no longer a guarantee that your credit card will be there as a backup if you need it.

If paying off your credit card with your savings means you have nothing left as a backup cushion, it's not a move I'd recommend. You can use some of the money in your savings, but by no means should you clean it out. Leave at least a thousand dollars in place in case you need it. Then, once you're debt free, start beefing that account back up until you have about six month's worth of expenses covered.

THE MATH

Here's why you need savings. Say you don't have an emergency fund, but you seem to be chugging along just fine without one. Your credit cards, thankfully, are paid off. Then you have one of those weeks. You know what I'm talking about: Your car breaks down, your dog needs to go to the vet, and you get two parking tickets inside of four days. How do you deal without a cushion to fall back on? The credit cards, of course.

Here's what it will cost you:

Veterinary visit for a dog: $99
Auto repair bill: $811
Parking tickets: $75 each

Total if you paid with cash from your emergency fund: $1060

Total if you paid with your credit card, then made minimum payments until it was paid off: $1,613. It would take you 6 years, 6 months at an interest rate of 15%.

I Also Need to Know . . .

Q: How can I keep my card active without running up debt?
A: Self-control. To keep your cards active, you have to use them. But I'm talking about responsible usage, not an excuse to spend

more than you can afford. Letting your card get dusty is an invitation for the company to cancel it, particularly in this market. Not only does that leave you without a reliable means of credit but it also dings your credit score because it reduces the amount of credit available to you. Buy a sandwich or a cup of coffee with your card once or twice a month, then pay it off immediately.

Q: How will I know if my card is canceled or my credit limit is cut?
A: Your credit card issuer will notify you by mail, or, if you signed up for online-only correspondence, they'll send you an e-mail. As part of the Credit CARD Act of 2009, they are required to notify you at least 45 days in advance of any major changes in card terms. Be sure to keep on top of all changes to your interest rate and credit limit, because not knowing your spending limit could allow you to go over, and then you'll be liable for big penalties.

46. Does my credit score affect how much I pay for insurance?

A: For home and auto, yes. For health, disability, life and long-term care, no.

Here's the deal: Auto and home owner's insurance companies (or property casualty insurers, as they are sometimes called) often use what's called an insurance score to help them determine how risky a proposition you are—information that plays into how much you'll pay in premiums and your eligibility for coverage (though it's typically not the deciding factor). An insurance score is different than the standard credit score that your credit card company or mortgage lender uses.

On page 161, I mentioned credit scores and Fair Isaac, the company that calculates the majority of them for the major credit bureaus. While Fair Isaac also sells insurance scores, most insurance companies use scores tabulated by a different company, ChoicePoint.

ChoicePoint pulls together your prior claim history and your credit history to develop your magic number, which is marketed to insurers but also to you as a ChoicePoint Attract Insurance Score. You can purchase your home insurance score or your auto insurance score for $12.95 each. As with your credit score, it comes with a detailed report, which in this case is called a CLUE, or Comprehensive Loss Underwriting Exchange report. There are separate scores and reports for auto and home insurance.

Right about now, you may be thinking: *What the heck does my credit history have to do with my eligibility for car insurance?*

It does seem kind of odd, but insurance companies have conducted study after study proving that customers with low credit scores file more insurance claims. They believe that your credit score is a better indicator of how much money you'll cost them over time than even your driving record. And because insurance companies need to make money, they shy away from extending coverage to people who have filed a lot of claims in the past, or people who they believe will file a lot of claims in the future. (Or they charge these people significantly more for the coverage.)

Keep in mind, though, that this number represents only a portion of what goes into determining your eligibility for coverage and the amount you'll pay for premiums. Companies combine the score with the other underwriting guidelines they use—your driving record with your state or your claim history as a homeowner—to evaluate your risk.

I Also Need to Know . . .

Q: **What's a good score?**

A: ChoicePoint's Attract scores go up to 997, and the higher you fall on that scale, the better. Here's how they break it down:

SCORE	RANKING
776–997	Good
626–775	Average
501–625	Below average
Less than 500	Less desirable

Q: **How long does information remain on my CLUE report?**

A: As with your credit report, there are federal laws specifying when and how things drop off your report. Missed payments and public records will stay on your report for 7 years, bankruptcy for 10 years, unpaid tax liens for 15 years, and inquiries into your file stay on the report for 2 years. Collection accounts remain for

7 years from the date that you initially missed the payment, and positive information can remain on your report indefinitely, although it generally drops off after 7 years as well.

Q: How do I get a copy of my Attract score or my CLUE report?
A: You are entitled to a free copy of your CLUE report once a year, which you can get by going to www.choicetrust.com (Choice-Trust is a division of ChoicePoint) and clicking the link "Review Your FACT Act Disclosure Reports." You can also request it by mail or phone:

CLUE Inc. Consumer Disclosure Center
Attn: FACT Act Request
P.O. Box 105295
Atlanta, GA 30348
1-866-312-8076

Just as you must with your credit score, you have to pay for your Attract score. Each score—home and auto—comes with a copy of your Equifax credit report.

Q: If my credit score is high, will my insurance score also be high? And do I need to buy both?
A: The scores have different focuses, so they're likely to vary. If you're concerned about your scores, you should buy both. Although ChoicePoint pulls its information from the three credit bureaus, your credit score really zeros in on whether you pay your bills on time and the amount you owe compared with the amount of credit you have available. An insurance score is likely to put more weight on the length of your credit history, because what they're really looking for is stability. They want to know that you've responsibly managed credit for a long time. Also, remember that ChoicePoint Attract scores range from 500 to 997, while FICO scores range from 300 to 850.

Q: What if I find an error?
A: If you want to challenge something on your report, you should contact ChoicePoint directly. ChoicePoint will go back to the company that reported the information and verify its accuracy within 30 days.

You also have the option of adding a personal statement to

your CLUE report, which can help explain your side of any negative records to insurance companies who pull the report.

In either case, you want to visit www.consumerdisclosure. com or call 1-866-718-7684.

Resources

Books

The Complete Idiot's Guide to Improving Your Credit Score, by Lita Epstein (2007)
Includes information on key ways to use credit and how to avoid credit scams; debunks common credit myths.

Credit Repair Kit for Dummies, 2nd edition, by Steve Bucci (2008)
Step-by-step advice and tools to help get your credit back on track.

How You Can Profit from Credit Cards: Using Credit to Improve Your Financial Life and Bottom Line, by Curtis E. Arnold (2008)
Information on how you can use credit cards to actually improve your financial standing.

Pay It Down! From Debt to Wealth on $10 a Day, by Jean Chatzky (2009)
Completely updated and revised in 2009. Learn how to pay down your debt with as little as $10 a day.

Credit Bureaus

Experian
www.experian.com
901 West Bond
Lincoln, NE 68521

TransUnion
www.transunion.com
2 Baldwin Place
P.O. Box 2000
Chester, PA 19022

Equifax
www.equifax.com
P.O. Box 740256
Atlanta, GA 30374–0241

Government Resources

Federal Reserve Board
www.federalreserve.gov/Pubs/shop/#aprs

Information from the Federal Reserve Board on how to understand credit cards and how to compare credit cards; your rights while using a credit card.

Federal Trade Commission
www.ftc.gov
1-877-382-4357

The FTC offers information on loans, facts on cosigning, credit card information, information on debt as well as information on credit card balance transfers.

Web sites

Annualcreditreport.com
www.annualcreditreport.com

Request a free annual credit report.

BankRate.com
www.bankrate.com
561-630-2400

Information on credit cards, several different credit calculators, comparisons of credit cards, tips on balance transfers, and credit card news.

Credit.com
www.credit.com
415-646-0000

Comparisons of credit card interest rates, information and tips on credit cards, a free credit score estimator, answers to FAQs, tips and tools for getting out of debt as well as information on balance transfers.

myFICO
www.myfico.com
1-800-319-4433

A division of Fair Isaac Corporation, at myFICO you can obtain your credit score; and their site features credit basics, calculators, credit Q&A, current news and more.

TransUnion
www.transunion.com

To obtain a free annual credit report: 1-877-322-8228. To dispute an item on your credit report: 1-800-916-8800.

CHAPTER 7

REAL ESTATE/MORTGAGES

47. Should I take money from my savings account and pay off my mortgage?

A: I generally think of this as an emotional decision, rather than strictly a financial one. Having a mortgage weighs on some people's minds—they lump it in with debt, a word and a concept with negative connotations.

But mortgage debt, in both my eyes and in the eyes of your credit report, is good debt. You're paying toward a home that you will eventually own outright. In many cases, that home will appreciate at slightly more than the rate of inflation (I know we haven't seen much of that lately, but things will turn around in time). You're also getting a tax advantage, because the interest you pay on your mortgage is tax deductible.

Finally, you're taking money that is liquid, that you can use if you have an emergency, and you're locking it up in your home. If, down the road, you suffer a job loss or an illness, or you just need a bit of quick cash, you won't have it available to you. Sure, you may be able to get a HELOC, but in some markets, that's not always a given.

So my answer here is no, with one exception: If you're retired, or getting close to it, you want to work to pay off your mortgage because you don't want that extra payment dragging you down. To read more, check out "Should I have a mortgage in retirement?" on page 177.

But when retirement is far off and your mortgage's interest rate is low, you'll be better off investing that money in a mix of stocks and bonds appropriate for your age and risk tolerance. What we're looking at here is the opportunity cost you're losing by leaving that money in savings (where it's likely earning 1% to 2% in recent years) or putting it into your mortgage (where, if you have a good rate, your return after the tax deduction will be 3% to 4%). Ask yourself: If I invested the money in another way instead—if I put it into my portfolio—could I do better? If you put it into a 401(k) where you could get matching dollars, the answer is an absolute yes. If you put it into another account where it could grow, tax deferred, the answer is probably yes. And if you put it into a taxable account, the answer has histori-cally been yes. History has shown that the return on your money will be worth more to you than the interest you're paying on your mortgage. In some cases, much more.

Which leads me to another question: How much money do you have sitting in savings anyway? More than enough to cover living expenses for about six months if you were without a job or a steady source of income? If so, you should consider putting the rest in the market where it can work for you. You can invest it through an IRA or Roth IRA, if you haven't already maxed those out, or you can open a brokerage account at any major invest-ment firm.

THE MATH

What's the real dollar difference between paying off that mortgage and investing the money?

Take a 30-year $250,000 mortgage fixed at an interest rate of 6%. The standard monthly payment would be $1,499, and all told, you'll pay $539,593.

If, after 15 years, you add an extra $1,000 a month to pay that mortgage off a bit faster, you'll save $49,781 in interest, paying a total of only $489,812. Your payoff period will be shortened by about 7.5 years.

Now let's say that instead, you decide to invest that $1,000 at an interest rate of 8%. In the 7.5 years that you could have paid off your mortgage, you'll have amassed more than $120,000.

Want to pay off even more? If you were to put $10,000 more a month toward that same mortgage, starting after 15 years, you'd save $115,313 total and shave more than 13 months off the life of the loan.

Investing that $10,000 a month instead at 8% for just two years, you'd have more than $259,000.

I Also Need to Know . . .

Q: **I've heard that some mortgage lenders charge a penalty for prepayment. Is that true?**

A: This practice used to be common, but these days, it's not so much. Still, you should check with your lender before you prepay just in case.

Q: **How do I deduct my mortgage interest?**

A: You deduct home mortgage interest as an itemized deduction (meaning you can no longer take the standard deduction, the amount you're automatically allowed to deduct if you don't have a lot of write-offs) on Schedule A of IRS Form 1040.

Mortgage interest, in the eyes of the IRS, is interest you pay on a loan secured by either your main or second home. This loan could be the mortgage, a second mortgage, a HELOC, or a home equity loan. To take the deduction, you have to be legally obligated to pay the debt and you have to write the checks. That means if you pay a mortgage for someone else—your children or an elderly parent— you can't deduct the interest unless you cosigned on the loan.

48. Should I get a reverse mortgage?

A: Only in specific circumstances.

A reverse mortgage allows you to draw on the equity in your home and turn it into cash—you can take that cash as a lifetime stream of payments, a lump sum, or a checking account that you draw on as you need it. If you move out of the home, you'll repay the loan; if you die, your estate will repay it. The amount you have to repay will never exceed the value of your home. If you sell the home for more than you owe, the difference goes in your pocket (or to your heirs).

This option is only for people 62 and older who have a substantial amount of equity in their homes. The ideal candidates for a reverse mortgage are people who are in their seventies who want to stay in their home and who don't have any other way of affording to do so. That's because the amount of the payouts hinge on the home owner's life expectancy; and the older the home owner, the higher the payouts will be.

While this sounds terrific, the downside of a reverse mortgage is the cost. You might pay 10% or more of the amount you borrow in fees alone, which means on a $200,000 mortgage, you could lose $20,000 to overhead. The AARP says that reverse mortgages cost $10,000 minimum to close.

At any age, though, you want to make sure that you exhaust all of your options. Could you take out a HELOC instead of a reverse mortgage? This loan will likely be cheaper. Could you sell the house and trade down to something smaller or in a less expensive neighborhood? Again, another good option. And why is it that you're so intent on holding on to the home anyway? If you're doing it for your children, you should be certain that they want it.

Note: Some states and local governments offer low-cost reverse mortgage options, so check with your city's or county's housing department about options in your area.

I Also Need to Know . . .

Q: **How do I receive the money from a reverse mortgage?**
A: You can elect to take your money as a lump sum, as a monthly paycheck of sorts, or as a line of credit (similar to a HELOC) that you can draw on as necessary. Most lenders will let you do a combination of all three, and if you change your mind and decide to switch between options, you usually have the ability to do so, although you may be charged a fee.

Keep in mind that you're paying interest on this money eventually, so the longer you have it in your hands, the more expensive this debt is going to be. Taking the lump sum means you have all of the money the entire time you have the mortgage, giving the interest a 10- or even 20-year time frame to accrue. If you don't need it all at once, an income stream or line of credit (the most popular option) would be better.

Q: How is my payout calculated?

A: How much you'll get depends on how old you are, how valuable your home is, and the interest rate on the loan. The older you are, the more you'll be able to borrow, because the assumption is that the lender will be paying you for a shorter amount of time (most reverse mortgages end when the borrower dies or moves into a nursing home or assisted-living facility). You can use the calculator on the Web site of the National Reverse Mortgage Lenders Association (www.nrmla.org) to get an estimate. Reverse mortgages can come with variable (more common) or fixed interest rates, so keep that in mind when you're shopping around.

Note: If you and your mate are co-borrowers, the age part of the equation will be based on the younger partner.

▶ An Example

A 65-year-old man who owns a $300,000 house in Richmond, Virginia, could get a lump-sum advance or credit line of $145,103 or a monthly payment of $915.

At age 75, he could get a lump sum or credit line of $177,744 or a monthly payment of $1,241.

At age 85, he could get a lump sum or credit line of $213,022 or a monthly payment of $1,895.

Note: This example is based on an interest rate of 4.70% (interest adjusts monthly).

Q: Can I get a reverse mortgage if I already have a current mortgage?

A: You can, but you will have to pay off your existing mortgage with some of the money you get from the reverse mortgage. So let's take the example already given of the 65-year-old man: If that man still had $100,000 left on his mortgage, he would be able to borrow $100,000 less overall because the first $100,000 would go toward paying that amount off. So his lump sum at age 65 would be $70,000; at 75, it would be $90,000; and at 85, it would reach $125,000.

Q: Is the money I get from a reverse mortgage counted as income for the sake of taxes?

A: The IRS does not consider this money income, since it is effectively a loan. However, Medicaid would count a reverse mortgage payment as an asset, particularly if you take the lump-sum option or if you allow your monthly payments to accumulate. You should check the Medicaid eligibility requirements in your state.

Watch Out for These!

- **Fees.** As I said, the extra charges on this product can be high. The fees are typically rolled into the mortgage, so you may not know what you're being charged. Ask to see a complete explanation of fees upfront.
- **Aggressive sales pitches.** Reverse mortgages are sold for commission, much like life insurance policies. Salespeople can come on so strong that the government requires you to meet with an approved counseling agency before signing on the dotted line. You can find a counselor through the U.S. Department of Housing and Urban Development (HUD) at www.hud.gov.
- **The notion that you should take out a reverse mortgage to pay for long-term care insurance**. You don't want to borrow to pay for an insurance policy.

49. Should I have a mortgage in retirement?

A: Not if you can help it. In retirement, you want to try to lower your monthly expenses as much as possible, and eliminating a mortgage payment will be a huge help. The lack of a payment will allow you to draw less money out of your retirement funds, giving them a better chance of lasting as long as you do.

THE MATH

Earlier in this book, I discussed the general rule when it comes to withdrawing funds in retirement: Most people can count on being able to pull out about 4% from their retirement accounts each year, plus adjustments for inflation. So let's say you're 65, you have $500,000 invested, and the 4% rule allows you to pull out $1,667 a month (more if the $500,000 grows, less if it takes a tumble). You also receive $1,100 in Social Security benefits. That gives you $2,767 to work with each month—fairly reasonable, especially for a retiree.

But let's say you're still paying off your mortgage, which requires a monthly payment of $1,000. Now you only have $1,867 left to work with—and that amount has to cover food, utilities, insurance, gas, and other general living expenses. Forget about traveling. Now you may need a part-time job. In order to meet the standard of living you would be able to have without your mortgage, you would have to pull significantly more from your retirement account, which means your savings would last about half as long.

I Also Need to Know . . .

Q: **What about the tax advantage of a mortgage?**

A: This is probably the one exception to the "no mortgage in retirement" rule. However, it's also a rare one. If you still have a fairly high income that puts you in a higher tax bracket, you may still want to capitalize on the tax advantages of having a mortgage, because you can deduct the interest paid on that loan. But in many cases, people not only retire to low- or no-tax states but they also have a small amount of taxable income, which means they don't get much of a tax deduction in the first place.

Q: **Wouldn't I be better off investing my money?**

A: That depends on your mortgage rate. In retirement, you are no longer investing as aggressively as you were when you were in your thirties or forties. If you're following the advice of most financial advisors, which is to shift the balance from stocks to bonds and cash as you get older, then you probably have at least 60% of your portfolio in bonds and cash and only 40% invested in stocks at this point. That means that your investments will probably return a little more than 6%. Those returns in a taxable portfolio put about 4.5% in your pocket—the same amount a mortgage at 6% (one where the interest is tax deductible) costs you. But your investment returns are not guaranteed. Paying off your mortgage is. That said, this is not an argument for *not* saving and investing year in and year out. In the best of all possible worlds, you save and invest habitually—and you pay off your mortgage by the time you retire.

50. What's a short sale? Which is worse for my credit score, a short sale or a foreclosure?

A: Under the terms of a short sale, you make a deal with your lender that allows you to sell the home for less than the amount you owe on the mortgage. The lender gets the money from the sale, you get nothing, but you walk away and—in most cases—no longer owe the balance on the loan (sometimes the lender can make you cough up some of the difference, which is something you need to work out at the onset).

You'll have to convince the lender that this is the best-case scenario, and that involves outlining your financial situation, with backup: paychecks, tax returns, and credit card and bank statements. If you have just been laid off, you'll need a letter from your former employer. If you have just gone through a divorce, you'll have to provide the paperwork. If you're suffering from a medical emergency, be prepared to prove it. You should be controlling your spending—high credit card debt, and particularly recent charges, can work against you, because if you're spending elsewhere, the lender will (justifiably) wonder why you can't afford your home.

A foreclosure, for comparison's sake, is when your lender takes steps to repossess your property, typically three to six months after your first missed mortgage payment. If you don't respond, the lender will file a suit against you, and you'll receive one final notice requesting payment. You have 30 days to pay up; if you don't, the home will be sold at auction.

To be clear: Neither of these options is ideal, for either you or the bank.

There are, however, a few benefits to a short sale: It allows you to avoid the lengthy legal process that accompanies foreclosure, and it may look slightly better to future lenders because it shows that you took initiative to talk to your lender and work out a deal.

But when you've reached the point that you're considering either of these options, your credit score has likely been pummeled.

When you miss a mortgage payment (or any other debt payment, for that matter), your lender reports it to the credit bureaus, and you lose points from your score. If you miss another one, more points. And so on and so forth. By the time you're facing foreclosure, your FICO score is likely already in the 500-point range, which is dismal.

The more important question for you now is how to build that credit back up. Understand that this process will take a good two to three years. There's no magic bullet. You should follow the steps in the question "How do I get my credit back on track after a settlement?" page 13.

One other note: Many borrowers don't realize this, but if you sit down and negotiate with your lender—for a short sale, for instance—one part of the conversation can be about how they report it to the credit bureaus. You can ask that they report the situation more favorably, so that your credit score is less damaged, and in some cases, they will. It's at least worth asking. Finally, always—always—get any deal you negotiate in writing.

I Also Need to Know . . .

Q: If I have tried—and failed—to sell short, are there any alternatives to foreclosure?

A: A deed in lieu of foreclosure allows you to hand over the keys and the title of the home to the bank. You no longer have ownership of the home, and the bank should waive the balance of the loan. Again, you need to get this agreement in writing, and it doesn't mean it won't affect your credit score. It's a tougher negotiation with the lender than a short sale, particularly in recent years. With a short sale, your lender gets cash, which is preferable.

Q: Are there tax consequences if the lender forgives my debt?

A: In general, if you owe debt and the amount is forgiven, you'll owe taxes on that amount. The IRS treats this money as taxable income. But the Mortgage Forgiveness Debt Relief Act of 2007 means that taxpayers can exclude income from debts forgiven on their principal residence in most cases. This act lasts through 2012 and includes up to $2 million of forgiven debt for singles or married couples filing jointly ($1 million for people married filing separately).

Q: I've seen advertisements for companies that are willing to help me avoid foreclosure. Are these legititmate?

A: I don't want to say that none of these companies are legitimate—although some are clearly scams—but there are free services available to help you navigate this system. If you're facing foreclosure, the last thing you need to do is cough up money when you don't have to, and these services will sometimes charge upward of $1,000. Instead, pick up the phone and call HOPE-NOW (888-995-HOPE; www.hopenow.com). You can talk to a HUD-certified housing counselor for free, and he or she will be able to answer all of your questions. There are other groups that offer free help as well:

- HomeFree-USA (www.homefreeusa.org; 1-866-696-2369)
- Neighborhood Assistance Corporation of America (www.naca.com; 1-888-302-6222)

51. What is the difference between a home equity line of credit (HELOC) and a home equity loan?

A: First, let's talk about how they are similar: Both of these products are secured loans, which means you're putting up your home as collateral for the money you borrow. Both offer fairly low interest rates, allow you to deduct the interest paid, and require great credit, as well as equity in your home. Both of these products are second mortgages: You're borrowing the equity in your home to use the cash.

Now, the differences. A home equity loan is relatively simple: You receive a lump-sum loan and pay it off through monthly payments over a set period of time, generally anywhere from 5 to 15 years, although many lenders offer periods as long as 30 years. The interest rate and the monthly payments will be fixed for the life of the loan. You probably want a home equity loan if you need a large chunk of money all at once to consolidate credit card debt or, better yet, make home improvements, the original intended purpose of home equity loans.

A HELOC, however, is more complicated. It is a pot of available money that you can draw on as you need it. It works much like a

credit card in that you pay interest only on the money you borrow.
The interest rate is generally variable (and tied to the prime rate),
which means your monthly payment amount will vary too.

Good candidates for HELOCs are people who want to have a
chunk of money in their back pocket should they ever need
it—an emergency fund of sorts (not, however, to replace the
equivalent of three to six months' worth of expenses that you
should have stashed in a liquid savings account)—or people who
have an ongoing home improvement for which they will borrow
over an extended period of time.

I Also Need to Know . . .

Q: **How do I know how much equity I have?**
A: The difference between how much you owe on your home and
your home's current value is equity.

THE MATH

Let's say you purchase a house for $300,000, and you put 10%, or
$30,000 down. For the rest, you take out a 30-year, $270,000 mortgage at an interest rate of 5%. At that point, your equity is $30,000.

After five years, if you continue to pay on your mortgage each
month, your balance will be $248,765, which puts your equity at
$51,235—if, and this if is big, your house is still valued at $300,000. It
may be worth more now, or it may be worth less. If, for example, it's
now worth $320,000, your equity will be $71,235. If it's only worth
$280,000, your equity will be $31,235.

Q: **Can I count on the money in my HELOC?**
A: Not always. In the financial crisis that started around 2007, many
people saw their home equity lines of credit frozen or cut off. Not
only were housing prices falling—which decreases the equity you
have in your home—but also people were feeling a squeeze on
their wallets and missing payments as a result. As with credit
cards, mortgage lenders can lower the amount of credit you have
available, and many will take advantage of that option in a bad

economy. After all, if you borrow more than you can afford, they risk taking a loss when you can't afford to pay it back.

If your HELOC is frozen, you should receive a letter from your lender letting you know how much of the line you're losing and why. It will include a phone number, and if you want to try to appeal, you should call to see if the lender will work with you. You might get a lower credit limit instead of a firm freeze, particularly if your home's value hasn't fallen that much (often lenders use a blanket system that assumes all values in a single area are down, which may not be the case). You can also shop around for another lender.

Q: **Is a home equity line or a HELOC a good way to pay off credit card debt?**

A: It could be, but only if you're disciplined. If you decide to pay off your credit cards with a home equity loan, you had better lock those cards in a drawer, stick them in a block of ice in your freezer, or somehow be absolutely, positively sure that you're not going to charge them back up again. If you do, you'll not only be stuck with even more debt than you had before but you'll also be putting your home on the line. For more on this question, see the question "Should I consolidate my debts?" on page 6.

Watch Out for These!

- **Minimum withdrawal amounts on HELOCs.** Amounts vary, but many lenders will require you to borrow at least a certain amount, which means you could end up taking on more debt than necessary. Look for a lender with a low minimum amount.
- **Fees.** You can find a lender that doesn't charge closing fees on a HELOC, but expect to pay such fees for a home equity loan. They will be rolled into the amount of the loan, so be sure you know what you're paying for and shop around for the cheapest lender. You should expect to pay between 1% and 3% of the cost of the loan, according to the Federal Reserve Board.
- **Introductory interest rates.** A rate might last for six months to a year, which is great if you can pay off your debt

within that time frame. If you don't, the rate will jump, so look at not only the introductory rate but also the standard rate on a HELOC.

52. Should I refinance my mortgage?

A: The answer varies according to how long you plan to be in your home (you want to be there long enough to recover in savings any money you spend to close the refi). To run the numbers, first answer these questions:

1. How much is your monthly payment?
2. What is the cost to refinance?
3. What would your new payment be?

Once you have the information you need in front of you—and for some of the specifics about the new loan, you may need to talk to your lender—you can figure out whether refinancing is worth it. To do that, you want to subtract the refinanced monthly payment from your current monthly payment, and divide the result into the closing costs associated with refinancing.

As long as you keep the new mortgage long enough to recover your closing costs, it makes sense to refinance. You typically want to aim to recoup your closing costs within about two years.

One final note: If you have a high-interest adjustable-rate loan, you should refinance and lock in a lower interest rate when you can. It will lower your monthly payments and help you sleep at night.

IS REFINANCING WORTH IT TO ME?

Use this worksheet to figure out whether refinancing is worth your time—and money.

A. Your current monthly mortgage payment: $_____

B. The new monthly mortgage payment, should you decide to refinance: $_____

C. A $_____ — B $_____ = $_____

D. Closing costs associated with your new loan: $_____

E. D $_____ ÷ C $_____ = $_____

An Example

Two years ago, Susan took out a $200,000, 30-year, fixed-rate mortgage with an interest rate of 8%. Her monthly payment is $1,467.53. Recently, she saw that she could refinance into another 30-year fixed loan, this time with an interest rate of 5.5%. This new mortgage would bring her monthly payment down to $1,115.82—a savings of more than $350 a month. It would take her a little less than nine months to recoup her closing costs. If she is going to be in the house longer than that, she should refinance.

I Also Need to Know . . .

Q: Should I refinance with my current lender?

A: Sometimes lenders offer a discount to current customers who refinance with them, so find out if yours does, and then compare your lender's terms with the terms offered by other lenders. By sticking with your current lender, you may also be able to get away with a "streamlined refi," which is more of a loan modification than a complete refinance. That can save you a significant amount in paperwork and closing costs.

Lenders are going to have to check your credit to give you an accurate rate, which means your credit score may take a hit. Do all your shopping within a 30-day period, though, and the credit scoring bureaus will count it as one inquiry instead of multiple inquiries.

53. How do I get the best deal on a home equity loan or HELOC?

A: I hate to sound like a broken record, but you'd better shop around.

If you visit Bankrate.com, you'll find an entire section dedicated to home equity loans and HELOCs. First, check the national averages. Then compare local ones. This step is key—the variation between the best rate and the worst in a particular local market can be as great as two percentage points. You'll see a list of lenders in your area, the rates they are offering, and the fees and conditions tied to the loan.

If you see something you like, contact the lender. But don't stop there. Bankrate.com doesn't list every bank and lender in the country, so call local ones as well as credit unions (for more on credit unions, turn to page 343). Once you know your options, consider the interest rate, the amount that lenders will allow you to borrow (or the credit line they'll extend), and the monthly payment, but pay close attention to fees as well: There are likely to be charges for the application, underwriting, appraisal, and document preparation, among others. Keep in mind that HELOCs typically come with variable interest rates, which means your monthly payment will fluctuate. The law requires a cap on how much your payment can increase and on how low it can fall on the basis of a change in interest rate.

It's okay to let the lenders know that you're shopping around; in fact, you should, because they may be willing to negotiate by waiving a fee or knocking back the interest rate slightly.

THE MATH

Use this worksheet to compare home equity loans:

Costs	Lender 1	Lender 2	Lender 3
Monthly payment			
APR			
Interest rate			
Application fee			
Underwriting fee			
Lender fee			
Appraisal fee			
Document preparation fee			
Broker fees			

(continued)

Costs	Lender 1	Lender 2	Lender 3
Miscellaneous fees			
Repayment term			
Total closing costs			
Late/missed payment fee			
Penalty for early repayment?			

APR = annual percentage rate.
Source: Federal Reserve Board.

Use this worksheet to compare HELOCs:

Costs	Lender 1	Lender 2	Lender 3
Variable APR			
How often adjusted			
Can you convert to fixed-rate loan?			
Application fee			
Appraisal fee			
Account maintenance fees			
Check-writing fees			
Nonusage fees			
Late/missed payment fee			
Penalty for early repayment?			

APR = annual percentage rate.

I Also Need to Know . . .

Q: How does my credit score affect my interest rate?

A: If your score is low enough (minimum requirements vary by lender, but less than 620 would have me worried), you may not qualify for a loan at all, or you may qualify with just one lender and your interest rate may be insurmountably high. Look at this differential from Fair Isaac Corporation (the company behind the FICO score) in the spring of 2009:

> 15-year, $50,000 home equity loan
> Credit score 740=APR of 8.086% and monthly payment of $480
> Credit score 620=APR of 12.411% and monthly payment of $613
> Difference in the monthly payment: $133
> Added interest over the life of the loan: $23,949

It pays to bring your credit score up before applying. For information on how you can do that, turn to "What's a good credit score? How can I improve mine?" on page 161.

Q: How much of my equity can I borrow?

A: That depends. You shouldn't expect to be able to borrow more than 80% of the current market value of your home, and that's including the primary mortgage and any other debt you owe on the property. If you have a home worth $250,000 and a mortgage that still has $100,000 left to pay down, you may be able to get a home equity loan for $100,000, but likely no more than that. Remember too that we're talking about the home's current market value—the lender doesn't care if you bought the home for $300,000—only how much the home is currently worth.

Q: Do you need a down payment for a home equity loan?

A: No. The equity in the home—which you're putting up as collateral to secure the loan—serves as your "down payment." But remember, if you don't pay the loan off, the lender could take your home.

54. Should I buy a real estate investment property?

A: There are a few things to consider in making this decision. Some are personal—are you the type of person who can thrive under the pressure of investing in real estate?—and others are objective, about the property itself.

First, you need to have an appetite for risk. How well do you sleep at night if you're not sure how well your investments are doing? Some people can stick their money in the stock market and ride through the inevitable ups and downs; others spend all day worrying about how much money they are losing. A real estate investor has to have a pretty high tolerance for risk, because not only do you have to worry about property values—which can go down as well as up—but you also have to worry about filling the property with tenants, and maintenance, which is never easy.

If you're taking on the landlord and management tasks yourself (some people outsource these tasks), you should also have a few specific personality traits, including, especially, the ability to talk to people. If you're shy or introverted, this might not be an investment for you. You need to be able to stand your ground with tenants as well as attract people to your property.

Finally—but perhaps most important—you need to evaluate your own finances. The better your credit score, the lower your interest rate on a mortgage (even a mortgage on an investment property, on which you'll pay a higher rate than you will on a primary loan). You also need a substantial cash cushion to fall back on in case the rent doesn't come through or unexpected fixes are needed on the property. No matter what happens, you need to be able to pay the mortgage, and even if you do your due diligence when it comes to approving tenants, there is still a chance that a rent check could be late or not come in at all. I'd aim for a cushion of at least six months' worth of expenses, ideally a year's worth.

Once you've checked these things off the list, you want to evaluate the property itself. Walk through this four-step process, used by professional real estate investor Robert Shemin:

1. **What is the property worth in today's market?** Talk to experts, look at comparable sales in the area, and find out what someone might pay for it right now.

2. **Are repairs necessary?** Find a good carpenter or contractor and do a walk-through together. This professional will be able to tell you what you'll need to fix and how much it should cost.

3. **What can you buy it for in today's market?** If you're trying to flip—not rent—the property, you want a big margin—a seller who will take 30%, 40%, 50% below value. If they will only take 10% or 15% below, the market could go down more, which means you'll either be stuck with the property or have to sell for a loss.

4. **What would your rental income be?** If you're planning to rent this property, this equation is simple: How much rent comes in versus how much money comes out, including the mortgage, taxes, insurance, vacancies, and repairs. To find out how much you can expect to charge for rent, look at other comparable rentals in the area.

55. How do I get a good deal on a mortgage?

A: First you need to figure out what kind of mortgage works for you. Then you want to compare rates on that kind of loan.

To figure out what kind of mortgage you want, first decide if you want a 30-year or a 15-year loan. Most people go with a 30-year, and that tends to be my advice. If you can afford a 15-year loan—which comes with higher monthly payments but will build equity faster and save you money on interest in the long run—you may want to consider that option, but many people can't. Remember, you need to be able to foot the bill on this loan, plus taxes, plus maintenance, plus other monthly expenses, and still have money to save for retirement and other goals. And note that most loans these days don't have prepayment penalties. So you can take a 30-year loan and prepay on a 15-year scale, which will save you interest but also give you the flexibility to scale your payments back if you get into a bind.

THE MATH

Let's compare the 15- and 30-year time horizons, using a $250,000 loan with a fixed interest rate of 6%.

15-year fixed-rate mortgage
Monthly payment: $2,109.64
Total interest paid: $129,735.57

30-year fixed-rate mortgage
Monthly payment: $1,498.88
Interest paid: $289,595.47

Difference in interest: $160,889.90

That 15-year mortgage sounds like a good deal, right? But wait just a minute. If you were to take the 30-year mortgage instead, your monthly payment would be $610.76 less each month. If you took that savings, and invested it at an interest rate of 8%, in 30 years you'd have $910,252.

Next, fixed versus adjustable rate. Fixed-rate loans have an advantage in that there are no surprises—the rate you get at closing is the rate you'll pay throughout the life of the loan, which means your payment won't change, unless your home owner's insurance policy payments and/or payments on your property taxes are added into your mortgage payments. ARMs can fluctuate with changing interest rates. Initially, the interest rate is generally lower than what you'll find on a fixed-rate loan, and it will stay that way for anywhere from a few months to 10 years. Then, it will adjust every so often—once a month, once a year, once every three years, depending on the loan's structure. You're taking a risk with this mortgage, because the interest could adjust up, leaving you with a monthly payment you can't afford.

Before you take on an ARM, ask yourself:

1. **Is your income enough to accommodate higher monthly payments?**
2. **How long do you plan to own this home?** If this is a starter house, an ARM may be better because you can get out of the house before the loan adjusts.

Once you know what you're looking for, you want to compare rates on that kind of loan. Cast a wide net that covers all possible sources.

Start online to get a sense of average rates, both nationally and in your area. The Web site www.hsh.com can give you both of those and point you toward the lenders in your area with good rates. You should also check with your bank as well as with credit unions. Finally, ask friends and family members, as well as your real estate agent, for a recommendation for a mortgage broker.

In the end, you should come up with at least three options: maybe one credit union, one bank, and one broker. A broker doesn't lend money directly; rather, he or she will work with a few lenders on your behalf. If you've ever used an insurance agent, it works in much the same way. Keep in mind, though, that brokers aren't obligated to find the best deal for you, so it's not a one-stop shop. That's why it's important to get a few quotes on your own as well. Also, some brokers will charge a fee for their services, typically in the form of extra costs at closing or an add-on to your interest rate. (Other brokers are paid by the lenders.) Likewise, some real estate agencies and home builders have in-house financing departments that may charge higher rates. Be sure to compare with outside lenders as well.

You should compare not only interest rates but other costs and fees as well:

- **Closing costs.** This is what you'll pay for everything needed to close on the loan: application fees, title insurance, property survey charges, costs to prepare the deed and mortgage, attorney's fees, appraisal charges, and credit report fees.
- **Down payment requirement.** Some lenders will require more of a down payment than others, and all will charge you private mortgage insurance if you don't put down 20%. This insurance protects the lender if you're unable to pay—be sure to ask about the cost of it upfront, because it will be added to your monthly payment.
- **Loan origination fee.** This fee is a percentage of the loan amount, charged by your lender to process the loan.
- **Points.** As the borrower, you pay these fees to your lender. One point is equal to 1% of the amount of the loan. You pay points at closing, or some lenders allow you to roll them into

the loan (which will raise your monthly payment slightly). You can also use points to buy down your interest rate.

Ask for what's called a "good faith estimate," which will outline the most you'll be charged in fees. That way, you know the worst-case scenario and whether you can afford it. Once you have all offers on the table, compare all around and pick the best deal. You can negotiate with lenders as well—often they'll waive a fee or lower your interest rate a notch or two. It's certainly worth asking.

I Also Need to Know . . .

Q: What kind of credit score do I need?
A: You should pull all three of your credit scores six months to a year before you estimate you'll apply for a mortgage—that'll give you enough time to dispute any inaccuracies as well as to work to bring your score up if necessary. A score of 760 and above is going to get you the absolute best rates; 700 and up will still get you pretty good rates. Below that, things start to look murky. It's worth it, actually, to take the time to bring your credit score up before applying for loans, because you could shave off a considerable amount on your monthly payment.

Q: Does shopping around hurt my credit score?
A: It doesn't have to hurt your score. Excessive requests for credit will bring your score down. But if you shop for mortgages within a 30-day period, the inquiries will be combined into one, meaning you'll be dinged only once.

56. Should I sell my house without a broker?

A: It depends on your situation. Can you look at your home objectively? Do you have time to put into selling the property? Is there a deadline attached to your move? What is the market like in your area?

If there is pressure to sell your home by a certain date, you probably want to work with a real estate agent, who will likely be able to sell your home faster. But if you're flexible, if you have time to do the work (warning: there's a lot), and if in your area, homes are selling, albeit a bit slowly, then I see no harm in giving it a go on your own. After all, using a real estate agent can cost a seller 6% of the purchase price. On a $300,000 home, that's $18,000. If your do-it-yourself efforts don't work, you can always try your luck with a real estate agent secondarily.

When you decide to sell your home yourself, your first step should be preparing it for market. That means keeping the grass cut, the bushes trimmed, and the leaves raked. Small investments that up your property's curb appeal are worth the money. Paint the shutters (or the whole house if it needs it), refinish the driveway. Adding planters or nice lawn furniture—even rocking chairs on your porch—are other inexpensive ways to improve its look. First impressions are key, and the outside of your home is the first thing a buyer notices. If it looks unkempt, many buyers won't bother to step inside.

Before you show the interior, you'll want to stage it. Clear any cluttered surfaces, make the rooms look as large as possible (if that means rearranging furniture, do it), and clean until the entire home is shining. Then, depersonalize it a bit by removing photographs where you can. You want buyers to be able to envision themselves—and their families—in the home. And again, if the walls are dingy, a can of paint can be a cheap fix.

Then set your price. You can get the advice of a licensed appraiser, which will run you about $300 or more (the price varies by area). It's an investment well worth the money, but if you can't swing it, ask a licensed real estate agent for what's called a free comparable market analysis (i.e., what they would list the home for if you signed with them) or purchase an online appraisal based on comparable sales. Also, look at the homes for sale in your neighborhood. Your home, unless it has many noticeable upgrades, shouldn't be too far off that track.

Finally, you need to market the property, by placing a few strategic ads in newspapers and online and spreading the word to friends and family members and even on Facebook, Twitter, and your blog. Put a sign in your yard, perhaps directing people to a listing you've placed online that includes pictures (FSBO.com is a good place to do this).

I Also Need to Know . . .

Q: **Are there tips for selling a home in a bad economy?**
A: One word: *price*. In a down economy, there are a lot of homes on the market, which means that as a seller, you're in a competition with your neighbors, whether you like it or not. You want to price your house attractively compared with the other places around yours—that will get you the first look from buyers, which is a key advantage. Often, you'll be able to spark a bidding war that will bring your final selling price much closer to your original goal.

Q: **How much do real estate agents charge? Can I negotiate?**
A: Generally, you can count on paying about 3% (for a discount agent) to 6% (for a full-service agent) of the sale price. You can and should negotiate. Invite three or four agents to your home and have them tell you how they would position it and how much commission they'd charge. Don't be unrealistic. If one broker tells you he or she can sell your home for significantly much more than the other three, chances are good that that particular broker is aiming too high.

Q: **How should I stage the home?**
A: Set the stage by putting out fresh flowers and playing calm music—even have an apple pie baking in the oven. (If you don't bake, put some cinnamon in a pot of water and let it boil on the stove . . . magic). Make sure the beds are made, the kids' toys are put away, and the rooms are decluttered. Then just show the buyers around—they'll have a lot of questions, and you should try to anticipate them in advance and prepare thoughtful answers. (Buyers won't hesitate to ask why you're moving. An answer like a divorce or a job loss will spell opportunity to them, so you may want to come up with something else beforehand.) Also, before a potential buyer arrives, put some time into thinking about the special features of your home that you'd like to point out. Make a list if it helps. Is there a big vegetable garden in the backyard? Do you have an outrageous number of closets or interesting molding around the windows and doors? Often, we get so used to our homes that we forget about these little details that can be attractive to other people.

One other note: When someone makes an appointment to see the home, you should be prepared with the paperwork for the off chance that the person wants to make an offer on the spot. Have blank purchase agreements ready, as well as the names of mortgage companies where a buyer can go to get prequalified. You can find offer-to-purchase templates online at Web sites such as www.docstoc.com.

Q: **What's your advice for negotiating with potential buyers?**
A: The buyer must make the initial offer, and depending on what you're asking for the home and the current real estate market, it can be well below your posted price or relatively in line with it. You then have the option to accept that offer, reject it, or make a counteroffer. In most cases, you're going to want to counter. Often, buyers will shoot low to test the waters, but they may be willing to spend thousands more. Your counteroffer should be slightly lower than your listed price but higher than the buyer's initial offer.

▶ An Example

Your home is on the market for $349,000. A buyer offers $300,000. That's more than a 10% discount off your asking price . . . in other words, too low for you. So you make a counteroffer of $335,000. The buyer comes back to you with an offer of $315,000. You agree to sell the home for $325,000.

Of course, negotiations can get much more complicated than that. You can drop your price by a little less but throw in another freebee, such as updated appliances or an offer to cover the buyer's closing costs. These are lucrative to buyers, but just make sure that you're calculating your final bottom line—closing costs can run thousands of dollars, and you might have been able to make the sale by simply dropping the price of your home by less.

57. How much should I offer on a home?

A: Before you make an offer on a home—or for that matter, any large asset—you should assess not only the home or other asset itself but also the market and, believe it or not, the buyer.

That means doing a little due diligence. If you're working with a real estate agent, he or she will be able to provide you with a lot of the data you need on the area. If you're not, you can get almost everything you need from Web sites (Zillow.com for pricing; Realtor.com for comparables) and open houses: how long homes have lingered on the market and how average selling prices have compared with asking prices. That way, you'll get an idea of how competitive the market is and whether it's tipped in the buyer's or seller's favor.

Next, look at the house itself. How is it priced? Has the price been lowered since it first went on the market? Is it competitive with comparables—other homes of the same size, in the same condition, in the same neighborhood?

Finally, try to glean everything you can about the seller or sellers. Are they in a hurry to unload the home? Has the home been on the market for a long time? Why are they selling? Real estate agents, who traditionally have worked for the sellers, aren't necessarily supposed to give you the personal lowdown on a seller's situation. That doesn't mean they won't. If you find out that they have a move deadline—maybe they are starting a new job in a month—and it's rapidly approaching, you can go a bit lower with your offer because you know that they're under a bit of pressure.

When you have all of this information in hand, make an offer that seems fair and reasonable to you, and most important, that you can afford. In a down market with sellers desperate to move on, try 30% below the asking price. In a good market, go 5% to 10% below. You may pay full price.

Remember, you don't want to lose the house of your dreams because you held out for an unreasonable compromise. In the same vein, any seller who still believes his home is worth what it was before the housing bubble burst is dreaming.

I Also Need to Know . . .

Q: **Are there other negotiating points?**

A: Absolutely. You can ask the seller to cover your closing costs—just make sure that your mortgage lender is on board—or install new carpet or appliances. These days, sellers are throwing in all kinds of extras to sweeten the deal, and even in a good market, if something isn't up to snuff, it doesn't hurt to ask for a fix. Just balance it out by the amount you offer (in other words, if you want all new appliances, you might offer a bit more).

You have even more room for negotiating if you've been preapproved for a loan, so get that preapproval from your mortgage company before you start making offers.

Q: I submitted an offer, but now I'm not so sure. Can I take it back?

A: Real estate laws vary by state. But in general, you can rescind on your offer up until the point that the seller accepts it. Your offer should contain a time limit so that the seller must make a decision within, say, two weeks. If they don't meet the deadline, it is revoked automatically.

Q: Do I pay a down payment when I submit my offer?

A: In most cases, yes. You'll submit a deposit with your offer so that the seller knows that you're serious. But it won't be the whole of your down payment; it will be more like 1% to 3% of the sale price. This amount varies by state (there may not be laws about this, but there are likely norms for your state or community). In a buyer's market, you might be able to put down less, but in a seller's market, when the competition is fierce and you want to attract the seller to your offer, you may want to offer to put down more. Once your offer is accepted, that deposit—often called earnest money—rolls into your down payment.

Note: You don't give this money directly to the seller; in most cases, you'll pay it to the real estate company. It will then be held in a separate trust until the offer is accepted. If it isn't accepted, it will be returned to you. Be sure to get a receipt.

58. How much will it cost me to own (rather than buy) a home?

A: The forgotten question of homeownership: How much will it cost me to live there?

There are all kinds of expenses that pop up when you own your own home. Some are the standard ones that you would expect, such as home owner's insurance. You want to insure your home for the cost to rebuild it, not the market value, and you don't need to include the cost of the land your home is on. For more, see "How do I save on homeowner's insurance?" on page 267.

Another expense you can plan for is property taxes. Every county calculates these differently, so go to your assessor's office to get an estimate of how much you'll owe (many counties also have calculators on their Web sites and real estate agents have these on their Web sites as well). That way, you can save in advance. And if your home's value ever goes up or down significantly, you should have the property reassessed. Some towns do assessments automatically once a year, but others let an assessment stretch as long as five years.

Other expenses, though, seem to come out of nowhere: your roof leaks or your driveway needs repaving or a tree needs to be removed before it falls on your garage.

Everyone needs an emergency fund, but if you own a home, you need one that much more for unexpected expenses such as these. You need to be able to reach into your savings account to cover these costs instead of digging out your credit card. If you don't have one already, start working toward the goal of six months' worth of expenses in a liquid savings or money market account. When you have that, set another goal: saving 1% to 2% of the value of your home each year to cover maintenance costs. (That's the amount that Harvard's Joint Center for Housing Studies estimates it'll cost.) So if your home is worth $300,000, you'd aim to set aside about $3,000 a year. And don't be fooled if and when you don't spend that money one year. These costs tend to be additive. The following year, you might spend double.

Then stay on top of the big things, so that you can plan for any huge maintenance costs in advance. If your central air conditioning is on the fritz and you know that replacing the main unit will cost more than you have, start saving up in the fall so that you can buy a new one if it kicks the bucket for good next summer.

Finally, don't forget upkeep. You can make everything from your appliances to your roof last longer if you keep up with routine maintenance. Make sure your gutters are clean, your windows and doors sealed tightly with caulk, your chimney cleaned once a year, and your smoke detector batteries replaced twice a year. Clean the filters in that air conditioning system, and have your furnace checked and cleaned once a year.

I Also Need to Know . . .

Q: Are there any improvements I shouldn't make?

A: Whenever you consider making home improvements, you have to consider resale value. Chances are, your first house won't be your last. At some point, you'll likely be ready to sell, even if you can't envision that time right now.

A lot of remodeling jobs add value. No seller is going to complain about updated appliances, retiling of a bathroom, or new kitchen cabinets. But combining two bedrooms into one can reduce the home's value significantly (by and large, buyers want homes with at least three bedrooms), as can removing carpeting.

You also want to make sure that you don't improve the home too much, because you can end up putting more money into it than the next seller is willing to pay. Maybe you did spend $75,000 on renovations, but if every house on your block is selling for $300,000 or less, most buyers won't pay $375,000 for yours. Your price should be within about 15% to 20% of the neighborhood average, if not below.

59. I'm considering buying a home in a new area. Is there a way to estimate how much it will cost me to live there?

A: This issue is important. Too many people purchase homes thinking only about the mortgage payment and not the big picture and wind up in deep, deep debt.

It's a vicious cycle—you buy your dream home in an expensive area, one that allows you to barely make ends meet. Then you're drawn toward the way of life in that area: Maybe your friends are members of the country club, so you want to be too, or the neighborhood children all play a certain sport. Before you know it, your finances are completely out of hand. On the outside, you have a beautiful home in a lovely neighborhood. On the inside, though, you're struggling to fill the refrigerator with groceries or keep the lights on.

To avoid this scenario, you need to do your research ahead of time, which isn't easy. Many cities and towns don't keep data on the cost of living in the area, most likely because it changes rapidly. Real estate agents will be able to give you a lot of information, because in addition to living there, they likely know the area better than most people. But remember, they're also trying to sell houses.

I'd take to the streets, and I mean that literally. The best way to get good information is by asking people. If you don't know anyone in the area, spend a weekend there. Go to the grocery store, check out restaurants, talk to people who live there. (You might feel timid about this, but trust me—most people love their neighborhood and are more than willing to answer your questions.) Ask them about their utility bills, the cost of groceries, and what people do in their downtime. If the entire community is centered around a beach club with sky-high yearly dues, it may not be for you or your salary. If there are lots of free activities— hiking trails, outdoor concerts, parks—it could wind up being the perfect fit.

One final note: The Web is an endless resource here as well. Although communities themselves may not track this kind of data, you can find a lot of what you're looking for online (although I'd still recommend a short in-person visit). Many sites that offer a cost-of-living analysis charge money, but one free one that I like is the Living Wage Calculator (www.livingwage.geog.psu.edu/). Put together by Dr. Amy K. Glasmeier, a professor of geography and regional planning at Pennsylvania State University, it will tell you the average hourly wage for popular fields as well as the cost of typical expenses in popular communities and how much you'll need to make on a monthly basis to support them. It isn't detailed, but it does have estimates available for a large number of cities and towns.

▶ An Example

I work in New York City, and I live a bit north of the city, in Westchester County. For my town, the Living Wage Calculator gives the following data:

Costs	One Adult	One Adult, One Child	Two Adults	Two Adults, One Child	Two Adults, Two Children
Living wage (hourly)	$13.39	$22.60	$18.45	$27.66	$34.65
Food (monthly)	$237	$386	$458	$607	$756
Child care (monthly)	$0	$624	$0	$624	$1,104
Medical (monthly)	$94	$186	$188	$280	$372
Housing (monthly)	$1,306	$1,519	$1,306	$1,519	$1,519
Transportation (monthly)	$278	$479	$556	$757	$958
Other (monthly)	$200	$393	$400	$593	$786
Annual taxes	$2,473	$3,959	$3,470	$4,971	$6,118
Monthly after-tax income required	$2,115	$3,587	$2,908	$4,380	$5,495
Annual before-tax income required	$27,853	$47,003	$38,266	$57,531	$72,064

Now, let's say I decided to pick up and move, and I'm thinking the South: Charlotte, North Carolina. Here's the data for that city, from the Living Wage Calculator:

Costs	One Adult	One Adult, One Child	Two Adults	Two Adults, One Child	Two Adults, Two Children
Living wage (hourly)	$18.73	$16.24	$13.17	$20.72	$26.96
Food (monthly)	$232	$378	$448	$594	$740
Child care (monthly)	$0	$572	$0	$572	$1,012
Medical (monthly)	$76	$151	$152	$227	$302
Housing (monthly)	$667	$740	$667	$740	$740
Transportation (monthly)	$232	$397	$464	$629	$794
Other (monthly)	$188	$369	$376	$557	$738
Annual taxes	$1,424	$2,504	$2,115	$3,264	$4,165
Monthly after-tax income required	$1,295	$2,607	$2,107	$3,319	$4,326
Annual before-tax income required	$18,164	$33,788	$27,299	$43,092	$56,083

I Also Need to Know . . .

Q: How do I adjust to a different cost of living?

A: It depends which way you're moving. If you're going to an area where the cost of living is higher than you're used to, my hope is that you're doing so because you've found a job to support that move. In general, employers pay more when the cost of living in an area is higher. You'll need to rework your budget on the basis of your new salary and your new expenses. It's difficult to set things right away, and I wouldn't suggest that you try. Instead, live lean for a little while so you know that you have enough money to cover your expenses. Then, once you've gotten a feel for how much you're going to be spending, you can start figuring out what portion of your salary you can save and, if there's any left over, how much you can afford to spend on luxuries such as entertainment.

If you're moving to an area with a lower cost of living, you may be able to save more money than you did before, provided you're staying at the same salary level. Again, you want to rework your budget. If you were strapped for cash in your old home, give yourself a little more wiggle room so that you can sleep at night in the new location, but up your savings as well and be sure you have a hefty emergency fund in place (three to six months' worth of expenses).

Q: What else should I check out about a place before moving?

A: Schools, schools, schools, if you have children or plan to have children while you're living there. Do you want to buy a home in an area where real estate prices will likely hold up? Pick the one with the best schools. A source for this research is SchoolMatch (www.schoolmatch.com). You type in the county, and the site's search engine will come up with a list of schools in that district, along with their addresses and contact information, the number of students enrolled there, and the number of full-time teachers. You can then buy a report card for the school district, for about $34, which will give you information on attendance rates, test data, school improvement plans, and public perceptions. It helps to supplement this information by talking to community members or other parents in the area to see what firsthand experiences they've had. (And don't hesitate to aim higher. We moved a lot when I was a child. Before my parents bought each house, my mother would meet with the superintendent of schools for the district to see where we might be best served.)

After that, you want to look at general quality-of-life issues. Are there good employment opportunities in the area? Even if you already have a job, this question is important, because you never know what's down the road. Does the area seem in sync with your lifestyle? If you enjoy being outdoors and hiking, you may not want to live in an urban jungle for long without knowing about nearby state parks. Can you tolerate the climate? How's the commute or the traffic? Is there a solid public transportation system, should you need or want one? What other services are available for residents?

60. I am behind on my mortgage payments. What should I do?

A: You're already on track since you're asking for help instead of hiding your head in the sand, so that's great. Your first step should be contacting your loan servicer directly. Many have workout departments with people trained to deal with your situation.

When you call, you should be armed with information. The servicer is going to want an overview of your financial situation and to want to know whether it is likely to be permanent or temporary. If a medical emergency has you out of work without pay for a month, you may just need a temporary solution. If you've recently gotten divorced or your income was reduced significantly because of a loss of overtime hours, you probably need a more permanent fix. The person on the other end of the line will ask for

- Proof of income, including Form W–2s, paycheck stubs, or bank statements
- Tally of monthly expenses, including utilities, food, other debt, insurance costs, and medical expenses
- Reason for default

To streamline the process, you should have all of this information in hand when you pick up the phone. You'll also need to submit the paperwork to the loan servicer, and the faster you do that, the faster you'll be able to get help.

In the meantime, I'd also pick up the phone and call a HUD-certified housing counselor. There's no cost, and this person will hold your hand as you navigate the system (it can be tricky). You'll be able to ask questions, and they will help you go over your budget. It's possible that they'll see something you don't—unnecessary expenditures, perhaps—or that they'll have suggestions for lowering your fixed expenses or even your debt payments. You can find one in your area at www.hud.gov or www.hopenow.com.

Once you've submitted documentation to your servicer, the company will review it, a process that can take up to 60 days. They may ask for additional information from you, including an appraisal of your home. Depending on your circumstances, you may then be approved for a loan modification or a repayment plan. If you are, you'll receive a letter detailing the servicer's proposal to you, including the new payment amount and due date. You'll need to sign a modification agreement to reinstate the loan.

If, however, you're denied, you need to start thinking about foreclosure alternatives. Your bank may allow you to do a short sale or a deed in lieu of foreclosure, which allows you to transfer the ownership of the property to the mortgage investor. For more on these, turn to "Which is worse for my credit score, a short sale or a foreclosure?" on page 179.

I Also Need to Know . . .

Q: **What is the difference between a loan modification and a repayment plan?**

A: A repayment plan will redistribute the payments you missed over the next several months. This is an option for people who are facing temporary financial troubles, because it will bring you up to date on your mortgage, but your payment will be increased for the near future.

THE MATH

Let's say your mortgage payment is $1,850 a month and because of an injury, you're unable to work for two months. You're on medical leave, without pay. Your emergency fund is inadequate, and during those two months, you're unable to make your mortgage payments. Once you go back to work and a regular income, the servicer grants you a repayment plan. The total amount of missed payments—$3,700—will be distributed across your standard payment for the next 10 months. Instead of paying $1,850 a month, you'll pay $2,220.

A loan modification, however, is a permanent change to your loan terms to make the payments more affordable. Your interest rate may be reduced or your loan term may be extended to lower your monthly

payment amount. Any interest you missed will be added to the unpaid balance.

Q: **What if I am not yet behind but am in danger of being there
soon?**

A: For a long time, there wasn't a whole lot of help for people like
you. Most of the foreclosure-prevention efforts were directed to
people already delinquent, and mortgage servicers often wouldn't
even speak to customers who weren't.

This strategy was bad for a number of reasons, including the
fact that it almost encouraged people to fall behind, and it damaged their credit scores in the process. But soon after President
Barack Obama took office, he instituted a program called Making Home Affordable (you can get more information at making
homeaffordable.gov). Under that program, you may be eligible
for what's called a Home Affordable Modification, even if you're
not yet delinquent.

To qualify, you must be the owner and occupant of the home,
the unpaid balance of the mortgage must be less than or equal to
$729,750, the loan must have originated before January 1, 2009,
and the mortgage payment must be more than 31% of your gross
monthly income. You also need to prove that the payment amount
is not affordable, because of a change in income or your expenses,
and that you are at risk of default, either because your loan payment is about to go up or your income has dropped significantly.

Note: If you have missed payments, you may also be eligible
for this program. In either case, you must contact your servicer to
see if you qualify.

Q: **How will my servicer determine if I'm qualified?**

A: If you meet the minimum eligibility criteria, outlined above, your
servicer will essentially go through the steps that I listed in answer
to the first question. He will gather your proof of income, add the
past-due charges (interest, insurance, and other costs, except for
late fees, which are waived here) to your loan balance, and determine what reduction in interest will bring your mortgage payment down to 31% of your monthly income.

He will then do some math to determine if the cost of doing
the loan modification under the Making Home Affordable program

is less for the mortgage investor than a foreclosure (there are financial incentives from the government for servicers who offer loan modifications). If so, you'll be given a trial period to see if you can make the new payments. If you do that successfully, you'll receive a permanent modification that will lower your interest rate for the next five years.

After five years, the rate may increase, but by no more than 1% per year. Your interest rate will be capped at the market rate on the day your loan was modified, and it can't surpass that cap.

Q: What if lowering the interest rate doesn't help?

A: If a lowered interest rate still doesn't get your payment down to 31% of your monthly income—or less—the servicer can extend your payment term, so that you have a 40-year loan instead of a 30-year loan. You'll pay more interest over time this way, but the monthly payments will be more manageable. The servicer can do what's called principal forbearance, which defers repayment on a portion of the loan amount until later in the repayment process. Or the servicer can forgive a portion of the debt. Note: This only happens in extreme cases and is completely optional. It's not by any means a requirement.

Q: I was turned down for a loan modification because I am laid off. Why?

A: A loan modification is designed to be a sustainable fix. It is designed to make your payment affordable for the long haul. When you don't have an income, a loan modification isn't likely to help you, because even after the loan is modified, you may not be able to pay (the servicer will, of course, run the numbers to see if this is in fact true). You should still keep the lines of communication open with your servicer, though, because the servicer may work with you for a couple of months while you're looking for work by putting off foreclosure or setting up a repayment plan.

Resources

Associations

National Association of Realtors
www.realtor.org
1-800-874-6500

Resources for both home buyers and sellers; includes current news, guides, and tools tips.

National Reverse Mortgage Lenders Association
www.nrmla.org
202-939-1760
An educational resource on reverse mortgages.

Books

Mortgages 101: Quick Answers to Over 250 Critical Questions About Your Home Loan, by David Reed (2008)
Answers to home loan questions; includes information on both simple and complex topics, definitions of the various loan types, and credit score explanations.

Mortgages for Dummies, 3rd edition, by Eric Tyson and Ray Brown (2008)
A comprehensive guide for anyone who might be entering into a mortgage; includes information on evaluating your creditworthiness, finding a lender, and refinancing.

Government Organizations

Internal Revenue Service
www.irs.gov
1-800-829-1040
Learn how to correctly make mortgage deductions; find answers to FAQs relating to real estate and mortgages.

Federal Trade Commission
www.ftc.gov
1-877-FTC-HELP (1-877-382-4357)

Federal Reserve Board
www.federalreserve.gov

U.S. Department of Housing and Urban Development (HUD)
www.hud.gov
202-708-1112
HUD aims to increase homeownership, support community development, and increase access to affordable housing free from

discrimination; visit its site to find an approved counseling agency to assist with your reverse mortgage as well as homeownership information for consumers.

Tools

Living Wage Calculator
www.livingwage.geog.psu.edu/

Developed by Dr. Amy K. Glasmeier, the Living Wage Calculator will tell you the average hourly wage for popular fields, as well as the cost of typical expenses in popular communities and how much you'll need to make on a monthly basis to support them.

Web sites

AARP
www.aarp.org
1-888-687-2277

Information about mortgages and retirement; includes a mortgage payoff calculator, recent mortgage news, and information on reverse mortgages.

Bankrate.com
www.bankrate.com
561-630-2400

Compare mortgage rates, use any of several mortgage calculators, read mortgage news, find a mortgage refinance rate, and more.

FSBO.com
www.fsbo.com
1-800-690-5802

The global For Sale By Owner real estate site. Buy, sell, or rent properties online; to list a property, packages start at $69.95.

HSH Associates Financial Publishers
www.hsh.com
1-800-873-2837

The nation's largest publisher of mortgage and consumer loan information; on the organization's site, you can search for a mortgage, find a loan, and access mortgage statistics, rates, information, articles, and calculators.

SchoolMatch
www.schoolmatch.com
904-230-3001

Find information on schools before relocating; access a list of and information on schools in a particular district; buy a report card for the school district (for about $34) that will give you information on attendance rates, test data, school improvement plans, and public perceptions.

CHAPTER 8

PAYING FOR COLLEGE

61. I need to take out a private student loan for college. Whom can I trust? What should I look for?

A: I must preface this answer by throwing a question back: Are you sure you need private money? Have you exhausted all of your other options? Let's check them off:

- **Federal loans.** These are the cheapest way to borrow money for college, and they come with all kinds of perks that private loans don't have, such as deferment if you are without a job and extended repayment terms. Look into the Stafford loan and Perkins loan for yourself, and PLUS loans for your parents.
- **Grants and scholarships.** Free money! There is more than $3.4 billion in scholarship money available, provided you meet certain requirements. Some scholarships are distributed on the basis of need, others on the basis of merit. For more on how to find one, see page 224.
- **P2P loans.** I talked about these loans a bit in the question "Is it safe to borrow from people whom you don't know?" on page 17, but many students are finding the money they need for college through peer-to-peer lending Web sites such as Prosper.com and LendingClub.com. So many, in fact, that there is now a service specific to college students that is worth checking out, called GreenNote.

If you've blown through all of these options and still need

money, then yes, your last option would be a private lender. Private loans come with higher and often variable interest rates, as well as longer terms—and they're tougher to come by during a credit crunch. That puts the onus on you to do your homework.

Start with your school's financial aid office, which should have a list of preferred lenders. Often, lenders will provide discounted rates to certain universities, so getting your hands on this list is important. But it doesn't mark the end of your research. You want to compare lenders, taking into consideration the following:

- **The term of the loan.** A low monthly payment on a 25-year loan may sound good, but not when you compare it with how much you'd save in interest if you went with a 20-year term instead.
- **The interest rate.** As I was writing this, interest rates on private student loans were averaging 10% to 12%.
- **Any perks the lending company offers**, such as a reduction in rates after you consistently pay on time for six months or a year, or a variety of repayment plans.

One note: Every time you apply for a private student loan, the lender looks at your credit history, which hurts your score a bit. Do a little homework first, both online and at your school's financial aid office, to narrow down your options. Then apply for just the financing that ranks highest on your list.

THE MATH

The average private student loan carries a variable interest rate of 10% to 12%. Subsidized federal Stafford loans disbursed after July 1, 2006, have a fixed rate of 6.8%, and those disbursed between July 1, 2008, and July 1, 2009, are fixed at 6%. Let's say you borrow $20,000 over the course of college. Here's a comparison:

Private loan:
Interest rate: 11%
Loan term: 20 years
Monthly payment: $206.44
Cumulative payments: $49,543.59
Total interest paid: $29,543.59

Subsidized federal Stafford loan:
Interest rate: 6.8%, fixed
Loan term: standard (10 years)
Monthly payment: $230.16
Cumulative payments: $27,619.31
Total interest paid: $7,619.31

As you can see, the difference in interest paid—$21,924.28—is huge. Wouldn't you rather have that money in your pocket?

I Also Need to Know . . .

Q: Do I need a good credit score to get a loan?

A: Federal loans aren't based on credit score, but private loans are, so yes, you need a decent credit score. The typical lender will have five or six credit levels for scores between 650 and 850. If your score is in the 650 range, you're looking at subprime borrowing, meaning you'll pay more in interest and possibly even fees. The higher your score, the lower your interest rate. However, most lenders will allow a cosigner. In fact, even if you're eligible to take out the loan on your own, you might ask a family member to help you out if he or she has a higher score. It could save you a lot of money in the long term.

Q: How can I get information on student loan forgiveness programs?

A: Loan forgiveness programs cancel all or part of your loan, but they are generally available only to people who work in public service, and only then for public, not private, loans. The list of jobs that may qualify includes public defenders, prosecutors, police, firefighters, teachers, and librarians. To find out more, ask your financial aid department or visit www.ed.gov, the Web site of the U.S. Department of Education.

If you don't qualify for loan forgiveness but you're struggling to make the payments on your loans, federal loans allow you to change the repayment plan to lower your monthly payments. For a list of repayment options, turn to page 216.

And finally, if things are looking grim, federal loans also offer forbearance and deferment, which can suspend or significantly reduce your monthly loan payments for a period of time. Typically you can do this for up to a year at a time and no more than three years total.

Q: **If my loan is forgiven, am I taxed?**
A: You will probably be taxed on the amount forgiven, as the IRS views it as income. But there are a few nitpicky exceptions, so you want to talk to an accountant before you file your taxes in the year of the write-off. In general, the forgiven amount won't be taxed as income if you were required to work for a set number of years in a certain profession in order to qualify.

62. What are the rules for consolidating student loans?

A: You might remember that there was a lot of buzz a few years ago about consolidating student loans, because nearly everyone had variable-rate loans, meaning that rates adjusted once a year. When that variable rate dipped lower than it had in years, borrowers rushed to consolidate and lock in the historically low rate for the life of the loan.

Now, all federal loans that originated after July 1, 2006, are fixed-rate loans, meaning that the interest will stay at 6.8% for the life of the loan. As a result, consolidating these loans isn't necessary—in fact, doing so will increase your interest rate by 0.075%. Not much, but certainly something.

If, however, you have federal loans that originated prior to July 2006, and you haven't consolidated, you may want to do so, provided that the interest rate you'll receive is lower than the one you have now. Look for a consolidator that provides a couple of perks for doing the deal—the first is an automatic reduction in your interest rate for electing to have your payments electronically drafted out of your checking account. It should be one-quarter of 1%. The second is a later reduction in your interest rate—typically a full percentage point or two—for making 24, 36, or 48 payments on time. Since you can ensure your timeliness with electronic payments, this decision is a no-brainer.

As far as rules go, there aren't many. Students and parents can consolidate education loans, although they must do it separately. The same goes if you're married—you can't consolidate your loans with your spouse's loans. Student loans may be consolidated during the grace period or in repayment, but parental loans can be consolidated at any time.

I Also Need to Know . . .

Q: Do I need to consolidate with my current lender?

A: You don't, and you may find that you can't. Many student loan companies have backed away from consolidation, because it's just not that profitable. You may need to shop around. Some lenders will require a minimum balance, generally $5,000 or more. You can also consolidate loans—federal or private—through the Federal Direct Consolidation Loan program at www .loanconsolidation.ed.gov, which is my recommendation. There is no minimum balance requirement.

Q: Does consolidating cost money?

A: No, and if a lender tries to charge you a fee, find a different lender.

Q: Why would I consolidate if I can't lower my interest rate?

A: To reduce your monthly payments. Consolidating can extend the life of the loan. Consolidation loans—and federal student loans—offer a variety of payment plans, so you can repay your balance over 10, 20, even 30 years. The longer the loan term, the lower your monthly payments will be—but the more you'll pay in total interest.

On the flip side, you can also prepay federal loans, just as you can prepay your mortgage, which will bring the term of your loan down and lessen the total interest. Just be sure to include a note to your lender that the payment should be applied to the loan principle, and note that you will need to continue to make monthly payments as usual.

A BRIEF GUIDE TO FEDERAL LOAN REPAYMENT PLANS

- **Standard:** You pay a fixed monthly amount for up to 10 years.
- **Extended:** Allows you to stretch out the loan term (anywhere from 12 to 30 years, depending on your loan amount). You'll

pay less each month but more overall because of interest. This is available only for loans greater than $30,000.

- **Graduated:** You'll start off with a lower monthly payment, which will gradually increase every two years. Again, the term is 12 to 30 years, and the monthly payment must be at least $25 or the amount of accrued interest each month, whichever is greater. The idea here is that as time goes on, you'll earn a larger salary.
- **Income-contingent repayment:** Payments are based on your income and the total amount borrowed. Monthly payments are adjusted as your income changes, and the loan term is up to 25 years. At the end of the 25 years, any remaining balance will be forgiven. Note: That amount may be taxable.
- **Income-sensitive repayment:** The loan term is 10 years, and the monthly payment is a percentage of total monthly income, before taxes.
- **Income-based repayment:** This is new as of July 2009. It is like income-contingent repayment, but it limits the monthly payments to a lower percentage of discretionary income.

► An Example

Jimmy has $35,000 in direct Stafford loans at a fixed interest rate of 6.8%. His income is $50,000 a year. Here are his monthly payments by repayment plan:

Standard
- Term: 10 years
- Monthly payment: $402
- Interest paid: $13,333
- Total paid: $48,333

Extended
- Term: 25 years
- Monthly payment: $243
- Interest paid: $37,879
- Total paid: $72,879

Graduated
- Term: 10 years
- Monthly payment: starts at $279; ends at $604
- Interest paid: $15,944
- Total paid: $50,944

---

63. What's the first step in saving for college for my child?

A: The first step is saving for retirement for you. I know that sounds selfish, but as I often say: There is no financial aid for retirement. There is plenty of financial aid for college. Once you've maxed out your 401(k) or IRA or other tax-advantaged retirement savings option, saving for college can begin.

And it should begin with a savings target, which means that you need an idea of how much college is going to cost and how much of these costs you aim to cover. Most parents don't foot the entire bill these days. But saving without a goal rarely, if ever, works.

The College Board (www.collegeboard.com) says that over the past decade, tuition and fees have risen at an average rate of 2.4 percent per year after inflation at private four-year colleges, and 4.2 percent at public four-year colleges. (You can view recent pricing trends at particular schools by doing a quick search at www.nces.ed.gov/ipeds/cool/.) Right now, one year at an in-state public college costs an average $18,326, while one year at a private college costs an average $37,390.

I have two teenagers, so I know: Those figures are scary. The reality is that most parents are not going to be able to save enough to cover the full amount, particularly if they have more than one child. If you're looking for a general guideline, aim to save one-third before your child goes to school, figure you'll pay one-third out of current cash flow, and that you'll borrow the remainder. If you overshoot the mark, all the better.

A QUICK GUIDE TO THE COMMON COLLEGE SAVINGS TOOLS

- **529 college savings plan:** Plans are developed by individual states, with every state offering at least one and some states offering more. In most cases, however, you do not have to invest in the plan in your home state if it doesn't meet your needs. However, you might get additional benefits for doing so, such as a deduction on your state income tax return. You'll make contributions to the plan with after-tax dollars, and if you use the money to pay for college, withdrawals can be made tax free. When you use money for purposes other than education, federal law imposes a 10% penalty and income tax on earnings. There are a few exceptions, though, including if the beneficiary of the account dies or becomes disabled, or if scholarships negate the need for the money. You can also change the beneficiary to another family member, in case one child decides to pass on college.

- **Coverdell Education Savings Account (ESA):** You make a nondeductible contribution into an investment account (you decide how the money is invested), and the money grows tax free. There is a contribution limit of $2,000 per child per year, and the money can be used for elementary and secondary education expenses, as well as for college expenses. However, if it's not withdrawn by the time the beneficiary reaches age 30, there will be penalties and taxes assessed. You can also no longer fund the account once the child turns 18. If the money is not used for college, the parents can't take it back—it is automatically distributed to the child named as the beneficiary. Note that unless Congress makes changes, certain benefits of the Coverdell are set to expire in 2010, including the ability to use the money for elementary and secondary education. The contribution limit will also be cut back to $500. There are bills being put forth by Congress to make those benefits permanent, but as I was writing this, they hadn't been passed.

- **UGMA account:** A product of the Uniform Gifts to Minors Act, this account contains money owned by the child—in other words, gifts from relatives and friends or money the child earns. Minors can't open an investment account in their own name, so parents or guardians are custodian of the funds until the child reaches adulthood. When your child is old enough (18 or 21, depending on the state), he or she will have total control over the account. In the meantime, though, the parent must file a tax return on behalf of the child, and income from the UGMA account will be taxed at the child's tax rate, often low or even zero. These assets are also considered the student's for financial aid calculations, which means they will hurt eligibility more than parental assets would. To avoid this issue, you can convert an UGMA account into a 529, called a UGMA 529 or a custodial 529. If you do that, the assets will be assessed at the parental rate, as they are with a 529 account.

- **Roth IRA:** For any parents trying to straddle the college–retirement line—a Roth IRA is a no-brainer. You put after-tax money into a Roth. It then grows tax free until you pull it out in retirement (you actually never have to withdraw from a Roth, as you can leave it to future generations). But you can also pull out contributions at any time (since you've already paid taxes) and earnings (after 5 years, although you'll pay taxes on the earnings if you use them for education and not retirement) and use the money for education or to buy your first house. That makes a Roth a terrific choice for anyone trying to save for college and retirement simultaneously. Annual contribution limits in 2009* are $5,000 for those younger than 50 and $6,000 for people who are older. You are allowed to make the full Roth contribution as long as you earn no more than $166,000 a year (if married, filing jointly; $105,000 if single). Once the money is in the Roth, you can invest it as you see fit. And note: In 2010, a traditional IRA can be converted to a Roth with no income restriction.

I Also Need to Know . . .

Q: What do you think about savings programs such as Upromise?

A: These programs work by depositing money in a college savings plan when you shop at certain retailers or buy certain products. I think that they're great, provided you're getting the bonus on things you'd be buying anyway and you're not being charged for the program itself. With most, you register your credit cards and the programs keep track of your purchases, giving you a little kickback when your spending qualifies for one. Some programs offer credit cards themselves, giving you the opportunity

* 2009 data is used when 2010 data was not yet available at press time.

to earn more rewards for your daily spending (a great bonus, but worth it only if you are paying off those cards each and every month).

Does that mean that you should buy a new television because you'll get cash back? No, but if you need a new television and one store participates in your savings program while another does not, then sure, you might as well spend your money at that first store and get a little boost for your college savings plan in the process. Check out the chart that compares a few of the bigger programs.

PROGRAM	COST	TERMS	NUMBER OF PARTICIPATING RETAILERS
Upromise: www.upromise.com	None	Register your credit or debit cards and get 1% to 25% back when you shop online through www.upromise.com; 8% back from restaurants; 1% to 3% back at the grocery store or drugstore on eligible items. You can invite your friends and family to join and contribute their rewards to you.	600 online retailers through www.upromise.com; 8,000 participating restaurants; more than 21,000 participating grocery stores
LittleGrad: www.littlegrad.com	None	You register and download a Little Grad Savings Manager that tracks your online purchases. Participating retailers give back a percentage that varies, usually 2% to 10%. You can ask friends and family to register and contribute to your account as well.	2,000 online services and stores.
BabyMint: www.babymint.com	None	Contributions range from 1% to 26% of total purchases. You can have your rebates sent to you by check, deposited into your college savings account, or applied as a payment on a student loan.	500 leading merchants, in areas such as travel, apparel, restaurants, electronics, home, pharmacies, and grocery stores.

(continued)

PROGRAM	COST	TERMS	NUMBER OF PARTICIPATING RETAILERS
Futuretrust: www.futuretrust.com	No annual fee, but because it's a credit card, you'll be charged interest if you don't pay off your balance each month. Interest rates vary depending on your credit history.	You must apply and be approved for the Futuretrust MasterCard. Once you are, you'll earn 1% of your purchases as a rebate into a 529 college savings account. Partner merchants offer an additional rebate, up to about 10%.	There are more than 500 partner merchants who offer additional rebates.

64. How can I figure out how much financial aid my children are likely to receive for college?

A: There are two tools that I'd recommend. The first is from the Department of Education itself. FAFSA4caster (www.fafsa4caster.ed .gov) allows parents to estimate eligibility early. It's aimed at high school juniors, but you can use it at any time. In fact, if your kids are young, you can even create scenarios that are based on future earnings.

The second is the Expected Family Contribution Calculator from FinAid.org. Also an estimate, this is based on the methodology that the federal government uses in calculating aid. As a result, it's pretty accurate. You can also run the numbers on the basis of what's called institutional methodology, which is close to the formulas used by most private schools.

THE FAFSA LINGO

- **Cost of attendance:** The total amount it will cost you to attend that college or university per year. As long as you're attending at least half time, the cost of attendance includes the tuition and fees, room and board (or living expenses for students not living on campus), books, supplies, transportation, loan fees, an allowance for dependent care (if the student has children who need to be cared for while the student is in class), costs related to disability, and study-abroad costs, if the student participates in international study programs. But you don't have to add these numbers up yourself—the school establishes them.

- **Expected family contribution (EFC):** This number is used to determine whether you're eligible for federal student aid, and how much you will receive. It's not, however, the amount that you will be responsible for paying. It helps a college calculate how much aid it can give you if you choose to enroll.
- **Financial aid package:** The college you choose to attend will wrap together all the aid you're eligible for to meet your cost of attendance. The result is the total money offered, including federal student aid and outside sources such as scholarships or grants.
- **Need analysis:** This process determines how much your family can reasonably contribute toward education, on the basis of income, assets, and living expenses. The result is the EFC. Combined with the cost of attendance, this number is used by the school to award grants, campus-based aid, and loans.
- **Student aid report:** Once you've completed your FAFSA, you'll receive this report, a summary of the information you submitted and the EFC that was calculated.

I Also Need to Know . . .

Q: What is a Pell Grant?

A: A Federal Pell Grant is for undergraduate students, and unlike a loan, it doesn't have to be repaid. These grants are need-based, and the amount awarded depends on your EFC, the cost of attending a particular school, and whether your child is attending full- or part-time. In 2009–2010, the maximum Pell Grant award is $5,350 (it was increased by $500 as part of the American Recovery and Reinvestment Act of 2009). This figure changes each year.

Once you receive a Pell Grant, that amount will be added to the EFC and any other aid you've received, and the total is subtracted from the school's cost of attendance. The result represents your remaining financial need.

Q: What about work-study programs?

A: Work-study can be helpful as part of a financial aid package. The program isn't available at every school (the Department of Education says there are approximately 3,400 participating institutions), but it is something to consider if your school offers the option. You'll earn money through a part-time job, either on campus or at a nonprofit or public agency that relates to your degree program, that you can use to help pay for school. It's up to the college to award work-study jobs to students on the basis of financial need. Students are paid by the hour (at least minimum wage).

THE STATS

- **$143 billion:** Amount of financial aid distributed to undergraduate and graduate students in 2007–2008.
- **$8,896:** Average amount of financial aid received by full-time undergraduate students in 2007–2008.
- **5.4 million:** The number of Pell Grant recipients in 2007–2008.

65. Where can I find scholarships and grants for college?

A: Start locally, as scholarships specific to your town, state, or county automatically cut down on competition. The fewer people who qualify to apply, the greater chance you have of winning. First, make a list of your interests, strengths, extracurricular activities, intended major, and anything else that sets you apart.

Then head to your school's guidance counselor, who can tell you about the awards for which you might be eligible. If you've worked or volunteered throughout high school, ask your employer or organization if it offers any money to employees or affiliates. Have your parents ask at their jobs, too.

Once you've maxed out the options locally, it's time to search on a national scale. There are a number of free scholarship search services out there, but my favorites are FastWeb (www.fastweb.com) and the College Board's search engine (www.collegeboard.com/scholarships). These sites have upward of $3 billion worth of scholarships listed in their databases.

If you've already decided on a college, or you have a few in mind that you like, call the financial aid office (or offices) and see what the school itself offers. You'll likely find a few that apply to you and your major.

THE MATH

Is spending your time searching for scholarships worth it? Without a doubt, yes. Take this small, $1,000-a-year, $4,000 total scholarship as an example. See what it saves you in borrowing costs:

- Stafford loan: $15,000
- Interest rate: 6.8%
- Loan term: 10 years
- Monthly payment: $172.62
- Total paid: $20,714.49
- Interest paid: $5,714.49

- Stafford loan: $11,000
- Interest rate: 6.8%
- Loan term: 10 years
- Monthly payment: $126.59
- Total paid: $15,190.52
- Interest paid: $4,190.52

Savings: $1,523.97 in interest; $5,523.97 overall

- Private student loan: $20,000
- Interest rate: 9%
- Loan term: 20 years
- Monthly payment: $179.95
- Total paid: $43,184.79
- Total interest paid: $23,184.79

- Private student loan: $16,000
- Interest rate: 9%
- Loan term: 20 years
- Monthly payment: $143.96

- Total paid: $34,547.83
- Total interest paid: $18,547.83

Savings: $4,636.96 in interest; $8,636.96 overall

I Also Need to Know . . .

Q: I found a scholarship-search Web site that charges a fee. Is it worth it?

A: No. Not only are there plenty of free ways to find scholarships, but if a site or scholarship charges you money, it may be a scam. Other scholarship-related red flags from the FTC:

- "The scholarship is guaranteed or your money back."
- "You can't get this information anywhere else."
- "I just need your credit card or bank account number to hold this scholarship."
- "We'll do all the work."
- "The scholarship will cost some money."
- "You've been selected by a 'national foundation' to receive a scholarship."
- "You're a finalist in a contest you entered to receive a scholarship."

Q: I'm in my thirties and want to get my degree. Are there scholarships for me?

A: There are. In fact, the bulk of scholarships out there don't have age requirements or restrictions. A recent search for awards on the College Board's scholarship site for "returning adult student" received 74 hits. FastWeb says it lists 50 awards that have a minimum age of 30, 230 that have a minimum age of 25, and 1,800 that have no age restrictions at all. You should also check with your employer if you're going to attend college while working part-time. Often companies offer internal scholarships, or they'll supplement a portion of your tuition if your education will help you advance at work.

You should also know that you're also eligible for federal student aid, which carries no age restrictions. In fact, since you're an independent student, you can take out even more in unsubsidized

Stafford loans—an additional $4,000 each year when you're a freshman and sophomore and $5,000 a year as a junior or senior.

66. How do I pick a 529 plan?

A: There are two kinds of 529 plans, both labeled 529 for the section of the tax code that created them.

- A 529 college savings plan, the more popular type, works like a 401(k) or an IRA. You'll make contributions into an account, and that money is then invested. You have control over the diversification of your investments, and your account's value will go up or down depending on the choices you've made and the market's fluctuations. Your contributions are made with after-tax dollars, but you may get a tax deduction—or some other benefit—for making your contribution, depending on the plan you choose. (More on this momentarily.) The value of the money in the account grows tax free to pay for education.
- A 529 prepaid tuition plan, however, lets you pay ahead of time either all or some of the tuition for in-state colleges. You lock into the cost of tuition at the time you pay it—which represents a large savings, considering that college tuition rates have been rising at about 6% annually during recent years. If your child decides that he or she wants to attend a private or out-of-state college, you can convert the prepaid plan so that the money goes toward that school. But depending on the plan and its rules, you may lose some or all of the growth on that money. Some colleges offer prepaid 529 plans of their own.

With both types of plans, should your child decide not to go to college, the money can be used to pay for education for another member of the family. If by the time that last family member hits age 30 it has not been used for education, you'll have to pull it out of the account and pay a 10% penalty as well as taxes on the income at your current rate.

Once you've decided on a 529, you need to pick a plan itself. Picking a 529 is a lot like picking a mutual fund. Most states have more than one 529 college savings plan. You'll want to compare and contrast the ones in your state with the ones in others across the United States regarding investment options, perks, expenses, and performance. Start with the plan(s) from your home state (they will be the only ones to offer you perks), but don't stop there.

- **Performance.** Some 529s came through the market meltdown of 2007–2009 with barely a scratch. Others did not. Go to www.savingforcollege.com or www.morningstar.com for a list of the best performing 529s. Look at how they handled the assets of young children as well as how they handled those of children ages 15 and 16.
- **Investment options.** Any plan you consider needs a menu of investments in line with your goals. If you're risk adverse, look for a plan that includes a CD so that at least a portion of the money that you invest is FDIC insured. If you're aggressive, however, you probably want a 100% equity option, which isn't offered by all states. Most likely, you're somewhere in the middle. I recommend looking for a plan with age-based investment options, which works like the target-date retirement fund you may be using in your IRA or 401(k). When the child is young, your investments will be heavy on stocks; as he approaches college age, the plan will rebalance to be more conservative.
- **Expenses.** Most plans are going to charge you a percentage of your money, but the exact amount will vary by plan and state. Shop around and compare the fee tables in the disclosure materials of a few different plans to get a good sense of how much you'll pay over time. Savingforcollege.com does an ongoing fee study comparing the lowest and highest 10-year expense totals for all direct-sold 529 savings plans. It's worth checking out, as the costs do vary. As I was writing this, fees accumulated on a $10,000 investment over a 10-year period ranged from $2,444 (Montana Pacific Life Funds 529) to $320 (Louisiana START).
- **Perks.** Many states offer incentives for people who save using the state 529 plan, including tax deductions or credits for contributions made. There are a few that will extend these tax incentives to people who invest in a plan out of state (Arizona, Kansas, Maine, and Pennsylvania), but that's more the exception than the rule.

If you find that your state's plan isn't up to snuff, you can go out of state and check out other plans to find one that suits your needs. Just check each plan's rules and regulations first. Some have residency restrictions.

I Also Need to Know . . .

Q: **Are there contribution limits or eligibility requirements for 529s that I need to be aware of?**

A: As these plans are set up by each state, eligibility requirements vary. But in general, anyone can open a plan, and contribution limits are quite high—often $300,000 plus for each beneficiary. There are usually no age restrictions or income limits, but withdrawals will be subject to a 10% penalty and taxes if the money isn't used for education.

Q: **My parents want to save for my children's education too. Can they contribute to a 529 plan as well?**

A: They can, and in fact, that is probably the best way for them to assist you. They can open a 529 plan in their own names, or they can make a contribution to your account if your particular 529 plan allows for that (some don't). The difference is that if they are the owner of the account, the money remains theirs, meaning that they have control over it and can change the beneficiary if they choose (Note: The money must still be used for education if they want to avoid paying taxes and penalties. But if, for instance, your children decide not to go to college or don't need the extra help, your parents can change the beneficiary on the account so that the funds go to another grandchild). Either way, the contributions are considered a gift to the account's beneficiary.

If they decide to give up control of the money and make contributions to your account, they'll need to send the check directly to the plan, making sure to follow the guidelines for third-party contributions (you can find these on the plan Web site or by calling customer service), or give cash that can be deposited into the account by the parents.

67. Is a high-priced private college worth the cost?

A: I think that every parent—and student—has this internal debate. Do you pay the big bucks for a name like Harvard, and then spend the next 20 years working your way out from under student loan debt, or do you go to a lesser-known in-state school and walk out with little or no financial stress?

Recent research from Princeton Review and *USA Today* (a study called "Best Value Colleges for 2009," found at www.usatoday.com/news/education/best-value-colleges.htm) shows that it may not be as much of an issue as we think. Ivy League schools such as Princeton and Yale come with a heck of a sticker price—more than $48,000 a year when you factor in tuition, room and board, books, and fees—but the school also gives out more than $35,000 on average in need-based grants. Ninety percent of those who request aid qualify for it, and for those who do, 100% of their need is met. You can find a list of the best-value public and private colleges on Princeton Review's Web site at www.princetonreview.com.

The lesson? Don't let a school's sticker price be its defining factor. One of the worst mistakes you can make, in fact, is crossing a college or university off your list because the cost doesn't seem feasible. There is no way to know how much assistance you'll be eligible for until you file that FAFSA form (for more on this, turn to "How can I figure out how much financial aid my children are likely to receive for college?" on page 222) and apply to the school.

That said, once you've been accepted to a few schools and you have the financial aid packages in hand, you do need to start making judgments. If the options are all workable financially, schedule a few visits. Not only do you want to look around campus and get a feel for the students, the landscape, the dorms, and whether you'd fit in, but you also want to spend some time with administrators and current students and ask questions:

1. Do they have the major you're interested in—or at least one that is similar? If not, there is no point in going further.
2. Do they have a study-abroad program? Even if the thought of a semester in a different country is overwhelming at this point, your interests may change over time. Having the option is valuable.

3. Are there clubs or activities you can see yourself participating in? If you play a sport, would you be able to join a
team, either on the college level or through an intramural
program?
4. Are the class sizes and structures conducive to the way you
learn best?
5. Where are the school's graduates working?
6. How soon after graduation are they able to find jobs?
7. What graduate programs are graduates attending?

I Also Need to Know . . .

Q: **Is there a way to find out about a college's typical financial aid
packages before I apply?**
A: Yes. You can find 200 schools in the study I mentioned earlier,
"Best Value Colleges for 2009" from Princeton Review; see www
.usatoday.com/news/education/best-value-colleges.htm and www
.princetonreview.com/best-value-colleges.aspx. It's a small group,
though, and if your school didn't make the cut, you'll have to take
matters into your own hands. For initial research, there are about
2,000 additional schools listed on the Princeton Review Web site
(www.princetonreview.com). If that doesn't satisfy your needs,
call the school directly or schedule an on-campus visit. Financial
aid representatives there should be able to tell you the average aid
package over the last few years.

Q: **I've heard that I should save my money on my undergraduate
years and then shell out for the big names for grad school. Is
this good advice?**
A: The idea behind this advice is that a graduate degree tends to
overshadow an undergraduate degree on your résumé. A potential employer may put more stock in the advanced degree and
in the college or university where you earned it. This is true, but
keep in mind one thing: You have to get accepted to a graduate
school first, and your undergrad grades and where you earned
them are integral to that process.

I'd pick a grad school exactly the same way I'd pick undergrad—
by evaluating financial aid packages, looking at programs, and
asking questions about the success and career paths of previous

graduates. Of course you want to make sure that the program you enter is well respected, but there are thousands of prestigious programs throughout the United States offered by schools you may never have heard of. It's worth it to do a little digging and see what you can come up with. If you're happy at the school, you'll likely do better.

Q: What about online degree programs?
A: They can be great if you're balancing a family and work or you want to save some cash. But you must make sure that the school you choose is legitimate; otherwise, it's a waste of money. A few points to check out:

- **Accreditation.** If the school isn't recognized as a legitimate institution by regional or national accrediting agencies, find another option. It won't help your résumé, and if you decide to transfer to a traditional school after a few classes, they likely won't take your credits. You may also have trouble getting financial aid.
- **Value.** People often assume that these online programs are less expensive than community colleges or local universities, and that may not be the case. Compare costs, and keep in mind that many traditional universities offer online classes now as well.
- **Customer service.** Someone should be a phone call away if something goes wrong and you need technical support. If no one is, or if the program won't give you a refund if you have to drop a class because of technical difficulties, that's a problem.
- **Interaction.** Learning at home without other students around and a professor looking over your shoulder may sound great, but you'd be surprised how much you learn by asking questions and interacting with other students. Try to sign up for a program that either has chat rooms—make sure they're active—or in-person meetings a few times a month.

Resources

Associations

College Savings Plan Network
www.collegesavings.org

A national nonprofit association dedicated to making college more affordable for families; access information about 529 plans, compare plans from many U.S. locales, and estimate costs with a college cost calculator.

Books

Best 368 Colleges, 2009 edition, by Princeton Review (2008)

A report on the top 20 schools in 62 categories based on ratings from students.

The Best Way to Save for College: A Complete Guide to 529 Plans, by Joe Hurley (2008)

Detailed information on 529 plans, includes a state-by-state comparison of all 529 programs.

The College Board Guide to Getting Financial Aid 2008, by the College Board (2007)

A step-by-step guide explaining how to get financial aid; includes explanations of key financial aid terms and assistance with filling out the FAFSA (Free Application for Federal Student Aid).

The College Board Scholarship Handbook 2008, by the College Board

Information for undergraduates on more than 2,100 scholarship, internship, and loan programs, also includes a planning worksheet to keep track of applications.

FastWeb College Gold: The Step-by-Step Guide to Paying for College, by Mark Kantrowitz and Doug Hardy (2006)

Learn how to develop a plan to pay for college, apply for loans, find scholarships and grants, and steer clear of financing scams.

Fiske Guide to the Colleges, by Edward B. Fiske (2008)

A guide to more than 300 colleges in which each college's listing is accompanied by an essay with information from students, administrators, and independent research; also includes a list of the 40-plus schools that deliver the best value for the cost.

Paying for College Without Going Broke, by Kal Chany (2008)

Advice on how to pay for college; includes the most recent financial aid forms, lists annual changes in tax laws, shows how to calculate your aid eligibility, and gives advice on how to negotiate with financial aid offices and information for those in special circumstances (single parents, independent students, etc.).

Government Organizations

FAFSA4caster
www.fafsa4caster.ed.gov
1-800-433-3243

Helps you estimate your eligibility for federal aid and provides advice on the financial aid process.

Federal Direct Consolidation Loan Program
www.loanconsolidation.ed.gov

Information from the government on how to consolidate your student loans.

Federal Student Aid
www.studentaid.ed.gov
1-800-433-3243

U.S. Department of Education's site for free information, with resources for preparing for and paying for college; features tools such as a college savings calculator.

Free Application for Federal Student Aid (FAFSA)
www.fafsa.ed.gov
1-800-433-3243

Detailed information on the Free Application for Federal Student Aid; provides instructions on how to complete the form and allows you to fill out the FAFSA form online.

Federal Trade Commission
202-326-2222

Information for parents and students on how to avoid scholarship scams.

United States Department of Education
www.ed.gov
1-800-872-5327
Information about loan-forgiveness programs and on federal student aid.

U.S. Securities and Exchange Commission
www.sec.gov/investor/pubs/intro529.htm
1-888-732-6585
An introduction to 529 plans, with answers to FAQs.

Alternative Lenders

GreenNote
www.greennote.com
1-866-711-5620
Students can connect with those in their social network to ask for small student loans, and for a fee (2% of the total loan amount), GreenNote will formalize the transaction.

Web sites

College Board
www.collegeboard.com
1-866-630-9305
Information for parents on how to help pay for college; articles, information, and tips on how to find scholarships and aid; college savings calculators; and information on the pros and cons of college savings plans.

College Savings Plan Network
www.collegesavings.org
A national nonprofit association dedicated to making college more affordable for families; access information about 529 plans, compare plans from around the United States, and estimate costs with a college cost calculator.

FastWeb
www.fastweb.com
Information on millions of scholarships.

FinAid
www.finaid.org

Detailed information on student aid, including information on consolidation, answers to FAQs, a scholarship search, a loan consolidation calculator, the Expected Family Contribution calculator, a calculator of prepaid tuition and of 529 college savings plans, and tips on saving for college.

Princeton Review
www.princetonreview.com

A wealth of information on undergraduate and graduate schools; includes free college test prep tools, a best-fit college search, information on choosing a major, rankings and lists, a scholarship search, a guide to financial aid, information on study abroad, and information on applying for college.

Savingforcollege.com
www.savingforcollege.com

Information on how to best prepare for college costs; includes information, tools, calculators, and a detailed guide to understanding 529 plans, including resources for comparing 529 plans and reviewing your state's plan.

SimpleTuition
www.simpletuition.com

Search for a student loan that meets your needs; the site includes recent industry news, a student loan glossary, and tips for planning, saving, and paying for college.

Student Loan Borrower Assistance
www.studentloanborrowerassistance.org
617-482-0850

The National Consumer Law Center's Student Loan Borrower Assistance project offers information for people who already have student loans and want to know more about their rights and options.

USA Today's "Best Value Colleges for 2009"
www.usatoday.com/news/education/best-value-colleges.htm

USA Today and Princeton Review joined forces to bring forth a list of the 100 best value colleges for 2009; includes information on each school, statistics, and why it's a great value.

CHAPTER 9

INSURANCE

68. What is a health savings account? Is it a good option for me if I don't have health coverage?

A: A health savings account (HSA) is a tax-advantaged savings account that's used to pay for medical expenses. But unlike regular savings accounts, HSAs don't stand alone. Rather, they are linked with high-deductible health insurance plans, which generally come with lower premiums than other insurance plans do.

Here's how it works: You purchase an HSA-compatible high-deductible health insurance policy, which has a minimum deductible of $1,200 if you're single and $2,400 for family coverage (in 2010; the deductible minimums are indexed annually for inflation). These plans are growing in popularity, so your employer may offer one: In fact, a 2008 survey by America's Health Insurance Plans found that 6.1 million Americans were covered by HSA-qualified plans, including 4.6 million as part of an employer-sponsored plan. That's up 35% from the year before. HSAs represented 27% of new purchases in the individual market, 31% of new enrollments in the small-group market, and 6% of new enrollments in the large-group market. If your employer offers this option, someone in the human resources or benefits department should be able to walk you through the process of setting up your account.

The idea is that you deposit the money you save on premiums—and any other dollars you can scrape together—into your HSA. Not only do you get a tax deduction for your contribution but also it can grow tax free, and withdrawals for qualified medical expenses are also tax free. In 2010, the maximum annual HSA contribution is $3,050 for an individual policy and $6,150 for family coverage. Individuals who are 55 or older can make catch-up contributions of $1,000 extra each year. There is no minimum contribution.

If you have an unused balance at the end of the year—and you might if you're healthy—the amount rolls over year after year. You don't lose the money, and it will continue to grow tax free.

THE MATH

How do a high-deductible plan and an HSA stack up against the standard individual health plan? Here's a comparison based on plans in four major cities:

City	Plan	Monthly Premium	Co-insurance	Deductible	Office Visits
Los Angeles	Individual	$123	40%	$900	$40
	HSA	$121	0%	$5,000	0% after deductible
Dallas	Individual	$159	25%	$1,000	25% after deductible
	HSA	$88	0%	$5,000	0% after deductible
Chicago	Individual	$212	20%	$1,000	$30
	HSA	$97.37	0%	$5,000	0% after deductible
Miami	Individual	$237.09	20%	$1,000	$15
	HSA	$146.84	0%	$5,000	0% after deductible

HSA = health savings account.
Rates as of May 1, 2009, from eHealthInsurance.com, for a 40-year-old man.

The beauty of an HSA is that you have full control over money in your account, and you can make your own health-care decisions until you reach your deductible with procedures or particular doctors approved by your insurer. You can also use the money to pay for any qualified medical expense (see box on page 239), many of which aren't covered by the typical insurance plan. And—perhaps better still—the money can be used to pay for medical expenses not only for yourself but also for your spouse or any dependents.

The downside? If you need to withdraw the money for an unqualified expense, you'll be taxed at regular income tax rates and you'll pay a 10% penalty if you're younger than 65. Once you reach age 65, however, you can use the money to pay for things other than medical expenses. Withdrawals will be taxable as income but not penalized.

An HSA is likely a great option for you if you're without coverage and the premiums on other plans you've found are just too expensive. A high-deductible plan may run you less than $100 a month this way. For more on finding a health insurance plan, turn to "How do I pick the right type of health insurance?" on page 241.

WHAT IS A QUALIFIED MEDICAL EXPENSE?

- An annual physical
- Medical supplies
- Birth control pills
- Chiropractor
- Contact lenses
- Dental treatment
- Glasses
- Laser eye surgery
- Prescription drugs
- Stop-smoking programs
- Therapy
- Transportation to and from medical care
- Weight-loss programs

I Also Need to Know . . .

Q: How do I open an HSA?
A: You can generally open one right at your local bank or credit union. You can do so on the first day of the month after your insurance coverage kicks in, or on the same day your policy becomes effective, if it starts on the first of the month (most do). Some accounts may require a minimum deposit, so make sure

you have that money available before heading to the bank. It is usually minimal, less than $50. If you are funding your account through work, your benefits department will take care of opening the account for you. Many employers will allow you to fund the account through a "cafeteria plan," which pulls the money out of your paycheck pretax. Keep in mind, though, that you can't also take a deduction on your income taxes for these contributions.

Q: **Is everyone eligible for an HSA? Are there income limitations?**
A: There aren't any income restrictions with an HSA. In fact, there isn't a requirement of having earned income at all. But not everyone is eligible. If you're covered by Medicare or you're claimed as a dependent on someone else's tax return, you can't open an HSA. And you have to have a high-deductible health insurance plan and no other health insurance coverage.

Q: **Can my employer contribute to my HSA for me?**
A: Employers can, and better still, their contributions are not taxable to you. In fact, if your mom, your grandmother, your husband, or anyone, for that matter, wants to contribute to your HSA for you, they can do so and you can deduct the amount they contributed from your taxes. All contributions are restricted to the limits I mentioned above.

Q: **Can I invest the money in my HSA?**
A: Yes. HSAs are self-directed, the same way that IRAs are. You can invest your contributions in a range of options, including stocks, bonds, mutual funds, and CDs, or you can just leave it in a money market or savings account. But remember that you may need easy access to this money one day for health care, so you don't want to take too much risk or tie it up so that you won't be able to get it if you need it. Earning a bit of interest by putting a small portion into a CD or choosing an account that has a high-interest-rate money market option is one thing, but investing the bulk of your health savings in the stock market is another.

Q: **Where does an HSA fall in my investment hierarchy? Should I put money in this account before or after I put it in my 401(k) and my child's college savings account?**
A: Your 401(k) comes first, particularly if your employer offers matching dollars. If you don't have a 401(k), an IRA or Roth IRA

gets first dibs on your money. Then you can fund—and max out, if you can—your HSA, because you may need that money for health expenses and it's another opportunity to (1) get a tax deduction and (2) allow your money to grow tax free.

Your child's savings account comes last, because, as hard as that may be to hear, there is plenty of money available for college in the form of financial aid and scholarships.

69. How do I pick the right type of health insurance?

A: Whether you're in the midst of open enrollment at your job or you're going at it alone, picking the right health insurance is all about knowing your needs, as well as the needs of your family, if you're selecting coverage for them.

You should start, very simply, by sitting down and making a list. Consider not only the coverage you need now but also what you might need in the future:

- How often do you see the doctor? And for what?
- Are you planning to have children soon?
- Do you take a lot of prescription drugs?
- Do you need dental coverage or coverage for contact lenses or glasses?
- Do you want a plan that pays for routine costs such as yearly checkups or just a broad safety net to pick up the tab for surgeries and major hospitalizations?
- Is there a particular doctor you want to be able to continue to see?
- Do you need mental health benefits?
- Are you covering only yourself, or are you covering your family as well?
- Do you need easy access to specialists, such as a chiropractor?

Once you've worked through these questions, you can start looking for plans that match the answers. Most large companies will offer two or three different plans to employees. If that's true of your employer, you want to go through each one and see where you're going to get the most from your contribution. Compare:

- Premiums
- Coverage amount
- Out-of-pocket costs, including deductibles

The goal is to pay as little as possible while still getting the coverage you need, so you need to do a little cost-to-benefit analysis. HMOs, or health maintenance organizations, which require you to visit in-network doctors unless you want to be charged a hefty copayment, are generally the least expensive. If you're single and your visits to the doctor are few and far between, this plan could be for you. PPOs, or preferred provider organizations, still involve a network of doctors, but it's easier for you to visit specialists because they don't require referrals. If you—or your family—go to the chiropractor or dermatologist regularly, this kind of plan is likely worth it. And high-deductible plans linked with an HSA come with inexpensive premiums and greater flexibility. They're good for people who have negligible health expenses (you'll pay out of pocket, from your contributions to the HSA, until you reach the deductible. For more on these, turn to "What is a health savings account? Is it a good option for me if I don't have health coverage?" on page 237).

Smaller companies, however, may only offer one plan, but that doesn't necessarily mean that you're stuck when it comes to cost and options. If your coworkers feel that the plan is lacking as well, you can talk to human resources—or, in most small companies, the owner or manager—and ask if they would be willing to add or change benefits the next time they negotiate the contract with the insurer. Sometimes, in the case of small businesses, if the employees agree on a change, it's easy to lobby for it to be implemented, as long as it doesn't cut into the company's bottom line. Or you can go it alone. Whether you work for a large or small company, these days it pays to compare the amount you're being asked to chip in for coverage with the amount it would cost you to go on a spouse's plan, if that's an option, or buy an individual or family plan on your own.

I Also Need to Know . . .

Q: **I'm a single parent, and I don't want to pay for a family policy at work for just my child and me. Is there a cheaper option?**

A: You're right; the choice at most companies is typically single coverage or family coverage, with no gray area. But you do have options here, as long as you're willing to do a little legwork. With the family option offered by most companies, the premium is the same no matter how many children you have—a great deal if you have five children, but not so good if you only have one. So shop around on your own—start at eHealthInsurance.com—and see if you can find an individual plan for your child. You will likely be able to find something inexpensive, provided he or she doesn't have a preexisting condition, and then you can sign yourself up for your employer's plan as a single. If your child does have a preexisting medical condition, you should still shop around, but you might find that it's cheaper to go with the family policy offered by your employer.

Also, if you fall into a low income bracket, you may be eligible for free or low-cost health insurance for your children through the U.S. Department of Health and Human Services. The eligibility rules vary by state, but in most states, uninsured children (age 18 or younger) whose families earn less than $34,100 a year are eligible. For information about your state's program, go to www.insurekidsnow.gov or call 1877-KIDS-NOW.

Q: **What is COBRA?**

A: COBRA, or the Consolidated Omnibus Budget Reconciliation Act, requires companies with 20 or more employees to let you stay on the group health insurance policy for at least 18 months after you lose or leave your job. You'll pay the full cost of coverage on your own, which is often considerably more than you're used to paying, because many employers pick up all or half of the health insurance tab for employees still with the company.

If you're young and healthy, you may be able to find coverage on your own for much less than your COBRA premiums. For more information, see "How do I buy my own health insurance?" on page 244. If you're older or you have preexisting conditions, you may be better off taking advantage of COBRA. On your own, you may pay more or be denied coverage altogether. Make sure you continue your policy using COBRA until you have found another way to cover yourself.

Q: **What is HIPAA?**
A: HIPAA (the Health Insurance Portability and Accountability Act) takes COBRA a step further: Under HIPAA, if you've been covered under a group policy in the past 63 days, you can't be turned down for different coverage, even if you're ill. That doesn't, however, mean that the coverage has to be affordable: If you're seriously ill, your premiums could be astronomical, depending on your state. You should shop around and compare your premiums under COBRA with quotes from individual policies.

70. How do I buy my own health insurance?

A: You may have heard that buying your own health insurance is impossible—or that it'll cost you an arm and a leg. In reality, finding an individual health insurance policy often isn't as bad—or as expensive—as you think. The number of carriers offering individual policies has grown in the past few years—in fact, eHealth Insurance.com, the biggest online marketplace, lists plans from about 175 companies and counting.

In fact, you may be able to get a better deal on coverage than you would from a group plan offered through your employer. In 45 states, insurance companies can accept or reject potential customers based on their health history. If you're healthy and live in one of these states, you'll get a better deal than you expect. If you're not, prices may be prohibitively expensive.

In the remaining five states—Maine, Massachusetts, New Jersey, New York, and Vermont—insurers are required to extend a policy to everyone, regardless of health status. This is called guaranteed issue, and as a result, even if you're healthy, you'll pay more if you live in any of those states.

Let's break it down. If you're healthy or you live in one of the five states with a guaranteed-issue policy, the first thing you want to do is figure out what kind of coverage you need. For more, turn to "How do I pick the right type of health insurance?" on page 241. Basically, you're going to figure out what kind of health-care consumer you are by answering a few quick questions.

Once you know what you need out of a plan, you can start shopping. First, head to eHealthInsurance.com or other comparison shopping sites such as Insure.com or Insurance.com. Type in your age, your ZIP code, your sex, and whether you are a smoker. A list of options will pop up, along with the various prices. You will want to narrow down the options. Individual plans generally come with a menu of options so that you can pick and choose.

When you have three or four plans in mind, compare them side by side to figure out where your dollars are best spent. Consider everything—copays, deductible, out-of-pocket expense limits—and make sure that the costs align with your needs. If you visit the doctor often, for example, you want to make sure office visits are covered. If you take a lot of prescription medications, be sure that the copay for those is low. When you have a plan that meets your budget and your needs, go ahead and apply.

But what if you have a chronic illness or you're otherwise uninsurable? If you're turned down for coverage, many states have state-sponsored health insurance pools that you can buy into, albeit at a higher cost. To find out if your state offers such a plan—and how much your policy would cost—call your state's department of insurance or visit it online.

Other options? You can join a professional association that offers a group insurance plan for members, although you want to shop around because the rates may not be better than those you'd find on an individual plan. Or you may be able to form your own small group if you own your own company. In many states, you can make a group with as few as two employees, including yourself, as long as each works a minimum number of hours per week. The rules vary by state.

I Also Need to Know . . .

Q: **Should I use a broker?**

A: Sure, if you can find a licensed broker who sells a wide range of policies from a number of different carriers. Going to a broker is free to you; the insurance companies pay them on a commission basis. But that's why it's so important to use one who has a large network of policies available—otherwise, you may be pressured into buying coverage that either isn't right for you or isn't the best value, just so the broker can mark down a sale.

To find a broker in your area, go to the National Association of Health Underwriters (www.nahu.org). All insurance advisors must be licensed, and they are regulated by state insurance departments.

Q: **Do you have any tips for saving on health insurance premiums?**

A: The best way to cut the cost of insurance premiums is raising your deductible. A deductible of $2,000 may save you 40% to 50% of your monthly premium, which is a significant amount of money. But you have to be able to pay for services upfront until you reach the deductible. One of the best ways to ensure that you can do that is by linking a high-deductible health insurance plan with an HSA (for more, turn to "What is a health savings account? Is it a good option for me if I don't have health coverage?" on page 237).

You should also take care to eliminate any coverage you don't need. If you're not planning to have children, cut out the maternity coverage. If you don't take a lot of prescription drugs, go with a plan with higher copays in exchange for lower monthly premiums.

Q: **Can I deduct the premiums I pay on my taxes?**

A: You can deduct the premiums if you pay them after tax, but there's a catch: Medical expenses are deductible only to the extent that they exceed 7.5% of your adjusted gross income. So if you make $40,000 a year and you spend $3,500 on your premiums and other unreimbursed medical expenses, you can deduct $500.

For most people, it's hard to make this mark, and it's easier to take the standard deduction. But if you have a lot of medical expenses, it's worth it to run the numbers to see if you qualify.

One exception to the rule: If you're self-employed, you saw a net profit in the year for which you are filing, and you're not eligible for coverage under either your own or your spouse's employer-subsidized health plan, you can deduct all of your health insurance premiums.

Q: Can you explain the different types of health insurance plans?

A: There are two main types of health insurance plans—and each has a few subtypes:

- An **indemnity plan** gives you the ability to choose your own doctors and hospitals. In most cases, you'll pay the bill out of pocket, and then your insurance will reimburse you for a portion of it, depending on your coverage. There is likely a deductible, and preventive health-care checkups (such as your annual physical) are generally not covered. The premiums also tend to be high—because you're paying for the freedom.

  Types of indemnity plans:
  - **Basic plans** will cover a hospital stay and care, including X-rays and medications administered. Surgery will also be covered. This is the least expensive option when it comes to your monthly premiums.
  - **Major medical** covers basic health care, as well as long-term care for an illness or injury and the inpatient and outpatient expenses related to it.
  - **Comprehensive plans** combine the features of major medical and basic plans, providing the most coverage.

- **Managed-care plans** tend to be more cost effective, with lower premiums and out-of-pocket charges such as deductibles and copays. But they give you less flexibility when it comes to choosing your doctors and hospital. If you have a doctor you love, you should make sure that he or she is affiliated with the plan before you buy a managed-care policy.

  Types of managed-care plans:
  - **HMOs** (health maintenance organizations) come with a network of doctors and hospitals. You pick a doctor from their list, and that doctor becomes your primary-care point person: You have to contact him or her—and often schedule a visit—before you can be referred to a specialist. You'll have a copay for office visits and prescriptions, but in general, HMO members have limited out-of-pocket expenses.

- **POS (point-of-service) plans** still involve your primary-care doctor making referrals to specialists within your plan, but if you need to visit a doctor out of network, you can. Those services will likely be subject to a deductible and your copayment will be higher—sometimes close to 50% of the cost of the service.
- **PPOs** (preferred provider organizations) involve lower costs if you use in-network doctors, but you don't have to. If you go out of network, you'll generally be required to pay the difference in cost. The PPO may reimburse up to 90% of costs in network but only 50% out of network. You don't need a referral to see a specialist, nor do you have to select a primary-care doctor.

Q: **What happens if I have a preexisting condition?**

A: As I write this, most individual health plans still come with an exclusion period for preexisting conditions. That may mean the plan won't cover medical costs related to your condition for a year or more. Some states limit the period to 12 months, but others let it stretch to 24 or even longer—in fact, in some states, insurers can attach riders to policies that permanently exclude preexisting conditions.

If you find yourself facing a period like this, you'll need to estimate what your medical costs might be during that time, using the worst-case scenario as your guide. Bank the cash so that you can cover your expenses and get all the care you can before you leave your prior plan, if possible. Then, particularly if the exclusion period in your state is open-ended, you should work with a broker to help you apply to multiple carriers at the same time. They all underwrite policies differently, so one may turn you down but another may accept you. A broker will know which carrier offers the best chance of acceptance.

71. How do I get my health insurance company to pay a claim?

A: We've all been in this scenario. You file a claim with your health insurer but instead of receiving a check, you receive a denial. Or worse, a bill. What do you do?

1. Make sure that the claim is actually covered by your policy. The book that came with your policy is likely the size of a phone book with a lot of fine print, confusing technical language, and vague statements. As a result, most people don't read these materials. But if you're having trouble getting a claim paid, you must be sure that it is on the menu. If you're uncertain, your benefits department at work should be able to answer the question. Or if you purchased the policy through an independent agent, you can ask for help there as well.

2. Once you're certain, or at least fairly certain, that you should be reimbursed, understand that there is an appeals process to follow. It varies by company, but in general, you'll need to act immediately. Most insurers limit the time you have to appeal—often to as few as 30 or 60 days.

   If you don't have a written denial from the company, send a letter requesting one. The letter should provide the reasons why your claim was denied. Next, call your doctor. He or she may be able to change the language on the claim to fit your benefits. Often just a different term for a procedure can solve (or cause) a big problem, so make sure the bill that your doctor is sending to the insurance company corresponds to the benefit outlined in your policy.

3. If that doesn't do the trick, it's time to file an appeal. Follow your insurance company's appeals process precisely. Often, you have to start by filing a complaint by phone, followed by a written appeal. At that point, an internal board will review your claim again and decide whether it should be covered.

4. If you're denied again and you want to continue to plead your case, you'll move onto an external appeal, which involves your state insurance department. If officials there rule that your claim should be paid, the insurance company must process the claim. Unfortunately, there's no compensation for the time and energy you'll spend pursuing your claim—although after all that work, it certainly seems like there should be!

Throughout the process, keep written records, including lists of all the people you've spoken with by phone, notes of when those conversations took place and what transpired, copies of any letters you've sent, the dates of your procedures, and the bills from your doctor.

I Also Need to Know . . .

Q: Is it worth it?
A: Absolutely. Some insurance companies seem to have a standard policy to deny claims the first time around, and all insurance companies make the occasional error. If you can see in black and white that your claim should be covered under your policy, you should fight until the end. In many cases, we're talking about thousands of dollars, and often more.

Q: My insurance company's process seems confusing. Is there someone who can help me sort through everything?
A: Yes. Many states have consumer assistants within their departments of insurance, so that's the place to start. If you strike out there, a handful of nonprofit organizations will serve as a liaison between you and the insurance company. The Patient Advocate Foundation (www.patientadvocate.org) is probably the best-known example. If you have a specific condition or disease and there is a not-for-profit advocacy group associated with it, that organization may have individuals who can help as well. Finally, if your dispute involves a hospital procedure or stay, most hospitals have patient advocates available to work with you on this issue, as well as on paying your medical bills over time if your claim is denied ultimately.

72. What's the best way to negotiate with a doctor or hospital about payment options?

A: If you don't have health insurance, your policy doesn't cover office visits or a treatment you required, or you just haven't met your deductible yet, discuss payment options with your doctor or hospital. Many will be more than willing to work with you. Here are a few tactics you can use to trim your bill:

- **Offer to pay cash.** Often, insurance companies can take three to six months to process payments and get the money in the doctor's hands. Avoiding that lengthy process may be worth 10% or 20% off, in the doctor's mind, so if you can pay cash upfront you might get a deal.

- **Pay the bill promptly and in full.** Some hospitals will give you 10% off if you pay the entire bill within 30 days.
- **Offer to pay the doctor the rate paid by insurance companies.** Insurance companies negotiate lower rates with doctors' offices than the full rates that the offices post in public view. That means that if you're going into an office without coverage, you may pay more in total than someone who has insurance coverage. If you offer to pay the rates charged to people who are covered by insurance, the doctor may take it.
- **Ask for a payment plan.** If you can't pay the total amount upfront but can chunk it down into three or four months' worth of payments, ask if the doctor could work out a plan with you. You may not get a steep discount, but you won't blow your entire month's budget on one visit either.
- **Know whom to talk to.** Start with your doctor. If it's a small office, he or she may work with you directly. If it's a hospital, your doctor will at least know where to send you. Understand: Sometimes the billing department makes a commission that is based on how much it can collect, which means the department will be less likely to issue a discount upfront.
- **Establish a relationship.** You'll be more likely to get a deal from a doctor who's seen you a few times and knows that you're a reliable payer.
- **If all else fails, ask for samples.** Even with insurance, prescriptions can sometimes run $50 or more, but doctors often have closets dedicated to sample medications. If you're being prescribed a medication to take for only a short time, you just might be able to get enough samples to avoid the pharmacy altogether.

73. Is there a formula that I can use to determine how much life insurance I need?

A: There are many formulas, but I don't like them. Just as it's hard to go by rules of thumb to determine how much you need to save for retirement, it's hard to use grids to figure out how much life insurance to buy. Don't get me wrong—you'll find plenty of these charts online. But their abundance doesn't mean that they are reliable.

Figuring out how much you need means taking a look at your current income and how much of it your dependents (children, partner, aging parents) would need to replace if you died. You must look at how many years they'd need to replace that income for, which raises additional questions about how close your children are to being self-sufficient, and whether your mate would be able to generate a higher income. And you need to look at whether you'd want your death benefit to pay for college, pay off the mortgage, or provide an inheritance for your spouse or your children.

Most of the formulas out there don't ask those questions. Instead, they tell you to multiply your income by seven or eight or they calculate a dollar amount that is only enough to cover the debt you have at this point. Instead, go through the process with a good online calculator—I like the ones at Insure.com and Insurance.com—or use the worksheet provided here. You may also want to go ahead and sit down with a life insurance agent or two to get a recommendation. (Just remember that these people sell life insurance for a living, so they have an incentive to get you to buy more than you may need or want. And keep in mind that term life insurance is far, far cheaper than cash-value life insurance and is perfectly sufficient for most people's needs. For more on the term-versus-whole argument, see "Which should I buy—term or permanent life insurance?" on page 258.)

THE MATH

Prefer pen and paper over online tools? Here's a worksheet that will help you ballpark your life insurance needs:

A. Total your spouse's (or family's) annual living expenses, including your rent or mortgage payments, utilities, groceries, insurance, clothing, entertainment, car payment and maintenance (including gas), and child care:
   $ _____

B. Total your spouse's salary and any other income, including estimated Social Security payments:

$ _____

C. Subtract B from A to get the amount of living expenses you'll
need to replace.

$ _____

D. Divide amount in C by 0.04 (a standard estimate) to estimate the
amount of death benefit you'll need:

$ _____

E. Estimate total expenses related to your death, including funeral
costs, hospital stays, estate taxes:

$ _____

F. Add an emergency fund of three to six months' worth of living expenses:

$ _____

G. If you plan to cover college tuition for your children, calculate
the amount that it will cost for each child to attend school for
four years, being careful to account for tuition increases. You can
base this amount on averages from the College Board, which
lists pricing trends at www.nces.ed.gov/ipeds/cool/. Current averages: in-state public college, $18,326/year; private college:
$37,390/year.

$ _____

H. Add any other outstanding debts not included in A.

$ _____

I. Add lines E, F, G, and H to get your total expenses.

$ _____

J. Add lines D and I. This figure represents your preliminary insurance needs.

$ _____

254 ■ MONEY 911

K. Calculate the value of other assets or insurance policies you own, including life insurance through your employer, pensions, savings, 401(k) and IRA plan, and any liquid savings accounts.

$ _____

L. Subtract the amount in K from the amount in J to get an estimate of your total life insurance needs:

$ _____

Source: USAA Educational Foundation, www.usaaedfoundation .org/.

I Also Need to Know . . .

Q: When should I buy life insurance?

A: When you need it. I'm not being flip. The time to buy life insurance is when you begin supporting someone else—and that person or those people would be hurting without your income. By this logic, singles do not need life insurance and children do not need life insurance. And yet there are many policies sold every year on the lives of singles and children, often on the basis of a sales pitch. Don't buy one. You're best off buying life insurance while you're healthy—as well as fairly young—and locking into a premium that is level for the next 20 or 30 years so that you don't have to go through an additional medical exam.

Q: How much should I expect to pay?

A: Your life insurance premiums will be based on how much coverage you need, the term of your policy, your current health (including whether you smoke), your family history of illness or disease, and the kind of life insurance you're buying. You should get personalized quotes from a few different companies before selecting a policy—you'll go through a physical only after you apply for particular coverage—but check out the chart on average annual premiums for a general idea:

$250,000 TERM LIFE POLICY AVERAGE ANNUAL PREMIUMS

	10 YEARS	20 YEARS	30 YEARS		10 YEARS	20 YEARS	30 YEARS
Female, age 30	$108	$148	$203	Male, age 30	$108	$148	$228
Female age 40	$130	$198	$308	Male, age 40	$130	$198	$335
Female, age 50	$250	$370	$585	Male, age 50	$250	$503	$768

$500,000 TERM LIFE POLICY AVERAGE ANNUAL PREMIUMS

	10 YEARS	20 YEARS	30 YEARS		10 YEARS	20 YEARS	30 YEARS
Female, age 30	$155	$235	$325	Male, age 30	$155	$235	$385
Female, age 40	$200	$305	$495	Male, age 40	$200	$335	$610
Female, age 50	$435	$680	$1,120	Male, age 50	$440	$945	$1,475

$1 MILLION TERM LIFE POLICY AVERAGE ANNUAL PREMIUMS

	10 YEARS	20 YEARS	30 YEARS		10 YEARS	20 YEARS	30 YEARS
Female, age 30	$230	$370	$550	Male, age 30	$230	$400	$670
Female, age 40	$320	$520	$820	Male, age 40	$330	$600	$1,150
Female, age 50	$755	$1,285	$2,100	Male, age 50	$810	$1,800	$2,830

Source: Insure.com, October 2008.

74. My 10-year term life insurance policy is expiring soon. What is the best option for me?

A: Many term life insurance policies allow you to renew your coverage when the policy expires, but not always at the same rate: Term life insurance policies are priced on your age and health—as well as market conditions—when you buy them. Ten, 20, 30 years down the road (if you opted for a long-term policy), re-upping will likely cost more.

A few months before your term policy expires, give yourself—and your family—a once-over. Do you still have children at home, or in college? Does your partner rely on your income? Do you have debt that would become a burden to your family if you weren't around? How healthy are you?

Once you outline the answers to these questions, it's time to do some research. You have four basic options: You can renew coverage with your current policy, you can convert to a permanent policy, you can purchase a new term policy, or you can forgo life insurance altogether. Let's break them down:

- **Purchase a new term policy.** If you are in good health, you can purchase a new term policy and you'll get rates similar to those if you were purchasing life insurance for the first time. (Incidentally, they may actually be lower than they were when you did purchase it for the first time, because term life insurance is very, very cheap right now.) To decide what term to purchase, figure out how much longer you're going to need the coverage. Consider factors such as your age, the age of your children, how long you'd like to provide for your family, any additional income from your mate, and your debt load. If you have a 10-year-old son, for example, and you want to provide for him until he gets out of college and starts to earn a living, you likely want a 20-year policy.

- **Convert to a permanent policy.** A lot of people think that if they get to the end of their term life policy and they're not healthy enough to buy another term of coverage, they're stuck. But that's not the case. Most term life insurance policies allow you to convert to permanent without having to undergo a medical exam (although you want to read your policy carefully—many require that you make the conversion before the term policy expires). While permanent policies can be up to four times more expensive than term life, yours may not be more expensive than keeping a term life policy that has expired and jumped to a higher rate. Weigh your options.

- **Renew the current policy.** If your health has changed for the worse and your policy doesn't allow you to convert to a permanent policy or you don't want to—say you need the coverage for only five more years, until your children graduate from college—you can continue your current term policy without a medical exam. The rates will jump substantially, sometimes by as much as 300% over the next few years. But if you don't need the coverage indefinitely, there's no need for a permanent policy. Again, run the numbers.

- **Forgo life insurance altogether.** Having life insurance for the past 10 years doesn't mean that you still need it. You may have more savings now than you did when you originally made your life insurance purchase. You may have paid off all of your debt, or you may no longer have anyone relying on your income. If that's the case and you have enough money to get yourself through retirement and leave whatever is necessary to your heirs to cover estate taxes or funeral expenses, you might decide to skip life insurance altogether. Just remember that if you change your mind, it will likely be either too late or more costly.

THE MATH

Let's see how some of these scenarios play out for a 40-year-old man looking for $300,000 worth of coverage:

If he's in good health and decides to purchase a new term policy, his annual premiums would be about $231 for a 10-year term, $369 for a 20-year term, or $446 for a 30-year term.

If he isn't in good health and wants to convert to a permanent policy, he would pay about $1,848 for a universal life policy.

If he isn't in good health and decides to continue his current policy after the guaranteed term, his premiums could jump to $504 for a 10-year term, $693 for a 20-year term, and $1,017 for a 30-year term.

I Also Need to Know . . .

Q: **What is guaranteed-issue life insurance?**

A: Guaranteed-issue policies are for people who couldn't get life insurance if they had to undergo a medical exam, because of health issues that would make them too risky in the eyes of the insurer. You may also have heard of quick-issue or simplified-issue policies, which ask applicants medical questions but don't require a medical examination.

If you're thinking that it sounds like there's probably a catch, you're right. Not only do guaranteed-issue policies come with more expensive premiums—sometimes three times as expensive—but also many have low benefit limits of $20,000 or so because they are designed to cover funeral expenses. They also tend to have age limits of 45 or 50. However, if you need coverage, and this is the only way you can get it, it's something to look into if you have the money.

Q: What is a "return of premium" policy?

A: With standard term life insurance policies, if your term expires and you're still alive, there is no benefit. For consumers who want the benefits of cash value coverage at a somewhat lower price, insurance companies have started selling term life policies with a "return of premium" feature. You'll pay more for one of these policies than you would for a standard term policy, but if you don't use the benefit—and many people don't—either all or a portion of it will be returned to you. Some companies cut you a check for the premium you would pay for a term policy—without the additional amount you paid for the return of premium add-on—and others will return the entire amount. Look into how long you have to keep the policy, before signing on. Many lock you in—otherwise you give up the benefit completely.

75. Which should I buy—term or permanent life insurance?

A: First, the differences:

- Permanent life insurance, also called cash-value insurance, is an option that stays in place until your death, whether that happens in 10 years or 50 years. You've likely heard of various types of permanent insurance, including whole life, universal life, and variable life. But what makes them permanent is that there are two components—a death benefit and an investment account. One portion of your premium goes to

funding the death benefit, and another portion is invested in mutual funds, stocks, bonds, or money markets. The hope—and often the promise—is that the interest you earn on your investments increases what's called the policy's "cash value."
- Term life insurance is life insurance that terminates. It consists of a death benefit, with no investment attached, and when the amount of time you purchase the policy for (which ranges from 1 year to 20 or 30 years) lapses, your coverage ends. If you are still living and you still want life insurance, you'll have to start again with another policy. Because term life provides only a death benefit, it is significantly cheaper than permanent life insurance. For most people, it is also the only affordable coverage.

The one notable downside of term insurance is that it becomes more expensive to buy as you age, particularly if your health declines. A policy that costs you very little when you are 30 and in prime condition may whack the budget when you're 55 and taking beta-blockers. For that reason, if you're buying term, you want to find a way to stabilize your premiums for as long as possible.

The easiest way to do this is with a level-premium term policy. Your premiums will remain the same throughout the term, whether that's 10 years, 20 years, or 30 years. How long a term you should purchase depends on how long you're going to need the insurance. Some people want to replace their income only until their children graduate from college. So if you have a toddler, you'd get a 20-year policy. If your youngest child is 15, you may need only a 10-year policy. To figure out the benefit amount you need, turn to page 251 and read "Is there a formula that I can use to determine how much life insurance I need?"

Q: What if you take out a term life policy and later decide you would have been better off with permanent insurance—or that you want to continue your insurance without taking another physical?

A: There's a solution for this dilemma, too. When you buy term insurance, make sure that it allows you to convert to permanent insurance without having to prove that you're still in good health. You have to do it during a specific period of time, though, and the conversion period is generally shorter than the length of your term coverage. If you have questions, call the insurer or the agent who sold you the policy to make sure you don't miss the deadline.

Q: **Are there scenarios where permanent insurance is best?**
A: Yes. If you have a child with special needs, you may need to provide survivor benefits for him or her whether you live for the next 10 years or the next 70 years, because that child will continue to be reliant on your income. In this case, it would make sense to buy a permanent life policy because you don't want to risk your term policy being unrenewable if you suffer a health setback in later life—or simply if you age.

Some people also use life insurance as a way to provide an inheritance for their heirs, special needs or not. It becomes part of an estate plan, and if you want life insurance for that purpose, permanent policies are best because they offer both a death benefit and a savings vehicle. They also stay in place whether you die in 10 years or 60 years. At that point, your heirs will receive your benefit. With a term policy, if the term expires and you're still alive, there is no benefit and thus no inheritance.

Q: **What is the difference between universal, variable, and variable universal life policies?**
A: These are all variations of a whole life policy, so they all have investment components. Here is how it breaks down:

- **A universal life policy** uses elements of term and whole life insurance. A portion of your premiums will be invested (fairly conservatively—your rate of return will be similar to that of a money market), and interest that is generated can then be used toward paying your premiums.
- **Variable life** allows the cash value to be invested in stocks, bonds, and money market mutual funds. You'll earn more in interest if the market is up, but you're also assuming more risk. If the investments take a hit, your cash value and your death benefit will as well. Look for a policy with a guaranteed minimum on your death benefit.
- **Variable universal life** is a combination of the two. You're taking more risk than you would with a universal policy, but

you can also adjust your premiums and death benefit on the basis of the policy's cash value.

Q: **Should I purchase a variable or variable universal life insurance policy as an investment for retirement?**

A: I don't think so. You're better off investing for retirement in other tax-advantaged vehicles—a 401(k), IRA, or Roth IRA—and letting life insurance do what it does best, which is support your family in the event of your death.

The problem with using your life insurance as a retirement investment vehicle is that these policies often come with hefty fees. Investment-management fees can be as much as 2% a year, annual mortality and expense charges are another 1%, and there are fees for insurance protection, which are nearly always more than you would pay for a standard term life policy. There may also be commission charges when you purchase the policy.

THE MATH

Take an example of a 35-year-old man in need of $500,000 worth of coverage.

- For a 10-year level term policy, he would pay an annual premium of $250.
- For a 20-year level term policy, his annual premium would be $380.
- A 30-year level term policy would put his annual premium at $455.
- A universal life policy with fixed premiums and coverage for life would be $2,265 annually.

76. Do I need insurance for long-term care?

A: There are two schools of thought here: those who believe you need insurance for long-term care no matter what and those who think you need it only if you fall into a certain income range.

I tend to agree with the second school, but let me lay out both arguments for you:

Those who say you need insurance for long-term care at any income or asset level do so because your having the padding of one of these policies can preserve your wealth for your heirs and save you a lot of heartache. Such insurance also gives you more freedom of choice if you should need to move into a nursing home or assisted-living facility, whereas Medicaid restricts your options considerably.

The second group argues that if you have a significant amount of assets—upward of $2.5 million or $3 million—you don't need insurance for long-term care because you'll be able to pay for your own care. If you have little to no assets—less than $300,000—you'll spend them down and then Medicaid will pick up the tab. Insurance for long-term care is pricey, with premiums north of $1,800 a year, depending on your age and health. And if you get coverage and one day find yourself unable to afford the premiums, in most cases, you're out of luck: The money you paid into the policy will be gone.

One thing that most people do agree on, though, is that no one is exempt from the possibility of long-term care itself. About half of Americans who live to age 65 will require some kind of long-term care. Nursing homes cost about $212 a day, according to a 2008 MetLife survey, and that number is rising each year. It's safe to say that you can expect to pay upward of $75,000 for a year's stay, and more in some areas: In Alaska, for instance, nursing-home care averages $577 a day; in Louisiana, the average is only $132.

So what's the answer? Insurance for long-term care is not for everyone. It is not for people who can't afford to maintain the premium payments. And it's not for people who can self-insure rather than preserve their inheritance for their children or other heirs.

You should evaluate your own personal circumstances. If illness runs in your family and many of your elders have lived out their last days in nursing homes, you may get your money's worth out of a policy, but in most cases, I'd go by the income thresholds I've mentioned. Here's a look at what premiums are likely to run.

AVERAGE ANNUAL PREMIUMS—LONG-TERM CARE INSURANCE	
AGE	ANNUAL PREMIUM ($)
55–64	1,877
65–69	2,003
70–74	2,341
75 or older	2,604
All ages	1,973

Source: U.S. Department of Health and Human Services.

THE MATH

How much money would you be able to sock away if you invested your money instead of paying premiums for insurance for long-term care?

Let's take the example of a 55-year-old woman, paying $1,877 a year in premiums for her long-term care policy. If she invested that $1,877 each year instead at an 8% return, she would have a nest egg of $254,219 at age 85.

I Also Need to Know . . .

Q: When should I buy insurance for long-term care?
A: The longer you wait, the more expensive your premiums will be, and if you develop an illness that might necessitate care, forget it—you won't be able to get a policy. The best time to buy, then, is your fifties. This is the time frame that will still allow you to get a good rate, but you won't be throwing money away by purchasing a policy too early and having to pay the premiums for 35, 40, or even 45 years.

Q: What should I look for in a policy?
A: Several things:

• **Coverage.** You can choose policies that pay only for home health aids, only for nursing-home care, or for a menu of options such as assisted-living facilities, adult day care, nursing-home stays, and home health care. The more benefits you are eligible for, the more expensive the policy, but if you're against living in a nursing home, you want to pay more for those additional options.

· **Benefits.** You want to purchase a policy with a daily benefit equal to the amount you expect to spend on care each day. For a good estimate, look at the average cost of a nursing home or assisted-living facility in your area and use that number to ballpark the benefits you buy.

You also want to look at the length of time that your benefits will be available. You can choose a benefit period; options generally start at two years and extend for the rest of your life. Again, the shorter the period, the cheaper your premiums. Most people who go into a nursing home end up staying there for 21 months, according to the American Seniors Housing Association.

· **Inflation adjustments.** The policy's benefits should adjust each year for inflation automatically, so you're not stuck with coverage priced for 2015 when you don't need it until 2030. The cost of care rises each year, and your policy should account for that.

· **Waiting period.** You can decide when your benefits kick in, and the longer the waiting period, the lower your premiums. If you can afford to foot the bill for a month, you'll save a bit of money. If you can afford to pay your bills for three months, even better. But note: the time you extend dictates the expenses you pay out of pocket.

Q: What is a partnership plan?

A: In most cases, before you qualify for Medicaid, you must spend down your assets. But if you live in a state that participates in the Partnership for Long-Term Care program, you can qualify for Medicaid without spending down your assets. Currently, there are four such states: California, Indiana, New York, and Connecticut.

Here's how it works: You must purchase a long-term-care insurance policy that falls within the guidelines outlined by your state (typically, it must provide basic benefits). If you require long-term care, that policy will kick in, protecting your assets.

Once your policy is exhausted, Medicaid will step in and pick up the slack. You are allowed to keep assets up to the amount of the long-term care benefits you purchased while still qualifying for benefits. So if, for example, you purchase $300,000 of long-term care coverage, you can keep $300,000 of assets and still qualify for Medicaid once your coverage depletes.

For more, go to Medicaid's Web site (www.cms.hhs.gov/home/medicaid.asp). We expect more and more states will pass these programs in the next few years.

77. Do I need disability insurance? What's the best way to buy it?

A: Disability insurance is the most overlooked type of insurance, but it's one of the most important.

By most estimates, if you're between the ages of 35 and 65, you have about a 30% chance of becoming disabled at some point. Disability insurance, if you have it, replaces a portion of your income if you become injured or ill and are unable to work. Policies vary—some cover you only if you are not able to work at all, others cover you if you are not able to work in your present occupation—but unless you or your family would be able to get by without your income, you should be considering disability insurance.

That means that if you're single and without another income to tide you over, it's a must. If you're the primary breadwinner and your partner couldn't easily transition into the workforce, it's also a must. If you and your partner both make good salaries and you could live off one of them if need be, it is not as necessary. The reason not enough people have it is that it tends to be expensive. But that's no reason to forgo it.

How do you find coverage? Start with your employer or benefits department. If your employer offers a group plan, it is likely to be much less expensive than individual coverage. Of course, you should evaluate what's offered. Many employer-sponsored plans are bare bones: They'll replace 60% of your salary but not bonuses; they come with a cap on benefits, usually less than $75,000; and they limit the amount of time they will pay benefits to as few as two years.

That means that if you make a salary of $50,000, you'll receive $30,000 if you're out of work for a year. If you make $200,000, you may receive only $75,000, and perhaps even less. Your benefits are also taxable, so in reality you'll end up with much less. And if you're not able to go back to work within two years, you either have to find another job that you can do in spite of your disability or prove that you can't work, period. Otherwise, your benefits will vanish.

None of these, though, is reason enough to turn down your coverage from work and hit the market solo. Instead, take your employer's policy and then add an individual plan on top of that.

To do that (or if you don't have employer coverage at all and are buying full coverage on your own), you should shop around. Insurance.com and Insure.com both offer disability insurance quotes. Many life insurance agents also sell disability coverage. You can also find an agent through the National Association of Health Underwriters, at www.nahu.org.

Disability insurance plans are fraught with complicated language and unfamiliar terminology. Here is a look at the lingo you need to understand to make a smart decision:

1. **Own-occupation coverage.** A policy with this option will pay if you are unable to perform the exact job you did when you became disabled. This coverage is more expensive than a policy that will pay if you can't work at all, but you get the benefit of not being told you are expected to get a job that pays significantly less.
2. **Partial/residual coverage.** The policy pays out if you are able to work, but your earnings are cut because your disability only allows you to work part time.
3. **Purchase option.** The plan allows you to buy more coverage as your income grows without having to prove that you're still in good health.
4. **Cost-of-living rider.** Your benefits should be automatically adjusted over time to account for inflation. This add-on, too, can be pricey, but worth it if you can afford it.
5. **Waiting period.** This is the amount of time you have to wait before the policy will begin to pay. The longer the period you elect, the less expensive your policy will be.

Q: **How much disability coverage do I need?**

A: Most policies will replace no more than 60% to 70% of your total taxable income. Why not more? Because the insurer wants you to have an incentive to return to work. As a general rule, you should aim to purchase enough to hit these percentages. However, if you think you can afford to live on less, you can purchase a smaller amount of coverage and save on monthly premiums.

You need to buy coverage only through age 65 when your Social Security Disability Insurance coverage (SSDI) will take over.

Q: **What's the difference between short-term and long-term disability insurance?**

A: Short-term disability policies generally have a waiting period of less than 14 days before coverage kicks in, and the benefit lasts for no more than two years. Long-term policies have an extended waiting period, and the maximum benefit period can vary, although it's generally either until age 65 or for the remainder of your life.

Q: **Any tips for cutting costs here?**

A: The best way to save on a disability policy—aside from shopping around to find the best rate in the first place—is by extending the waiting period before coverage kicks in. If you go from 30 days to 60 days, you'll save about 30% off your premiums. Going from 60 to 90 days will save you another 10%, and extending from 90 to 180 days will shave off another 10%. Just be sure you have enough resources to get you by in the meantime.

THE STATS

- **20%:** the percentage of workers who will be out of work for at least a year before age 65 because of an illness or accident
- **$1,684:** the average annual premium of a noncancelable individual disability insurance policy, which comes with a benefit of $4,242 a month.

78. How do I save on homeowner's insurance?

A: Before we can talk about saving money, we need to talk about getting the right amount of coverage on your home. There are two basic types of homeowner's insurance—replacement-cost coverage and cash-value coverage. When you buy cash-value coverage, you buy enough insurance to pay you back for the depreciated value of your home—and your personal property—should there be a total loss. It's cheaper than replacement-cost coverage but not a better deal. With cash-value coverage, you sacrifice the ability to rebuild your home completely.

With replacement-cost coverage, you're insuring your home for the cost to rebuild it, not the market value. That's an important distinction. If your home would sell for $500,000 but you could rebuild for $300,000, you need a policy that covers only $300,000. Why the difference? The value of your home is determined by factors other than the home itself—schools, the neighborhood, the amount of land surrounding it. When it comes to homeowner's insurance, you're not covering the land you own, only the home itself.

To find your magic number, you do a walk-through (with an appraiser from your insurer, typically) and estimate the replacement cost. Be sure that this person takes note of any features you would want to replicate if you had to rebuild, such as molding, expensive flooring, and upgraded appliances.

Once you know how much you need, you can begin to shop around. There are two rules to follow: (1) cast a wide net and (2) ask for discounts. If you already have an auto insurer that isn't currently providing insurance on your home, that's the first place to begin. As long as you're a good customer with a decent claims history, you can expect a discount of 10% to 15%.

Next, survey the marketplace. Web sites such as Insure.com and Insurance.com allow you to request quotes from several different carriers and see who offers you the best premiums.

At that point, it's time to take the top two or three and pick up the phone to see if you can drive the cost down further by pointing out the sorts of discounts for which you might be eligible. Your insurance premiums are based on the level of risk the insurance company is taking on by offering you a policy. To get the best price on that policy, you need to minimize the risk you represent. You can lower your risk profile by

· **Installing a security system, deadbolts, and smoke detectors in your home.** Each can net you about 5% off.

- **Keeping your credit score high.** Insurers consider something called an insurance score when calculating your premiums. It's slightly different from your standard credit score, but it still considers factors such as debt load and payment history. For more on this issue, see "Does my credit score affect how much I pay for insurance?" on page 166.
- **Raising your deductible.** Deductibles usually start at $250, but increasing yours $500 or $1,000 can save you up to 25% on your premiums.
- **Minimizing claims.** If you are considering filing a claim for just a little more than your deductible amount—or less than about $1,000—you're better off footing the bill yourself. Why? Because filing claims generally causes your premiums to rise.
- **Stop smoking.** Some, but not all, insurers will charge higher premiums for smokers, as there is a greater risk of fire.

But remember, cost isn't the only consideration here. Once you have a few quotes in hand, check your state's insurance department for the number of complaints filed against the companies you are considering. Most offer online guides for consumers, where you can find the number of complaints filed with each company. If a particular policy is cheap but the company is notorious for a delayed response to claims, you're better off paying a little more. You also want to check the financial health of all insurers via the Web site of insurance ratings agencies Standard & Poor's (www.standardandpoors.com) or Moody's (www.moodys .com). Look for a rating of A or higher from Standard & Poor's and at least AA from Moody's.

THE MATH

See how making just a few tweaks can cause your premiums to take a dive:

Install a security alarm, deadbolt lock, smoke alarm, or fire extinguisher
  Savings: 5%

Raise your deductible from $250 to $1,000
  Savings: 25%

Ask for a loyalty discount if you've been a good customer for several years
   Savings: 5%

Inquire about discounts for retirees. Because it is assumed that you'll be home more often, most insurers offer them.
   Savings: 10%

   Overall savings potential: $299, based on the average home-owner's insurance premium of $764

I Also Need to Know . . .

Q: What exactly does my policy cover?
A: A standard policy will cover

1. The structure of your home (which is why you need to have its value assessed before taking out a policy)
2. Your personal belongings
3. Liability if you—or your pet—were to hurt someone or damage someone's property
4. Living expenses if there is a fire or other disaster that forces you to live elsewhere while your home is repaired

   Your belongings are generally insured for up to 70% of the amount of insurance you have on the home. So if you valued your home at $300,000, your belongings would be covered up to $210,000. If you don't think that is enough, you should do an inventory of your home and buy additional coverage.
   As a general rule, you want to purchase about $300,000 worth of liability coverage.

Q: How often should I revisit my coverage?
A: It's a good idea to look over your policy once a year, particularly if you've made any major changes to the home—an addition or the remodeling of your kitchen will increase the home's replacement value. Most insurers will automatically adjust your coverage for inflation.

Q: Does my homeowner's policy cover belongings in my child's college dorm room?

A: It should, yes. If your child's belongings are destroyed in a fire or burglary, your policy will likely cover them, but only while he or she is living in the dorm. If and when your child moves into his own apartment off campus, he or she (or you) will need to look into purchasing a renter's insurance policy. For more on renter's insurance, see "How do I know if I need renter's insurance?" below.

79. How do I know if I need renter's insurance?

A: If you rent your home or apartment, you need renter's insurance. Most landlords won't cover your belongings after a fire or break-in, so buying your own policy makes sense. You may not think you have many valuable possessions, but if you add up the cost of your computer, television, camera, jewelry, and a few other items, they'd be worth a lot more than you realize. And because you're only covering your possessions, as opposed to the physical building, the premiums on policies for renters tend to be low.

There are two categories of renter's insurance. The first, called actual cash value, pays to replace what you lost, after a small deduction for depreciation. The second, called replacement cost, will pay the real cost of replacing your belongings, without taking depreciation into consideration. This option is more expensive but it's worth the extra money, particularly if you have older electronics such as a television. You might have spent $500 on it, but if it's worth only $200 now, that's all you're going to get with a cash value policy.

If you experience a disaster, such as a fire in your home, a good policy will also step in and cover your living expenses if you're forced out of your home. Costs such as hotel bills, another rental, and meals (within limits) qualify. Most renter's policies also provide liability coverage, so if you or your pet injures someone, either in your home or out, the injured person's medical bills should be covered, as well as any legal costs you incur if the person decides to sue. The exception: liability from car accidents, which would be covered under your auto policy.

As far as the possessions covered, you need to take an inventory to figure out how much your belongings are worth and then buy a policy that is based on that number. Add up the value of everything you own, keeping in mind that there will be coverage limits on valuable items such as jewelry and art. Most companies will put a cap of $1,000 or $2,000 on these items. If you have items worth more, you'll have to purchase additional coverage with an add-on policy called a rider.

I Also Need to Know . . .

Q: How do I buy renter's insurance?
A: Just as you would with any other insurance product, you want to shop around. You can use Web sites to request a number of quotes and then compare them side by side. What to look for:

- **Standard coverage limits.** This will tell you limits on jewelry and other valuable items.
- **Deductible.** How much do you pay out of pocket before the insurance policy kicks in? A higher deductible means lower premiums, but it's not worth it if you can't afford to pay the deductible, if necessary.
- **Distance.** Some companies will give full coverage to your belongings no matter where you go. Others won't. If you travel a lot, you may want to pay extra for this security.
- **Premiums.** You will pay this amount each month, quarter, or year. Make sure you compare apples with apples, though—if a company offers more coverage than another, the premium should be higher.

Keep in mind that if you bundle your policies, you may get a deal. Check with the company that handles your auto insurance and see if it will give you a discount for adding another policy.

Q: How much will it cost?
A: You can generally find basic coverage for about $200 a year.

Q: How can I reduce my premium?
A: The easiest way is to increase your deductible, which means you'll pay more before the insurance kicks in. But many companies will also give you a discount if you have an alarm system, smoke detectors, and other safety mechanisms in place.

Q: **Does my policy cover flooding?**

A: Probably not—most homeowner's and renter's insurance policies don't—and if it does, it may not cover enough. You must buy a separate policy if you live in a designated flood zone (for more information, check out www.floodsmart.gov).

THE STATS

- **$193:** The average renter's insurance policy premium, according to the most recent data from the National Association of Insurance Commissioners
- **46%:** The number of renters who own renter's insurance
- **66%:** The percentage of homes that are underinsured

80. Do most homeowner's policies cover my jewelry or other valuables?

A: Most policies have a provision that will cover only a portion of valuable jewelry and art—often only up to $1,500. The same goes for other big-ticket items: pricey electronics, furs, instruments, antique furniture.

Check with your insurer about any valuable items you own, and if they're not covered completely, discuss purchasing a separate policy called a "rider." Generally this provision will also cover you if you lose the item yourself, which is a major plus when it comes to jewelry.

The annual premium on a rider or stand-alone policy for jewelry, for instance, will probably be about $10 to $15 per $1,000 of coverage, but it depends where you live. In a big city, where there tends to be more loss and more theft, you'll pay more. For example, in New York, where I live, I might pay $20 per $1,000 of jewelry coverage. Still, it's inexpensive in the grand scheme of things: You can cover a $5,000 piece for about $50 to $125 a year, a $10,000 piece for $100 to $250 a year, and a $50,000 piece for $500 to $1,250 a year. You can also fiddle with your deductible to lower the price, but remember that if you want to replace the item if lost, you'll have to pay the deductible before the insurance company steps up.

You also need to increase the value of your policy annually to account for inflation. If you don't, and you lose your engagement ring ten years after it was purchased, the insurance will only cover the purchase price, not the current value of the ring. There could be a big difference, particularly if the price of gold is on the rise. The same, of course, is true for art, which may appreciate. Electronics aren't as likely to follow suit—and may even decrease in price. But your insurance agent will help you calculate the increase amount. You'll likely want to have most items reappraised every few years.

QUESTIONS TO ASK ABOUT A RIDER OR STAND-ALONE POLICY

1. Is there a deductible? There likely will be, but you can tinker with the amount to raise or lower your premiums.
2. Are there any exclusions to the coverage? Some policies may limit coverage in certain instances, for example, if you're traveling overseas with jewelry. Others won't cover musical instruments or cameras used for profit.
3. How are claims settled? Most companies will just cut you a check for the value of the items, but others may replace the items. You want to go with a policy that will pay out a cash settlement.
4. Do you require an appraisal? How often? Most companies will require that the item is appraised, particularly if you're buying coverage for more than a few thousand dollars. You may also have to get it reappraised annually.
5. Does the coverage apply to repairs? This question primarily relates to jewelry insurance. You can find policies that cover both repair and replacement, if that's what you want.

---

81. How do I get the best deal on automotive insurance?

A: First things first: Figure out how much coverage you need. Auto insurance requirements vary by state, but most states require that you have liability insurance at the bare minimum. Liability coverage is expressed by three numbers, each representing thousands, and looks something like this: 100/300/50. The first number is the maximum that the insurance company will pay per person for bodily injury from an accident, the second number is the maximum amount that the insurance company will pay per accident for bodily injury, and the last number is the maximum amount covered for damage to someone else's property.

Why are these coverage amounts important? Because if an accident is your fault and the costs exceed your coverage, the difference will come out of your own pocket.

▶ An Example

Kate has liability insurance for her Toyota Camry. Her coverage is 50/100/50, the amount required in her state. She runs a red light and gets into an accident that causes $20,000 worth of damage to the other vehicle. She's covered, because her liability insurance covers up to $50,000. But let's say she injures three people in the other vehicle, and their medical bills add up to $150,000. Her insurance will cover $100,000, but she's going to have to come up with the remaining $50,000.

Lesson: The bare minimum isn't always the best option. You have to look at your financial situation. If you have assets to protect, you want to get enough liability coverage so you don't have to tap into those if you're in an accident. Otherwise, attorneys for the injured party can go after your assets to recoup the cost of their medical bills (or worse, pain and suffering) not covered by your insurance. If you don't have a lot of assets, your state's basic requirements may meet your needs.

The other main components of any auto insurance policy are collision and comprehensive insurance. Collision insurance pays for damage to your car itself—and if you have this coverage, your car is covered no matter who is at fault. Comprehensive coverage pays for theft, fire, and vandalism. If you don't have comprehensive coverage and your car is stolen, you'll foot the bill for a replacement. If you have a new car, you want both collision and comprehensive coverage. Generally, it's not necessary for old models or those where the cost of paying for this insurance is more than one-tenth the value of the car.

Once you know what kind of coverage you want, start with the company that handles your home owner's or renter's insurance.

You'll likely get a discount of up to 15% for bundling the policies.

But don't stop there. Hop on the Internet and do a little searching. Get quotes from four or five companies, using an online service such as Insure.com or InsWeb.com. Then, check the complaint history of those companies by visiting your state's insurance department. Price is important, yes, but service is right up there with it. If you have a claim, you need to know that it will get processed, and quickly.

The rest, I'm afraid, is in your hands. Insurance companies take a range of factors into consideration when calculating your premiums, because they're basically evaluating the risk involved in extending a policy to you. There are some risk factors you have no control over, such as the accident statistics in your area, but others are malleable. Your credit score, driving history, number of claims filed, and the type of car you drive all play a role. The higher your credit score, the lower your premium, so keep working on paying your bills—all of them, not just your insurance premium—on time (for more information, turn to page 161). The fewer accidents you have and claims you file, the better, so small scratches are best handled on your own. And cars that cost a lot to repair or that are of a make or model that tends to be stolen often will cost you more. Your insurance company can give you more information on this.

I Also Need to Know . . .

Q: Can I ask for a discount?
A: Not all companies will offer discounts, but most do. Try your luck with these:

- **Group or association.** Often if you're a member of a professional association, the military, a union, or even an alumni group from college, you can get a few bucks shaved off your monthly premium.
- **Loyalty.** Many companies will give you up to 10% off after you're a customer for a year or two.

- **Defensive-driving class.** Taking and passing one that's recognized by your carrier could get you another 10% off.
- **Retirees.** Because it's assumed that your commute has been eliminated or at least shortened because you've stopped working, you may get a portion shaved off your premium. By the same token, if you drive less than the average number of miles per year, you could see a discount, retired or not.
- **College students.** If your son or daughter is on your policy and he or she goes away to school sans car, ask for a discount because that young driver will be behind the wheel significantly less.
- **Security.** Sometimes an insurer will shave a bit off your premium if you install an alarm on your car and have comprehensive coverage.

Q: **Should I raise my deductible?**

A: If you have collision or comprehensive coverage, raising your deductible is a great way to lower your premiums. Bumping your deductible up from $200 to $1,000 can save you more than 30%.

Q: **Should I be buying more liability coverage than my insurance company offers as a standard option?**

A: You've probably heard the expression "We live in a litigious society." That's why the answer to this question is a resounding yes, if you have significant assets—maybe a nice home, a large investment portfolio, and significant savings. The policy you want is called an umbrella liability policy, and it will provide liability for both your home and your car at once. The good news is that umbrella policies are cheap—only about $100 to $200 per million dollars of coverage.

Q: **What is uninsured or underinsured motorist coverage?**

A: Another component of some auto insurance policies. It will cover your expenses if you're in an accident and the driver at fault either doesn't have insurance or doesn't have enough coverage, or if it was a hit-and-run. A few states require you to have this coverage, but it isn't the norm. However, if you can afford it, you should probably include this feature in your policy. It's estimated that about 25% of drivers are uninsured, and if they don't have any assets—or they flee the scene—you may be stuck with the bill.

The price of this coverage varies by state, mainly depending on the percentage of drivers who are uninsured in that state.

Resources

Associations

National Association of Health Underwriters (NAHU)
www.nahu.org
703-276-0220

NAHU represents more than 20,000 licensed health insurance agents, brokers, consultants, and benefit professionals; on this site you can search for a NAHU member in your community, browse a glossary of terms, and access guides and a database with information on different types of health insurance.

National Association of Insurance Commissioners
www.naic.org
1-866-470-6242

Detailed insurance information for people in all stages of life who are considering buying insurance; includes guides, tips, and more.

Books

101 Health Insurance Tips, by Michelle Katz (2007)

Tips from health insurance expert Michelle Katz on how to find the best health-care plan for your budget.

The Insurance Maze: How You Can Save Money on Insurance—and Still Get the Coverage You Need, by Kimberly Lankford (2006)

Insurance explained in simple terms; learn how to avoid insurance pitfalls and make the most of your insurance policy.

Questions and Answers on Life Insurance: The Life Insurance Toolbook, by Anthony Steuer (2007)

Answers to life insurance questions covering topics such as how to differentiate between policies, evaluating policies and companies, hiring an agent, and monitoring your policy.

Government Organizations

Internal Revenue Service
www.irs.gov
1-800-829-1040
Detailed information on HASs and other tax-favored health plans.

Insure Kids Now
www.insurekidsnow.gov
1-877-543-7669
A national campaign to provide uninsured children (from birth to age 18) with free or low-cost health insurance; through Insure Kids Now, you can be put in direct contact with your state's children's health insurance program and get answers to FAQs about insurance for minors.

U.S. Department of the Treasury
www.ustreas.gov
For HSA questions involving individuals, call the IRS toll-free assistance line at 1-800-829-1040; for HSA questions involving businesses, call 1-800-829-4933.
Information about HSAs; includes a fact sheet, answers to FAQs, information on IRA-to-HSA transfers and the full contribution rule, and current news.

U.S. Department of Labor, Employee Benefits Security Administration
www.dol.gov/ebsa/
1-866-444-3272
Information on various types of insurance, fact sheets, answers to FAQs, and current benefit news.

Web sites

AARP
www.aarp.org
1-888-687-2277
Information, resources, and research on insurance for long-term care.

Consumer Federation of America
www.consumerfed.org
202-387-6121
Information on variable universal life insurance.

eHealthInsurance.com
www.ehealthinsurance.com
1-800-977-8860
Get quotes on individual, family, and small-business health insurance plans; compare plans; and apply for coverage online.

Edmunds.com
www.edmunds.com
Compare auto insurance rates; read auto insurance articles, insurance forums, and answers to auto insurance questions.

Insurance.com
www.insurance.com
1-866-533-0227
Research insurance products, get comparison rates from top car insurance companies and tips on when to buy insurance, learn how to save money when buying insurance, read insurance news, get insurance quotes, find answers to FAQs, and use a life-insurance calculator.

Insure.com
www.insure.com
1-800-556-9393
Consumer insurance information, insurance articles, answers to FAQs, an insurance glossary, and interactive tools; obtain insurance quotes and purchase insurance from the company of your choice.

Insurance Information Institute
www.iii.org
212-346-5500
Use a glossary of insurance terms, search for an insurance company in your state, read information on insurance and financial planning priorities at different life stages, and read answers to FAQs about insurance.

Kiplinger
www.kiplinger.com/money/insurancecenter/

Insurance information, interactive tools, advice on how to save money by lowering insurance costs, quizzes, videos, and a directory of state insurance regulators.

Moody's
www.moodys.com
Check the financial ratings of any home insurance company.

National Patient Advocate Foundation
www.npaf.org
202-347-8009
A national nonprofit organization that provides patients with a voice in health care through regulatory and legislative reform; read recent news, learn about research, and use tools to help you become an advocate for quality health care.

Patient Advocate Foundation
www.patientadvocate.org
1-800-532-5274
A national nonprofit foundation that acts as a mediator for patients, helping them obtain financial stability when dealing with a life-threatening or debilitating disease; find disease-specific information and support, information on insurance, and recent news.

Standard & Poor's
www.standardandpoors.com
Check the financial ratings of any home insurance company.

CHAPTER 10

RETIREMENT

82. I have nothing set aside for my retirement. Where should I start?

A: 1. **Tax-advantaged, retirement-specific buckets.** These accounts allow you to contribute money, generally before you pay taxes on it (the Roth IRA is an exception to this rule), and then grow it tax deferred (or tax free in the Roth case) until you withdraw the funds at retirement. Does your employer offer a 401(k) or 403(b) or 457? If so, these are some of the best tools available for retirement saving. In 2009, you can contribute up to $16,500 ($22,000 if you're older than 50) to these accounts. That might sound like a reach, but it's likely that your employer is going to help you out with matching dollars. Although some companies have fallen on such tough times that they've reduced or eliminated their 401(k) match, many companies will match your contributions to their 401(k) program—sometimes by as much as 50%—which means free money.

   If your employer doesn't offer a 401(k) or similar program, an IRA will be your best bet. An IRA, or individual retirement account, is an account that you establish on your own to save for retirement. The contribution limits are a little lower, at $5,000 (again, $6,000 for those older than 50), but depending on your income and what kind of IRA you choose, they may be tax-deductible. Here are your IRA options:

- **Traditional deductible.** A Traditional IRA is available for anyone younger than age 70½ who has earned income. Contributions are tax deductible up to the limits, and the money grows tax deferred until you withdraw it at retirement. At that time it will be taxed at your current income tax rate. To be eligible to contribute the maximum to a traditional deductible IRA, your modified adjusted gross income must be less than $55,000 if you're single or $89,000 if you're married filing jointly (amounts are for 2009). After that, contribution limits are reduced until you're no longer eligible at a modified adjusted gross income of $65,000 for single filers and $109,000 for married filing jointly. If you or your spouse aren't also eligible for an employer-sponsored retirement plan, there are no income limitations.

- **Traditional nondeductible IRA.** If you earn more than $65,000 as a single filer or $109,000 as a married joint filer and have an employer-sponsored plan, you can still contribute to an IRA; you just can't deduct your contributions on your income tax returns. The money will grow tax deferred until you withdraw it.

- **Roth IRA.** There aren't any age requirements when it comes to a Roth IRA, but there are other restrictions. For you to be eligible to contribute the maximum to a Roth, your modified adjusted gross income can't exceed $105,000 if you're single or $166,000 if you're married filing jointly (again, these are the limitations for 2009). You're no longer eligible to contribute at all if your modified adjusted gross income hits $120,000 for single filers or $176,000 for married filing jointly. Other differences? Your contributions to the account won't be tax deductible, but your money grows tax free—when you pull it out in retirement, you won't have to pay taxes on it. You are not forced, as you are with a traditional IRA, to ever make withdrawals, which means that you can pass this money on to your heirs. And you can make preretirement withdrawals for education and for your first house, as long as the money has been in the account for 5 years, without penalty. You can also pull out your contributions, but not your earnings, at any time, penalty free.

2. **Tax-advantaged, nonretirement ways to save.** Once you max out your ability to contribute to accounts designated for retirement, you should look at other tax-advantaged ways to save. No, they don't specifically say they're for retirement, but in fact all accounts that allow your assets to grow in a tax-deferred way aid retirement. Why? Because they enable you to not have to use those retirement-specific assets for other life needs.

- **529 college savings account.** Each state offers at least one version of this savings plan. This plan allows your investments to grow tax free, as a Roth IRA does. Contributions aren't deductible on your federal return, but your state may offer tax breaks for contributing to their plan. The best part? Distributions used to pay for the account beneficiary's college education are tax free. If you don't use the funds for college, however, you'll pay a 10% penalty and income tax on earnings, but you can change the beneficiary to another qualifying family member at any time.
- **Health savings account.** If you're covered by a high-deductible insurance plan, you're likely eligible for an HSA, which allows you either to deduct your contributions or make them on a pretax basis, depending on your employer. There are no income restrictions, but for you to have an HSA, your deductible must be $1,200 for individual coverage and $2,400 for family coverage. You can then contribute $3,050, if you have self-only coverage, or $6,150 if you have a family plan. Once the money is set aside, you use it for qualified medical expenses—everything from doctor visits to over-the-counter medicines. If the money is used for anything else, you'll be taxed, and if you're not older than 65, penalized 10%. Once you turn 65, you can use your account for other expenses without penalty.

3. **Non-tax-advantaged ways to save.** If you still have money to sock away for retirement, good for you. First, think about whether you have any self-employment in-

come. If so, there are other tax-advantaged options for you. See "I'm self-employed. What's the best way to save for retirement?" on page 291. If not, it's time to open a plain-vanilla savings, money market, or brokerage account. You'll pay taxes every year on the money you earn on your savings or investments in these baskets.

Now that your baskets are established, you need to start funding them. In my book, there is only one way to fund retirement accounts: *automatically*. If you are putting money into a 401(k) or other employer-based retirement account, that means doing your funding through automatic paycheck withdrawals. If not, however, you need to set this up yourself. Call the bank or brokerage firm that houses your IRA or Roth or 529 and ask to have a certain amount of money transferred automatically to the retirement account every month. You have to make this call only once, and it will continue to happen until you stop it (which you shouldn't). The miracle is how fast your savings manage to add up.

THE MATH

Want to make sure you max out your Roth or Traditional IRA? Start early and automatically contribute $416.66 a month if you're younger than 50, or $500 a month if you're older. By the end of the year, you'll have hit your target.

I Also Need to Know . . .

Q: **Which is a better option for saving for retirement, a 401(k) or a Roth IRA?**

A: Assuming you're eligible for both—in other words, you have a 401(k) through your job and you are within the income requirements for a Roth (less than $120,000 if single and $176,000 if married filing jointly)—you should look first at that 401(k). If it has an employer match, contribute enough to that account first to grab all the matching dollars. After that, the advantage to the 401(k) is its higher contribution limits ($16,500 versus $5,000), which means you'll be able to save more if your income allows for that. The advantage to the Roth is flexibility (you can get at the money if you need it) and investment choice (you're not limited to the choices on your employer's menu).

But here's an important point: You don't have to choose, because you can, and should, have both. A Roth IRA has more than a few advantages that you don't want to pass up, particularly the fact that your money grows tax free and you can withdraw your contributions at any time without penalty for something such as a down payment on a house or education expenses.

My advice to you is to tag-team your retirement. Contribute enough to your 401(k) to grab your match, if your employer offers one, and then shift your focus to your Roth. If you hit the limit on the Roth and have money left over, go back to the 401(k) until you reach the limit there.

Q: What is a Roth 401(k)?
A: Essentially, it's the best of both worlds. A Roth 401(k) is set up through your employer, although because it is a relatively new concept (it was introduced by the Economic Growth and Tax Relief Reconciliation Act of 2001), only about 12% of employers offered it in 2007. Like a traditional 401(k), it has a $15,500 cap on contributions ($20,500 for those older than 50) and no income restrictions.

But like the Roth IRA, contributions are made with after-tax dollars, meaning that your savings grow tax free.

How do you know whether to go with a Roth or traditional 401(k) if your employer offers both? It's a matter of hedging your bets. If your income, and thus your tax responsibility, is low now, you're probably better off going with the Roth, because you'll lock in that low tax rate. If you make a good bit now and expect to have a lower tax rate in retirement, put off your tax responsibility by going with a traditional 401(k). If you can't decide, you do have the option of contributing to both, although your contribution limit is still $15,500 combined.

Q: I heard that the Roth 401(k) is going to expire soon. What happens to my money if it does?
A: The law authorizing the Roth 401(k) was set to expire in 2010, but it's since been made permanent, so there's no need to worry.

Q: What is my modified adjusted gross income, anyway?

A: This term comes into play only when you're talking about IRAs. It is used not only to figure out eligibility for Roth IRAs but also to determine what portion, if any, of your contributions to a traditional IRA will be tax deductible. You can figure out yours by taking your adjusted gross income—found on your most recent tax return—and adding back certain items, including student loan deductions, IRA contribution deductions, deductions for higher-education costs, and foreign income. The higher your modified adjusted gross income is, the less you'll be able to deduct when it comes to your Traditional IRA contributions. You may also eliminate your ability to open a Roth IRA if you reach the income limitations ($120,000 for single filers, $176,000 for marrieds filing jointly).

Q: I'm only 25. Why do I need to think about retirement already?

A: The earlier you start investing, the more you'll have amassed when it's time to retire. Obvious, right? But what might not be so obvious is that the earlier you start investing, the less you have to contribute overall. That's right, you're actually saving money by saving money. Let me show you what I mean:

Let's take two people, both your age. We'll call them Jane and Bob. Jane starts investing $100 a month at age 25 and continues investing that same amount until she retires at 65. Bob, however, puts off saving for retirement until he's 40, at which point, he starts investing $350 a month for the next 25 years:

TOTAL CONTRIBUTED BY AGE . . .	JANE	BOB
25	$1,200	$0
30	$6,000	$0
35	$12,000	$0
40	$18,000	$4,200
45	$24,000	$21,000
50	$30,000	$42,000

(continued)

TOTAL CONTRIBUTED BY AGE . . .	JANE	BOB
55	$36,000	$63,000
60	$42,000	$84,000
65	$48,000	$105,000
Total contribution	$48,000	$105,000
Total value of retirement account	$351,428	$335,079

Total earnings are based on an 8% return on investment.

You're not seeing things. Bob contributes twice as much as Jane but ends up with less money for retirement. That's the power of compound interest: Jane's investments are boosted by the time they have to grow.

Q: **Which kind of IRA is better for me?**
A: Generally speaking, if you're eligible for the Roth, that's going to be your best bet, particularly if you're younger than 50. You'll lose the tax deduction, sure, but the advantages are greater overall. Going forward, we don't know what tax rates will be, but we know what they are now, and it's a safe bet that they won't go any lower. That means that it makes sense to get your money in a tax-free account if you can. And note: If you haven't been able to contribute to a Roth because you earn too much money, 2010 presents a great opportunity. You can convert a Traditional IRA to a Roth regardless of income. You'll have to pay income taxes on the conversion; as long as you don't have to raid your IRA to do so, this is a good idea.

83. I am a married, stay-at-home parent. How do I save for retirement?

A: As a nonworking spouse, you can save money in what's called a spousal IRA as long as you and your spouse file a joint tax return and his or her income is at least as much as your contribution. There are limits to how much you can contribute each year to an IRA, and currently they are set at $5,000 if you're younger than 50 and $6,000 if you're 50 or older.

Your spousal IRA can be in the form of either a traditional IRA (where your contribution is tax deductible in the year you make it, and you pay the taxes as you withdraw the money once you're retired) or a Roth IRA (where you pay taxes on the money as you earn it, but the money can then grow tax free forever). If you qualify for the Roth, that would be my pick. Not only is the tax treatment advantageous but also the Roth is flexible. You can pull out your contributions at any time for any reason, and you can withdraw income on those contributions for education or to buy your first home after five years. However, the adjusted gross income on your joint return must be less than $166,000 for you to contribute the maximum to a Roth.

A traditional IRA doesn't have income limits. But if your spouse is also covered by a qualified retirement plan at work, the tax deduction on the contribution starts to phase out at a modified adjusted gross income of $166,000 (in 2009). You are no longer eligible for the tax deduction if your modified adjusted gross income is $176,000 or more.

THE MATH

A contribution of $5,000 a year may not seem like much, especially when compared with the amount your partner contributes to his or her 401(k) each year, but it adds up over time:

- In 10 years you'll have $74,721.
- In 15 years you'll have $143,225.
- In 20 years you'll have $243,796.
- In 25 years you'll have $393,630.
- In 30 years you'll have $616,861.

I Also Need to Know . . .

Q: Why do I need my own retirement plan if my spouse is saving enough to cover us both in retirement?

A: Just like having your own bank account in a marriage, having your own retirement savings account gives you a bit of independence. You have control over your own retirement, and not only does that feel good but it also protects you against the unexpected. Trust me—once you start to see the balance tick up because of your contributions, you won't want to stop saving. It's also in your best interest when it comes to taxes, because in most cases you'll be able to save up to twice as much money in a tax-advantaged way.

Q: **Will I get Social Security benefits that are based on my husband's income? How are those calculated?**

A: Probably. A spouse who hasn't worked at a paying job or who has accumulated low earnings throughout his or her career is typically entitled to up to half of the working spouse's benefit amount. You'll start to receive your benefit when your husband starts taking his or at age 62, whichever comes last.

One thing to note, though, is that if you're eligible for your own benefits—say you decide to go back to work once the kids are settled in school—the SSA will pay you your own benefits first. If that amount happens to be lower than what you'd receive from your husband, the SSA will combine the two benefits to equal the higher amount, but you won't get the total of both.

If you're at full retirement age and you're eligible for both your own benefit and your husband's, you can choose to receive his now so that your benefit continues to grow. (Social Security benefits increase by as much as 8% for each year you delay taking them between ages 62 and 70. For more on how this works, see page 316). You can file for your own benefits in a few years and your monthly check will be higher because it will be based on the delayed benefit.

► An Example

Shannon is 62 years old. On the basis of her earnings, her Social Security monthly benefit is $998. Her husband, Jack, who is 68, just began taking his benefit in the amount of $2,842 a month. That means that because her benefit from Jack's Social Security is higher, the SSA will pay Shannon all of her own monthly benefit, plus $423 of her spousal benefits from Jack, for a total of $1,416—50% of Jack's monthly benefit.

Shannon could maximize her benefits by delaying taking her own Social Security benefits and just taking her $1,416 in spousal benefits as Jack's wife for a few years. That way, when she reaches age 70, her own monthly benefit will be $2,494 (adjusted for inflation). What's the difference?

- If Shannon takes $1,416 starting at age 62, which is based on a combination of her husband's benefits and her own, and she lives 30 more years, she'll receive a total of $509,760.
- If Shannon takes $1,416 starting at age 62 from her husband's benefits, delays taking her own until she's 68, and lives 30 more years, she'll receive a total of $820,224.

The difference? A whopping $310,464.

Q: What if my husband and I get divorced? Do I lose my stake in his Social Security benefits?

A: No, provided you were married for more than 10 years. However, if you remarry, you generally cannot collect benefits that are based on your former spouse's benefits.

84. I'm self-employed. What's the best way to save for retirement?

A: There is one big downside to being self-employed when it comes to saving for retirement: You lose the employer match that many employees get when they contribute to a company-sponsored 401(k).

Fortunately, there are a lot of upsides, starting with the fact that you can contribute more each year than a person who works for someone else.

If you're eligible for a Roth IRA (to make the maximum contribution, your modified adjusted gross income must be less than $105,000 for single or married filing separately or $166,000 for married filing jointly), start there. But that accounts for only the contribution limit of $5,000 a year ($6,000 if you're 50 or older).

For the rest of your retirement savings contributions, look to the solo 401(k). This option allows you to contribute up to $16,500 in 2009 as an employee (i.e., your own employee). That's the same contribution limit as a 401(k). Then, as the business owner, you can also contribute 20% of your self-employment income, up to a combined maximum of $49,000 (in 2009, these limits adjust each year for inflation). And if you're older than 50, you can make catch-up contributions of an extra $5,500 each year. All in all, if you had a good year, you could contribute $70,000.

Better still, contributions to a solo 401(k) are tax deferred. You'll be taxed when you withdraw the money after age 59½; as with a traditional 401(k), you'll incur a 10% penalty if you withdraw the money earlier.

A solo 401(k) can be a great option for sole proprietors, but if you have any employees (other than your spouse), you're not eligible. In that case, you should consider something called an SEP (simplified employee pension) IRA. This account allows you to contribute 20% of your business income, up to $49,000 in 2009, but doesn't allow you to also make an employee contribution for yourself. Your contributions will be tax deductible, and you can open plans for your employees and contribute on their behalf. You'll incur the same penalties as you would with a 401(k) if you make an early withdrawal.

Other options include Keogh plans, which tend to make sense only for high-income business owners with low-income employees (for instance, a doctor might open a Keogh because while his income is likely good, he may pay his receptionist very little). A SIMPLE (savings incentive match plan for employees) IRA is the opposite of what its name implies—it is quite complicated—and is a better option than a SEP only if you have a good number of employees. That's because with a SEP IRA, you're contributing your own money to your employees' accounts. With a SIMPLE IRA, the contribution is a salary deferral, which means they are contributing their own money. To be eligible for a SIMPLE IRA, you must have fewer than 100 employees.

One thing to keep in mind with all of these: You want to think about the big picture. Maybe you don't have any employees now, but do you envision a time when you might? If so, you should probably think ahead and go with a SEP IRA instead of the solo 401(k).

THE MATH

What's the tax benefit here? Let's take a look. The chart below compares Shawn and Mary. Shawn makes the maximum contribution to his solo 401(k) each year, while Mary doesn't. They both have business incomes of $100,000.

	Shawn	Mary
Net income	$100,000	$100,000
Deductions	$33,650	$33,650
Solo 401(k) contributions	$35,087	$0
Taxable income	$21,263	$66,350
Tax due	$3,854	$9,118
Self-employment tax due	$15,300	$15,300
Total tax	$19,154	$24,418
Tax savings	$5,263	$0

Source: T. Rowe Price.

I Also Need to Know . . .

Q: **Can my spouse contribute to my solo 401(k) if she works for the business?**

A: Yes, if she is paid by the business. And if she can afford it, she should contribute for herself too, because it doubles the amount that you can put away for retirement. A good deal, any way you look at it.

Q: **I work full time and I have a 401(k) through my employer. Can I also have a SEP IRA or a solo 401(k) for my self-employment income?**

A: Yes. If you choose a solo 401(k), though, your contribution limits may be reduced. If you want to contribute to a solo 401(k) and an employer-sponsored 401(k), your contributions to both as an employee have to fall under that year's limitations. However, you can still contribute the additional 20% of your self-employment income. So if you contributed, say, $10,000 to your employer's 401(k), you could still contribute $6,500 to your solo 401(k), plus 20% of your business income.

Q: **If I decide to leave my full-time job to start my own business, what should I do with my 401(k)?**

A: You can leave it in place, if you want, but your best bet is to roll that money over into either a SEP IRA or a solo 401(k), whichever tool you've chosen to continue your retirement savings. For more information about rolling over these assets, turn to "How do I roll over a 401(k)?" on page 300.

85. What is an annuity?

A: An annuity is an insurance product sold as an investment. You deposit a certain amount of money with an insurance company, then receive it back at a later date, sometimes in a lump form, other times in the form of "paychecks" at regular intervals. There are several basic types of annuities—and many varieties, one of the reasons that the world of annuities can be tough to decipher. But one thing is clear: You should understand what an annuity is before you tackle the next question, which is "Should I buy one?"

- **Variable annuity.** A variable annuity takes the money you deposit and invests it, generally in mutual funds. The performance of those investments ultimately determines your payouts. If the stock market rises, your payout likely will too, and vice versa. There is sometimes a minimum return, or a guarantee, that is set at the time of purchase. You may pay extra for this feature, however. Fees on variable annuities are often high (higher than they are on mutual funds outside of annuities). Be sure that you understand the costs of making this investment.
- **Fixed annuity.** A fixed annuity takes the money you deposit and invests it, guaranteeing a return. Your payout will be the same each month and is based on how much you contribute, your age, and the interest rate when you purchased it.

These annuities are for individuals who have a lower tolerance for risk than those investing in variable annuities. Fees are generally built into the interest rate, much as they would be with a standard savings account. The bank earns 6% on your money, for example, but gives you an interest rate of 5%. The fee schedule is generally not as complicated or cumbersome as with a variable annuity, but you still need to understand how much making this investment will cost you.

· **Deferred annuity.** A deferred annuity is one type of fixed annuity or variable annuity. It allows you to put off payments for a period of time, essentially until you need them, which is why it is often sold for long-term retirement planning. The money invested in your account grows tax deferred and when you're ready (and contractually able), you will start receiving payments. This kind of annuity typically comes with a death benefit—if you die, the beneficiary of the account is guaranteed the principal and investment earnings.

· **Immediate annuity.** An immediate annuity gives you your paycheck right away in return for your investment of a lump sum—hence the name *immediate*. You can pick the length of time—five years, your lifetime, even your spouse's lifetime—that you'll receive your payments. The longer the time frame, the lower your payments. You pay taxes only on the part of your annuity payment considered earnings, not the principal. These can also be fixed or variable.

Keep in mind that while the stream of income you receive from any annuity may be steady as advertised, it could be eroded by inflation, because while you'll get the same amount of money, it won't go as far. Most annuities will give you the option to have your payouts increased each year to account for that. You will pay more for that guarantee.

Q: **Are annuities safe?**

A: Before 2007, nearly everyone you asked that question would have answered yes. Now, after the fall of insurance giant AIG, we're not so sure. But insurance companies are regulated tightly, and most states cover insurance companies if they fail. Coverage amounts vary by state, but ranges from $100,000 to $500,000. If the value of your annuity is less than that, or if you have two annuities with two different insurance companies valued at less than that, you're covered much like the FDIC covers money in your bank account.

And if the value is not? Much depends on the financial health of your annuity provider. Check out the ratings on Web sites such as A.M. Best (www.ambest.com/) and Moody's (www.moodys.com), but keep in mind that these are just ratings and not guarantees. (They, too, let us down in recent years.) Understand where the rating falls on the charts as well. An "A–" may sound good, but at A.M. Best, it's only the fourth highest rating behind AAA, AA, and A.

Q: **How do I buy an annuity?**
A: Annuities are sold by insurance agents but also through some financial planners, banks, and life insurance companies. Whoever you work with, make sure that he or she is licensed by your state's insurance department. And if you feel pressured to buy or do not fully understand what you are buying, walk away.

Watch Out for These!

- **Fees.** The fees charged on annuities tend to be high—more than what you'd pay for your standard investment account. Actual costs vary, but expect to pay an annual fee upward of 2% of the assets you deposit, as well as surrender fees if you want to withdraw your money early. These tend to go down every year—they generally start at 7% in the first year and go down 1% each year thereafter until you've left the money in place for seven years.
- **The fine print.** Annuities are complicated—so complicated that even many of the people who sell them do not understand them well enough to explain them to you. That doesn't mean you shouldn't buy one—only that you shouldn't buy one if you don't understand it. And if the person pitching you doesn't have the ability to explain it to you, you should find another source.
- **The suggestion to put an annuity into an IRA.** Annuity funds grow tax deferred; therefore, you don't need the double protection of an IRA.

86. When should I cash out my 401(k)?

A: Let's be clear: You shouldn't. You don't want to "cash out" your 401(k) (or your IRA or any other retirement account) all at once. Instead you should consider taking distributions from your 401(k) without penalty when you reach age 59½. (Understand, though, that you don't have to begin taking distributions until you reach age 70½.)

How do you make the decision on when to begin distributions? The first and most important question: Do you need the cash? If you need the money to live on, or if you've stopped working and aren't yet receiving Social Security benefits, or if you are receiving Social Security benefits but they're not enough to meet your needs, then it's the right time to start.

But remember, this is simple math: You have a certain amount of money, and you need it to last an estimated number of years. The sooner you start pulling it out and spending it, the less money you'll have down the road. For more information, turn to "How do I make my retirement funds last as long as I do?" on page 311.

Next, look at how your investments are doing. If they're way down, you will want to put off pulling money out of that account if possible. That will give your money more time to grow—and come back—tax deferred.

Bottom line: If you're worried that your money isn't going to make it to the end of your life and if you can continue to work or you have adequate personal savings to support yourself for a while, go ahead and spend that down before you tap into your 401(k) or your IRA.

Once you've decided that it's time to start taking distributions—or you turn 70½—you want to pull your money out in a way that minimizes your tax liability. Distributions from 401(k) and IRA accounts are income, and they are taxed as such.

That means that you must consider your tax bracket. If you're on the cusp of moving to a higher bracket and if taking a certain amount in distributions will push you there, then it's worth cutting your distribution back a bit—and possibly your spending as well—to stay in the less-expensive bracket. In general, retirees tend to have less in earned income as they get older, which means that as time passes, you might have a bit more leeway to pull out more.

One other factor to consider: Social Security benefits. In general, these aren't taxable, unless you have enough additional income to push them over the threshold. Your income from 401(k) and IRA investments could do that. Here's how to do the math:

1. Add half of the total benefits you received to all of your other income, including any tax-exempt interest and other exclusions from income.
2. Then compare that total amount with the base amount for your filing status:

   - If married filing jointly: $32,000
   - If single, head of household, qualifying widow/widower with a dependent child, or married, filing separately, and you did not live with your spouse at any time during the year: $25,000
   - If married filing separately and you did live with your spouse at any time during the year: $0

If the total is more than your base amount, some of your benefits may be taxable.

▶ An Example

Josh is single and 65, and his monthly Social Security benefit is $1,150, or $13,800 a year, about the average. He can also pull $18,100 out of his retirement accounts each year—as long as he has no other income—without his benefits being taxed.

THE MATH

Jackie is 60 years old, and every year, she and her employer contribute $10,000 to her 401(k). She now has $600,000 in her account. She can retire now and begin taking distributions, or she can continue to work for a few more years. She needs at least $2,000 a month to get by.

If she opts to retire now and pull that amount out each month, her money has only a 75% chance of lasting until she is age 95. If she wants a 90% chance—and she should—she must reduce her living expenses so that she can pull out only $1,750. Or she can continue to work for a bit longer. In fact, if she waits just five years and continues to stash away that $10,000 a year, she'll be able to pull out $2,588 a month without worrying.

Source: T. Rowe Price Retirement Income Calculator.

I Also Need to Know . . .

Q: I've heard that I should pull my money out of my retirement accounts sooner rather than later because taxes are low . . . and likely to go up. Thoughts?

A: There are varied opinions on this question: Some people say that because taxes are relatively low right now (as I wrote this, the tax cuts from the administration of George W. Bush were still in place), and there's a good chance they'll only go up from here. That would mean that paying taxes on money now rather than later is a good gamble. Other people think that delaying your withdrawals to allow for additional tax-deferred growth is the key, no matter what. Me? I can understand both sides of the argument. But in the end, I'm in the second camp. Delaying taxes has almost always been the better bet, except if you are in a very low tax (10% to 15%) bracket to begin with. If that's the case, it likely won't make much difference either way.

Q: What are the other rules in regard to distributions?

A: You might have heard that required minimum distributions were suspended in 2009, which means you're not required to pull money out of your retirement accounts during that year.

Under normal circumstances, the IRS requires that you withdraw a certain amount from your tax-deferred retirement accounts each year, beginning when you turn 70½, or the year that you retire—whichever is later. If you have an IRA or you own more than 5% of the business sponsoring your plan, you must begin withdrawing at age 70½, regardless of whether you're still working.

These rules apply to 401(k), 403(b), and 457(b) accounts; traditional IRAs, SEP IRAs; and SIMPLE IRAs. They do not apply to Roth IRAs as long as the owner of the account is still alive.

Next, you have to do a little math. You have to calculate the amount you're required to withdraw. This is based on the account balance at the end of the prior year and your life expectancy factor, as determined by the IRS (you can find yours at www.irs.gov). Essentially, you're dividing your account balance by your life expectancy factor. One thing to note: There are three tables of life expectancy factors used by the IRS. The first is for account beneficiaries, the second is for account owners who have a spouse more than 10 years younger than they are, and the third is for singles and account owners with a spouse less than 10 years younger than they are.

► An Example

Let's take Richard. Say that on December 31 of the year before he turns 70½, he has $500,000 remaining in his 401(k). His wife, Sally, is 65. According to the IRS, Richard's life expectancy factor is 27.4. That means that his minimum distribution for this year is $18,248.18.

Q: I have a lot saved for retirement, but I don't need the money right now. Is there any harm in waiting to take distributions?
A: Not really. You have two risks. The first is that by leaving the money invested, you could potentially lose principal. But you can solve that problem by making sure you move any money you could potentially need in the next five years into safe havens within your retirement accounts (an exercise you should repeat annually, by the way). The other risk is that you'll delay living. It's a tricky balance between making your money last until the end and not pinching pennies throughout retirement only to wind up with millions on your deathbed. You want to enjoy life, and if you have the money to do that without tapping your retirement fund, then so be it. But if you're passing up vacations or other enjoyable experiences because you have the money but don't want to spend it, you may regret that later on. Consider your priorities carefully.

87. How do I roll over a 401(k)?

A: First, good for you for asking. Too many people—almost 50%!—choose to cash out their 401(k) when they leave a job, then blow the money and set themselves back years when it comes to saving for retirement. I did it myself, in fact, after I left my first job back in my early twenties. It's a huge mistake, because not only are you spending money that should be earmarked for retirement but also you're losing a lot of it (20% to 30%, depending on your income) in taxes. Add that to the 10% penalty you'll pay for pulling out of the plan early if you're younger than 59½, and you've lost nearly half your money to the government. Ouch!

When you leave a job you have these better options:

1. Leave your money in your former employer's plan. Some companies will allow you to leave your money in its 401(k) plan even though you no longer work there. You typically must have $1,000 to $5,000, minimum, in the plan for this to be an option. If you like your investment options, and the fee structure is palatable, this is a fine choice.
2. Move the money to your new employer's plan. Again, this option hinges on the investment options offered. If you like them, this move can make your life easier administratively, particularly if you'll be contributing new money to this new employer's plan.
3. Roll the 401(k) into an IRA. This will give you more investment options, because IRAs tend to offer more flexibility than company-sponsored plans. Also, administratively, rollovers simplify life. Think about it this way: Over the course of your career, you're likely to have 12 different jobs. If you had 12 different 401(k)s with 12 different employers, your head would spin from all the paperwork (or if you've automated, all the e-mails). And keeping your asset allocation in line across all those accounts would be next to impossible. Rolling all the 401(k)s into a single IRA, however, streamlines your investments.

Rolling over is a simple process. It starts with sitting down with human resources or the plan administrator at your former job. They'll have you fill out some paperwork, and then you can have them cut a check in the amount of your account balance and send it to an IRA account you've opened with a brokerage firm or bank. To select the home for the IRA, look at the administrative fees for the account. They can be as much as $50 a year, but most banks will waive them if you reach a certain account balance, so it pays to shop around. And, if you plan on actively trading stocks in your account, look at trading costs as well. They average about 4% or 5% of the amount you trade at full-service brokerage firms and $7 to $20 at discounters.

An important note: When you pull the trigger on the rollover, you want to make sure that the company doesn't cut the check to you personally. If they do, it will be treated for tax purposes as income, as if you cashed out. If you take possession of the check, you'll also have only 60 days to deposit it into an IRA—if you miss the deadline, you'll be hit with a 10% early withdrawal penalty.

THE STATS

- **45%:** The percentage of 401(k) participants who cash out when they leave a job
- **32%:** The percentage who leave the money in their current 401(k)
- **23%:** The percentage who roll the funds over into an IRA or other retirement plan

THE MATH

How much damage can you do by cashing out your 401(k)? Lots!

Take a 35-year-old in the 28% tax bracket who expects to retire at age 65.

- His 401(k) balance is $50,000.
- If he cashes out, he'll net $31,000.
- If he rolls the money into an IRA and invests it at 8%, at retirement he will have $546,786

The difference: $515,786

Q: As part of my compensation package, I have employer stock. Can I roll that over as well?
A: You can, but you probably don't want to. This is, in fact, the major

caveat when it comes to rolling over your 401(k): Company stock gets special tax treatment under the employer-sponsored plan. Luckily, you can roll a portion of your 401(k) over and leave the company stock behind. Here's how it works:

Say you were given $10,000 worth of company stock, and it's now worth twice as much. If you roll that $20,000 worth of stock into an IRA, when you withdraw the money down the road, it'll be taxed as ordinary income and you can lose up to 35%. But leave it in the 401(k) and only the original investment—$10,000— will be taxed as ordinary income when you take distributions. The rest won't be taxed until the stock is sold, and then only at a long-term capital gains tax of 15%.

That can mean big savings. In this example, the employee would eventually pay $7,000 by rolling the company stock into an IRA. If the employee keeps it in the 401(k) plan, the tax will only pay $5,000 in taxes, a savings of $2,000. This math assumes that the employee is taxed at the highest rate of 35%. The more the stock grows, the more the employee saves.

Q: **I'm changing jobs. I want to roll over my 401(k), but I was told that I can't keep my employer's contributions. Why not?**

A: Many employers require you to remain with the company for a specific length of time to be eligible to take matching dollars with you when you leave (this is called vesting). If you don't meet that threshold, you can roll over the money you've contributed out of your own paycheck, but you're going to leave behind any contributions made by your employer.

Nearly half (44%, according to a 2007 study by Hewitt Associates) of companies offer immediate vesting to their employees, but that means that more than half don't. Commonly, companies will offer graded vesting over five years, which means if you leave after one year, you'll get to keep 20% of their contributions; after two, you'll keep 40%; and so on. At other companies, you're vested after three years—leave before, and you'll get nothing from their end, but stick it out and you can keep it all. If you can, it often pays to hang around, but you have to weigh a variety of variables, including your own happiness, your career, and your salary. In some cases, a bump in compensation is enough to make up the difference.

88. My employer is going to stop or reduce matching my 401(k) contributions. What do I do?

A: Unfortunately, many companies can no longer afford their matching programs in the current economy. Some are cutting back on contributions, others are eliminating them altogether.

That doesn't mean you should stop contributing. As you know, your 401(k)—with its annual cap on contributions of $16,500 for 2009—allows you to kick in about three times the money you can put into any sort of IRA. That makes it a valuable asset as you prepare for retirement. Instead, look into the following.

- **Your investment choices.** Some 401(k)s offer a wide menu of terrific, low-cost investment options. Others pale by comparison. Meager choices matter less when your employer is offering you an instantaneous return on your investment in the form of a company match. When that match goes away, however, choices matter more. If you have never liked your choices, take the first $5,000 off the table ($6,000 if you're older than 50) and contribute that money to an IRA or Roth IRA instead. See "I have nothing set aside for my retirement. Where should I start?" on page 282 to figure out which is right for you. Put any the difference between that $5,000 (or $6,000) and the rest of your retirement-designated funds into your 401(k) and pick the best of the options on your limited menu.
- **Contributing more.** Chances are you've run some scenarios on your retirement. You've figured out how much money you need to make your retirement work—and you've figured matching dollars into those equations. (If you haven't run your retirement numbers, you can get started on page 307 with "How much do I need to set aside for retirement?") If your employer is no longer contributing, making that retirement date will require increased savings.

I Also Need to Know . . .

Q: Any ideas for finding the money to increase my contribution?
A: Sure. Unless you can take on a part-time job or work overtime,

you're going to have to find the money in your own wallet, so to speak. Comb over your expenses and see where you can cut back. When you come to something that's discretionary—for example, you enjoy having cable television but you can live without it—think about whether you can eliminate that expense or, failing that, cut back on it. If you really want the cable, maybe you keep it but cancel HBO. The goal is to cut as much fat as possible by making conscious choices that allow you to keep the things that matter most in your life while eliminating those that are not so meaningful but often expensive.

THE MATH

If you make $45,000 a year and save 10% of your salary in your 401(k), that's $4,500 a year. Let's say your employer usually matches half, but after some financial trouble, no dice. Want to make up that $2,225 on your own? Here's how to get it done:

- **Bring your lunch to work just twice a week**
  - *Found money:* $13/week
  - *In the pot:* $676/year

- **Clip coupons for the grocery store**
  - *Found money:* $10/week
  - *In the pot:* $520/year

- **Cancel your landline phone service—you have a cell, right?**
  - *Found money:* $45/month
  - *In the pot:* $540/year

- **Dine out one less time each month**
  - *Found money:* $50 or more a month
  - *In the pot:* $600/year

Total: $2,336

Q: Do I pay taxes on the money my employer contributes to my 401(k)?

A: With a 401(k), all contributions grow tax deferred, whether they come from you or from your employer. You'll pay taxes when you withdraw the money in retirement.

89. I have accepted early retirement benefits from my employer. These benefits include a lump-sum retirement distribution. What should I do with the money?

A: Nothing, until you read this answer. Even then, I want you to move slowly. You don't want to make a rash decision, as this money likely represents a big chunk of your retirement. And once it's gone, you can't get it back.

Lump-sum retirement payouts are a more frequent occurrence these days, largely because of the economy. It's overwhelming, handling a check that big, particularly when all or part of your standard of living in retirement is riding on it. To start, I'd put the money in an FDIC-insured savings or money market account. If you're looking at more than $250,000 (the current limit on FDIC insurance), put it in two or three or more accounts at different banks so that you don't run afoul of those limits. FDIC insurance is important because it protects your money in case of a bank failure.

Then it's time to plan. You need to answer some important questions:

- What does this money represent in terms of your retirement nest egg? Is this it? Will you continue to work and add to it?
- How much will you need each year to live in retirement? How much of that money will come from this nest egg and how much from other sources such as Social Security?
- How much do you need this money to grow to satisfy your retirement needs?

These are complicated questions with complicated answers, which is why I want you to talk to a financial advisor. If you don't already have a financial advisor, hire one, even if it's just on a temporary basis. For advice on how to do that, see "I'd like to hire a financial advisor, but after all the frauds in the news recently, I'm nervous. Can you help?" on page 37. An advisor will be able to look at your whole financial picture, including your assets, such as retirement funds and other savings accounts, and your liabilities, such as a mortgage, and determine how the money can best be put to use.

One option an advisor might suggest is an immediate annuity, which provides an infinite stream of income. For people used to receiving a paycheck, I recommend using part, not all, of that lump-sum payout to buy yourself a stream of income that's guaranteed to last for the rest of your life. An immediate annuity works best when you use the annuity payouts in combination with Social Security benefits to cover fixed expenses—housing, food, utilities, transportation—then invest the remainder of the lump sum so it can continue to grow. For more on this subject, see "What is an annuity?" on page 294.

Bottom line: Give yourself plenty of time to process your decisions, think about the best way to put it to use, and talk over your options with an expert. Whatever you decide to do, have a detailed plan in place before you act.

90. How much do I need to set aside for retirement?

A: If only there were an easy answer to that question, more people would be able to reach their retirement savings goals. For many, pinpointing a number seems so complicated, and they'd rather sit back and do nothing or pull a goal out of thin air.

But that's a huge mistake. If you don't calculate how much you'll likely need in retirement, chances are you're not going to get anywhere close. A recent study by Hewitt Associates projected that fewer than one in five—one in five!—workers are saving enough to meet their retirement needs.

We're living longer than past generations did, so we need more money at our fingertips than ever before. Financial advisors used to have people strive to replace 75% to 80% of their income in retirement. Now that's not nearly enough, especially if you want to travel extensively or don't have adequate medical coverage. The Hewitt study suggests that men need to replace 123% of their final salaries and women need to reach 130%. That's per year—so if your final salary is $100,000, you should strive to replace $123,000 a year if you're a man or $130,000 a year if you're a woman.

You may find those numbers out of reach, but that doesn't mean you shouldn't try to get close. Shoot for replacing 100% of your income, and if you end up with more, great.

To ballpark how much you need to save, figure out how much you'll get from the SSA. You can do that by estimating your benefit with the calculator at www.ssa.gov (choose the option that allows you to see your monthly benefit in inflated dollars). You'll notice that the longer you put off taking your benefits, the more you get per month. For more on why that is, and how you can work it to your advantage, turn to "When should I begin to collect my Social Security benefits?" on page 314.

Once you have an estimate of your Social Security benefits, fill out the Ballpark E$timate worksheet below, from the American Savings Education Council.* If you're married, each partner should fill out a separate version. Be sure to understand that this figure is just an estimate, and if you fall way short, you can always work a little longer, invest more aggressively, or put off collecting Social Security benefits for a few years.

BALLPARK E$TIMATE WORKSHEET

1. How much annual income will you want in retirement?
(Tip: You'll need at least 70% of your current gross income to maintain your standard of living. If you want to travel or you need to cover your medical insurance, aim for 90%. If you need to cover all of your health-care costs, want a lifestyle that is more than comfortable, and need to save for long-term care, aim for 100% to 130%.)
2. Subtract the income you expect to receive annually from:
Social Security benefits $ _____
(Tip: If you make less than $25,000, enter $8,000; $25,000 to

* The Ballpark E$timate worksheet was developed by the American Savings Education Council and the Employee Benefit Research Institute, and is a registered trademark of EBRI. Further details can be found at www.choosetosave .org. Used with permission.

40,000, enter $12,000; and more than $40,000, enter $14,500. Note for married couples: The lower earner should enter the higher of either the lower-earner's own income or 50% of the spouse's benefit.)

Traditional employer pension: $ _____
Part-time income: $_____
Other: $ _____
=$ _____

This is how much you need to make up for each year in retirement.

3. To find out how much you actually need in the bank when you retire, multiply the amount above by the factor below:

Age You Expect to Retire	Choose Your Factor on the Basis of Life Expectancy (at Age 65)					
	Male, 50th Percentile (Age 82)	Female, 50th Percentile (Age 86)	Male, 75th Percentile (Age 89)	Female, 75th Percentile (Age 92)	Male, 90th Percentile (Age 94)	Female, 90th Percentile (Age 97)
55	18.79	20.53	21.71	22.79	23.46	24.40
60	16.31	18.32	19.68	20.93	21.71	22.79
65	13.45	15.77	17.35	18.79	19.68	20.93
70	10.15	12.83	14.65	16.31	17.35	18.79

Note: This assumes a real rate of return of 3% after inflation and that you'll begin to take Social Security benefits at age 65.

$ _____

4. If you expect to retire before age 65, multiply your Social Security benefits from part 2 by the factor below:
   At 55, your factor is 8.8
   At 60, your factor is 5.7
   +$ _____

5. Multiply your savings to date by the factor below (including the money you've stashed in a 401(k), IRA, or other retirement plan):
   If you plan to retire in
   10 years, your factor is 1.3
   15 years, 1.6
   20 years, 1.8
   30 years, 2.4

35 years, 2.8
40 years, 3.3
–$ _____
Total additional savings needed at retirement: $ _____

I Also Need to Know . . .

Q: Why do women need to replace more income than men?

A: Women live an average of seven years longer than men, they are paid less throughout the course of their career—about 81 cents for every dollar a man makes—and they often don't take as much risk in their investments as men do. Add to that the fact that many women leave work for extended periods of time to have children and care for their parents. In the end, women have to work harder to save for retirement.

Q: What if I'm not on track to have enough?

A: Well, for starters, you're certainly not alone, as I said earlier. But that doesn't mean that you shouldn't do all you can to try to catch up. My first tip may sound too simple, but the best way to make up for lost time is to save more. Pinch your pennies, cut out extras, and put that money into your retirement accounts. Understand that you can spend $100 on a pair of shoes or you can instead allow that money to grow tax free in an IRA. Those pumps may look snazzy as you're trotting about town today, but down the road, that $100 could grow enough to pay a year's worth of gas or water bills.

Here are a few more ways to make up for lost time:

- **Work a little longer.** Putting in a few more years of 9 to 5 can have a huge effect on the balance in your retirement fund. If you can delay taking Social Security benefits as well, you'll be even better off.
- **Plan to pick up a part-time job.** You might find that once you're retired, having all that time on your hands isn't all it was cracked up to be. If that's the case—or you need some extra cash—why not find some part-time work you enjoy? Look for something you've always wanted to do, so it's more hobby and less chore.

- **Scale back.** Maybe your dream is to travel a few times a year. Instead you limit yourself to twice a year to save a little extra cash. You can still do the things you want to do, just do them less frequently or find other ways to loosen up your budget.
- **Bank your windfalls.** The average annual individual tax refund is more than $2,000 a year. If you put that money into an IRA every year, it would go a long way toward supplementing your retirement funds. Ditto for holiday bonuses, birthday checks, or the money you free up when you pay off your car and have an extra $300 or $400 a month.

Q: **Are the retirement calculators on the Internet legitimate?**

A: As always, it depends on which site you're visiting, but most personal finance magazines and financial institutions offer a version. If you stick to well-known and well-respected sites, you'll be able to generate a good estimate like the one above. In fact, I like to see people use a few different calculators to come up with a consensus estimate, so to speak, of what they need to save.

91. How do I make my retirement funds last as long as I do?

A: This question tops everyone's list when it comes to retirement. We're all living longer these days, and unexpectedly cruising by age 85 or 90 can have you struggling to make ends meet during your final years. There are a few things you can do to budget your way through retirement so that you're covered until the end.

- **Know what you're aiming for.** You can use a calculator on the Internet to figure out your life expectancy (I like this one, from Wharton: gosset.wharton.upenn.edu/mortality/) or you can just play it safe and plan on living to be 90 or 95. If you have a strong family history of longevity, plan to be 100. If your family is prone to disease, go slightly shorter. When in doubt, however, it's best to overshoot by a year or two.
- **Withdraw like a skinflint.** In general, you can withdraw 4% of your retirement savings each year and know your money should last as long as you do. That 4%, however, is a

moving target. If the market is down and your accounts are down as a result, your 4% this year will be less than it was last year. If the market is up and your accounts are similarly up, your 4% will be heftier.
· **Give yourself a checkup.** Even if you're adhering to the 4% rule, every couple of years take a look at where your portfolio stands and whether you're on the right track. You can use the Ballpark E$timate once again, or T. Rowe Price has a helpful tool on its Web site, at www3.troweprice.com/ric/RIC/.

Immediate annuities, that will take some of your money and return it to you in a guaranteed stream of income. For more on this, see "What is an annuity?" on page 294.

I Also Need to Know . . .

Q: Is it possible to save too much for retirement?
A: People always say you can never save too much, but that's most likely because the majority of Americans aren't in danger of saving too much. Most Americans save way too little. But you can, in fact, be too conservative when it comes to retirement. If you funnel every last cent into savings for the majority of your working life, you're probably going to miss out on meaningful experiences, such as family vacations. You don't want to shortchange the present for the future. Second, your retirement should be an enjoyable time, but the idea isn't to make it to the end with hundreds of thousands of dollars left over, only to look back and wish you'd taken that cruise when you had the chance. It's all about balance. Remember, as you age, you're likely to get less and less mobile, which makes hiking in Tuscany a reach.

Q: Should I continue investing in the market up until the day I retire?
A: Yes. Unless you have more than enough to sustain you, you need the growth of the market to keep you ahead of taxes and inflation. In general, you'll want to reduce your exposure to the market by 1 percentage point for each year you age. So, while at age 55 you'd want to have 45% of your assets in a diversified stock

portfolio, when you hit 65 that number drops to 35%, and at 75, you should be at 25%.

THE STATS

- **24%:** The amount by which Americans entering retirement will have to reduce their standard of living if they don't want to outlive their money.
- **$60,000:** The typical balance in the retirement plan of a 55-year-old.
- **$229:** The typical monthly retirement contribution that a 55-year-old makes.
- **70%:** The percentage of older workers who are planning to work in their retirement years.

92. Where should I live when I retire?

A: We spend a lot of time saving for retirement. We crunch the numbers to see how much we're going to need, and we put strategies in motion to make sure that money lasts as long as we do. Where we live plays a big role in that equation. One way to be sure that your money lasts a longer period of time is to move somewhere less expensive.

You need to start this quest with a little soul searching. Are you thinking of a tropical paradise or of a small town instead? Do you want a condo in a retirement community? Do you want to be near your family? What do you plan to do in your retirement? If you want to volunteer, take classes, or even work, you need to look at an area that would support those opportunities.

Once you figure out what kind of atmosphere you're looking for, think about your cash flow. Life expectancies are going up, which means that your money needs to last longer, which means that you need to spend less, save more, or work longer. More than ever, there's pressure to stay within your budget, because the last thing you want is to be overextended financially. Make sure you evaluate not only the cost of the home you buy or rent but also maintenance, taxes, and the cost of living in that area. (For more on how to make these estimates, turn to "I'm considering buying a home in a new area. Is there a way to estimate how much it will cost me to live there?" on page 200.)

Finally, think long term. You want to consider whether there is a good hospital nearby, and if there is a public transportation system that can get you around if you're no longer able to drive. Spend a week—or better yet a summer (rent something)—in the town or city to see what activities are available and what the other residents are like in terms of age and interests.

I Also Need to Know . . .

Q: I've heard that I should pick a state that doesn't have income tax. Is that true?

A: Don't base your entire decision on income taxes, but it is a factor to consider. Although many retirees opt for no-income-tax states, nothing in life is free. Many of these places charge higher property taxes, so that's something to look into if you buy, and sales taxes are often higher as well.

Q: What should I look for in the home itself?

A: You want to make sure you can afford it. But beyond that, look for features that could accommodate you as you age. You may be able to get around just fine now—I know plenty of people in their sixties who still go the gym daily— but you need a home that will support you when that's no longer possible. That means gravitating toward single-level houses and apartments. You should also look for wide doorways that will accommodate a wheelchair, should you ever need one, and bathrooms that will allow you to install handrails and a larger shower stall with a seat, if need be. The rooms should be small enough and laid out in a way that you can get from place to place easily.

93. When should I begin to collect my Social Security benefits?

A: You can start collecting anytime after age 62—but that's not necessarily when you should. In fact, there is no magical age when it comes to tapping Social Security, but there's one thing you need to keep in mind: The longer you wait to take your benefits, the more your monthly check will be.

For each year you delay collecting, the Social Security formula increases the amount of your payments by about 8%. On top of that, the amount is also adjusted yearly for inflation. That means you could feasibly get a 9%, 10%, or even 11% increase for each year you wait.

Here's what that difference looks like:

| BIRTH YEAR | BENEFIT AT AGE 62 | | BENEFIT AT AGE 66 OR 67 | | BENEFIT AT AGE 70 | |
	TODAY	ADJUSTED FOR INFLATION	TODAY	ADJUSTED FOR INFLATION	TODAY	ADJUSTED FOR INFLATION
1946	$993	$993	$1,368	$1,576	$1,905	$2,494
1956	$1,126	$1,582	$1,587	$2,503	$2,121	$3,795
1966	$1,171	$2,382	$1,712	$4,030	$2,151	$5,570

Benefits are based on a $50,000 annual salary at retirement.

Bottom line: If you can hold off until you reach full retirement age at 66 or 67 (depending on when you were born), great. Wait until you're 70, and that's even better. In fact, quick math reveals that depending on how your retirement accounts are allocated, you may be well advised to spend down your own investments before tapping into Social Security benefits, because few investments can be counted on to provide a yearly guaranteed return that large.

THE STATS

- **$1,089:** The average monthly benefit for a retired worker, as of November 2008
- **$536:** The average monthly spousal benefit, as of November 2008.

I Also Need to Know . . .

Q: **How are my benefits calculated?**

A: The amount you receive from the SSA is based on the earnings throughout your time in the workforce. First, the administration adjusts the earnings to account for changes in average wages over time, and then it averages your 35 highest-earning years. This is why if you retire early after working only from ages 22 to 50, for example, your Social Security benefits may decrease because you only worked 28 years, not 35. Those seven years when not bringing in a paycheck will be factored in as zero income, dragging your overall average down.

Q: **If I start collecting Social Security benefits at 62, will that affect my spouse's benefit amount as well?**

A: It will. Your spouse will see even more of a reduction in benefits than you will if you begin collecting at 62. He or she could lose up to 35%, or $175 from a $500 monthly check. Check out the chart below, from the SSA, that shows what a $500 spousal benefit would be reduced to if the retiree takes benefits at age 62 instead of at full retirement age:

RETIREE'S BIRTH YEAR	FULL RETIREMENT AGE	SPOUSE'S MONTHLY BENEFIT	PERCENTAGE OF REDUCTION
1946	66 years	$350	29.17%
1956	66 years 4 months	$341	31.67%
1966	67 years	$325	35.00%

Q: **I've heard that if I started taking Social Security benefits early, I can have a do-over. How does that work?**

A: This is called double-dipping. Essentially, if you jumped the gun and started taking your benefits at age 62—as many people do— you can file a form 521 now (or after you hit full retirement age) and pay those benefits back, no interest required. You'll then be eligible to receive the larger benefit as if you'd been waiting all along.

There are, however, a few things you need to know. For starters, timing matters. If you take early benefits at 62 and pay them back at 70, you're going to increase your standard of living far more than if you took the benefits at 62 and paid them back at 76. Why? Because your life expectancy at age 76 is going to be shorter. So you'll receive the bigger payments for a shorter period of time. Not only that, but the longer you wait to file the 521, the more money you'll have to pay back. So you want to aim to pay the money back by age 70, if you can.

Also, it's important to note that this takes a lot of foresight. The key to making it work is having the money in pocket to pay back. Some people see double dipping as a strategy. They take the money starting at age 62, stash it where it will earn some interest for the next seven or eight years, and then pay it back. It's an interest-free loan from the government, more or less, and it's made even more attractive by the fact that the amount you pay back isn't even adjusted for inflation. But if you end up squandering the money or losing it in a risky investment, you're stuck with the lower benefit for life. You have to plan well and have another source of income you can draw on in the meantime—a retirement account or part-time job.

Last, there is always the chance that the government will eliminate this loophole in the Social Security system, sticking you with the lower payout, though it doesn't seem likely. When I called the SSA, I was told that the agency is very willing to accept 521 forms.

THE MATH

Let's take the retiree from the chart on page 315.

He had a final annual salary of $50,000. He elects to take the $993 a month starting at age 62. According to the SSA, his life expectancy is about 19 more years. Over those years, he'll collect a total of $226,404.

Now, if he pays back his benefits at age 70 ($95,328) and begins taking the adjusted monthly amount of $2,494 instead, he'll collect $329,208 during his remaining 11 years.

He comes out $102,804 ahead if his life expectancy remains the same.

But these days, more and more people are outliving their life expectancies by 5, 10, and even 15 years. If he lives just another 5 years, add $149,640 to his pot. Another 10, and you can multiply that by two for a total of $533,160 collected from the SSA. Had he continued to take the $993 and lived this long, he'd have only taken $345,564 in benefits.

94. How do I earn money in retirement without losing Social Security benefits?

A: If you're under full retirement age—which, according to the age stipulated by the SSA, will be set for the next 18 years or so at age 66—$1 will be deducted from your benefit for every $2 you earn above the annual limit. In 2009 and 2010, that bar is set at $14,160. Note that the SSA looks at your gross, not net, wages when making these calculations, which means your full salary, before deductions for taxes, insurance, and 401(k) contributions.

This calculation is where it starts to get a bit complicated. The rules change when you enter the year that you will reach full retirement age (January 1 of the year you turn 66.) At that point, you can earn more, up to $37,680 for 2009 and 2010. Above that amount, $1 will be deducted from your benefits for every $3 you earn.

Once you turn 66, you will begin to get your benefits regardless of your earnings. From that point on, you can earn as much as you want and your Social Security benefits will remain the same.

▶ Example 1

Let's say your birthday is in September and you'll be 66. You earn a salary of $60,000 a year, which is $5,000 a month. You'll earn $40,000 from January through August, and your Social Security benefits should be $1,400 a month. You'll receive $773 less this year because your income from work during the months that you are still younger than full retirement age is $2,320 over the annual limit.

▶ Example 2

You're 64, earning the same salary of $60,000 per year. Because you're earning $45,840 over the annual limit of $14,160, your benefit is wiped out. You would have to earn less than $28,000 to earn any benefit whatsoever.

Unfortunately, there is no way to get around losing a portion of your benefit if you're still earning decent money under age 66. But my advice to you, if you'd like to continue to work, is to delay taking your benefit, if at all possible. Not only does your benefit see a hefty increase for each year you put off taking it until you reach age 70, but also, if you're going to be losing a portion—or even all—of your money anyway, you're better off waiting. You can read more about the advantages of delaying your Social Security benefits on page 314 in response to the question "When should I begin to collect my Social Security benefits?"

I Also Need to Know . . .

Q: **What if I retire in the middle of the year?**

A: If you retire in the middle of the year, a monthly income threshold replaces the annual limits. In 2009, the monthly limit is $1,180 (the yearly limit, $14,160, divided by 12). You can receive full benefits in any month that you do not earn more than that, regardless of how much you earn the rest of the year.

Q: **What income counts toward those totals?**

A: Any income you earn from work or self-employment will count against your Social Security benefits if you're younger than 66. But investment income, such as IRA or 401(k) distributions, interest, pension, and inheritances, won't be included. These are considered "nonwork" sources of income and they don't affect your Social Security benefits.

95. How do I transition into Medicare?

A: If you're already receiving Social Security benefits, you'll be enrolled in Medicare when you turn 65. You don't need to do a thing, except watch the mail for your Medicare card, which should come about three months before your birthday.

If you haven't tapped into your Social Security benefits, you need to apply for Medicare by calling 800-772-1213. If you want to apply for both at the same time, you can do that online at www.socialsecurity.gov/applytoretire.

Note: Your full retirement age in the eyes of the SSA isn't until age 66, but you'll still be eligible for Medicare at 65 as long as you've paid into the Social Security system for at least 10 years or you are eligible to receive benefits because of your spouse's earnings. (This is a requirement of Medicare at any age, not just 65.)

Once you're enrolled, of course, you need to navigate the system. Medicare has four parts:

- **Part A:** This is hospital insurance that helps cover inpatient care in hospitals, as well as nursing facilities, hospice, and home health care. It does not, however, cover long-term care if you end up in a nursing home. You typically will not pay a premium for this coverage, as long as you or your spouse paid Medicare taxes while you were working. If you didn't, you can usually buy part A coverage. In 2009, the premium is up to $443 a month, and in most cases, you will also have to purchase part B.
- **Part B:** This is medical insurance for doctors' visits, outpatient care, and preventive care. You will pay a monthly premium for this service, $96.40 in 2009. (If your income is above $85,000 as a single filer or $170,000 as a joint filer, your premium will be higher. The amount increases with your income, with the highest premium at $308.30 for single filers who make more than $213,000 and joint filers who earn more than $426,000.) There is also an annual deductible of $135 in 2009, and you will typically pay 20% of the cost of whatever service you receive upfront.
- **Part C:** The Medicare Advantage Plans of part C are like HMOs and are run by private health insurance companies. They include a combination of parts A and B, and often D. The cost will vary depending on the individual provider, and you must have parts A and B to join. You will have a network of doctors and hospitals to choose from.
- **Part D:** Prescription drug coverage, which defrays the cost of prescriptions. This part is a rider to parts A and/or B—you can't get it alone. You'll pay a monthly premium, a deductible, and copayments, all of which vary by plan.

So how do you know what you need? The first step is deciding whether you want what's called Original Medicare, which can include part A or B, or a Medicare Advantage Plan, which includes the services of A and B and is provided by a private insurer. Compare the costs and the coverage and remember that under Original Medicare, you'll have your choice of doctors and hospitals, while under a Medicare Advantage Plan, that option will be limited to your particular plan's network.

Then you must decide if you want prescription drug coverage, and believe me, you do. If you've chosen a Medicare Advantage Plan, you can get it through your provider, and if you've gone with Original Medicare, you can join Part D.

Medicare has a helpful tool on its Web site that can help you compare plans. Go to www.medicare.gov and then click on "Compare Health Plans and Medigap Policies in Your Area" or "Compare Medicare Prescription Drug Plans." You can also get free counseling through your State Health Insurance Counseling and Assistance Program. Find yours on Medicare's Web site at www.medicare.gov/contacts/staticpages/ships.aspx.

I Also Need to Know . . .

Q: What isn't covered under parts A and B?
A: You can find a full list on Medicare's Web site, but here is a sampling:

- Chiropractic services
- Dental care and dentures
- Eye exams and glasses
- Hearing exams and aids
- Insulin
- Yearly physicals (a one-time physical is covered)
- Foot care

To fill in all or some of those gaps, you can purchase what's called a Medigap policy, which are sold by private insurers. It's an extra expense, but it will help cover the services that Medicare won't, plus a portion of your copayments and deductibles. You'll pay separate monthly premiums—one for part B and one for the Medigap coverage. If you think you need a Medigap policy, you should buy one during the first six months after you turn 65 and enroll in Medicare. After that, your ability to buy gap coverage is often limited. For more information about Medigap policies, see www.medicare.gov/medigap/Default.asp.

Note: You don't need a Medigap policy if you are enrolled in an advantage plan (part C).

Q: **My employer is one of the few still providing coverage after retirement. Do I need Medicare? And what if those benefits go away sometime in the future—can I join then?**

A: Check with your employer's human resources department to find out exactly how the company's coverage plays into Medicare, but in general, health insurance through your former employer is treated as secondary. In other words, it fills in the gaps left by your Medicare coverage. In most cases, you'll probably want Medicare parts A and B, and then your private health insurance will most likely cover prescription drugs and anything else.

If your benefits are canceled, you have the right to enroll in part C or part D. You must do so within two months of cancellation of coverage from your former employer. One other thing to keep in mind: If your benefits are canceled and you don't already have part B, you'll have to wait until the next general enrollment period to sign up. This period occurs in the first quarter of each year, and your coverage won't start until July. To avoid gaps in your retiree benefits—particularly if you anticipate changes—get a jump on things so that you don't experience a lapse in coverage.

Q: **I can't afford Medicare's prescription drug coverage. Do I have any options?**

A: Yes. There are federal programs to assist you, provided you fall under the income limitations to qualify.

FEDERAL LIMITS IN 2009

- **Single:** Your 2008 income must have been less than $15,600 and your assets (investments and balances of savings and checking accounts) must be less than $11,990.
- **Married and living together:** Your 2008 income must be less than $21,000 and your assets must be less than $23,970.

Once you qualify, you have to join part D, and then you'll receive assistance to meet the premium, help meeting your yearly deductible, and a reduction in coinsurance and copayments.

Aside from this assistance, your state will also offer what's called a Medicare Savings Program. These programs vary by state, but in general, they will help you pay your premiums and in some cases, your deductibles and coinsurance. To qualify, you must be enrolled in part A and meet income limitations.

LIMITS FOR MEDICARE SAVINGS PROGRAMS IN 2009

- **Single:** Your monthly income must be less than $1,190 and your assets must be less than $4,000.
- **Married and living together:** Monthly income must be less than $1,595 and your assets must be less than $6,000.

To find out information on your state's program, you can call your state's Medicaid office. You can also find links to the Web sites for many states' Medicare Savings Programs at www.medicare.gov/contacts/staticpages/msps.aspx.

96. How long will I live?

A: That is the million-dollar question. (Along with its all important codicil: Will my money last as long as I do?) There are all kinds of life-expectancy calculators out there—do an online search on the words *life-expectancy calculators* and you'll see what I mean—but how accurate are they and how should they factor into your retirement planning?

What most of these calculators tell you is how long the average person with your demographic profile will live. The U.S. Census Bureau has life tables that tell you roughly the same thing. Unfortunately—or perhaps fortunately—you are not the average person. Basing your retirement solely on these numbers could leave you pinching pennies your whole life, only to have millions at your death, or running out of money well before you're ready to kick the bucket.

What do you do? Consider other factors as well. For starters, your health. If you're healthy—you don't smoke, you don't have high blood pressure, you exercise, you're within a normal weight range, and you practice good health habits on a regular basis (one glass of wine, not three)—you probably want to plan on living a little longer than the number that the calculator shows you. Your lifestyle choices are given a weight of about 75% in estimating your life expectancy.

Then consider your family history. Genetics is given a weight of about 25% in this estimation, and if you have a family history of cancer or other terminal illnesses, you should take that into consideration. That family history is far from a death sentence, but combined with your habits, it could mean that you don't have to plan to live quite as long.

Then, to make your money last, think about the other things that are going to play into how much money you need, because, believe it or not, it's not all about age. You also must consider where you plan to live, the cost of your living expenses, whether you'll work in retirement, and how much you'll withdraw each year. For more information, turn to page 311 and read the question "How do I make my retirement funds last as long as I do?"

AVERAGE LIFE EXPECTANCY AT BIRTH—U.S. CENSUS BUREAU			
YEAR	TOTAL	MALE	FEMALE
1970	70.8	67.1	74.7
1975	72.6	68.8	76.6
1980	73.7	70.0	77.4
1985	74.7	71.1	78.2
1990	75.4	71.8	78.8
1995	75.8	72.5	78.9
2000	77.0	74.3	79.7
2005	77.8	75.2	80.4
2010*	78.3	75.7	80.8
2015*	78.9	76.4	81.4
2020*	79.5	77.1	81.9

*Projections.

I Also Need to Know . . .

Q: Does my life expectancy change over time?

A: The twentieth century had the most dramatic increases in life expectancy of any century so far, and we haven't seen many changes yet in this century. But there are sure to be some, and it doesn't hurt to run your numbers every once in a while—every five years or so.

Q: Why do women live longer than men?

A: The big reason is that women seem to develop cardiovascular disease later in life than men. Typically, women develop heart disease in their seventies or eighties, while men tend to do so in their sixties or even fifties. There are other, more technical reasons that scientists have uncovered. But there are also these factors: More men than women smoke; men tend to take in more cholesterol through their diets than women do; and men's suicide attempts tend to be more successful than women's do.

Q: I didn't expect my parents to live this long, and they didn't either. Now I feel squeezed between their needs, my own retirement, and my kid's college expenses. What comes first?

A: This is increasingly a problem, and one that's even been given a name: You're a member of the sandwich generation, people squished between elderly parents and their own needs.

Here's my advice: Your parents need food. They need shelter, and the utilities to keep the lights on, the water flowing, and the heat or air conditioning pumping. They also need health care. If they can't meet these needs on their own, you—and your siblings—are going to have to lend a hand. If they have any assets you can sell—possibly downsizing to a smaller, less expensive home, getting rid of a car they no longer use, or draining bank accounts until they qualify for government assistance—that will help. You can also give them up to $13,000 in money or property per year without having to worry about the tax implications. If you can afford it, that is.

Once you have that taken care of, go back to focusing on your own retirement. As hard as this is to hear, your children come last, because there is financial aid for college and they will be able to borrow the money they need or apply for scholarships or grants to get some for free. You can't do that for retirement.

If that makes you squirm, think of it this way: Do you want your kids to have to take care of you one day the way you're taking care of your parents? Probably not. Putting your retirement needs first is doing them a favor in the long run.

One final note: If you're taking care of your parents financially, you could see a tax advantage. If you provide more than 50% of their support, you can claim them as a dependent, even if they live separately.

Resources

Associations and Organizations

Pension Rights Center
www.pensionrights.org
202-296-3776

The nation's only consumer organization dedicated exclusively to protecting and promoting American retirement security. The Web site features fact sheets on pension and retirement, links to reports related to pensions and retirement, information on the organization's public policy initiatives, and more.

Books

Buying a Second Home: Income, Getaway or Retirement, 2nd edition, by Craig Venezia (2009)

Tips and information on purchasing a second residence.

Kiplinger's Retire Worry-Free: Money-Smart Ways to Build the Nest Egg You'll Need, by the editors of *Kiplinger's Personal Finance* magazine (2008)

Tips and tools to teach you how to prepare financially for your retirement.

Nextville: Amazing Places to Live the Rest of Your Life, by Barbara Corcoran with Warren Berger (2008)

Information on the best places to retire, how to make smart real estate choices when relocating and how to find out what's most important to you when looking for the next place you'll live.

Retire in a Weekend, by Bill Losey (2007)

Losey answers the 10 most popular retirement questions in simple terms and also addresses the 5 main concerns individuals have about retirement.

The Savage Number: How Much Do You Need to Retire? by Terry Savage (2007)

Advice to help you determine the amount you need to retire; includes tips on how to control your finances, find reliable financial advice, protect your retirement fund, and set up an estate plan.

The Smartest 401(k) Book You'll Ever Read: Maximize Your Retirement Savings—The Smart Way! by Daniel R. Solin (2008)

Solin presents readers with comprehensive information on the most common deferred compensation plans, annuities, and other retirement investments while showing those in those plans how to create the best portfolio. Includes new rules for investing and retirement and information on how to determine your needs, gain control of your finances, avoid scams, and get income out of tax-deferred plans.

Social Security, Medicare & Government Pensions: Get the Most out of Your Retirement & Medical Pensions, by Joseph L. Matthews and Dorothy Matthews Berman (2008)

A guide to finding retirement benefits and figuring out the best time to claim them.

Spend 'Til the End: The Revolutionary Guide to Raising Your Living Standard—Today and When You Retire, by Larry Kotlikoff and Scott Burns (2008)

Draws on economic thought to abolish conventional retirement strategies and suggest that you might be saving *too much* for retirement, that you shouldn't take Social Security benefits until you turn 70, and more.

The Truth About Buying Annuities, by Steve Weisman (2008)

A guide to annuities with information and explanations of all types and advice on the impact they have on things such as Medicare, Medicaid, other retirement plans and long-term care.

Your Complete Retirement Planning Road Map: A Comprehensive Action Plan for Securing IRAs, 401(k)s, and Other Retirement Plans for Yourself and Your Family, by Ed Slott (2007)

Facts, checklists, and questionnaires to help you plan for your retirement.

Government Resources

Internal Revenue Service (IRS)
www.irs.gov
1-800-829-1040
Detailed information on taxes; calculate your life expectancy factor.

Social Security Administration (SSA)
www.ssa.gov
1-800-772-1213
Apply for Medicare, compare health plans, search for free counseling through your State Health Insurance Counseling and Assistance Program, and access the Social Security Retirement Planner, which includes tools to find your retirement age, a retirement estimator, a benefit calculator, information about Social Security programs, retirement options, retirement benefits, and more.

Retirement information from USA.gov
www.usa.gov/Topics/Seniors/Retirement.shtml
1-800-333-4636
General information on retirement, setting aside money, benefits, pensions, IRAs, and more.

U.S. Department of Labor (DOL)
www.dol.gov
1-866-444-3272
The DOL's online publication "Taking the Mystery Out of Retirement Planning," at www.dol.gov/ebsa/publications/nearretirement.html, features information specifically designed to help individuals who are approximately a decade away from retiring.

Web sites

401k.com
www.401k.com
Fidelity's 401(k) site featuring information on 401(k)s and several relevant calculators.

401khelpcenter.com
www.401khelpcenter.com
Detailed information on all aspects of 401(k)s.

AARP
www.aarp.org
1-888-687-2277
Recent retirement news, a retirement nest egg calculator, Social Security benefits estimator, a retirement income calculator, information on Medicare, and more.

A.M. Best Company
www.ambest.com
A worldwide information and insurance rating agency (the Web site has articles on retirement, but you have to purchase access to them).

Bloomberg.com
www.bloomberg.com/invest/calculators/retire.html
Use the company's retirement planner calculator to estimate what it will take to attain a secure retirement.

Choose to Save Ballpark E$timate
www.choosetosave.org/ballpark/index.cfm?fa=interactive
Choose to Save, a national public education and outreach program, offers the Ballpark E$timate worksheet to help you identify approximately how much you will need to retire.

CNNMoney.com
cgi.money.cnn.com/tools/retirementneed/retirementneed_plain.html
Visit CNNMoney.com to estimate how much you'll need to retire.

ESPlanner.com
www.esplanner.com
A different approach to financial planning that seeks out the highest standard of living you can maintain through time; for a fee, you can obtain the ESPlanner (the Economic Security Planner) financial planning software.

Insurance Information Institute
www.iii.org
212-346-5500
Facts, statistics, and answers to FAQs on annuities.

IRA Help
www.irahelp.com
1-800-663-1340
Informational retirement downloads and a free discussion forum where you can post your retirement questions.

Life calculator
gosset.wharton.upenn.edu/mortality/
Enter your health information to calculate an estimate of how long you will live.

Moody's
www.moodys.com
212-553-0300
Moody's is a publisher of financial strength ratings on insurance companies.

The Motley Fool
www.fool.com/retirement
Tips to prepare for retirement, advice on where to invest your money, information on how to estimate how long your savings will last, and more.

My Retirement Success
www.myretirementsuccess.com
1-866-786-2521
Many free resources, including a retirement newsletter, article archives, and more than 20 calculators to help you plan for retirement and other financial events.

RolloverSystems
www.rolloversystems.com
1-888-600-7655
An independent provider of rollover services, RolloverSystems will roll over your 401(k), 403(b), pension, or other employer-sponsored plan to an IRA for free. The company's Web site also features free retirement education and planning tools, including a glossary of retirement terms and answers to FAQs.

T. Rowe Price
www.troweprice.com
1-800-225-5132
You'll find retirement guides, investment tips, and financial tools

at this Web site. Use T. Rowe Price's free retirement income calculator to figure out how much you may have to spend each month while in retirement, to determine whether your savings will last throughout retirement, and identify actions you can take to avoid coming up short. The calculator can be found at www3.troweprice.com/ric/ric/public/ric.do.

CHAPTER 11

SAVING AND INVESTING

97. How much cash should I keep on hand in case of an emergency?

A: Some people say three months. Some say six. Some say three to six, and as unemployment soared in 2008 and 2009, I've even heard a year. I tend to think that in general, three months' worth of living expenses is enough for a two-income family. Single-income families should shoot for six. During an economic downturn, two-income families want to aim for six no matter what, and single or one-income families want to shoot for nine.

But let me be clear, because I know those amounts sound intimidating. When we are talking about your emergency cushion, we are talking not about the amount of money that you spend each month during good times. We're instead talking about the amount you'd need to cover basic living expenses. You need enough money to cover your mortgage or your rent, your food, your utilities, and your bills, but not enough to go the movies, buy a new pair of shoes, or go out to dinner. When you're in an emergency situation—you've lost your job or you have large medical bills—you're not going to be thinking about entertainment or the latest fashion trends.

For more on establishing your emergency cushion and where to find and then put the money, turn to "How do I create an emergency fund?" on page 333.

I Also Need to Know . . .

Q: **How much of my income should I be saving in total?**

A: As a general guide, aim for 10%. It helps to use an online calculator, particularly when it comes to saving for things such as retirement and college, which will help you run the numbers and get you a close approximation of where you need to be. And it's okay to start small and work your way up. Starting at all is half the battle.

Q: **Should I be keeping cash at home in case of a bank failure?**

A: When banks fail, your money is still protected by FDIC coverage, provided you stay under the limit of $250,000 per depositor. For more on the FDIC, turn to "What are the FDIC and SIPC? How do they protect my money?" on page 357.)

You no doubt remember when IndyMac failed in 2008. There was a great deal of news coverage, specifically with footage of people standing in line to pull out their money. This, in fact, was largely unnecessary—customers could still use ATMs, their debit cards still worked, and within a few days, they were able to transfer their accounts to another bank.

The best thing you can do to protect yourself against a bank failure is to spread your money around in advance, so that you stay under the FDIC limits by banking at a few different institutions.

That said, if you can't sleep at night without some money within your reach, go ahead and keep some cash at home. How much? Maybe a month's worth of living expenses, tops. Less— enough to get you through a week or two—is probably plenty. And keep it in a safe. (For more on safes, turn to "Which financial papers should I keep? Which should I toss? And on what timetable?" on page 58).

98. How do I create an emergency fund?

A: A little bit at a time. Unless you've been lucky enough to receive a windfall, you're going to have to establish your emergency cushion bit by bit. Your ultimate goal is to have three to six months' worth of living expenses, in cash, that you can draw on if and when you need it. But you can work your way there by socking away a little bit each pay period.

THE MATH

How much do you need in emergency funds? Probably not as much as you might think. Use this worksheet to find your goal:

Rent or mortgage:	$ _____
Car payment:	$ _____
Cost of bare-bones transportation (for job hunting, say, but not commuting):	$ _____
Food (not eating out):	$ _____
Health insurance (COBRA payment):	$ _____
Other insurance (home, auto, life):	$ _____
Utilities:	$ _____
Children's necessities:	$ _____
Total:	$ _____
×3 for two-income families:	$ _____
×6 for one-income families	$ _____

Q: **Where do I put the money?**

A: In a savings or money market account that pays a decent rate of interest, but not the same one I advised you to open in "How do I save for a goal?" on page 54. Why? Because you want to keep your emergency money separate. If you start blurring the line, your emergency fund could become your vacation fund, and all of a sudden, you're tan but back to square one when it comes to protecting yourself. Open a separate account for this money, and try to get a competitive interest rate (go to Bankrate.com) while still keeping the money safe and liquid. You need to be able to get at the money whenever you need it, which is why CDs are not as appropriate for your emergency cash as money market accounts.

Q: **I have great credit. Why can't I use my credit card or home equity loan in a pinch?**

A: You can, but you shouldn't. Staying out of debt is the point of an emergency fund. Unexpected expenses always pop up. Your car breaks down. The roof springs a leak. Your cat needs surgery. If you have savings, you can afford to write a check for these expenses. If you don't, they go on the card, and if you can't pay them off right away (and I mean that month, before interest starts to accrue), you could end up paying twice as much in the end. Don't believe me? Turn to "Which is more important, paying off my credit card debt or having money in the bank?" on page 164 for an eye-opening example.

On top of that, these days, you just can't rely on your lines of credit to be there tomorrow. Limits have been cut—often by $5,000, $10,000, even $20,000—and as a borrower, you don't have much in the way of recourse.

99. How do I teach my children to save money?

A: **Step 1.** Talk to them about money and savings. These days, with so much of our banking done electronically, it's more important than ever. Chances are, they never see you put checks in the bank, because your pay is directly deposited; they only see you pull cash out. And they may not see you pay bills if you do it online from the office or on the computer after they're in bed. The problem with all of these technological advances is that unless you explain things to them, your children may think that there's an unlimited source of funds behind that ATM wall. And that nobody has to pay bills, ever.

Step 2. Start an allowance. I'm a believer that all children should receive some form of an allowance on a regular basis.

You can't, though, just start passing out bills every week. An allowance needs to be prefaced with an explanation that you'll be giving them X number of dollars on a set schedule, and that this money is intended for Y period of time. The X and Y are up to you but dependent on each other.

When you start an allowance, you must decide that there are certain things you used to pay for that are now going on your children's tab. This list should be simple to start (candy, comic books) but should grow as they age. And as it grows, so should the amount of money. You can put saving money or giving to charity on the list too; you just have to give your children enough money to cover it. The trick is in the balance. You want to give them enough money to buy some—but not all—of the items on their list every week. If they want all of the items on the list, they have to progress to Step 3.

Step 3. Let them work to earn more. Unfortunately (and I have learned this lesson through experience), no money you give your children and no money they get for their birthdays or Christmas will mean as much to your children as money they earn themselves. Children aren't as eager to save your hard-earned money as they are theirs. When they are young, pay them to do things you might otherwise pay strangers to do (walk the dog, wash the car). And when they get older, encourage them to work outside the home. Students can excel at school and hold down a part-time job simultaneously.

Along the way, talk to your children about having goals. Little kids can save for something small at the dollar store; older kids might work toward a new toy or even an MP3 player. Once they save up enough money to make the purchase, they'll feel that sense of accomplishment that comes with buying something for which they've worked hard. It doesn't hurt to tell them about some of the goals you're saving for yourself, like a family vacation or a new car.

Finally, as far as where to stash the cash, for younger children, it helps to have a fun savings bank so they can count their money and watch it grow. Once they reach age 9 or 10, they're old enough to have a savings account at the bank. Talk to them about interest at that point, and explain that the bank pays them for leaving their money in an account. Show them the interest they're accruing on a regular basis.

I Also Need to Know . . .

Q: How much should I give as an allowance?

A: As I said, an allowance should be used to shift the responsibility of some purchases from the parent to the child. So the amount of the allowance is going to depend on what your children need to cover. Keep track of what you're spending on your children for a few weeks, and then pinpoint one or two things that they should be able to pay for out of an allowance. Maybe it's a bag of chips from the vending machine at lunch, or a movie out with friends. And explain to them, in detail, the change that is under way. Make sure they understand that the portion for spending is to last until it's time for the next allowance; otherwise, they're out of luck. And then whatever you do, don't bail them out. If they blow it all on candy the first day, no more money for the rest of the week. If you give them more, they'll never learn.

To teach them how to budget, you might want to consider lengthening the time between allowances as they grow up, so that they learn to make their money last for a longer period of time. Young children might get their allowance every week, but in junior high you might stretch it to every two weeks, and in high school you might make it once a month. Giving them a bigger chunk of money on a less frequent basis forces them to stretch it.

Q: At what age should children begin getting an allowance?
A: I'd take a cue from their environment. If children at school are getting an allowance, you probably want to consider giving one. If you have a few children and the age span is rather wide, the younger children might want an allowance when they find out the older one is getting one, and that's okay, too. As a general rule, I think children are ready for a small allowance when they start school.

Q: I tie my children's allowance to chores—if they don't do their chores, they don't get paid. Is this a good way to go about it?
A: I shy away from tying my kids' allowances to their chores because I believe they should do things to help out around the house because they live there, not because they're getting paid. Chores serve a different purpose, in my mind: They help kids develop a work ethic and teach them to juggle a few different tasks and responsibilities at once. An allowance, however, is a way to teach them how to budget, save, and spend money wisely.

Also, to be honest, I find that tying an allowance to chores doesn't always work unless you have one of those children who is primarily motivated by money. You'd be surprised how often kids are willing to give up a few bucks so they don't have to unload the dishwasher or clean their rooms. That's why I tie chores to things my children seem more passionate about, such as video games and television watching.

100. What is a CD?

A: A CD (certificate of deposit) is a low-risk method of investing, similar to a savings account but without the liquidity. You deposit money into a CD for a set amount of time—generally six months, a year, or five years—and in exchange, the bank pays you interest for the life of the CD. If you pull out your money early, you'll pay a penalty. This penalty varies by bank, but you might forfeit three months' worth of interest for a six-month or one-year CD, and six months' worth for a longer-term CD.

The interest rate on a CD is generally more than you'd earn from a plain-vanilla savings account, sometimes more and sometimes less than the rate you'd earn on a money market account. As I was writing this, interest rates on six-month CDs were averaging about 1.75%, and one-year CDs were at 2.19%. At that rate, your money won't keep pace with inflation, so while it's important to have a low-risk aspect of your portfolio, you need to diversify with a mix of stocks and bonds as well.

THE MATH

Let's say you put $5,000 in a six-month CD for an upcoming vacation. At the current average interest rate of 1.75%, you'll have $5,043.56 when the CD matures.

Put the same amount in a one-year CD at the average interest rate of 2.91% and you'll have $5,109.50 after a year.

Put it into a five-year CD, which is averaging 2.80% right now, and you'll have $5,750.31 at the end of the term.

I Also Need to Know . . .

Q: **Are CDs FDIC insured?**
A: They are, up to FDIC limits, which are $250,000 per depositor.

Q: **How do I know what term CD to purchase?**
A: You want to invest in a CD as part of an overall financial plan. Sit down and think about what you're saving for and when you're going to need the money. If you're planning to go on vacation in two years, a CD might be a good place to stash your

money so it earns interest but isn't exposed to the ups and downs of the stock market. If, however, you're looking for a place to keep some emergency money, a CD isn't the best option, because you're locking up that money for a set period of time and an emergency could surprise you. You're better off opening a savings or money market account with easy access.

Watch Out for These!

- **Terms.** Get the term of the CD in writing, and make sure you understand what it means. Know the penalty for early withdrawal as well.
- **Callable CDs.** These CDs tend to offer higher interest rates, so they can be tempting. But they also allow the bank to terminate your CD after a specified time. If they do, you'll receive your deposit amount back plus interest. Generally this call occurs after a fall in interest rates, which means you may not be able to find another product offering the rate you had before. If a fluctuation in rates was acceptable to you, you would have put your money in a money market account to begin with.
- **Variable-rate CDs.** Make sure you understand how and why the interest rate might change. These CDs often track stocks or commodities, which means although you won't lose principal, you may be taking more risk than you thought. They also may set a limit on the amount of interest you can earn.

101. What is a brokered CD?

A: A brokered CD is a CD purchased through a brokerage firm or through an independent broker. Brokered CDs often have higher interest rates than the products offered through your bank because the broker negotiates directly with the bank and generates more business in exchange for higher rates. Brokered CDs can also carry longer terms. But they can be a bit more complicated than bank CDs and they tend to come with more risk.

When you're evaluating brokered CDs, you want to consider the same factors that you would with a CD from your bank (interest rate, term, and penalties), and then some:

- **Fees.** Some brokers will charge you more in fees than you'd pay a typical bank. And those fees may be rolled into the interest rate, which means it can be hard to figure out how much you're paying. Ask for a specific breakdown and compare it with the rates at your bank.
- **Broker reputation.** Just about anyone can claim to be a deposit broker, the term for an independent broker of these CDs. You always want to check out any broker you're considering. The best place to start is with the online database at FINRA (the Financial Industry Regulatory Authority—www.finra.org/brokercheck). You can also contact your state's consumer protection office.
- **Additional risks.** It's possible that if you want to access your money early, the broker will sell your CD to another investor. If interest rates have changed, you could lose not only your interest, but some of your principal. Be sure to find out upfront what happens if you need to pull money out early.

I Also Need to Know . . .

Q: **My broker says I'm purchasing a CD with other people. What does that mean?**

A: This distinction is another big difference between bank CDs and brokered CDs. Often, your broker will pull a group of investors together to buy one large CD with a higher interest rate than is available on a smaller one. That means you own a piece of the CD, instead of the whole thing, and you may earn a higher rate of interest than you would if you were investing alone. But the downside is that if you need out, the broker will have to sell your piece, which means you may take a loss depending on current interest rates. If interest rates are lower, you'll usually be okay. But if they've risen, your CD's lower rates won't be as attractive to other investors. That's why it's always important to understand that you're locking up your money for a set period of time. Pulling out early could negate any interest you've earned.

Q: **Are brokered CDs FDIC insured?**

A: Like bank CDs, they are, up to $250,000 per depositor per institution. Take care here: Even though your broker is investing this money for you, you need to know where it is held. FDIC coverage limits include all accounts under your name at one banking institution, which means that if your broker purchases a CD for you at a bank where you already have money invested, it could put you over the edge when it comes to FDIC coverage.

▶ An Example

John has $150,000 in a money market account at Bank of Florida. He is covered under FDIC limitations if Bank of Florida fails. His broker comes to him and says that he can get him a 5% interest rate on a two-year CD if he deposits $150,000. The CD will be held with Bank of Florida as well, which means that if John were to make the investment, $50,000 of his money wouldn't be insured because he is over the FDIC limitations at that particular bank. Instead, John should have his broker look for a similar CD at another bank so that he is fully covered.

---

102. How do I find the best interest rate on savings accounts, money market accounts, and CDs?

A: There's no magic here. I like to start with the bank that already hosts my checking account. Since I'm already a customer, they may give me a good rate—it's okay to ask for more than they're advertising—and at the very least, it will be a bit easier to link the two accounts if I want to transfer money back and forth.

Once you have savings account and CD rates in hand, you can look at the accounts offered by other banks in your area and see how they compare. The business section of your local paper likely carries advertisements with rates. Otherwise you can simply look at the signs in the branch windows.

Then, jump on your computer and compare rates online at the Web site www.Bankrate.com. These days, you're not limited to local banks. Online banks such as HSBC Direct and ING Direct can offer higher rates of interest because they've eliminated the overhead associated with brick-and-mortar branches. The downside? You won't be able to walk into a branch anytime you want. Also, some provide ATM access; others don't. You may also need to maintain a checking account at a brick-and-mortar bank

SAVING AND INVESTING

and transfer money from the online one (which takes a few days) to access your funds.

Understand, CDs and savings and money market accounts are different savings vehicles and should be evaluated as such. Savings and money market accounts allow you access to your money at any time. CDs lock your money up for a prescribed period—anywhere from 3 months to 10 years. If you want to get the money early, you'll need to "break" the CD and pay a penalty. That means that you want to compare savings accounts against savings accounts and CDs against CDs.

When you look at savings accounts and money markets, note not only the interest rate but also the minimum opening balance requirements and service fees. While it's preferable to find an account that doesn't charge service fees, some charge fees only if you don't have a minimum average balance. Avoid these as well, unless the threshold is low and you know you can consistently make it. Otherwise, you'll negate a good chunk of your interest.

When it comes to CDs, compare interest rates and penalties for getting your money out early. And be sure to compare like to like: compare a one-year CD to a one-year CD and a five-year to a five-year. Bankrate.com maintains charts of these as well.

If you are inclined to put your money into a CD because you know you won't need it for that period of time, it still pays to look at money market accounts. Some banks offer better rates on their money markets than they do on CDs. It's worth the comparison. Just know that if interest rates go up and you have your money in a money market or savings account, you'll reap that gain. But if they go down, so will your interest rate. With a CD, you get what you signed up for. So in a declining-interest-rate environment, CDs tend to be the better bet. Once you've done this research, it should be simple to choose a place to stash your cash.

THE MATH

What does a little difference in interest mean? A lot. When writing this book, I plugged my own city and state into Bankrate.com's comparison tool and found that my best option was an online bank offering 2.63% and my worst was a local bank offering only 0.10%.

- If you put $5,000 in the online bank, after a year you'd have $5,133.
- After 5 years, you'd have $5,702.
- After 10 years, you'd have $6,502.

- If you put that same $5,000 in the local bank, after a year you'd have $5,005.
- After 5 years, you'd have $5,025.
- After 10 years, you'd have $5,050.

You're reading that correctly. You'd earn more than twice as much in one year at the online bank than you would in 10 years at my local one.

Finally, a word about credit unions. Federal credit unions are nonprofit financial institutions essentially owned and operated by members—a co-op of sorts. Because they aren't for profit like banks, they can sometimes charge less interest on loans and more on savings accounts.

Most credit unions have what's called a field of membership, or restrictions on who can join. For instance, you may be eligible to join a credit union in your area because of where you work, your school, your church, or even just because you live in that county. To find a credit union likely to admit you in your area, do a search on www.findacreditunion.com or through the Credit Union National Association at www.cuna.org. Both sites will generate a list for you, and then you can call around or visit the credit unions in person to find out what products they offer and compare interest rates.

INTEREST RATES: CREDIT UNION VERSUS BANK		
PRODUCT	CREDIT UNION NATIONAL AVERAGE (%)	BANK NATIONAL AVERAGE (%)
Regular savings	0.5	0.35
Money market	1.04	0.65
1-year CD	1.97	1.6

Source: Datatrac National Rate Index, April 28, 2009.

I Also Need to Know . . .

Q: Is the interest rate guaranteed?

A: For many CDs, the interest rate is locked in for the term of the CD, but there is such a thing as a variable-rate CD, so you want to check (for more on CDs, turn to "What is a CD?" on page 338).

Savings and money market accounts, however, are a different story. Savings and money market account interest rates can fluctuate. You may have noticed that throughout 2008, your savings account interest rates dropped steadily. That's because every time the Federal Reserve cut interest rates, your bank did too. (For more on the effect these Fed cuts have on your finances, turn to page 51.)

In general, when your interest rate changes, you'll get a notice from your bank. At that point, you can start shopping around for a higher rate, if you think it's worth it. If you have a lot of money in your account or are adding to your savings regularly through automatic contributions, a quarter or half a percent can make a significant difference. If you don't, it's probably not worth the trouble.

Q: What's APY?

A: APY stands for *annual percentage yield*, which is the amount you earn annually on your savings or investments, based on the interest rate. This annualized rate is important because compound interest comes into play. Your bank will calculate your interest on a regular basis and add it into your account balance. Then the next time your interest is calculated, it will be based on the new amount.

This compounded rate is the reason it's so important to start saving early. The longer your interest has to compound, the more you'll end up with.

► An Example

Most banks will compound and credit your interest on a monthly basis. If you deposit $5,000 into a savings account that pays 2% interest, then after one month, your balance will have grown to $5,007.93. The next month, the bank will pay you 2% interest on the new amount, bringing your balance up to $5,016.86. After a year, you'll have earned $100 in interest, with a balance of $5,100. Leave the money in place for five years, and you'll have $520.40 in earned interest, for doing nothing at all.

103. What should I do with my tax refund?

A: First of all, you shouldn't be getting a tax refund. At least not every year. If you've filled out your W-4 correctly, that money will be distributed in your paychecks throughout the year, which means you'll get a little bit more each month. That way, you can put it in a high-interest savings account or invest it for retirement, so it's working for you throughout the year instead of for the government. When you get a refund, you've essentially given the IRS an interest-free loan for a year. Don't you think that the IRS already takes enough of your money?

THE MATH

The average individual federal tax refund in 2008 was $2,429. If that amount was instead split into monthly increments and invested tax-deferred into the market and earned an average 8% annually, by the end of the year, you'd have $2,515.

- Do the same thing for the next five years, and you'll have $14,842.
- After 10 years, you'll have $36,955.
- After 20 years, you'll have $118,982.
- After 30 years, you'll have $301,053.

- Now let's say that you just invested your refund each year as a lump sum. After five years, you'll have $14,335.
- After 10 years, you'll have $35,693.
- After 20 years, you'll have $114,919.
- After 30 years, you'll have $290,771.

Again, a valuable lesson in compounding—the time value of money. Even having the money in hand for a few additional months each year can be worth thousands of dollars many years in the future. (For more on compound interest, turn to "I'm only 25. Why do I need to think about retirement already?" on page 287).

But let's get back to this year, because you already have the money in hand and it's too late to change that. A tax refund, depending on its size, is a windfall, and you should treat it as such. Whenever you have a good-sized chunk of money on your hands, you want to ask yourself a few questions:

1. Do I have a liquid emergency cushion of at least six months' worth of living expenses?
2. Do I have credit card or other high-interest-rate debt?
3. Could my retirement savings use a boost?

Then you want to put the money to use, typically in that order. There's no guarantee that if you put your money toward paying off those credit card bills that the card issuer would not reduce your credit limit. That would sap your ability to use those credit cards as a back-pocket emergency cushion. So, emergency funds first.

High-interest-rate debt is next because it costs a lot of money, and paying it off is like an instant return on your investment: If you have a card with a 18% interest rate, for example, paying it off is like earning 18% on that amount, because you won't have to pay it to the credit card company or lender.

I Also Need to Know . . .

Q: How do I know what my withholding should be?

A: You want to as closely as possible match up your withholding to your estimated tax liability. If you continuously get a large tax refund—or you typically owe a big chunk of money—you probably have the wrong withholding amount. The lower your withholding, the less that is taken out of your paycheck each month. Factors such as whether you're single, if you have children, and if you made an investment profit during the last year will factor into your withholding. A good way to run your numbers is by using the Withholding Calculator on the IRS Web site: www.irs.gov/individuals/article/0,,id=96196,00.html.

Q: How often should I review my withholding?

A: You want to look things over about once a year, particularly if you received a big refund or tax bill the year before or if you've experienced one or more of these major life changes:

- Marriage
- Divorce
- Birth/adoption of a child
- Purchase of a new home
- Retirement
- You or your spouse stopped working or took a second job
- You earned a significant amount of income from investments or capital gains
- There have been changes to your deductions (i.e., you can now deduct items such as student loan interest or alimony, or you can no longer claim children as dependents)

THE STATS

- **107,569,000:** The number of refunds issued by the IRS in 2008
- **$261,320,000,000:** The amount of total refunds issued by the IRS in 2008
- **$156,053,000:** The total number of tax returns processed by the IRS in 2008

104. How do I start an investment club?

A: Investment clubs were first made famous in the 1980s (remember the Beardstown Ladies?), but they are still much around today. It's a way to pool assets and buy stocks, as well as share advice and research. Maybe you each chip in $50 each meeting—some groups do less, some more—then use that money to buy stocks.

To kick things off, you need a good core group of members. Keep in mind: This group isn't just any old club. When money comes into the picture, things can get tricky, so you need to make sure that the members are like-minded when it comes to their willingness to research these investments. You also want members who are in sync when it comes to their investment strategies. If you have a day trader in one corner and a long-term investor in the other, you're bound to have conflict.

Once you have your members, you should set up a meeting schedule. I'd suggest once a month. If you can do it physically, great, but time is tight these days and meeting virtually works too, either through online chat rooms or a free service like Yahoo! groups.

At your first meeting, you should elect officers. Having a president and treasurer is key. You should also get the legal paperwork out of the way. You need to draw up an agreement for members to sign (the National Association of Investors Corporation, a nonprofit, has example documents in their book, *The NAIC's Official Guide to Starting and Running a Profitable Investment Club*. You can also join for a $40 annual fee, plus $25 or $79 per club member depending on level of service, and they will provide you with computer tools, accounting forms, and educational materials. The group's Web site is www.betterinvesting.org).

At each meeting, you'll pool your investment dollars, discuss one or two stocks members have agreed to research, and decide to purchase (or not to purchase) one or more. You may also opt to sell out of prior positions or add to positions you've previously taken. Joining an investment club can be a great learning opportunity. Most successful clubs assign each member a stock to watch, and then he or she can fill in the rest of the members every meeting. You can also assign members topics to read up on, so they can teach everyone else what they learn. This way, you're all pitching in to learn as much as you can in the shortest amount of time.

You'll invest your money through a brokerage firm, and I suggest going with a discount brokerage. You'll pay a lot less for trades (under $20; sometimes as little as $7 or $8) and because part of the idea is learning and doing the research on your own, you don't really need the services that a full-service brokerage provides.

I Also Need to Know . . .

Q: What about the tax liabilities?

A: As a partnership, you aren't liable for taxes as a group, but you'll have to include your individual losses and gains, as well as your portion of the investments, on your tax return.

Q: **How many members should we have?**

A: I tend to think 10 to 15. It's a good idea to match the number of members with the number of stocks you plan to hold in your portfolio. That way, you can each be assigned one stock to track. Tracking several stocks can be a bit of a full-time job, but if you work as a group, it's not as much of a burden. It's important that all members participate.

Q: **What if I—or another member—want to get out?**

A: You'll need to withdraw from the partnership, which means selling your share of the stocks. Think of it like a mutual fund: You have a pool of money invested in an assortment of stocks. When you no longer want to own those stocks, you sell. The club will write you a check in the amount of your share of the club portfolio's value at the time you sell. That means that just as if you were investing on your own, it's not a good idea to walk away from a club when your investments are down.

Q: **I'm not sure I want to invest with other people, but I'd like to learn about stocks and investing in a group. Are there clubs for this?**

A: There are, and you can certainly start one. These are more along the lines of study groups: You don't pool money, but you get together on a regular basis to talk about stocks and investment options. You can still assign each person a stock to follow, as you would with a traditional investment club, and you can even invest in the same stocks, but you can do it in separate accounts.

Another option, and one I advocated in my book *Make Money, Not Excuses* is to form a group of people to meet on a regular basis and talk about money in general, whether that means investing, insurance, saving, real estate, or spending. I call it a Money Group. You can cover a different topic each meeting, and assign members to do research and report back. You can share money-saving tips, talk about your money fears, and just open up the lines of communication about your finances, something we don't do enough.

SAVING AND INVESTING

105. How do I put together an asset-allocation plan?

A: An asset-allocation plan sounds complicated, right? Not so much. "Asset allocation" is just a fancy term for a straightforward process: Taking the money you have to invest and spreading it among different investment categories in a way that fits your investment goals and your risk tolerance.

You've heard not to put all your eggs in one basket, and that's what asset allocation aims to avoid. If you invest all of your money in stocks and the stock market takes a major dive, your entire nest egg is at risk. Ditto with bonds. And if you put all the money in cash, you'll no doubt lose money after taxes and inflation. That's a risk too. But if, however, you have a mix of stocks, bonds, and cash, you'll be protecting yourself against exactly that scenario.

Figuring out your asset allocation means figuring out what mix of assets is right for you. A typical asset allocation includes stocks for long-term growth, bonds for income and security, and cash for short-term needs. You can get every one of these components in mutual funds, index funds, or exchange-traded funds. Let's run through each category separately:

- Stocks, or equities, are shares in public companies that trade on a stock exchange. They are the highest risk investments, but have also historically provided the highest returns. According to Morningstar, from January 1926 to March 2009, U.S. stocks had an average annual return of 9.4%%, bonds returned 5.6%, and cash returned 3.7%. Money invested for the long-term (10 or more years) generally belongs in stocks because you want to be able to maximize your ability to pull in those bigger returns while still having time on your side in case you need to recover from losses.
- Bonds allow you to buy the debt of a company or government agency for a set period of time and interest rate. Picture yourself as a lender. The money you earn on that bond is the interest paid to you for allowing that company to borrow your money. If interest rates go up, making it more expensive to borrow money, you can sell your bond at a higher price. If they go down, the bond will become less valuable—not the

time to sell. But if you hold on to it until the maturity date, you'll get your money back, plus interest. That makes bonds less of a risk than stocks, but they also aren't as lucrative.
· Cash investments, like money market funds and CDs, are the safest investments because they aren't subject to outside risks. You won't earn a great deal in interest, but you won't lose principal, either (3.7% average annual return).

When you create an asset-allocation plan, you're finding a mix of these three categories (sometimes supplemented with gold or real estate) that, when pieced together, can help you get the maximum return on your investment with the appropriate amount of risk. In general, the younger you are, the more you should have invested in stocks. Investors nearing retirement age should have more in bonds and cash for safekeeping. An easy way to do the math is to subtract your age from 100. The number you have left is the percentage you should be investing in stocks. The rest should be in safer havens.

I Also Need to Know . . .

Q: Can I set it and forget it?
A: You set your allocation, but even if you make no changes, it can get out of whack. Not only does the stock market rise and fall, leaving you with too much or too little in risky investments, but you'll age, or your risk tolerance may change. Periodically—once a year—you need to go back and update your asset allocation to keep it on track. This is called rebalancing. And it could have saved a lot of people a lot of pain—and money—during the most recent market downturn. When you rebalance you move money out of the category that has performed best (i.e., sell your winners), take some profits, and plow those gains back into categories that haven't performed as well. This manuevering enables you to lock in some gains.

If the idea of having to rebalance each year turns you off, you should consider a lifestyle or target date retirement fund. These funds do the work for you: You'll select an initial objective for the money—typically the year in which you plan to retire—and then the fund will put your asset allocation on autopilot, and adjust it automatically as you age.

Q: **What is diversification?**
A: After you've allocated your assets, your work isn't done. Within your asset classes, you need to make sure you have a mix: different kinds of stocks (U.S.-based companies, international companies, small companies, large companies, and companies in varied industries) and a few different kinds of bonds (U.S. Treasuries, inflation protected, corporate). This minimizes your risk, because if an entire industry or sector goes up in smoke—the auto industry, for example, or technology—you won't be all in.

One of the easiest (and one of the cheapest) ways to diversify is to put your money into index funds or exchange-traded funds (ETFs), which invest in a plethora of stocks and bonds in one swoop. You might buy a domestic total stock market index fund, a total bond market index fund, and a global stock fund. How much of your money goes into each goes back to your asset allocation: If you're 40, you'd probably want 50% of your money in the domestic stock fund, 40% in the bond fund, and 10% in the international fund.

Note: The target-date retirement fund that I mentioned earlier will do all of this for you as well.

▶ An Example

Early in your career, your investments might look like this:
- 50% Total Stock Index Fund
- 20% International Stock Index Fund
- 20% Total Bond Market Index Fund
- 10% Cash or Money Market Fund

In the middle of your career, they might look like this:
- 45% Total Stock Index Fund
- 14% International Stock Index Fund
- 30% Total Bond Market Index Fund
- 10% Cash or Money Market Fund

Late in your career or early in your retirement, they might look like this:
- 35% Total Stock Index Fund
- 10% International Stock Index Fund
- 40% Total Bond Market Index Fund
- 15% Cash or Money Market Fund

Retirement (80 or older) they might look like this:
- 25% Total Stock Index Fund
- 5% International Stock Index Fund
- 40% Total Bond Market Index Fund
- 30% Cash or Money Market Fund

---

106. What is the difference between stocks and mutual funds?

A: When you buy a stock, you're buying a partial ownership—called a share—in one particular company. If the price of the stock goes up between the time you bought it and you sold it, you'll turn a profit at the sale. If the value of the stock goes down in that time period, you lose money when you sell. You're putting your faith in that company to perform in a way that will increase the value of your stock. (Note that stock prices—particularly in the short term—are based on many factors in addition to the performance of the company: faith in management, the underlying economy, interest rates, and the general attitude toward the markets to name just a few.)

When you buy a share of a mutual fund, however, you aren't buying a piece of a single company; you're buying a piece of a basketful of investments. Those investments may be stocks, but they may also be bonds (debt instruments), government securities, real estate, or precious metals or some combination of these things and others. Because you're not buying one stock, for instance, but instead, buying into the basket, the risk you're taking is more diversified. In other words, if one stock performs poorly, the hope is that the others will continue to do well.

Your mutual fund will have a manager—or several—who will pool your money with that of other investors and use it to make investments. The manager is then responsible for making the day-to-day decisions that will affect your money. If you wanted to invest in all of a particular mutual fund's holdings on your own, it would take a lot of cash—and a lot of time and research. For people who don't have the time or the patience, selecting a solid mutual fund is like hiring a manager to do the work for you.

Of course, that costs money. When it comes to mutual funds, the primary cost to consider is the "expense ratio." This represents what it costs the investment company to operate the fund— the operating expenses divided by the average dollar value of the fund's assets. The higher the fund's operating expenses, the less return on your investment. According to Morningstar, the average expense ratio for all actively managed mutual funds was 1.25% in April 2009. Don't go too far beyond that.

I Also Need to Know . . .

Q: How do I know what mutual fund to invest in?

A: One of my favorite tools for selecting mutual funds is Morningstar (www.morningstar.com). Although the site has a subscription component, much of the information is available for free. The site allows you to look at Morningstar's analysis of any mutual fund you're interested in. You can make it easy on yourself if you're clueless by looking directly at their picks—they have lists for the top performers in the last month, year, three years, and five years, as well as in each fund category. If you are investing in a retirement plan, such as a 401(k), and have been given a list of fund options to choose from, this site can point you in the right direction.

What you're looking for:

- **No-load:** This designation means the fund's shares are sold without sales charges or commissions. The less you pay in fees, the more you earn. Some investors, however, choose to go with load funds because they'd rather pay a little more for the advice of a broker or investment advisor.
- **Performance:** Make sure the fund has performed in the top one-third of its class during the last one-, three-, and five-year periods.
- **Expense ratio:** The lower the expense ratio, the better. You should pay no more than 1.5% for actively managed

funds and 0.50% for index funds. Interestingly enough, some research has shown that the lower the expense ratio, the better the performance.

· **Management:** Remember, someone else is making the buying and selling decisions when you buy into a mutual fund. Experience is worth taking into consideration.

Q: **Does a mutual fund make me automatically diversified?**

A: No—and this is a common misconception. Diversification means building a portfolio of investments that will—the hope is— react differently to the ebbs and flows of the market. You'll have exposure to many industries and companies, so if one sector takes a hit, the others will continue to do well. If you own five different mutual funds, and they're all heavy with technology stocks, you are more vulnerable than if you own one mutual fund that spans a few industries and holds a good mix of domestic and foreign companies, small and large companies, mature companies and start-ups.

107. What are the differences between an exchange-traded fund and an index fund? Which is better?

A: First, let's define each. Then we'll talk about the pros and cons.

An exchange-traded fund (ETF) is a basket of stocks that track an index—often the S&P 500. It works much like a mutual fund, in that you're buying a piece of the market instead of buying the stock of one company. But it trades on the market like a stock. You pay commissions, not expense ratios. For this reason, they're inexpensive.

An index fund is a mutual fund (for more on mutual funds, turn to "What is the difference between stocks and mutual funds?" on page 353). But it's a mutual fund that tracks an index again (the S&P 500, maybe, or the Dow Jones Industrial Average). That eliminates the need for a pricey fund manager skilled in picking stocks and making trades. Because the manager or management team is paid to track the index, expenses are lower than for managed mutual funds.

There are similarities. Both are relatively cheap. Both are good for long-term investors. And both come in many varieties. Today there are index funds and ETFs that track everything from the Wilshire 5000 to the FTSE All-World Index.

Now the differences. You can buy an index fund only once per day, because they are only priced once a day. Also, some (not all) index funds come with high minimum investments— sometimes as much as $50,000.

ETFs, however, can be bought and sold throughout the day, and they have no minimum investment. You can buy a single share. Often, more hands-on investors opt for ETFs because they can trade in and out all day.

I Also Need to Know . . .

Q: I've heard that ETFs have a tax advantage. Is that true?

A: It can be. When you invest in a mutual fund, such as an index fund, and a fellow shareholder wants out, the fund has to sell shares to raise the money to allow her to pull out. That generates capital gains for you—even though you didn't do anything—and that money is taxable. One of the advantages of index funds versus actively managed mutual funds is that index funds have fewer trades because they adhere to the index. That results in fewer capital gains. But ETFs still have the edge versus index funds when it comes to taxes.

Because ETFs are traded like stocks, when an investor wants out, she just sells her shares to another investor, which doesn't affect other owners of the ETF. You'll still be liable for any taxes on your own earnings, though.

Note: If you hold the ETF in a tax-advantaged account, such as a 401(k) or IRA, this tax question doesn't matter.

Q: What do *load* and *no-load* mean?

A: *Load* means a commission. So a load fund, a term you'll often hear, charges a commission each time you buy shares. You're purchasing the fund through a broker, and you're going to pay for the broker's service. There are two types of loads—front-end, which is what you pay when you purchase the fund shares, and back-end, or deferred loads, which is what you pay when you pull your shares out. With a front-end load, the amount of money you have to invest is reduced because the fee is taken out at the beginning.

When you buy shares that charge a back-end load, all of your money is invested, and the fee isn't charged until you sell your shares. In most cases, the fund will calculate the back-end sales fee on either the value of your initial investment or the value of your investment when you sell, whichever is less. So if you lost money, you could end up paying less in fees with a back-end load.

A no-load fund, however, doesn't charge sales fees each time you buy in because you purchase directly from the mutual fund company—no middleman, no broker. With a no-load product, more of your money will go to the investment, and less to fees. Always a good thing.

▶ An Example

If you have $15,000 to purchase a mutual fund and you choose a no-load fund, all of that $15,000 will be invested. If, however, you purchase a load fund that charges 5%, only $14,250 of your money will be invested. $750 will automatically be lost to commission.

Q: **Why would I ever pick a load mutual fund over a no-load mutual fund?**

A: Novice investors buy load mutual funds and pay the fees involved because they don't want to take on the decision making. They want a financial advisor or broker to hold their hand through the process. And that's okay. If you don't have time to do your own research, or the inclination to do it and understand it, it's likely worth your money to pay someone to help you.

108. What are the FDIC and SIPC? How do they protect my money?

A: The FDIC, or Federal Deposit Insurance Corporation, is an independent agency of the federal government that insures the money you deposit in a bank. For years, the limit has been $100,000 per depositor per bank, which means that you can have up to $100,000 in a bank under your name without having to worry about losing that cash to a bank failure like the ones of 2008 (and in fact, we see bank failures most years; they just don't make as much news as they did in recent times). In 2008, the FDIC raised the limit on insured deposits to $250,000. If you want to put more money into a savings, checking, CD, or money market account, you'll either need to open another account at a different bank or add a joint account holder to your existing account. That last move doubles your existing FDIC protection.

So what, exactly, does the FDIC cover?

- Checking accounts
- Savings accounts
- Money markets
- Trusts
- CDs
- IRAs, excluding investments in mutual funds (stocks, bonds, or money market mutual funds)

The FDIC does not cover:

- Mutual funds
- Treasury securities
- The contents of safe-deposit boxes
- Annuities
- Stocks, bonds, or other investment products

That's where SIPC, the Securities Investor Protection Corporation, steps in. SIPC is not a government agency but a nonprofit that protects investors when brokerage firms, not banks, fail and owe money to customers.

When a brokerage firm goes bankrupt and customer assets are lost in the fray, the SIPC will work to retrieve your assets. (Some of the investors in financier Bernard Madoff's notorious funds were able to recover money this way.) Keep in mind, though, that this isn't coverage for when your stocks or other investments don't perform as well as you expected. In that case, you're either taking a loss or waiting until the market rebounds. The SIPC goes to work only when your money goes missing because of a brokerage firm's failure.

Cash and securities, like mutual funds, stocks and bonds, held at a brokerage firm are covered by SIPC up to a limit of

$500,000 per customer, including a maximum of $100,000 for cash claims.

I Also Need to Know . . .

Q: **Does SIPC cover the amount I paid for my investments or instead the amount they were worth when the brokerage firm failed?**

A: Neither, actually. Here's how it works: When a firm becomes insolvent, a federal court will appoint a trustee to liquidate the firm. Your coverage is based on the amount your investments are worth when that trustee is appointed. That could be more or less than what you paid for them, depending on the movement of the market.

▶ An Example

You purchase 50 shares of a stock worth $100 a share, an investment of $5,000. Your brokerage firm goes bankrupt, and on the date the trustee is appointed to liquidate the firm's assets, those 50 shares of stock are now worth only $75. Your claim to SIPC will be for $3,750.

Q: **Under FDIC and SIPC, when will I get my money back?**

A: SIPC claims that it tries to get back money—usually in the form of the investments held—in less than three months. The FDIC tries to make deposit insurance payments within two business days of a bank failure. Understand, this timing may vary because each situation is unique and dependent on a lot of moving parts.

THE STATS

- **$5 trillion:** The amount of total deposits insured by the FDIC in U.S. banks and thrifts
- **$15.7 billion:** Total assets recovered by SIPC since its creation in 1970
- **3,583:** The total number of bank failures since the FDIC was established in 1934

109. What is the difference between a money market account and a savings account?

A: Largely, these products are similar. Money market deposit accounts and savings accounts are both bank savings tools, which means they come with FDIC protection.

The main difference is that money market accounts tend to pay more in interest. Unlike savings accounts, money markets also come with checks but limit the number of them that you can write each month (generally to three) and limit the number of total withdrawals from the account each month (generally to six). Many also have a higher minimum balance requirement than savings accounts.

Savings accounts tend to pay a lower rate of interest. They don't come with checks. And though there may be a limit on the number of withdrawals per month (again, the number is usually six), there isn't always. Minimum required balances also tend to be lower.

Keep in mind that both of these accounts are for money you want to save, not spend, which means you may not—and you should not—need to withdraw money once a month, let alone six times.

I Also Need to Know . . .

Q: **What is the difference between a money market mutual fund and a money market deposit account?**
A: A money market mutual fund is an investment vehicle, not a bank savings vehicle, which means it is not insured by the FDIC.

Money market mutual funds are short-term mutual funds that invest your money in government securities, CDs, or other liquid investments. You'll earn interest—sometimes more than you would with a money market deposit account—on the basis of the performance of these investments. And while money market funds were for many years thought to be no-lose propositions, we learned in the 2007–2009 recession that that is not always the case if the value of the investments in the fund falls.

In late 2008, the value of a prominent money market mutual fund—the Reserve Primary Fund in New York—fell below $1 per share, which means investors lost money. This occurrence is called "breaking the buck," and it's rare enough that the government stepped up and issued a temporary guarantee that investors would receive at least their original investment back if they were invested in money market mutual funds. This program, though, applies only to money market funds that paid a fee to join, and it protects only those assets invested prior to September 20, 2008. You can find out if your money market fund qualifies by contacting your fund company.

Q: Are money market mutual funds safer than other mutual funds?
A: Yes, because they invest in stable products such as CDs and U.S. Treasury bonds, not stocks. The potential returns, however, are much lower than for other mutual funds.

Q: What's the difference between a taxable and a tax-free money market mutual fund?
A: If you have money in a taxable money market fund, any returns you receive will be taxed as regular income, both federally and at the state level. Tax-free money market mutual funds are always exempt from federal taxes, but not necessarily state and local ones. A money market fund that is exempt from federal and state taxes is called "double tax free," and one that is exempt from federal, state, and local taxes is called "triple tax free." Tax-free funds tend to have a lower yield because you won't be taxed at the end. They do not belong in tax-deferred or tax-free retirement accounts, where the protection is unnecessary.

110. How do I check out a broker?

A: This question has been at the top of every investor's mind since the Bernard Madoff scandal broke in December 2008. All of a sudden, we all wondered if we'd checked out our brokers, money managers, financial advisors, and investment bankers thoroughly enough.

Brokers work for brokerage firms and are paid to buy and sell your investments as you direct. To check out a broker, go to the Web site of FINRA, the Financial Industry Regulatory Authority.

There you'll find a tool called BrokerCheck, at www.finra.org/ Investors/ToolsCalculators/BrokerCheck/index.htm, which allows you to input a name and get information on licensing, how long a broker has been in business, and whether there have been any complaints filed against the broker (a major red flag).

An investment advisor is someone paid to provide advice about investing in securities (stocks, bonds, and so on). Advisors must be registered with either the U.S. Securities and Exchange Commission (if they manage more than $25 million in client assets) or their state's securities agency. To find out if your advisor is properly registered, look at their "form ADV," which lists information about the advisor's business and whether the advisor has had complaints from regulators or other clients. It will also list the advisor's services and fees. You can find the ADV form of your advisor on the SEC's Investment Advisor Public Disclosure Web site (www.adviserinfo.sec.gov). Some investment advisors are also brokers.

A money manager will choose and manage your investments for you, developing a strategy that meets your needs and goals and buying and selling investments as needed. Money managers don't work for commissions based on what is bought or sold; rather, they take a percentage of the assets they have under management. This arrangement eliminates a conflict of interest because the manager won't be tempted to favor investments that will earn him the most in commission. Money managers should be registered with the SEC or the state securities agency.

A financial advisor can help you with everything from retirement planning to investments to general budgeting. There's a range of professional designations used (for a complete list and definitions, go to FINRA.org). Certified financial planners must be certified by the Certified Financial Planner Board of Standards. For more on finding a financial planner, turn to page 37.

In all cases, you should do a thorough background check. Ask for references—and call them—and make sure they are licensed (if necessary). To find a financial planner, you can contact trade organizations like the Financial Planning Association (www.fpanet.org) or the National Association of Personal Financial Advisors (www.napfa.org) and search by Zip code.

I Also Need to Know . . .

Q: **What else can I do to protect myself and my investments?**
A: Diversify—not just your investments but also your investment firms. We've discussed not putting all your eggs in one basket. A range of investments means that you're taking less risk. The same rules apply to your money manager: You don't want to place your life savings in the hands of one broker or one firm.

Also, pay attention to where your money is going. An independent institution, not your financial advisor or money manager, should hold your money, and you should be writing deposit checks to that third party. Look over your quarterly statements and make sure that they are coming from the custodian firm, not your advisor.

Watch Out for These!

According to FINRA, these strategies are used by scammers trying to con people into forking over cash:

- **Exaggeration of credibility.** Con artists often go out of their way to make people believe that they are reliable, successful, and popular.
- **Social consensus.** If everyone else is doing it, why shouldn't you? This strategy encourages investors to feel comfortable, so they no longer think it necessary to do their homework.
- **Scarcity.** If the money manager goes out of his or her way to make it seem as if his or her firm is exclusive—perhaps turning you down or making it difficult for you to schedule a meeting—it's likely a red flag. The firm should be vying for your business.
- **Pressure.** There are few investments where urgency is absolute, and if you're given a limited time to respond, it could be a tactic to limit the amount of due diligence you can do.

Q: **I don't really understand my investment options, no matter how many times my financial advisor explains them. What can I do?**
A: Find another advisor. You should never, ever invest in a product

you don't understand or with an advisor who can't explain it to you in plain English. This is a major red flag.

Q: My portfolio is way down. Should I switch advisors?
A: Not necessarily. What is the rest of the market doing? Your portfolio should largely track the market, and if the market is way down as well, you may be okay. What should cause raised eyebrows is if the market is up, up, up on a continuous basis, and your portfolio is still falling out of the sky.

That said, there's no reason not to pick up the phone and give your advisor a call. He or she should be ready and willing to answer any questions you have about why your portfolio is performing the way it is and whether you should change your asset allocation. (If you can't sleep at night, you're probably taking on too much risk.)

Note: If your advisor seems to hide when times get tough, that is reason enough to switch. He or she should be prudent about returning your calls, even if it means being the bearer of bad news.

Resources

Books

The Difference: How Anyone Can Prosper in Even the Toughest Times, by Jean Chatzky (2009)
Based on a study of more than 5,000 people, *The Difference* uncovers the habits of people who have moved from the lowest economic stratum to the highest and teaches you how you can implement these same habits in your own life to achieve financial freedom.

Easy Money: How to Simplify Your Finances and Get What You Want Out of Life, by Liz Pulliam Weston (2007)
A guide to help you take control of your finances, attain financial security, and combat overspending; includes checklists, charts, and tables to help get you organized.

Investing in an Uncertain Economy for Dummies, by Sheryl Garrett (2008)

Investment strategies to help you meet your financial goals; learn how to accumulate wealth, consolidate and protect gains, and make the best investment allocations.

Raising Money-Smart Kids: What They Need to Know About Money and How to Tell Them (*Kiplinger's Personal Finance*), by Janet Bodnar (2005)

Bodnar explains what's important to tell your children about money and how you should go about telling them.

Government Organizations

Federal Deposit Insurance Corporation (FDIC)
www.fdic.gov/about/learn/learning/index.html
1-877-275-3342

Detailed information for parents, educators, and children about the FDIC, banking, and finances.

The Federal Reserve
www.federalreserve.gov/kids/default.htm

The Federal Reserve's kids' page provides FAQs about the Federal Reserve as well as a quiz to test children's knowledge.

Internal Revenue Service
www.irs.gov
1-800-829-1040

Taxpayer information, tips, and tools, including a tax withholding calculator (the withholding calculator, which can be found at www.irs.gov/individuals/article/0,,id=96196,00.html).

Kids.gov
www.kids.gov

Educational money resources for kids, divided by grade level; includes games and guides.

U.S. Securities and Exchange Commission
www.sec.gov
1-888-732-6585

Investor information, current news, and information on laws and regulations.

Web sites

Bankrate.com
www.bankrate.com
561-630-2400

The Web's leader in financial rate information provides free rate information on more than 300 financial products, including money market accounts, checking and savings accounts, certificates of deposit, and credit cards. The Web site offers a variety of financial calculators.

BetterInvesting
www.betterinvesting.org
1-877-275-6242

The nation's largest nonprofit organization dedicated to investment education. For a fee ($6.95 a month, $79.00 a year) you can become a member and receive unlimited access to BetterInvesting's online stock and mutual fund analysis tools, a subscription *Better-Investing Magazine*, access to member-only Web site content, and more. You can also apply to start your own investment club (clubs must pay $40 annually in dues, and each member must pay either $25 or $79 annually, depending on the level of service the member would like to receive).

Financial Industry Regulatory Authority
www.finra.org
301-590-6500

The largest nongovernmental regulator for all securities firms doing business in the United States; the organization's Web site features investor news, tips on investing, and market data.

iMoneyNet
www.imoneynet.com
508-616-6600

Money market fund information and analysis.

Investopedia.com
www.investopedia.com

Free investing tips and tools, including answers to FAQs, investing strategies, financial calculators, articles, and a dictionary of financial terms.

Morningstar
www.morningstar.com
1-866-486-9750

For free, you can access investment research, stock and fund information, data and tools, and company investing and financial news. For a fee, you can sign up for a premium membership, which allows you to access additional resources.

Securities Investor Protection Corporation
www.sipc.org
202-371-8300

A nonprofit membership corporation whose aim is to restore funds to investors with assets in the hands of bankrupt and otherwise financially troubled brokerage firms.

CHAPTER 12

CAREERS/WORK

111. How do I ask for a raise?

A: Asking for a raise is daunting, even when you've more than earned it. But the best way to calm your nerves is by doing your homework so that you walk into your negotiation prepared.

First and foremost, take a look back at your performance and make a list of your accomplishments over the past year or two (or however long it's been since you had a review). Despite what you may think, this review is not about the calendar. Being with a company for six months or a year does not guarantee you a raise. It's about the work you've produced and your employer's financial situation. If you've seen signs around the office that your employer is being affected by a downturn or a decline in business—layoffs, scaled-back bonuses, no more birthday cakes—now is not the best time to have this conversation. Raising the issue may make you look as though you're out of touch.

If you decide to go for it, schedule a meeting with your boss. Scheduling in advance will communicate to your boss that you know that his or her time is valuable. Then research, research, research. You need to know what you are worth. A good place to start is by finding out the salary range for someone else in your position in your same location. You can do so by referencing the U.S. Department of Labor's *Occupational Outlook Handbook* (www .bls.gov/OCO/), PayScale (www.payscale.com), or Salary.com. Don't forget to take into account any special skills or certifications that are an asset to your job.

Go back through your calendars and compile a list of what you've accomplished in the time since your last review. Anything that is an example of how you added to the bottom line or saved the company money should go at the top of the page. Also make note of anytime your performance has been commended. You should take that piece of paper to the meeting.

Next, practice. Before the meeting, rehearse what you plan to say. Go back to that list and name at least three specific achievements. Talk about what you do every day that affects the bottom line of the company—now is the time to brag a little.

The rest is in your employer's hands. If you get shot down, ask if you can revisit the possibility in six months. Ask what you need to do in that time frame to improve your chances. Then follow up with an e-mail, saying thanks and recapping the goals you've set together.

I Also Need to Know . . .

Q: How can I accurately assess what I'm worth to my employer?
A: I mentioned using Salary.com and PayScale to get an idea of what you're worth. It's a good idea to use both sites and average the two salary numbers they provide you with to get a more accurate assessment. You can also ask people in similar positions at other companies what they make. But don't phrase it like that. Ask: "How much would someone with my skills likely earn at your company?"

Q: How much of a pay increase is the typical raise?
A: The average increase in wages is 3% annually, which just about covers inflation. It's okay to shoot a little higher, but in this economy be prepared to settle for less.

Q: Besides a raise, what else is open to negotiation?
A: You can ask for a better title, a nicer office or work space, to work at home a day or two a week, a department change, more vacation time, or even tuition reimbursement or coverage of commuting expenses.

112. I recently lost my job. How should I budget my money until I have a steady income again?

A: Before you start making a budget, you must take stock of where you stand. You need a clear idea of what, if any, money is coming in and how much how much you have in liquid, accessible savings. You then need to know how much you spend on a monthly basis.

Your spending gets divided into two categories: fixed expenses, which would include items such as mortgage or rent, student loan and credit card bills (minimum payments), car payment, insurance, communication (cell phone, Internet service provider), gym, utilities, and child support. And variable expenses such as the money spent on eating out, clothing, and entertainment. Even groceries are a variable expense, as you can find ways to save money with coupons or generic brands.

Look over your bank statements, as well as your credit and debit card usage from the last month or two. Pay attention to how much cash you've been pulling out of the ATM on a monthly basis. That will give you some indication of where your money *has* been going.

Once you know where the money is going, it'll be easier to find ways to cut back. Start with your variable expenses. The restaurants and entertainment go, for starters. The coffee shop, new clothes, spontaneous trips to the mall or bookstore do too. Then turn to the fixed expenses that are not so fixed: Can you do without the land-line phone and use your cell phone? Can you do without cable and watch TV via the Internet? Finally, look at the interest rates you're paying on your preexisting debts. Are they as low as they can be? If you haven't tried negotiating for a better deal, do it now before your creditors realize you are out of work.

What if you're still low on money? Desperate times call for desperate measures, as they say, and that could mean getting rid of the extra car, moving to a more affordable apartment (if you rent), even renting out the room over the garage. You almost certainly want to be cutting back at the grocery store and clipping coupons whenever you can (for more tips on how to save at the grocery store, turn to page 124). Bottom line: You have to get creative to make the money last as long as you can.

I Also Need to Know . . .

Q: Can I negotiate my severance package?

A: You can and you definitely should, but the best time to do that is before you leave the office. If you see a layoff coming, do some research about severance packages in your industry (and at the company) before you have your discussion so that you know what you should aim for. Your employer might even expect you to negotiate, so ready your case. And if more money doesn't seem forthcoming, ask for other considerations: use of the office for the rest of the month, the ability to keep the company laptop, an extension of health benefits. Figure out what is meaningful to you and then ask for it. And if you can't do it yourself, hiring an employment attorney to negotiate for you may be well worth the money.

Q: What should I do if I can't pay my creditors?

A: Be honest with them. You are not the only person out of work—and your creditors know that. What separates the people they want to help from the people they don't is communication. So first, prioritize your debts and pay the ones that have the ability to take the most away from you: That means the mortgage, the car payment, and the doctor you want to be able to visit in a pinch.

Next, contact the creditors who are going to get stiffed. Explain the situation, being careful to point out that your situation is temporary. They may be willing to help, either by negotiating a lower monthly payment or, in extreme cases of credit card debt, settling for an amount that is less than the total amount due. But you need to initiate the talks. If you wait for the phone to start ringing or the letters to come, it may be too late.

Q: Should I collect unemployment?

A: Absolutely. Part of that huge chunk that's taken out of your check each pay period goes to unemployment insurance, which means that this money is money you've earned. It's not much—the average is $292 a week, according to the Department of Labor—but if you've paid into the system, it's your due. Your first order of business, in fact, when you're laid off should be to head to your local unemployment office. It can take a few weeks for payments to kick in.

113. For years I have been a stay-at-home parent. I am now ready to reenter the workforce. I'd prefer a flexible schedule—but I'll do whatever it takes. Do you have any suggestions?

A: Call a family meeting, gather everyone around the table, and hash it out. Talk about how you can make it work for everyone and make sure you address logistical questions, such as whether you'll need child care to fill in the blanks or if your mate will have to make schedule adjustments.

Then assess what you yourself need to do to prepare for the change. Your skills likely need a spit-polish, so think about classes that you can take to get up to speed. Attend networking events in your field, put feelers out to friends and friends of friends (often the best source of leads) to let them know you're looking for work, and update your résumé.

At that point, you can start hunting for a job. Remember that if you want a flexible schedule, you must be flexible as well. That could mean working atypical hours, taking a lower salary, or working in a position you might not have considered before.

The first stop in your search should be your former employer. See if the company has any positions available. Hit the big job boards such as Monster.com and listing sites like craigslist (www .craigslist.com). And know that there are companies such as Mom Corps (www.momcorps.com) or Women for Hire (www .womenforhire.com; they deal with men too) that offer vetted opportunities on their Web sites for flexible and at-home jobs.

If you have a particular skill—writing, say, or photography—you might consider working on a freelance basis. Consulting is an option as well. For the most part, these fields allow you to set your own hours. Jobs that operate on shifts or pay hourly typically allow for flexible schedules as well. If you have school-age children, working for a school district may be a good option, as you'll have the same time off as your children.

One note: Your search will be easier if you focus on where the jobs actually are—and the fields expected to grow in the future.

TEN FASTEST-GROWING OCCUPATIONS: 2006–2016

1. Network systems and data communications analysts. Typical education requirement: bachelor's degree.
2. Personal and home care aides. Typical education requirement: short-term on-the-job training.
3. Home health aides. Typical education requirement: short-term on-the-job training.
4. Computer software engineers. Typical education requirement: bachelor's degree.
5. Veterinary technologists and technicians. Typical education requirement: associate's degree.
6. Personal financial advisors. Typical education requirement: bachelor's degree.
7. Makeup artists (theatrical and performance). Typical education requirement: postsecondary vocational award.
8. Medical assistants. Typical education requirement: moderate-term on-the-job training.
9. Veterinarians. Typical education requirement: first professional degree.
10. Substance abuse and behavioral disorder counselors. Typical education requirement: bachelor's degree.

Source: U.S. Department of Labor.

I Also Need to Know . . .

Q: What's the best way to reconnect with my old contacts?

A: First, pick up the phone. Apologize that you haven't been in touch, and ask if you can meet for coffee or lunch. (Note: You can do this only once per person.) Then keep the relationship going by following up with e-mail and checking in once in a while by phone or e-mail to schedule additional coffee dates.

If the contact information you have is outdated, many companies have alumni Web sites for former employees that open up a slew of new networking opportunities. But with the advent of networking sites such as LinkedIn (www.linkedin.com) and Facebook (www.facebook.com), you can create your own. Join both of these sites, then start searching around for old colleagues or clients. As long as you keep your presence on these sites professional, they are a great way to network.

Q: How can I explain a return to work to my children?
A: The answer to this question depends on how old they are. If you have younger children—say, younger than 5—talk to them in terms they will understand. Explain that you're going back to work so that they can have the things that they like—their favorite toys or trips to the movies or museum. As your children get older, it's important to convey to them that you need to work for your own enrichment. Tell them what you do at work and why you enjoy it.

Q: What's the best way to go about finding reliable and affordable child care for my kids while I'm at work?
A: Three words: Word of mouth. Talk to people you trust to get recommendations—other parents at the park, friends, colleagues. Find out where they take their children and what they like about it, and then visit a few of the places to see the setup and employees with your own eyes. Try to schedule your visit during rush hour, when parents will be dropping off or picking up their children. They'll most likely be happy to talk to you about their experiences, and it will be a more reliable opinion than a reference from the day care provider, as it will be uncensored.

And finally, as a mother, I have to tell you: Don't ignore your gut instincts. They're usually spot on.

SEVEN QUESTIONS TO ASK A POTENTIAL NANNY

1. What is your experience or prior training?
Answer: Decades of experience aren't necessary, but you certainly want someone who has worked with children before, and several times. If he or she has worked with one family on a long-term basis, even better. Get the contact information of multiple references and call them.

2. How do you generally discipline?
Answer: The nanny's philosophy should be in line with yours, whatever that may be. If he or she takes a completely different approach, it will be confusing for the children.

3. **Why are you a nanny?**
   Answer: You obviously want someone who likes children, but a good nanny gets something out of the job (aside from money). If he or she doesn't want to be there, your children's experience will suffer.
4. **Why did you leave your last position?**
   Answer: It's okay if he or she didn't mesh well with the last family, as long as you understand the reasons why.
5. **Can you describe an average day when you're caring for my child?**
   Answer: What you're looking for depends on what kind of parent you are, but you don't want someone who is going to park the kids in front of the television. The nanny should be able to suggest multiple interesting and educational activities he or she would do with your children, both in and out of your home.
6. **What are some of your rules?**
   Answer: Again, they should be in line with your own. Too rigid and you'll constantly be at arms; too loose and you'll have trouble disciplining your children when the nanny's not around. The last thing you want to hear all the time is "But she lets us do it!"
7. **Finally, ask about any requirements that are important to you—** whether he or she has her own car, whether the nanny can prepare lunches or help with schoolwork, and so on.

---

114. I work on commission, which results in a fluctuating paycheck. How should I budget?

A: When the amount you bank fluctuates each month, budgeting can be a challenge. So instead of waiting to see what comes in each month, you need to know what comes in during an average month and then attempt to live on less than that.

Begin with your take-home pay from the past year. Add it up, then divide it by 12. This amount is your average income per month. This is assuming that the last year was typical—if it was atypical, even on the upside, take the last six typical months and average those. This will be the number you'll work with to create your monthly budget.

Now, you need to map out your monthly expenses. You can't do much of anything if you don't know what's going out. So for one month, track every penny you spend. (For more information, turn to "How do I set up a monthly budget?" on page 117.)

Once you know where you're spending, you can not only scale back any shockingly extravagant extras—$100 on sandwiches for lunch? $50 in ATM fees?—but you can also estimate how much you need to get by each month. Be sure to overshoot just a bit, because it's better to budget too much—you can just move the extra to savings—than too little, which will have you scrambling to pay the bills.

The next step is simple subtraction. Take your average month's income, subtract the month's expenses, and look at it. Can you live on that amount? If you're cutting it too close, you may need to make some more spending cutbacks. If you have money left over, you'll want to work on paying off any debts you have, or if you're debt free, put the extra into savings.

Finally, you put the system into practice. I think it works best if you deposit your commission checks in a savings account, then pay yourself once each month. The logistics are simple: You can set it up with your bank so that a certain amount is moved from savings to checking each month. That way, you can simulate a regular paycheck. If it's easier for you to get paid less frequently, you can choose to do so twice a month. (Be careful of every two weeks— that works out to 26 yearly payments, so if you go this route, you need to divide by 13 rather than 12.) And tell yourself that the days of dipping into that savings for an extra purchase are over: You'll regret those shoes later if you're short on the electric bill.

Finally, don't forget about an emergency fund. Everyone should have enough to cover six months' worth of living expenses socked away, but for people who have an unpredictable income, this fund is even more important. That way, if you have a sudden expense, you can pay in cash rather than credit. Read more on how to set up an emergency fund, and where to put the cash, on page 333 in response to the question "How do I create an emergency fund?"

THE MATH

Use this worksheet to budget your commission so that it lasts all year:

Monthly Income
A. Enter the total amount that you can reasonably expect to earn this year in commission: $ _____ .

B. Enter any additional income: $ _____.

C. Add A $ _____ and B $ _____.

D. Divide the total of C by 12 months $ _____.

Monthly Expenses

E. Add up fixed expenses, including insurance, utilities, cell phone charges, car payments, mortgage or rent, and other debt repayment: $ _____.

F. Enter the total of your variable expenses, which is based on the tracking that you did for one month. This amount includes items such as entertainment, dining out, coffee, and any other expenditures: $ _____.

G. Enter contributions to savings: $ _____.

H. If you noticed anything you'd like to cut out or scale back in either E or F, enter the total amount those changes will save you each month here $ _____.

I. Add E $ _____, F $ _____, and G $ _____, and then subtract H $ _____.

Now compare the number in item D (your monthly income) to the number in item I (your monthly expenses). If I's number is greater, you need to go back through your expenses and make some more cuts. If it's less, that's great. Make sure that you have a cushion of about $100 or so, then shift the remaining money to paying down high-interest-rate debt, if you have any, or savings.

I Also Need to Know . . .

Q: Would I set a budget for my severance the same way?

A: Yes, with one exception. When you're living off a severance, you need to scale back. Big-time. Particularly in an economy when the job market is bleak, you need that severance to last for as long as possible. That means taking an even closer look at your monthly expenses and making difficult decisions: Forgoing cable, for example, or clipping coupons, eliminating restaurants, and hosting game nights with friends instead of going out for drinks. You can read more about budgeting your money between jobs on page 370.

Q: What should I look for in the savings account where I keep the bulk of my money?

A: Interest rate and accessibility. This money needs to be liquid. You're going to be drawing on it each month and moving it around quite a bit. So you want it in either an online bank that allows transfers easily—most do, and offer above-average interest rates to boot—or a brick-and-mortar bank in your area. You can compare interest rates in your area and online on Bankrate .com, and I'd definitely do that before making a final decision. After all, this money might as well be working for you, right? Even 1% or 2% in interest can add up.

One note: Some banks allow you to link a savings account to a checking account. That can be convenient, but if you can find better interest rates elsewhere—and often you can—it may be worth having two banks. Just make sure that both allow you to make bank-to-bank transfers free.

115. Can I afford to stop working after having a baby?

A: It depends on your situation. Staying in the workforce has obvious benefits: an additional income, coworker camaraderie, and the enrichment that comes with working in a field you enjoy. But going back to work also comes at a cost. You'll likely have to pay for child care if you don't have a family member who can help you out, work clothes, and commuting costs.

That said, staying home isn't free—not only because of a loss of income but because of increased utility bills. Thinking forward, you may lose some of your future earning power if you stay out of the workforce for too long. So the best way to make this decision is to crunch the numbers.

THE MATH

Use this worksheet to calculate whether one partner can afford to stop working.

A: Enter your monthly take-home pay: $ _____
   Your spouse's monthly take-home pay: $ _____
   Your monthly take-home pay combined: $ _____

B: Enter your anticipated monthly
   expenses post-baby (overestimate, if possible):
   Mortgage or rent: $ _____
   Car payments and insurance: $ _____
   Utilities and cell phone bills: $ _____
   Other insurance (life, home owner's,
   disability): $ _____
   Groceries: $ _____
   Miscellaneous (entertainment, dining
   out, gym membership): $ _____
   Debt repayment: $ _____
   Child-related expenses, not including
   child care: $ _____
   Savings, not including retirement
   contributions automatically deducted
   from your paycheck: $ _____
   Total: $ _____
C: Enter the amount you expect to pay
   for child care each month if both
   spouses were to work: $ _____
D: Enter the amount the spouse who would stay home pays in com-
   muting and other work-related costs each month (wardrobe, your
   daily latte): $ _____
E: Subtract the total in B and C from your combined monthly take-
   home pay in A: $ _____
F: Subtract the total in B from the monthly take-home pay of the
   partner who will continue to work: $ _____
G: Add the total in D and F: $ _____

Now look at which figure is greater: D or G? Remember, you want
a little bit of cushion here, so if it looks like you're cutting it close, go
back and see if you can cut some of your variable expenses in B. If
there isn't any wiggle room, staying home, at least full-time, might
not work. Perhaps there's a part-time work option.

Pushing the math aside for a minute, there are other factors
you need to consider before you make the decision not to go back
to work. Would your health insurance coverage be affected if you
didn't return to work? Will you be able to get back into your field
when you want or need to work again? And, finally, do you have

an emergency fund? The best thing you can do if you're planning to have a child and stop working is to practice living on one income beforehand. You should do so, ideally, for the entire pregnancy, banking the second income. By the time the baby's arrived, you not only know how to live within a tight budget but you've also built up a considerable savings to fall back on if need be.

I Also Need to Know . . .

Q: **What is the cost of raising a child?**

A: There are more than a few calculators online that will help you tally the cost here, but I like the one from BabyCenter.com (www .babycenter.com/cost-of-raising-child-calculator). This calculator lets you input your specific information (number of children, marital status, location, whether you expect your child to attend public or private college), and the results estimate the total cost, as well as the cost in the first year. You'll also find a breakdown of major budgetary components, such as food, transportation, and clothing.

Q: **Is there anything I can do from home to make up for the lost income?**

A: Many stay-at-home parents make up for at least part of their lost income by getting part-time or occasional work or taking a position that allows them to work from home. (For more information on working from home, see the question "What Web sites have information on legitimate stay-at-home jobs?" on page 384). If these aren't options, pitch in another way. My suggestion? Become the money manager for your household. While your partner will be the one earning the income, you can be the one to make sure that the bills are paid and the insurance is handled. You'll monitor spending, scour for good deals on household necessities, and take on the responsibility of making sure that your family lives within its means.

Q: **Any tips for making this a smooth transition?**

A: If you're making the switch from working to staying at home, you need to prepare financially. But you also need to think about the social aspect: Staying at home is going to be a huge transition.

There will be times when you miss your peers. To help keep a balance between parenthood and your social life, make it a point to meet up with friends or former colleagues, whether it's just for coffee or a night out on the town. Even a quick phone call or e-mail to maintain contact may prove to be vital if you find yourself wanting to return to the workforce in the future.

From a financial standpoint, practicing living on one income for a while and saving the other before the baby comes goes a long way here. It's also important to check that you have enough Social Security credits under your belt in case you don't ever return to the workforce. You need 40 to collect your benefits when the time comes. (Note: While spouses can collect benefits that are based on their partner's earnings, that right is granted in the case of divorce only if your marriage lasted more than 10 years.)

Q: **I'm afraid if I don't return to work right away, I'll lose my job. What are the laws?**

A: According to the federal Family Medical Leave Act, employees are allowed to take up to 12 weeks of unpaid leave (during any 12-month period) with their job protected, to care for a newborn child. Not all companies or employees are covered by this law, so you're going to want to read the Family Medical Leave Act section of the U.S. Department of Labor Web site (www.dol.gov/esa/whd/fmla/index.htm) to see if you and your employer qualify.

116. I need a career change. Where do I start?

A: If you have a stable job but you're feeling the itch—maybe you watch the clock all day or you're just unfulfilled by the work—start brainstorming before you take the plunge.

Try to put your finger on your passion. Do you have a hobby that could be turned into a moneymaker? Do you have a fantasy career you've always wanted to pursue? In what other industry or business might your talents and experience be of value?

Once you have a good handle on what you want to do and what your skills will allow, research the types of careers that fit the bill. Start with the U.S. Bureau of Labor Statistics' *Occupational Outlook Handbook* (www.bls.gov/OCO/), which offers descriptions of hundreds of different careers. Once you've narrowed it down, talk with people in the fields you're considering. Ask about the pros and cons of their positions to get an accurate sense of what their job entails and whether you'd be interested in doing something similar.

Then—and this is crucial—take a realistic look at what is available in the current job market. Pay attention to news headlines to see what industries are hiring. Seek out jobs in your area by talking with the local chamber of commerce and local businesses. And start looking at the big job boards daily. Monster.com, CareerBuilder.com, and HotJobs.com are my favorites.

The idea is to come up with 25 to 50 employers you'd be interested in working for. Then start tapping into your networks, both professional and social. Let people know about your career change goals. Often, they'll know about jobs that aren't advertised. Make use of social networking tools such as LinkedIn or Facebook to reconnect with old contacts and make new ones. And call your college's alumni association. They may be able to put you in touch with an alumnus currently working in your desired field.

When it comes time to start applying, make sure you're not submitting a one-size-fits-all résumé. Print out the job description and highlight key words and phrases specific to the position. Then, look at your own résumé and make sure that those same words and phrases appear. Many companies screen potential candidates through electronic applicant tracking systems, which look for key word matches. If your résumé has the same language as the job posting, the odds that you'll get a call from human resources increase. But if you don't get a call, go ahead and follow up anyway.

I Also Need to Know . . .

Q: **Should I see a career counselor?**

A: A counselor can be a great resource if you're struggling with decisions surrounding your career change. He or she will evaluate your education, training, skills, work history, interests, and personality traits to help you find work that's a good fit. A counselor can also arrange for you to take aptitude or achievement tests to better home in on your interests and qualifications. Then the counselor will work with you to develop your job-search skills and help you locate and apply for jobs.

Plus, if you're feeling stressed about the job change, it might be worth your while to schedule an initial meeting and talk things out. If you don't get anything out of it, you don't have to go back.

Q: **Where can I find a career counselor?**

A: I'd start with a call to your local college or university career center. Even if you didn't attend the school, staff members there can provide you with referrals for career counselors in your area. If they can't, as with anything else, you can do a search online for counselors in your area. Call the counselors to get an idea of what they charge and the specific services they offer, and then meet them in person to see if you're a fit.

Q: **How do I assess what type of job I'm best suited for?**

A: O*NET's online "Skill Search" (online.onetcenter.org/skills/) can help you match your skill set to in-demand jobs where your skills could be of use. The site also features an "Interest Profiler" (www.onetcenter .org/IP.html) that can help you determine what type of occupation you might find most interesting.

Q: **How long does it typically take to change careers?**

A: If you want to enter a field where your current skills can be of use, the change can be made quickly, perhaps in a matter of months, depending on the job market. If you're switching to a career that requires additional education, you may need to go back to school for one to four years, and possibly longer if you don't attend full time.

Q: **What if all this research teaches me that I don't want to work for anyone but instead want to start my own business?**

A: Well, now is not the time to quit your day job. But that doesn't mean you can't start a job on the side. If you walk instead of run, you can slowly launch your business while still having your salaried gig as an insurance policy of sorts. If you don't have an idea in mind, here are a couple to consider:

Direct selling: Think Mark cosmetics or The Pampered Chef. These companies allow you to sell their products, either to friends, family members, and coworkers, or to strangers through in-home parties or Web sites. You take a cut of the profit, and there is little upfront cost to you. It's also something you can do on the weekends and evenings, based on your own schedule. To find a company that matches your interests (it's important to be excited about the products you're selling!), head to the Direct Selling Association's Web site at www.directselling411.com.

Online expert sites: These are new, and the key players right now are LivePerson (www.liveperson.com) and Guru.com (www.guru.com). They allow you to share your expertise with others, for a fee. You can dish out financial planning advice by the minute or hour, for example, or counsel people on health issues or teach computer skills. You do need to be a credible source (for instance, you need the correct certification to sign up as a financial planner), and you'll be carefully vetted.

One thing to keep in mind: While you still have your day job, make sure there isn't a conflict of interest with your side job. You must to do them during different hours, of course, but avoiding conflict of interest also means that you must not compete against your employer. If you work in Web design for a firm, for example, your employer probably won't be thrilled if you launch a Web-design company on the side.

117. What Web sites have information on legitimate stay-at-home jobs?

A: First, let's talk about what's not legitimate: Web sites that claim to offer work-from-home jobs but ask you to hand over your billing or credit card information first. They are sure to be a scam.

Luckily, you can sidestep these by using two sites that I recommend often: Women for Hire (www.womenforhire.com) and Mom Corps (www.momcorps.com). Both offer lists of legitimate stay-at-home jobs. You can also look directly at Web sites of corporations for work-from-home opportunities. Many, such as JetBlue, have customer service agents who work remotely.

Beyond that, you can try a general Internet search, but proceed with caution. Many sites oriented to working from home feature ads that are tough to differentiate from editorial content.

If you find something that looks like a good work-from-home opportunity but you still have some lingering doubts, check the company's legitimacy with the BBB (www.bbb.org/us/).

I Also Need to Know . . .

Q: What are the most common stay-at-home jobs?
A: These days almost anything goes when it comes to work-from-home jobs. On the basis of availability and popularity, the top (legitimate) work-from-home jobs are

- Direct sales
- Virtual customer service
- Virtual assistant
- Home companion
- Virtual technical services

Q: What other red flags should I look for to spot scams?
A: These should serve as serious warning signs:

- Having to pay for your own training
- Waiting a month before you get your check
- An employer's inability to provide you with the contact information of a former employee so that you can contact her to get a feel for what the potential job might entail
- Claims that you can make a lot of money with little or no experience
- Claims that you can make a lot of money while putting in only a few hours
- A requirement that you front money for instructions or supplies

Q: How much can I expect to make from a stay-at-home job?
A: As with traditional office jobs, that varies. Some people can make minimum wage by answering calls, while others are attorneys or tax accountants who work from home. The amount you make will depend on your position, skill level, and the amount of hours you put in.

386 ■ MONEY 911

Q: What supplies will I need to work from home?

A: A computer with Internet access and a phone line solely for work purposes. Sometimes your employer will provide you with these things, but not always. To be successful working from home, you're going to need to have a dedicated work space. Your dining room table, for example, should not double as your desk. A dedicated space will give you a separation between work time and personal time. When you're working from home, you will need the rest of your family to recognize that you're on company time.

Q: I currently work in an office, but I think I could do my job from home. How should I go about approaching my boss with the idea?

A: You need more to your argument than just a desire to work from home, so do some brainstorming before you schedule this meeting. What's your reason? Do you think you could be more productive? Would you save on commuting costs? Would the company save money by eliminating your work space?

Next, look at your performance. If there's a chance that your boss could say that it's been subpar, you should hold off on having this conversation until it has improved significantly. Your boss has to trust you to get the work done when you're not being supervised.

Finally, look at the company you work for. Do other employees work from home? If you're proposing something that's brand new, it might be harder and you'll need to present a rationale that benefits the company more than you to get the answer you want. Think about how you would make working from home work. Would it be full time or part time? Would you have everything you need to work from home? Would the company need to install anything? How would people contact you? It's important to think about the logistics before making the proposal to your boss.

It's also helpful to anticipate any reasons your boss could say no. Preempt these responses by creating a proposal in writing. This way, he or she can mull it over, and if it's necessary to discuss your plan with other higher-ups, a written proposal will let you rest assured that all your important arguments are included.

One thing to note: It's easier for your boss to say yes to a trial period than it is to a permanent, immediate change. If you sense hesitation, suggest working from home three days a week for three months. To chart your progress with the trial, offer to schedule a weekly review with your boss. At the end of the trial period, the two of you can sit down and make a decision that is based on the way things went over the past several months.

Q: **Help! I think I'm the victim of a work-from-home scam. What do I do now?**

A: Before you panic, ask the company for a refund. If your contacts refuse, let them know that you plan to notify the appropriate law enforcement officials. My hope is that you've kept careful records of all transactions and conversations you've had, because your case is going to be stronger if you've documented the phone calls, e-mails, and even the original advertisement that hooked you. You should have copies of paperwork, such as letters and receipts, and a record of costs you've incurred, including the time you've spent. When you're ready to make your case, you can file your complaint with the following agencies:

- Your local BBB branch
- Your local or state consumer affairs agency
- The U.S. Postal Inspection Service
- Your state's attorney general's office or the office in the state where the company is headquartered
- The advertising manager of the publication that ran the ad you answered

Resources

Books

The Stay-at-Home Survival Guide: Field-Tested Strategies for Staying Smart, Sane, and Connected While Caring for Your Kids, by Melissa Stanton (2008)

Tips on how to manage everything from your emotions to your finances while being a stay-at-home mom.

Surviving a Layoff: A Week-by-Week Guide to Getting Your Life Back Together, by Lita Epstein (2009)

A week-to-week timeline for getting your life back on track after a job loss; includes information on how to cope with the emotional aspect of a job loss, how to conduct a job search, how to explain your situation to family and friends, how to reorganize your schedule, and how to handle finances.

Who Gets Promoted, Who Doesn't and Why: 10 Things You'd Better Do if You Want to Get Ahead, by Donald Asher (2007)

A guide to career advancement; includes tips on how to make an impression on your employer, strategies to advance your career, advice on how to avoid career mistakes, and interviews with human resources managers showing how corporations make hiring and promotion decisions.

Will Work from Home: Earn the Cash Without the Commute, by Tory Johnson and Robyn Freedman Spizman (2008)

A guide to making working from home work for you; includes a step-by-step plan, helpful tips, and advice on how to avoid scams.

Government Organizations

Career Voyages
www.careervoyages.gov
1-877-872-5627

A Web site dedicated to informing visitors about occupations that are experiencing growth and have an increasing number of job openings; also provides information on how you can train or become further educated to obtain one of these positions.

GovBenefits
www.govbenefits.gov
1-800-333-4636

Determine eligibility and access additional information on unemployment insurance.

United States Bureau of Labor Statistics
www.bls.gov
202-691-5200

Employment and economy information, statistics, research, and tools for people at all stages of their career; also features the *Occupational Outlook Handbook*, with detailed information on hundreds of different jobs.

BabyCenter.com's Cost of Raising Your Child Calculator
www.babycenter.com/cost-of-raising-child-calculator

Estimate how much it will cost to raise a child.

United States Department of Labor
www.dol.gov
1-866-487-2365
Employment resources and information, including answers to FAQs, statistics, and more.

USAJOBS
www.usajobs.gov
The official job site of the U.S. government; search jobs, tips on how to create a standout résumé, interview tips, and more.

Job Search Web Sites

Career Builder
www.careerbuilder.com
1-866-438-1485

Monster.com
www.monster.com
1-800-666-7837

Simply Hired
www.simplyhired.com

HotJobs.com
www.hotjobs.yahoo.com

Web Sites

Mom Corps
www.momcorps.com
1-888-438-8122
Search for a job (includes work-from-home jobs and part-time jobs) with a flexible schedule.

O*NET Online
www.online.onetcenter.org
Developed for the U.S. Department of Labor by the National Center for O*NET Development, O*NET Online offers helpful career tools including the Skills Search (online.onetcenter.org/skills/) and the Interest Profiler (www.onetcenter.org/IP.html).

PayScale
www.payscale.com
1-888-219-0327

Get a free customized salary report to assess what you're worth to your employer or potential employer.

Salary.com
www.salary.com

Career tips, tools and articles, the Salary Wizard to help you estimate your value to current and future employers, a benefits calculator, job search wizard, the Performance Self-Test, and more.

Women for Hire
www.womenforhire.com
212-290-2600

Access job postings, career advice, tips, tools, and more.

CHAPTER 13

TAXES

118. Can I deduct my home office as a business expense? (I'm worried about the IRS.)

A: If you have a place in your home used to conduct business that you don't do anywhere else, you should be taking a home office deduction. Not doing so is leaving free money on the table. But you're right to be cautious. In years past, the home office deduction has been an audit flag for the IRS. You have to play by the rules.

That means that if your home is your primary place for conducting this business (it doesn't have to be your primary occupation; it can be a sideline), you want to designate an area of it specifically for work. If you have three bedrooms and one can be turned into an office, you're in luck, but if you have a corner of your bedroom that can be cleaned out and designated as office space, that can work as well. The idea is to establish a space in your home used only for business. Your kids can't use the desk to do their homework. You can't keep personal files on the computer. And don't write off the entire room—just write off part of it—if it includes a pull-out sofa and turns into a guest room when you have visitors.

CRITERIA FOR CLAIMING THE HOME OFFICE DEDUCTION

Ask yourself these questions before you write off your home office:

1. **Do you use this office regularly?** This doesn't necessarily mean daily, but you should be using it on an ongoing basis for business

or work. If the IRS asks, you should have records of calls you've made from your office over the last year or e-mails on the computer that prove you've worked in that space on an ongoing basis.

2. **Is the space used exclusively for work?** As already explained, the IRS is strict here, and you shouldn't be mixing business with pleasure or even personal activities like paying bills.

3. **Is your home office your principal place of business?** This means that you don't perform the bulk of your work at another location. You must use your office to handle administrative tasks such as invoicing and bookkeeping.

Once you have your office space carved out and you've let the rest of the family know that the area is off limits, you can start adding up your deductions. The IRS allows you to deduct what's called the business percentage of your home expenses, items such as rent, mortgage, home owner's or renter's insurance, related utilities, and real estate taxes. There are two methods for figuring out your business percentage:

1. You can divide the area (length multiplied by width) of your home office by the total area of your home.
2. You can divide the number of rooms used for business by the total number of rooms in your home. This really works only if the rooms are all the same size; otherwise, you may be way off.

Keep in mind that you can't deduct more than your gross income from this business when you deduct the business use of your home.

▶ An Example

Finding the Business Percentage

Example 1
Stacy's home is 2,000 square feet. As an independent financial advisor, she works out of her home daily and uses a spare bedroom as her office. The bedroom measures 300 square feet.

300 ÷ 2,000 = 0.15

Stacy's business percentage is 15%.

Example 2
Sam doesn't know the square footage of his apartment, but it's made up of four rooms that are relatively the same size. He runs his real estate business out of an office he's set up in one of the rooms.

1 ÷ 4 = 0.25

Sam's business percentage is 25%.

THE MATH

How much can a home office deduction be worth? Let's use Stacy, from the example, to find out.

Stacy's monthly expenses:
- Rent: $1,000
- Electricity: $80
- Cable Internet service: $35
- Two phone lines with long distance: $150
- **Total: $1,265**

Stacy can deduct 15% of her rent, electricity, and cable Internet service (unless she never uses it for personal reasons; then she can deduct 100%). She can deduct all of the phone line and related charges used for the business, so we'll assume that that's one phone line, or $75 worth of charges. Her total deductible expenses each month, then, are $242.25. That means that for the year, Stacy can claim a total of $2,907 for the home office deduction.

I Also Need to Know . . .

Q: What kinds of records should I keep in case I'm audited?
A: The IRS requires you to keep records that prove which portion of your home is used for business and that it is used exclusively and

regularly as your principal place of business or as the place that you meet with clients or customers in your regular business affairs. You'll also need to prove any business-related expenses that you claim. That means that you must save receipts, canceled checks, and any other proof of expenses.

If you own your home, you also want to keep records that show depreciation. Keep paperwork that shows when and how you purchased the home, what you paid for it, and any improvements you've made.

In general, all of these records should be kept for either three years from the date you filed your taxes or two years after the taxes were paid, whichever is longer.

Photos are also good. An audit may happen several years down the road. For that reason, it's a good idea to photograph your home office in use. That way, should the space become a nursery, say, you have proof of its former use.

Q: What if I don't own the business, but I work from home as an employee because my boss doesn't have office space?

A: You'll likely still be able to take a home office deduction. To qualify, you must be working from a home office for the convenience of your employer. But if you work from home two days a week because your children are home from school but you have a perfectly acceptable desk for your use in your employer's office, you're not getting a tax break.

119. How do I determine the value of items I donate to charity?

A: To take a tax deduction, anything you donate must be in good used condition or better. What you're looking for is what the IRS calls the "fair market value," which is essentially what the item would go for if it were sold in today's market. So if you gave a used bicycle to Goodwill, the fair market value of the bike would be what a buyer would pay for it, taking the bike's age and condition into consideration.

That's where it gets complicated, because you as the donor don't usually have a good idea of what the item will sell for, and many people tend to under- or overshoot. Often, something may hold a great deal of sentimental value for the donor that doesn't translate to a buyer.

The easiest way to satisfy the IRS requirements (and leave your feelings out of the equation) is to use a free online program such as TurboTax's ItsDeductible (turbotax.intuit.com/personal-taxes/ itsdeductible/index.jsp). The Salvation Army also has a valuation guide for common items on its Web site (go to www.salvationar myusa.org and click on the "Ways to Give" menu on the home page, then choose the "Donation Receipts: Valuation Guide" link). You'll be given a general range of the fair market value of items similar to your donation, and you want to give your best estimate within that range.

FAIR MARKET VALUE RANGE OF COMMON DONATIONS		
ITEM	LOW ($)	HIGH ($)
Radio	7.50	50
Children's bicycle	15	65
Women's coat	10	40
Women's shoes	2	25
Men's raincoat	5	20
Men's suit	15	60
Sofa	25	200
Desk	25	140
Bedspread	3	24

Source: The Salvation Army.

If the item you're looking to value isn't in these databases, search for the items in the "recently completed auctions" section of eBay. Each auction closed at a price that someone is willing to pay for the item; find one in which an item like yours was sold. Print out the sheet as backup, and use that—as well as an estimation of the condition of your item compared with the one that sold—to get to your price.

One thing to note: Cars are an exception to this rule. Up until a few years ago, you could deduct the fair market value of those as well, but the rules changed in 2005. Now, if the car is valued at more than $500, the deduction is based on the charity's actual selling price. The charity will provide you with what's called a statement of sale, which you then need to attach to your tax return in order to take the deduction.

I Also Need to Know . . .

Q: **What kind of documentation do I need?**

A: That depends on the value of the donated items you want to deduct. No matter what you donate, you always want to get a receipt from the organization. It may not list the value of the donation, but you'll still be able to prove that you gave the property away in case the IRS asks for backup. And if you donate more than $250 to an organization in either goods or cash, you need written acknowledgment from the group that you didn't get anything in return.

If the total of your donations reaches $500 or more, you must file IRS Form 8283 with your return. If you're claiming a deduction of more than $5,000, you must get the item appraised before you donate it, then attach the appraisal to section B of that form. Keep a second copy of the appraiser's report with your own records in case you need it. You can deduct the appraisal fees as a miscellaneous itemized deduction, as long as your combined miscellaneous deductions exceed 2% of your adjusted gross income.

Q: **How do I know if I'm donating to a legitimate organization?**

A: Sad to say, but these days, it's a little tough. Less-than-scrupulous groups often use names or symbols that make them appear to be a charity when they're not. It's particularly important to be wary when it comes to unsolicited mailings, phone calls, or e-mails, or even those drop boxes that you see outside of strip malls and supermarkets. All of these should list contact information for the organization, including a phone number (if you're worried about legitimacy, be sure to try it out), a mailing address, and a Web site where you can do a bit more research. If you're still not satisfied, check with the BBB (www.bbb.org/us/) to see if it has any information or complaints on file about the group. The Web site reports on more than a thousand charities, and your local office will have details about even more, particularly smaller groups in your area.

Q: **Is there anything I shouldn't donate?**

A: Most large charities will post their donation rules on the Web, and smaller ones will be able to answer any questions you may have directly. As a general rule, make sure any clothes you're giving away are clean and that there aren't any missing buttons, broken zippers, obvious rips, or stains. You could actually cost the charity money if it has to spend a lot of time sorting through donations to get rid of your old socks or that ripped concert T-shirt from 10 years ago.

Generally, though, there seem to be groups out there for almost every donation as long as you do a little research. A few examples: the Glass Slipper Project (www.glassslipperproject.org/) in Chicago focuses on used prom dresses, Soles4Souls (www.soles4souls.org/) will happily take your gently used shoes, and Baby Buggy (www .babybuggy.org/) in New York is the place to get rid of your baby gear and clothes you no longer need.

120. How do I choose which charities to support?

A: It's fine to allow your heart to lead you down the path, but you have to allow the final decision to be made by your head. Why? Because when you are considering giving away a limited resource— and your money and your time both fall into this category—you need to understand there are more than one million organizations in the United States with their hands out. And they are not all equally deserving of your efforts.

It's perfectly fine—smart, even—to start by making a list of the causes that hit close to home. That could mean your children's school, your alma mater, or a friend's organization. Or it could be more vague: cancer, hunger, the homeless.

If it's a small-scale group, such as a local school, you probably have a good idea of where the money is going and for what it's going to be used. You're funding the basketball team or the debate club's trip to a national competition. You don't feel the need to do a whole lot of digging.

But if you're in the camp of people who support a cause or two but don't necessarily know where to put your money, you need to do some research. Before you write the check, hit the Internet.

Start at Charity Navigator (www.charitynavigator.org). Type in the name of the charity that interests you, and it will spit back a report detailing the group's mission, efficiency in tackling it, and how it spends donated money. You can see how much money the organization took in during the past few years, who heads up the organization, and how much that person is paid. And you can read the ratings given to that charity by the folks at Charity Navigator, as well as comments from other donors. Another solid charity Web site is GuideStar (www2.guidestar.org/).

There are a lot of numbers in each Charity Navigator report. Focus on:

- **Program ratio.** This number tells you what percentage of the charity's income goes to programs, as opposed to administrative costs and other overhead. It's a great place to start, but understand that you shouldn't line up charities of all shapes and sizes and pick the one with the higher program ratio. If you're going to compare groups by this number, you need to compare apples with apples, food banks with the food banks, the homeless outreach programs with the homeless outreach programs, and the museums with other museums. Why? Because some causes incur more administrative costs. A museum, for instance, needs security, a large building, insurance, and a cleaning staff. A food bank doesn't.
- **Growth.** Revenue growth and growth in program spending should go hand in hand. Consistency from year to year signals a healthy organization—healthy, financially speaking. Struggling charities, while in need of donations, may not be around long enough to use the money in the way you want them to.
- **Capital.** Look for charities that have at least six months' worth of savings, so they can fund their operations if they experience a slowdown in donations.
- **CEO pay.** Charities are required to disclose how much their CEOs earn, but again, you want to compare similar charities, not across the board. If one food bank's CEO earns $200,000 and a handful of others earn only $50,000, it's safe to assume that something might be amiss.

If the numbers add up, you can start asking the tough questions. Any good charity will be open to talking to a potential donor. Ask about the group's short- and long-term goals, how it plans to reach them, and what progress it has made in the past. These answers, combined with organizations' financial statements, should help you single out the group most deserving of your money.

I Also Need to Know . . .

Q: **Can I spread my charitable donations among a handful of groups?**

A: You can, but it's often better to select one or two. In general, your dollars are more useful if you give a smaller number of larger donations rather than a larger number of smaller donations. It costs the charity money to solicit and process your donation, and that means a greater percentage of your money is going to administrative costs and overhead instead of the cause you want to support.

Q: **Money is tight. Is it okay to skip out on my usual donations this year?**

A: Of course it's okay, but you may not want to. Often when we're feeling strapped for cash, it helps psychologically to give a little bit to people who are less fortunate. It brings financial matters into perspective and makes you value what you have even more. Also, when you're struggling to keep up, your favorite charity is likely struggling right along with you, particularly human services charities, such as food banks, homeless shelters, and soup kitchens. That doesn't mean that you need to scrape together the exact amount you gave last year, but if you can come up with something, it will make a big difference, both to your mental health and to the charity.

But don't forget that there are other ways to give as well—free ways. If you have a few hours a week or even a month, see if you can volunteer. If you have used clothing or extra cans of food, donate them. Every little bit helps.

Q: **How do I deduct on tax returns the money that I donate to charities?**

A: You can deduct cash donations to charity when you file taxes for the year in which the donation was made. If you give more than $250, you need a written receipt from the charity, and it has to list any goods or services you received in return. For example, if your contribution was part of a benefit dinner, you can deduct the amount of your ticket, less the value of your meal.

For you to be able to take a deduction, the organizations you support must be recognized by the IRS. Most are, but you should double-check before writing the check. You can do that by searching on the IRS Web site (www.irs.gov) or by calling the IRS directly (877-829-5500).

Q: How much is the deduction worth?

A: That depends. The deduction goes against your income tax, which means the amount that it is worth to you depends on your adjusted gross income and what tax bracket you fall into. The more money you make, the more of a deduction you'll receive for money given to charity. Consult the chart below for a few examples:

TAX RATE (%)	DONATION ($)	ACTUAL COST AFTER DEDUCTION ($)
15	100	85
	500	425
	1,000	850
25	100	75
	500	375
	1,000	750
28	100	72
	500	360
	1,000	720
33	100	67
	500	335
	1,000	670
35	100	65
	500	325
	1,000	650

121. We owe the IRS back taxes. What do we do?

A: Pick up the phone and call the IRS (1-800-829-1040). Hiding from this debt will do you no good. Explain your situation. There are a number of things that the IRS can do to help you, including postponing a collection action against you, putting you on a payment plan, or allowing for skipped or reduced monthly payments. Take careful notes, including the names of the people you speak to. The IRS is an enormous operation, and if you're promised something that doesn't materialize, you're going to want to be able to retrace your steps.

A payment plan is available, generally, to anyone who owes less than $25,000 and believes they will be able to pay that debt off within five years. You can apply for this option using IRS form 9465 (available at www.irs.gov), but you can't send it in electronically. This form must be sent in the mail.

If your call falls flat—or you've already been put on a payment plan and you're still behind—you probably need to take more drastic measures. That could mean selling assets, if you have any, to pay off debt, or it could mean negotiating what's called an offer in compromise, which is an agreement between you and the IRS that settles your debt for a reduced amount.

An Offer in Compromise works only in extreme circumstances, after you've exhausted other options. Essentially, you—or your tax attorney, if you have one—will be required to make an offer to settle, which must be more than the amount the IRS would be able to glean from selling your assets and draining your bank accounts but can be less than you owe. Understand that not every offer is accepted, and you may end up on the hook for the full amount of your debt—or more, because in some cases, there is a $150 application charge. You should also be prepared to hand over 20% of the amount you offer the IRS immediately.

One note: If you know you're going to owe but you can't afford to pay, you still need to file your taxes on time. The penalties for not filing are greater than the penalties for not paying.

I Also Need to Know . . .

Q: **Does the IRS charge interest?**

A: Absolutely. When you are accepted into a payment plan with the IRS, you'll pay interest at a rate set every three months at the federal short-term interest rate plus 3%. It is compounded daily and adds up fast.

There is also a monthly late payment penalty, which is assessed at 0.5% of the tax owed. If your return is more than 60 days late, there is a minimum penalty of either $100 or 100% of the tax owed, whichever is less.

THE MATH

How much could your tax bill end up costing you if you don't pay up on time? Let's say you owe $10,000 from that 401(k) withdrawal. As I write, the IRS's interest rate is at 6%.

- Pay in full by April 15 and you'll pay $10,000.
- Pay one month late and you'll pay $10,096.96.
- Pay six months late and you'll pay $11,420.25.
- Pay a year late and your bill will total $15,519.46.

Q: **Do I need a lawyer or an accountant?**

A: Not necessarily, particularly as that is just an added expense that could go toward paying down your tax bill. If you feel overwhelmed, an independent organization within the IRS called the Taxpayer Advocate Service (www.irs.gov/advocate/) can help answer your questions and take you through the steps of working out a payment plan or filing an offer in compromise. The service can be reached by calling the toll-free case intake line: 877-777-4778.

Q: **What happens if I don't pay?**

A: If you don't pay at all—let's say you try to hide from the debt—the IRS can do one of three things. The easiest is to garnish any future tax refunds, if you're entitled to them. If that doesn't work, the IRS will either issue a tax lien against your property, which can do some significant damage to your credit score and prevent you from being able to sell that property if you want to, or issue a notice of levy, which allows the IRS to sell your property and use the proceeds to pay off your debt. The agency may sell real estate or your car, or it might garnish or tap into your paycheck, you bank accounts, your Social Security benefits, or your retirement accounts. You're better off negotiating a payment plan.

Q: **Is there any property that can't be levied?**
A: There is a short list of exempt property, including child-support payments, workers' compensation, unemployment benefits, some annuity and pension benefits, and some clothing. Additionally, only items expected to bring in money over and above the cost of liquidating them can be levied.

Resources

Books

The Better Business Bureau's Wise Giving Guide
A quarterly magazine published by the BBB Wise Giving Alliance; includes summary of the latest results of the Alliance's national charity evaluations. To obtain your free copy, send a postcard or note with your name and address to
BBB Wise Giving Guide
4200 Wilson Blvd, suite 800
Arlington, VA 22203

Home Business Tax Deductions: Keep What You Earn, by Stephen Fishman (2008)
Basic information on how different business structures are taxed and how deductions work, including information on various expenses.

J.K. Lasser's 1001 Deductions and Tax Breaks 2009: Your Complete Guide to Everything Deductible, by Barbara Weltman (2008)
A straightforward guide to tax deductions and breaks; explains tax benefits along with their eligibility requirements; includes tips and new tax law alerts.

The Retirement Savings Time Bomb . . . and How to Defuse It: A

Five-Step Action Plan for Protecting Your IRAs, 401(k)s, and Other Retirement Plans from Near Annihilation by the Taxman, by Ed Slott (2007)

IRA expert Ed Slott shares his tips for protecting your retirement savings.

Government Resources

Internal Revenue Service
www.irs.gov
1-800-829-1040

Information on how to file taxes, online tools to assist in the process, an online small-business tax calculator, information on what donations are deductible, and information on how to deduct donations from your taxes.

Internal Revenue Service Taxpayer Advocate Service
www.irs.gov/advocate/
1-877-777-4778

The Taxpayer Advocate Service can help answer your questions, take you through the steps of working out a payment plan, or help you file an offer in compromise.

Web sites

American Institute of Certified Public Accountants Tax Center
tax.aicpa.org/

Tax tips, recent news, and information on legislation and tax practice tools.

Better Business Bureau
www.bbb.org/us/
703-276-0100

Check out a business or charity, inquire about or file a complaint about a charity, read answers to FAQs, and find tips and additional resources for donors.

Charity Navigator
www.charitynavigator.org
201-818-1288

Evaluations of more than 5,300 of America's largest charities, tips and resources on giving to charity, articles, and a glossary of terms related to giving.

Goodwill
www.goodwill.org
1-800-741-0186

Information on tax-deductible donations and a valuation guide for donated items.

GuideStar
www.guidestar.org
757-229-4631

With a basic GuideStar membership, you can access information to determine a nonprofit's legitimacy, learn if your donation will be deductible, view a nonprofit's recent Form 990, and more.

Nolo.com
www.nolo.com

Answers to FAQs about small-business taxes and articles on how to pay taxes for a small business.

Salvation Army
www.salvationarmyusa.org
1-800-SAL-ARMY

Donation information, including a valuation guide for donated items.

TurboTax
www.turbotax.com

Access TurboTax's ItsDeductible online program, which helps you track your donations for free.

CHAPTER 14

MARRIAGE

122. Should my mate and I have separate or joint bank accounts?

A: I'm a big advocate of both, actually. You have a joint account for general household and shared expenses—groceries, the mortgage payments, utilities, saving, and the like—and separate accounts for your individual saving and spending.

Why? We all need some financial independence, a little money that is all ours, so that we can do whatever we like with it without having to answer questions or ask permission. You can use funds from your account to buy that new pair of shoes you've had your eye on, and your spouse can bring home a new set of golf clubs without asking. It's easy, it works, and it allows you both to have a hand in your finances because you need to manage the joint account—and your contributions to it—together.

To do that, have your paychecks directly deposited into your separate checking accounts, and then have your bank automatically deposit a set percentage into the joint account each month. You should each contribute the same percentage of your earnings to the joint account—but not necessarily the same amount.

First, sit down and figure out how much the joint account needs each month to stay afloat by adding up your monthly expenses (mortgage, car payments, saving, day care, dinners out for you both, groceries, etc.). Once you have your goal—be sure to allow for a little wiggle room—figure out what percentage of each of your salaries will need to be deposited to meet it.

THE MATH

Say that after taxes and retirement contributions, your take-home pay is $2,800 a month. Your spouse, however, brings home $4,000 a month.

Total: $6,800/month

Your monthly expenses account for $4,000 a month, or 58% of your total take-home pay. That means you both need to kick in 58% of your individual income to meet the mark.

His: $2,320
Hers: $1,624

To be sure you're covered, I'd add an extra $200 or so from each of you on top of that. The rest of the money is yours to spend or save how you please.

I Also Need to Know . . .

Q: What about saving?

A: If your employers offer 401(k) plans, you should take advantage of those, and those contributions will be kept separate. The same goes for IRAs. But if you're saving for a goal—a down payment on a house, for example, or a vacation—you should work out a plan so that you do that together, in a high-interest savings account or a money market. You'll want to use the same approach: Figure out your goal amount and date, and how much you need to save each month to reach it. Then calculate what percentage of your take-home pay must be contributed to savings each month to meet your goal. This money comes out of your pay after taxes, retirement contributions, and monthly expenses.

Q: What if one of us doesn't work?

A: It's still possible to have your own accounts. Basically, you're going to reverse the system above. The working partner's paychecks, after taxes and retirement savings, will be deposited into the joint checking account. Then you'll have a preset amount funneled into your separate accounts each month, leaving enough in the joint account to cover monthly expenses with a little cushion.

How do you determine the amount? You'll have to discuss your needs. If the working partner wears suits on the job, he or she will need a little extra to cover clothing. Likewise, if you have a gym membership that has to be paid each month, you'll have to take that into consideration. It's all about compromise, really, and talking it out.

One more thing to note: The nonworking mate, if qualified under the law, should be contributing to a spousal IRA. For more, see "I am a married, stay-at-home parent. How do I save for retirement?" on page 288.

123. I am getting divorced. What are my first financial steps?

A: The answer to this question depends on a few factors. Is the divorce amicable? Are you the primary earner? Are your finances merged? Let's go through each scenario separately:

If the split is on friendly terms—or, at the very least, you're not worried about your spouse raiding your bank account—you don't have to be too concerned with splitting up your bank accounts right away. Instead, you should focus on how exactly you're going to begin the divorce proceedings and how you'll pay for an attorney. One scenario, and you should consider this option only if you've already agreed on the terms of the split, is to file for divorce on your own, without attorneys. You can first go to family court to decide custody and child-support arrangements, and then go to court to finalize the divorce. You'll pay only court fees, considerably less than the cost of an attorney. But you should agree to go this route together, and only if you're on the same page about how you'll split up your assets and the custody of your children. As a general rule, if you have enough assets to afford attorneys, you should probably hire them. You can still sort out the details amicably, through mediation or a process called collaborative divorce (more on this topic on page 411).

If the divorce is hostile and it's possible that your spouse could try to drain your bank accounts, you want to take precautions. In most states, you can remove all or some of the funds from a joint account, provided that you have legitimate reason to feel that the assets are in jeopardy, and place the money in another account for safekeeping. This isn't the time to go on a shopping spree. The court will ask you to prove that you moved the money to protect it, not spend it. You'll also need a legitimate reason for feeling that you had to do so, and spite is not a sufficient reason. Talk to your attorney before making any major moves.

If you are what a divorce attorney would call the moneyed spouse (in other words, you bring home the bulk of the family's income), you may want to start to segregate some money. You don't want to cut your husband or wife off completely, but it makes sense to open up an account in your own name and start funneling a reasonable portion of your paychecks in that direction, leaving your spouse enough to cover his or her living expenses. Certainly, if you get a chunk of money separate from your standard paycheck, such as a bonus, you'd want to put it into a separate account. Now, that doesn't mean that the money won't be considered joint funds in court—it likely will—but at least you'll have it for safekeeping in the meantime.

If you're not the primary earner—maybe you're the one who stays home with the kids—you want to make a summary of your budget. You must figure out how much you need to live on, so if you end up having to fight for your fair share, you'll know where to start negotiations. You also need to start thinking about how you'll bring in an income when you have a home to maintain on your own.

Finally, both parties should make themselves aware of the family's financial situation and assets. Gather all important information, such as past tax returns, bank and retirement plan statements, and credit card or loan balances. The idea is to get a rough estimate of what the marital estate is worth, inclusive of your home, if you own it, your 401(k) and IRA balances as well as your spouse's, your mortgage or other debt, your regular bank accounts, and any other assets or liabilities.

I Also Need to Know . . .

Q: How do I find a divorce attorney?
A: I'd go about it the same way I would if I were looking for a doctor or a new accountant: Ask your friends and family. Judging by the

divorce rate in the United States, I'm sure you know a handful of people who have gone through the process, so see if they'd recommend the attorney they used. If that effort comes up short, you can call your local bar association and ask for a list of names. Either way, you want to set up consultations with two or three lawyers (this initial meeting is often free). Do it in person so that you can get a feel for what it would be like to work with each attorney. Make sure you feel comfortable enough to ask the lawyer questions and share the personal details and circumstances of the split.

Six Questions to Ask a Divorce Lawyer

1. **How long have you been practicing?**
   Answer: You want someone with a lot of experience, but make sure that the lawyer you choose is staying up to date on the latest trends and changes in the industry and the laws in your state. Ask what's changed since the person started practicing. You can also flip through a couple of past copies of your state's law journal to see if any of this person's cases have been included.
2. **How would you handle my case?**
   Answer: Some lawyers prefer to go to trial; others like to settle. Settling is cheaper. You should go with someone whose preference is in line with your own.
3. **How many cases have you handled this year?**
   Answer: Try to aim for someone who has handled at least 20 cases a year.
4. **Do you use mediation?**
   Answer: If you're not interested in that route, you don't need a lawyer who actively mediates. But if it's something you want to consider—and going through mediation is often cheaper than hiring two attorneys—you want someone with the right experience.
5. **What is a reasonable resolution in my case?**
   Answer: The lawyer should be honest about how he or she thinks the case will proceed, including anything that might work against you. False promises are a red flag.

6. **What are your fees?**
Answer: Make sure that you can afford what the lawyer charges, keeping in mind that he or she may work more hours than you planned for. Ask the lawyer if he or she would be willing to work out a payment plan if you need one.

Q: How much does it cost to get divorced?
A: It varies, depending on whether you go to court, how long the proceedings take, and how many hours the attorneys put in. If you handle the details of the separation yourself and just go to court to have it finalized, you could pay less than $500, depending on the state you live in. If you're able to work things out through mediation or collaborative divorce, you might pay $5,000 or so, with the total being based on the number of times you meet and the length of each session. And if you have a contested divorce or a lengthy case, you can expect to pay upward of $10,000 to $20,000, perhaps significantly upward.

Q: What is collaborative divorce?
A: Collaborative divorce is an alternative to a traditional divorce, which often ends in court. In a collaborative divorce, you take the court out of the equation and work together—with your attorneys involved—to come up with a settlement. Before starting talks, you both will have to agree to collaborate and communicate openly about what's best for each other and your children.

There are generally only four people in the room—you, your spouse, and your respective lawyers. The lawyers are there to keep things fair and help you reach a decision. You'll want to hire an attorney specifically trained in collaborative divorce; you can find one through organizations such as the International Academy of Collaborative Professionals (www.collaborativepractice.com/). In many cases, you and your attorneys will need to sign an agreement saying that you won't go to court. If the conversation and the negotiations turn ugly and you end up needing a judgment, your attorney will likely withdraw from the case and you'll need to find a new one.

Keep in mind that while it sounds wonderful—and in some cases, it can be—it's not for everyone. By the time divorce enters the equation, many couples have already reached the point where they can't talk without arguing, and collaborative divorce attempts to eliminate the hostility and find a solution. If both parties can't agree to do that, you're better off leaving your situation in the hands of lawyers who can fight for you or, in the worst case, a judge. You have to be on the same page, or at least similar pages, about how you're going to work out this separation for collaborative divorce to be effective.

Q: **What's the difference between collaborative divorce and mediation?**

A: Mediation involves one third-party individual who will help you negotiate and settle the case. The mediator can't give you legal advice or take sides; he or she listens and works with you to reach an agreement. You can go to mediation with or without lawyers, and when you've settled on an outcome, the mediator will draw up the terms.

In collaborative divorce, there is no third party. You'll work together and with your lawyers to come to a settlement and then the lawyers will outline an agreement. In both cases, you must be willing to talk openly and meet your spouse halfway.

124. My ex refuses to pay child support. How do I get the money?

A: Laws related to child support can vary by state. In all states, though, the district or state attorney is required to help you collect, so that's the place to start. That attorney will likely serve your ex-spouse with papers that require arrangement of a payment schedule with the district or state office.

If that fails, the attorney will be able to go after the money in other ways, including garnishing wages or tax refunds. Extreme enforcement measures include suspending a business license, if there is one, and refusing to issue a passport. In some states, a driver's license can be garnished as well. If you incur a lot of legal fees in your battle for the money, the court may require that your ex-spouse pay those as well.

It's far better, of course, to avoid this whole song and dance. When the court rules that you'll receive child support, you can ask that it be paid through your state's child support-enforcement agency, which means you don't have to do anything at all. The agency will collect your ex's payments and send them to you. If your former spouse doesn't pay, the agency will intervene and go after the money. The agency will also automatically seek cost-of-living increases. For these services, you'll pay a small administrative fee, generally $25 a year. And if you didn't take advantage of this service at the time of divorce, it's not too late. You just have to go back to court and make the change.

I Also Need to Know . . .

Q: Is there a way to figure out in advance how much my child support will be?

A: Child support is based on a percentage of income—in other words, it's a basic mathematical calculation, and there isn't much wiggle room. If you have joint physical custody of the child and you both make similar incomes, you likely won't have a child-support arrangement. However, if one person makes considerably more than the other, that person may be required to pay child support, even if you share custody.

The exact arrangements will be determined by a judge, but most states have a child-support calculator online, so you can plug in your numbers to see how much you will pay or be paid each month.

▶ An Example

Let's say that Mark and Mary, residents of Indiana, decide to get divorced. They have one 10-year-old daughter and a joint-custody arrangement that splits their time with her evenly. Mark's gross weekly income is $2,000, while Mary's is half that at $1,000. They each spend $200 a week on after-school child care. According to Indiana's basic calculations, Mark would pay Mary $165.86 each week in child support.

Q: I can no longer afford the amount of child support that I'm required to pay. Is there anything I can do?

A: You should first talk to your ex-spouse. If he or she is aware of your situation, you may be able to work out an alternative arrangement. If you do, you'll have to get it approved by a judge.

If you can't agree, you can go back to the court and ask to have your payments modified on the basis of a change in circumstances. You're going to have to prove that there was, in fact, a change in circumstances: a layoff, a reduction in hours, a new lower-paying job, or an illness—whatever the case may be. The court may award you with a temporary modification—until, for example, you find a higher-paying job—or a permanent one, if your circumstances won't change.

Keep in mind that this system works both ways. If you ever come into a situation that allows you to pay more in child support, instead of less, your ex-spouse can go back to the court and ask for a modification. It may not be granted, but it's a possibility.

Q: **What is the difference between child support and alimony?**
A: Alimony, also known as spousal support or maintenance, has nothing to do with children. It is a way of providing money for living expenses to the lower-income spouse, typically determined by a judge based on each spouse's income, ability to earn money, health, and on the length of the marriage.

Alimony and child support are also treated differently for tax purposes. If you pay alimony, you can deduct it on your taxes, and if you receive it, you must pay income taxes on it. Child support, however, isn't deductible or taxable.

125. How can I save money on my wedding?

A: The best way to cut costs on a wedding and reception is to cut your guest list. Let's say you're having a sit-down dinner at $75 a head. Eliminating just 10 people will save you $750. Plus, you're getting rid of an entire table, which means you're slashing costs on decorations (centerpieces can run upward of $50), favors, linens, and more.

But let's be honest. It's not always easy to cut people off your list. Maybe you're already at the bare-bones minimum, that precarious line where feelings could start to get hurt. Or maybe you have a huge family that comes as a pack—either you invite them all or invite no one. In that case, try these suggestions:

- **Time it right.** If you avoid the busy wedding months— generally May, June, September, and October—you'll save money. Not only will venues be less expensive but also vendors will be more likely to negotiate with you because they are happy to have business at all. August, January, and February tend to be the cheapest months to walk down the aisle. You might save 20% a head.

- **Pick a nontraditional day.** Plan your party on a Thursday or Friday night instead of a Saturday. You'll be able to get the same kind of deals because Friday isn't the traditional day to have a wedding.

- **Cut back all around.** If you eliminate one big element— flowers, say, or music—trust me, your guests will notice. But go with seasonal, local flowers instead of calla lilies, or smaller bouquets, and you'll fake everyone out. The exception? I'd cut out favors, if you need to make a total elimination. Often they get left behind on tables anyway.

- **Use an e-mail save-the-date.** You can make one on your own, or you can use a template from The Knot (www.theknot .com). Either way, you'll save money, stamps, and paper. I wouldn't advise e-mail for the invitation itself (too informal, in most cases), but it's perfect for a save-the-date.

- **Make a wedding Web site.** You can get free space for a mini Web site of your own from Web sites such as The Knot or mywedding.com. You pick the design of your choice, enter the details of your wedding, and then direct your guests there on the invitation instead of incurring extra printing charges for a sheet explaining the directions and accommodations.

- **Always overbudget.** Little expenses are going to pop up, and it will do a lot for your mental health if your budget has some flexibility. And don't forget to include tips and tax in the overall breakdown. These can run hundreds of dollars.

SAMPLE WEDDING BUDGET

Use this worksheet to allocate your budget. Remember, all of these items are not requirements.

Total Budget $_____
Reception 50%
    Venue/rentals $_____
    Food $_____
    Bar $_____
    Cake $_____
    Taxes and tips $_____
Décor 10%
    Flowers for ceremony $_____
    Bride's bouquet $_____
    Bridesmaids' bouquets $_____
    Boutonnieres/corsages $_____
    Reception decorations $_____
    Lighting $_____
    Taxes and tips $_____
Attire 10%
    Gown, veil/hat/headpiece, alterations $_____
    Tux $_____
    Bride's accessories $_____
    Groom's accessories $_____
    Hair and makeup $_____
    Taxes and tips $_____
Photography 10%
    Photographer $_____
    Videographer $_____
    Prints and albums $_____
    Taxes and tips $_____
Ceremony 2%
    Site fee $_____
    Officiant $_____
    Miscellaneous $_____
Music 10%
    Ceremony music $_____
    Cocktail-hour music $_____
    Reception music $_____
    Equipment rental $_____
    Taxes and tips $_____
Favors/Gifts 3%
    Welcome bags $_____

Bridal party gifts $_____

Stationery 2%
   Save-the-dates $_____
   Invitations $_____
   Programs $_____
   Place cards $_____
   Menu cards $_____
   Thank-you cards $_____
   Postage $_____

Rings 2%
   His $_____
   Hers $_____

Transportation 1%
   Limo $_____
   Shuttle for guests $_____

Watch Out for These!

Hidden fees. Or even not-so-hidden fees. As I mentioned earlier, taxes and tips can eat away at a budget before you know it, so make sure you account for them. Who should be tipped? In general, anyone who provides a service: The wedding planner, hair and makeup stylists, delivery staff, DJ or band, and limo driver all expect a little extra. Catering contracts often have the service charges built in, so check before tipping.

Other fees or charges to watch out for:

- **Cake-cutting charges.** These can run $1 a slice.
- **Delivery charges for the cake.** These can be $50 to $100.
- **Liability insurance.** If your venue requires it, this can be about $200.
- **Overtime.** Most DJs, bands, and photographers and videographers will charge time and a half or even double their hourly rate for any hours not booked ahead of time.
- **Prints of your pictures.** To save money, buy a package that includes prints or purchase the rights to your photos from the photographer and print them yourself.

I Also Need to Know . . .

Q: Is there anything I can do myself?

A: You're limited only by your creativity and your time. Chances are, you're not going to want to bake a cake the day before the wedding or make flower arrangements the week of. But small things that can be done in advance can save you a lot of money in the long run. A few ideas: Order simple invitations and personalize them with a rhinestone in your wedding colors or a custom stamp of your initials. If you're making welcome bags for hotel rooms, you can personalize the water bottles yourself rather than buying expensive versions online. Make your own favors, if you're having them, and enlist the help of family members. That aunt who wants a job? Ask her to make her famous chocolate chip cookies for the goodie bags.

Q: Is it still traditional for the bride's parents to foot the bill?

A: No. More and more couples are contributing to the cost of their own wedding—about 75%, according to The Knot—largely because people are marrying at an older age these days and thus have full-time jobs and the resulting income to cover wedding expenses. As you start your planning talk to both sets of parents to see what they intend to contribute, then build your budget from there.

THE STATS

- **2.5 million:** The number of weddings that take place each year in the United States
- **$28,000:** The average wedding budget
- **175:** The average number of invited wedding guests

Resources

Associations

International Academy of Collaborative Professionals
www.collaborativepractice.com
602-953-7881

Information on how to resolve a divorce without going to court, through the use of collaborative practice; search for a collaboration professional or a collaboration practice in your area.

American Bar Association
www.abanet.org
312-988-5000
The Web site has a special section covering family law; offers answers to FAQs, assistance in finding a lawyer, and charts that summarize the basic laws in each state by topic, including grounds for divorce, custody, and alimony.

Association for Conflict Resolution
www.acrnet.org/
202-464-9700
A professional organization whose mission is to enhance the practice and public understanding of conflict resolution; search the Web site for a family mediator and browse resources on conflict resolution.

Books

The Complete Divorce Handbook, by Brette McWhorter Sember (2009)
Answers to hundreds of divorce-related questions in layperson's terms.

How to Debt-Proof Your Marriage, by Mary Hunt (2008)
Information for couples on how to successfully manage their finances and avoid debt.

Government Resources

Office of Child Support Enforcement (of the Administration for Children and Families, under the U.S. Department of Health and Human Services)
www.acf.hhs.gov/programs/cse/
202-401-9373
Information on child support, including handbooks and assistance in establishing support orders and collecting support payments.

Web Sites

Brides.com
www.brides.com

Wedding budget and planning guides; create a free, customized wedding budget with the site's budget advisor.

divorce360.com
www.divorce360.com

Resources, advice, and a community for those in all stages of divorce; includes guidance on legal issues, spousal support, and the emotions that surround divorce.

The Knot
www.theknot.com

Create your own personalized wedding budgeter and access articles and content about money-saving tips, wedding budget advice, and more.

Nolo.com
www.nolo.com
1-800-728-3555

Features a section on family law, with a lawyer directory, checklists, a glossary of legal terms, and recent articles on family law and divorce.

CHAPTER 15

MILESTONES

126. I'm graduating from college. How do I establish myself financially?

A: These days, many—if not most—college students have checking accounts and even credit cards. But if you don't, you want to open both a checking and a savings account at your local bank, as well as get a credit card (as soon as you turn 21, or sooner if your parents will cosign) to start establishing a more comprehensive credit history. If you have student loans, you likely already have a file, but lenders like to see that you're capable of managing different types of debt.

Look for a checking account that is free (most accounts are, particularly if you elect to have your paychecks direct deposited or you use your debit card a few times each month) and a savings account that pays you a decent rate of interest. (For more information, see the question "How do I find the best interest rate on savings accounts, money market accounts, and CDs?" on page 341.)

As for that first credit card: Look for one with a low or no annual fee and a low interest rate. Without an established credit history, you may be offered a low credit limit, and that's okay. The purpose of this card is not to go wild or spend more than you make. It's to use it every once in a while and then pay off your balance each and every month, in full and on time. That way, you're building a solid credit score and will look appealing to future creditors. If you have student loans, paying them on time will help as well. Don't even think about rewards cards. They typically charge annual fees and an interest rate higher than you can find on other cards. They're not what you need right now.

If you can't get a card because you lack a credit history, apply for a secured card, which allows you to deposit a lump sum of money as collateral. That money, on which you should earn interest, becomes your credit limit. Look for a card that will automatically convert into a regular credit card after 18 to 24 months of your paying your bill on time.

Then, assuming that you have your first full-time job and thus your first steady stream of income, you need to build a budget. Start by listing your take-home pay and your fixed monthly expenses side by side (your rent, your utilities, your car payment and insurance, and anything else you pay for month in and month out). To that, add your variable expenses—groceries, entertainment, gas—and then subtract all of your expenses from your total take-home pay.

Do you have money left over? If you do, that gets stashed in your savings account each month so that you can build an emergency fund equal to three to six months' worth of expenses. This fund is key to staying out of credit card debt, because if an unexpected bill comes your way—your car breaks down or you went way over your cell phone minutes—you'll have money to cover it.

If you're just breaking even—or worse, you're in the hole—go back over your expenses and see where you can cut back. It helps to track your spending for a few weeks to see where the leaks are. For more on the basics of budgeting, see page 117: "How do I set up a monthly budget?"

I Also Need to Know . . .

Q: **How much should I be saving?**

A: A good rule of thumb is 10% of your income, but if you can't get there, start where you can and work your way up. If your employer offers matching dollars for contributing to the 401(k) plan, at the very least contribute enough to grab those. The average 401(k) match is 50% of your own contribution, up to 3% of your salary. Once you've hit that mark, put anything else you can scrape together each month into that savings account that I just mentioned, with the goal of amassing three to six months' worth of expenses. When you do, you can shift back to the 401(k) and try to max out your contribution for the year.

Q: Should I live with my parents to save money?

A: More and more recent grads are taking this route. A survey by the job-search site CollegeGrad.com found that 77% of 2008 graduates moved back in with their parents. No doubt it does save money to live at home for a year or even a few years after college, but it also pushes off responsibility to some extent. At some point, you're going to have to learn to live on your own and learn how to make ends meet when you have rent and groceries to think about. And in many ways, living at home takes some of the pressure off, pressure that might otherwise make you more productive: After all, are you really going to do your best to save money and advance in your career if you know that your parents will always be there to support you?

Here's my take: If you want to live at home and your parents are open to the idea, then go ahead and do it, if—and this is a big if—you're going to save the money that you would be spending on rent and other expenses if you were to live on your own. Every cent should be socked away in a savings account at a decent rate of interest, and you should have a goal date in mind for when you're going to move out. If you're not going to do that, go ahead and get an apartment with a roommate or two. You'll still cut down on your expenses, but you'll be doing it on your own.

I also think that your parents should charge you something to live there, even if the amount is small, and that you should be sure to contribute around the house in other ways.

Q: Do I need any insurance?

A: You do. If you move in with your parents, their home owner's insurance will cover your belongings, but if you're out on your own, you need renter's insurance. If you ever experience a fire or theft, you'll thank me. For more on renter's insurance, turn to "How do I know if I need renter's insurance?" on page 271.

Another nonnegotiable is health insurance. Many college students are on their parents' health insurance plan as a dependent, and unfortunately, many of those same insurers give students the boot upon graduation (double check, though, as some have age

424 ■ MONEY 911

limits instead). If you're lucky, you'll land a job that picks up part of the tab for your own coverage, but if you're an hourly employee without benefits—or you're still looking for a job—you need to find an individual plan. You can do so fairly inexpensively in most states if you don't have any preexisting conditions, but no matter what the cost, it's worth it. For more on finding individual health insurance plans, turn to "How do I buy my own health insurance?" on page 244.

127. When starting a new job, how do I make the most of my benefits?

A: When you start a new job, the company's human resources department (or your boss, if it's a small organization) should sit down with you and go over the available benefits. If no one offers to do that with you, ask. Here are the topics you should discuss:

- **Health insurance.** Some companies will offer just one option; others will offer a few. If you have a choice, you should consider both your needs and the needs of your family as well as the price. There's no sense in paying more for a plan with benefits that you know you'll never use. Think about the future as well as the present: Do you have doctors you're particularly loyal to, and do they accept patients covered by these plans? Do you take certain prescriptions on a regular basis, and do these plans cover those? For more in-depth advice on picking your health plan, see "How do I pick the right type of health insurance?" on page 241.
- **Other insurance on the menu.** Many employers offer other forms of insurance as well, including life and disability. Group life policies offered through employers typically don't provide a huge death benefit, but they often have the advantage of being inexpensive, not requiring a physical, and, should you change jobs, allowing you to continue the coverage at a reasonable rate—again, with no health exam. As for disability, if anyone relies on your income, including you, disability insurance is worth paying for. If you don't—say you and your partner both work, you have no dependents, and you could comfortably live off your partner's salary if need be—then you

likely don't. Depending on the plan, a portion of your income will be replaced for a set amount of time if you cannot work. You may need to purchase additional coverage on your own to fill in the blanks. ("Do I need disability insurance? What's the best way to buy it?" on page 265 has more details).

· **The retirement plan.** If your employer offers a retirement plan, you'll want to enroll as soon as possible and contribute at least enough to catch any matching dollars offered. The goal is to max it out each year if you can swing it. And if you already had a 401(k) plan at your previous job, be sure to roll that over into an IRA or into your new employer's plan instead of cashing it out. Doing the latter, assuming you're younger than 59½, could cause you to lose 30% to 40% of every dollar in penalties and taxes.

One final note: Don't forget to inquire about and take advantage of other employee benefits that can increase your bottom line. Small things add up fast, so if your new job's building has a fitness center and you can cancel your current gym membership, go for it. Other things to look out for: the option to telecommute, which could save gas; tuition reimbursement; concierge services or discounts on things such as car rentals; and flexible spending accounts, which allow you to pay for child care and some health-care expenses with pretax dollars.

I Also Need to Know . . .

Q: **I turned down a benefit, and now I regret it. Can I change my mind?**

A: Most companies allow you to add, drop, or change your benefits for the following year—including insurance and the retirement plan—during a period of time called open enrollment, which usually falls in the fourth quarter. The process is simple, and even if you have no regrets about the choices you made originally, you should go back over your benefits just to be sure. It's possible that the health plan you enrolled in has changed (even in price) or that new options have been added that are more lucrative.

Q: **What if my work-based health plan is too pricey?**

A: If the coverage that your employer offers becomes too expensive, look elsewhere. Most people assume that group plans are always cheaper, but that's not always the case: Because they are obligated to accept everyone, the premiums (if you're healthy) are often more than you'd pay on the open market. In five states—Maine, Massachusetts, New Jersey, New York, and Vermont—individual health insurance is expensive because insurers are required to give coverage to everyone, regardless of their health. This drives up the price across the board.

But if you live in one of the remaining 45 states and you're healthy, you can often find a policy on your own that is less expensive than what you would pay for your group plan at work. One of the best places to start shopping is eHealthInsurance.com, which will take your information and generate a few quotes on the spot. Compare those with what your group plan charges you—after any contribution from your employer—and see which option is less expensive.

For in-depth information on shopping for an individual plan, turn to "How do I buy my own health insurance?" on page 244.

128. We're getting married! How do we chart a good financial course?

A: · **Talk money.** You should ask the following questions about your beloved's financial life. What do you own? What do you earn? What do you owe? And what do you spend? *These are personal questions,* I hear you arguing. Yes, they're personal, but so is marriage. And not being willing to share this information with the person with whom you've chosen to share your life is the leading reason that so many marriages end up in divorce. Why? If your spouse-to-be has a lot of undisclosed debt (and the shaky credit report that goes with it), that's not information that you want to learn only when you apply for a mortgage and are denied.

· **Talk goals.** The money conversation is the hard one. *This* conversation is fun. When you are talking about your goals, you are sharing your dreams for the future. Where do you envision living? What kind of house would you like to own? How many children would you like to have, and when? When do you think you might retire? You may not think of these as financial questions, but every one of them has a price tag. And knowing that your spouse's priorities are in sync with yours will help you work together to amass the funds you need to achieve them. For help, see "How do I save for a goal?" on page 54).

• **Talk tactics.** Before the wedding you should have discussed how you're going to merge your finances. Will you keep separate accounts, have one joint account, or use a combination of both? I'm a fan of this last approach. For more, turn to "Should my mate and I have separate or joint bank accounts?" on page 406.

• **Talk benefits.** In fact, do more than talk. You and your soon-to-be spouse should conduct a benefits audit to figure out if it makes sense for you to swap your two single health plans for a family plan from one of your employers. This swap works best if one spouse works at a company where the employee contribution is small. You could save hundreds of dollars.

• **Talk savings.** You should also look at everything else that you pay for separately and see if those things can be bundled. If you didn't live together before you walked down the aisle, you're going to now, and that means one rent or mortgage payment instead of two, and a significant decrease in utilities. You may want to get a joint cell phone plan, so that you can share minutes and talk to each other for free, or start commuting together if it's convenient to save on gas (you might even be able to get rid of a car, depending on where you live and how much you drive).

I Also Need to Know . . .

Q: Should we file our taxes jointly or separately?

A: If you get married at any point within a year, you're considered married for the whole year in the eyes of the IRS. That means that you can no longer file as single. Instead, your options are married filing jointly or married filing separately. Most couples benefit from filing jointly. If you don't file jointly, you'll lose some big tax deductions, such as the one that allows you to write off student-loan interest.

There is, however, one instance where you might benefit from filing married filing separately: if one of you has a great deal of medical expenses. That's because you can deduct medical expenses only when their total exceeds 7.5% of your adjusted gross income. It's much easier to reach that mark on one income instead of two.

My advice? If you're confused about which scenario puts you on top, have your accountant run the numbers for you, or use an online tax software program such as TurboTax to run both scenarios on your own.

Q: **What about the marriage tax penalty?**

A: Getting married used to hit your wallet when it came to taxes, particularly for couples who earned comparable incomes. But for the most part, this scenario has been phased out by Congress over the years, and it really isn't a concern. In fact, there can be a tax benefit to getting married, particularly if you have disparate incomes. The lower earner's income can help drag the higher earner into a less-expensive tax bracket.

THE MATH

Joe and Susan get married. Joe makes $90,000 a year as a lawyer, and Mary, a teacher, brings in $35,000. As a single filer, Joe would pay about $18,000 in taxes. Susan, however, would pay only $3,500 in taxes.

As a married couple, they can now file together, which means Mary's income will drag Joe's down into a lower tax bracket. With a combined income of $125,000, their total tax liability would be about $19,500, saving them $2,000 in taxes.

Q: **Do I need to change my retirement planning strategy?**

A: At the very least, you should add your new spouse as your account beneficiary. That way, if you die, the money in those accounts will go to him or her. The beneficiary designation on your retirement accounts overrules your will.

You should also think about your investment strategy as a combined effort, even though you have separate retirement accounts. Try to diversify your investments not only within your individual accounts but also between each other's accounts. You'll at least reduce the risk of both portfolios taking a huge hit at the same time.

129. How can I prepare financially for a baby?

A: Bringing a child into the world means two things, financially speaking: You need to prepare for the future, and you're going to have more and different expenses than ever before. Although these two issues affect each other—having more expenses today means having less money to save for tomorrow—let's tackle each separately.

Preparing for your child's future requires the following:

· **Crafting a basic estate plan.** Once you are a parent, you need a will. It's the only document that allows you to name guardians for your child. And while you're at it, prepare a living will and durable powers of attorney for health care and finance. To read more about all three of these, turn to pages 85.

· **Getting the right insurance.** You'll need to make the necessary changes to your health insurance, so that the child's medical expenses are covered. If you're married and both you and your spouse have health insurance, look over the policies to see which provides the best coverage and value for the child. If you don't have health insurance, each state has a program that provides free or low-cost health insurance for children. Eligibility rules vary by state, but you can find out more about your state's program by visiting www.insurekidsnow.gov. You should also look into inexpensive term life insurance so that if something happens to you or your spouse, a pool of money would replace that income and enable you to support the child (for more information, see page 85).

· **Thinking about college.** Notice, I didn't write "saving for college." You're not there yet if you're not steadily saving for your own retirement. There is plenty of financial aid for college, but no one is going to finance your retirement. So max out your 401(k) contribution at work, or at least contribute enough to grab your employer's matching dollars, and then open a Roth IRA. It will allow you to pay for your own retirement, as well as—or instead of—college. If you're on track to a great retirement nest egg by the time your kid reaches his senior year in high school, you can pull money out of that Roth to help him pay tuition.

If you still have money left over, you can open a 529 plan, which will help you save for college in a tax-advantaged way. While you're at it, sign up for an account with a company like UPromise, which will deposit a percentage of your everyday purchases into that 529 plan to boost your balance. (There are various companies that do this; UPromise is just the best known. On page 221, I've put together a chart that compares the company with its competitors so that you can find the perfect fit.)

Budgeting for having a child means tackling the following list:

- **Use your pregnancy to save.** Pregnancy (I know, I've been there) is a long nine months. Use it to sock away as much as you can in additional savings. And if you're thinking that you or your partner would like to stay home with the child after the birth, try to live on the single remaining income during the pregnancy. Why? This regimen not only allows you to supercharge your savings but also shows you whether you can make the one-earner model work.
- **Run the new numbers.** Adding a child to the mix can add $500 a month to your expenses. Where is that money going to come from? What are you going to cut back on to stay afloat? Pregnancy is a great time to prepare a new budget. Go through line by line and ask yourself: Will I spend more or less on work clothes? Commuting? Insurance? (If you're planning to stay home, your home owner and auto insurer may be willing to give you a lower rate.) How much do I expect to spend on diapers, equipment to outfit the baby's room, child care? Ask a friend who's been through the experience recently to share how it's impacted his or her finances.
- **Claim the child tax credit.** Some of these new-to-you expenses will be offset by the child tax credit. Married couples who file jointly, have one child, and earn no more than $110,00 a year can claim $1,000 annually, in addition to the $3,500 exemption that you can claim for each dependent.

BUDGETING WORKSHEET FOR NEW PARENTS

A. Child Care

Amount you expect to pay for regular child care: $_____/month

Amount you expect to pay for an occasional babysitter: $_____/month

Total: $_____ × 12 = $_____/year

B. Supplies:

Amount you expect to pay for diapers: $_____/month

Tip: Ask friends for estimates that are based on their experience, as costs vary. Note that cloth diapers are considerably cheaper than disposable, particularly if you wash them yourself. You can save almost 75% that way.

Amount you expect to pay for wipes: $_____/month

Amount you expect to pay for clothing: $_____/month

Tip: Budget about $50 a month for this, and be on the lookout for hand-me-downs from friends. Babies grow fast!

Amount you expect to spend for formula: $_____/month

Tip: This isn't a news flash, but breastfeeding is cheaper!

Amount you expect to spend on baby food: $_____/month

Amount you expect to spend on medicine: $_____/month

Tip: Shoot high here—at least $20 a month. We all hope our baby is healthy, but plan for the worst just in case.

Amount you expect to spend on bath essentials: $_____/month

Amount you'd like to budget for extras (toys, etc.): $_____/month

Total: $_____ × 12 = $_____/year

C. Other Costs:

These are things that you'll generally have to buy only once.

Stroller	$_____
Car seat	$_____
Baby backpack or carrier	$_____
Diaper bag	$_____
Bouncy seat	$_____
Crib	$_____
Blankets and sheets	$_____

Bassinet	$_____
Nursery monitor	$_____
Changing table	$_____
Bottles	$_____
High chair	$_____
Bibs	$_____
Plates, bowls, and other utensils	$_____
Breast pump	$_____
Baby bathtub	$_____
Safety supplies for your home	$_____
Total	$_____

D. Add together the totals for A, B, and C to get the total budget for the year: $_____

Finally, because I don't like surprises—and there are always surprises when it comes to children—I'd up the total by 10% or 15% just to be safe. That way, you have a bit of wiggle room.

Sources: BabyCenter.com and personal parenting experience.

I Also Need to Know . . .

Q: Any money-saving tips?

A: As a parent of two children myself, I have tons of them. First of all, borrow, borrow, borrow. If you have friends who were recently pregnant, many of them will happily lend you maternity clothes as well as hand-me-downs for the baby when the time comes. You can give them back when your baby outgrows them, pass them on to someone else, or keep them if you plan on having more children. You can also buy great clothes from consignment or used-clothing stores, which seem to be popping up more and more these days. Children outgrow their clothes so fast that it doesn't make sense to splurge. And don't forget that you'll likely receive lots of nice gifts from friends and family members. In fact, I'd hold off on any purchases you might make on your own until after your baby shower.

Q: **I've heard people talk about flexible spending plans. What are they?**

A: Flexible spending plans are accounts that you open through your employer and fund with pretax dollars. You can then use the money to pay for expenses such as over-the-counter medicines and child care. If you pay for your child care through your flexible spending account, for example, you can cut the cost by 25% or more, because of the tax savings.

There are three types of flexible spending accounts: Health Care Flexible Spending Accounts (HCFSAs), which can be used only for qualified medical expenses; Limited Expense Health Care Flexible Spending Accounts (LEX HCFSAs), which can be used only for qualified dental and vision-care expenses; and Dependent Care Flexible Spending Accounts (DCFSAs), which are used to pay for child-care costs that are necessary so you or your spouse can work or attend school. You cannot have both an HCFSA and a LEX HCFSA. You must elect one or the other.

To find out if your employer participates in this federal program, ask the human resources department. If your employer does participate, you can enroll during the federal benefits open season, which is held each year in November and December. You have to reenroll every year if you want to continue having these accounts, and any money not used during the year will be lost. You must calculate how much you think you'll spend and then deposit only that much—or even a little less. If you end up forfeiting money, you could negate any tax benefits of contributing.

Q: **Is there a limit on how much I can contribute to a flexible spending account?**

A: Yes, there are annual maximums. You can contribute up to $5,000 for the HCFSA or $5,000 for the LEX HCFSA. The DCFSA allows a contribution of up to $5,000 per household or $2,500 per person if you're married, filing separately. All accounts require you to contribute at least $250.

130. What financial steps are needed when there's a death in the family, particularly of a parent or partner?

A: When a member of your immediate family passes away, you're left with not only grief but also a lengthy list of things to do.

It's important to prioritize. Some things must be done right away, but others can be put off for a while. This sort of loss is overwhelming enough without piling on unnecessary pressure. I'm highlighting the big stuff here. On page 435, I provide a checklist of sorts that you can follow to make sure everything in the larger picture is covered as well.

In the Case of a Parent

If this was your last surviving parent and he or she never remarried, you (and your siblings, if you have any) are going to be in charge of closing out your parent's affairs. You will have to phone friends and family members to inform them of the death. You should bring in other family members to help spread the word and to get back to people with information once the funeral is planned. If your parent left specific instructions for a funeral, follow those. It's not only respectful but it will also make decisions much easier. If there are no instructions, contact a funeral director and put together a service that you and other family members feel is fitting. A funeral director can also help you write an obituary and provide you with original copies of the death certificate. I suggest getting 10 certificates, because you'll need them for financial institutions that will require proof of death, and copies won't suffice.

Then, you want to secure your parent's property and belongings and make sure that all the insurance policies—particularly homeowner's—are paid up (if something were to happen—a fire, for instance—and the policy had lapsed, you could lose a great deal of the estate).

Next, complete an inventory of assets and liabilities. If your parent had a will (fingers crossed), it should name an executor, and if it's you, you're responsible for completing this inventory (though an estate-planning attorney can assist), as well as for taking care of any debt that needs to be paid off from your parent's estate. You'll also have to file the life insurance claim, divvy up the remaining assets according to the will, and notify any sources of income your parent had (Social Security benefits or a pension, for instance) that he or she has passed away. It's important to do so within a few days of death. (Note: if there is no will, the laws vary by state, but typically a court hearing will appoint someone to this post.)

If there is a surviving spouse—your other parent or a stepparent—that person is going to have to redo three important documents: his or her will, his or her durable power of attorney for finances, and his or her health-care proxy. For detailed information about how to help him or her do these things, turn to the question "How do I write a will?" on page 83. He or she will also have to update the beneficiary designation on any retirement accounts and life insurance policies.

If a Partner Dies

Many rules are the same. You still have to phone friends and family members, of course, and work with a funeral director to carry out plans for the service, if your partner wanted one. You'll also need to contact your partner's employer, bank, lenders, and insurance providers.

If he or she had life insurance, contact the company about your benefits. To do so, you'll need copies of your marriage certificate or certificate of domestic partnership (if either applies in your situation), which you can get from the county clerk's office or city clerk's office that issued it.

You'll also have to switch the ownership of things—the cars, the insurance policies, the house, bank accounts, and credit cards—into your name only.

And don't forget to redo your own will, durable power of attorney for finances, and health-care proxy, and be sure to update your beneficiary designations.

CHECKLIST: WHAT TO DO WHEN A PARENT DIES

- Notify family and friends
- Arrange care for dependents and pets, if any
- Secure the parent's home, if empty, and belongings (many security experts advise having someone stay at the home during the funeral)
- Have the parent's mail held for a week or two to give yourself time to catch up

- Review the parent's funeral wishes and discuss them with the funeral director to arrange for a service and burial or cremation
- Obtain 10 copies of the original death certificate
- Write and send an obituary to relevant newspapers
- Keep close records of all expenses and time spent (if you are the executor, you can choose to be paid by the estate for your time)
- Locate wills, trusts, life insurance policies, and safe-deposit boxes
- Locate other important documents that outline investments, debt, insurance, and bank accounts (if the parent has a financial advisor, call him or her for this information)
- Notify the Social Security Administration, Medicaid, and former or current employer if parent was receiving a salary or pension
- Investigate Social Security and life insurance benefits
- Deal with insurance on parent's property, including home and vehicle
- Prepare an inventory of assets, accounts, and debts
- Cancel credit cards and charge accounts
- Obtain appraisal of assets, if necessary

Source: Health and Elder Law Programs (H.E.L.P.; www.help4srs.org).

I Also Need to Know . . .

Q: Am I responsible for my parent's debt after he or she passes away?

A: No. To the extent that your parent's estate can pay off the debt, you'll have to make good. But if it's not enough, a creditor cannot require you to dip into your own assets, nor should you feel obligated to do so. This includes any life insurance settlements that were paid out to you. Creditors can't make a claim on that.

The creditor will, though, likely ask for documentation from the court that proves that the assets of the estate are not enough to satisfy the debt. Credit card companies have special departments that deal with this situation, and they're well versed in it.

Q: I am the executor of my parent's estate, and my siblings are already arguing. What should I do?

A: Money can polarize families like nothing else, and unfortunately, it's hard to see it coming. But you must remember—and your siblings must too—that you're not making any decisions here; you're merely carrying out decisions that were already made by your parent. The will is the final answer, and you should feel free to contact the attorney who helped your parent draw it up. He or she is knowledgeable about the terms and legal language and should be able to help you sort things out.

The potential for this rancor is why it's so important that when writing your own will and choosing your own executor, you choose only one person, someone whom you know can manage conflict well. You should also make it clear how you want assets to be divvied up, and I mean everything from the bank accounts to your favorite chair, which may have sentimental value to your family members.

Resources

Associations

Books

The AARP Crash Course in Estate Planning: The Essential Guide to Wills, Trusts, and Your Personal Legacy, by Michael Palermo (2008)
Covers every aspect of planning an estate and a will.

A Guide to Elder Planning: Everything You Need to Know to Protect Yourself Legally and Financially, by Steve Weisman (2003)
A guide for elders and their children on how to handle the legal and financial issues that accompany aging.

Government Agencies

Internal Revenue Service
www.irs.gov
1-800-829-1040
Research the tax advantages of owning a home.

Federal Flexible Spending Account program
www.fsafeds.com
1-877-372-3337

Detailed information on the Federal Flexible Spending Account program; use the Web site to determine eligibility, access forms, and enroll in the program.

Web Sites

AARP
www.aarp.org/families/end_life/
1-888-687-2277

Visit AARP's End of Life section for information on issues surrounding aging for both elders and their families. Includes tips on estate planning, caregiving, and legal issues, as well as how to handle the emotional aspect of a loss.

H.E.L.P.
www.help4srs.org
310-533-1996

A nonprofit education and counseling service created to help older adults and their families deal with elder care, law, finances and more; the group's Web site features information on issues affecting elders and their families, a schedule of free informational classes, and more.

National Endowment for Financial Education
www.nefe.org
303-741-6333

An independent, nonprofit foundation whose Web site features financial news, resources, research, and more.

SmartAboutMoney.org
www.smartaboutmoney.org
303-741-6333

An independent, nonprofit foundation, the National Endowment for Financial Education hosts the SmartAboutMoney.org Web site to provide Americans with information on a broad range of financial topics.

ACKNOWLEDGMENTS

This book would not exist without its corresponding series on *TODAY*. For that series, we thank Rachel DeLima, who pushed it forward; Jim Bell and Marc Victor, who gave it the green light; Jackie Levin, who gave it her full support; Amanda Mortimer, Lindsay Sobel, Amanda Avery, and Gil Reisfield, who worked with Rachel to produce it; Al Roker, Ann Curry, Natalie Morales, and Amy Robach, who fielded the questions; David Bach, Carmen Wong Ulrich, and Sharon Epperson, who rounded out the panel; and Don Nash and Joe Michaels, who cheered it on.

As always, we are greatly indebted to our incredible sources. For this book, as for the Money 911 series on *TODAY*, big thanks go out to: Gail Cunningham, VP public relations, NFCC; Gerri Detweiler, credit advisor, Credit.com; Charles Phelan, founder, Zipdebt.com; John Ulzheimer, credit expert, Credit.com; Asheesh Advani, former CEO of Virgin Money; Greg McBride, senior financial analyst, Bankrate.com; Stephen Elias, attorney and author of *Special Needs Trusts: Protect Your Child's Financial Future and How to File for Chapter 7 Bankruptcy*; Henry Sommer, president, the National Association of Consumer Bankruptcy Attorneys, and supervising attorney, Consumer Bankruptcy Assistance Project; Pam Villarreal, senior policy analyst, National Center for Policy Analysis; Robin Davis, CFP and author of *Who's Sitting on Your Nest Egg?*; Art Spinella, president, CNW Research; Lois Liberman, matrimonial attorney in New York; Cathy Middleton-Lewis, attorney and author of *Girl, Get That Child Support*; Brette McWhorter Sember, author of *The Complete Divorce Handbook*; Kal Chany, founder of Campus Consultants and author of *Paying for College Without Going Broke*; Barbara Blouin, cofounder, *The Inheritance Project*; Mark Eskin of Janney Montgomery Scott; Doug Roberts, founder, Channel Capital Research Institute and author of *Follow the Fed to Investing Success*; Liz Pulliam Weston, author of *Easy Money*; Alicia Rockmore, cofounder, Get Buttoned Up and coauthor of *Everything (Almost) in Its Place*; Ross Levin, founding principal of Accredited Investors Inc. and author of *The Wealth Management Index*; Ted Beck, president and CEO, the National Endowment for Financial Education; Peter Greenberg, author of *The Travel Detective* series and *Don't Go There!*; Olivia Mellan, psychotherapist and founder of Money Harmony; Stephen Rhatigan, estate and special needs planner, Stedmark Associates; Todd Gentry, CFP and MetDESK Specialist (MetLife's division of Estate Planning for Special Needs Kids); Betsy Broder, assistant director, FTC's Division of Privacy and Identity Protection; Scott Mitic, ID theft expert and CEO, TrustedID; Jay Foley, executive director, Identity Theft Resource Center; April Benson, author of *Stopping Overshopping*; Robert Hobbs, deputy director, National Consumer Law Center; Alexis McGee, president, foreclosures.com; Barbara Corcoran, real estate expert and author of *Nextville: Amazing Places to Live the Rest of Your Life*; Mark Kantrowitz, founder, FinAid.org; Joe Hurley, founder, Savingforcollege.com; Robert Franek, Princeton Review; Amy Danise, editor, Insure.com; Jack Hungelmann, author of *Insurance for Dummies*; Michelle Katz, author of *Healthcare for Less* and *101 Healthcare Tips*; Christine Fahlund, senior financial planner, T. Rowe Price; Mac Hisey, president, AARP Financial; Bill Losey, CFP and retirement expert; Anja Winikka, editor, TheKnot.com; Dr. Robert Butler, president and CEO, International Longevity Center; Marc Savitt, president, National Association of Mortgage Brokers; Faith Schwartz, executive director, Hope Now; Steve Weisman, attorney and author of *A Guide To Elder Planning* and *The Truth About Avoiding Scams*; Michael T. Palermo, CFP, attorney and author of *AARP Crash Course in Estate Planning*; Dennis Genord, director of education and chapter development, National Association of Investors Corporation; Dick Gaylord, 2009 immediate past president, National Association of Realtors; Michael Malkasian, president, FSBO.com; Sheryl Garrett, founder, Garrett Planning Network and author of *Personal Finance Workbook for Dummies*; Peter Post, director, Emily Post Institute; Paul Golden, spokesperson, National Endowment for Financial Education; Ric Edelman, author of *Rescue Your Money*; John Rother, policy director, AARP; Thomas Ochsenschlager, CPA and VP of taxation, American Institute of Certified Public Accountants; Ed Slott, IRA expert and founder, IRAhelp.com; Ken Berger, president and CEO, CharityNavigator.org; David Reed, author of *Mortgages 101*; William J. Bernstein, author of *The Four Pillars of Investing: Lessons for Building a Winning Portfolio*; Miriam Arond, director, Good Housekeeping Research Institute; Dr. Steven Weisbart, senior vice president and chief economist, Insurance Information Institute; Jeff Yeager, author of *The Ultimate Cheapskate*; Phillip Reed, Edmunds .com; Jon and Eileen Gallo, authors of *The Financially Intelligent Parent: 8 Steps to Raising Successful, Generous, Responsible Children*; Dr. Pamela York Klainer, executive coach and workplace consultant, Klainer Consulting; Allison O'Kelly, CEO, Mom Corps; Tory Johnson, CEO, Women for Hire; Donald Asher, career expert and author of *From College to Career*; Melissa Stanton, author of *The Stay at Home Survival Guide*.

The team at Harper: Ben Loehnen, Carrie Kania, Cal Morgan, Jen Hart, Alberto Rojas, Teresa Brady, Matthew Inman, and Hollis Heimbouch.

And, for their help with this project and all we do: Michael Falcon, Richard Pine, Richard Leibner, Adam Leibner, Sarah Compo, David Rollert, Lisa Manganello, Rob Densen, John St. Augustine, Gary Koops and the crew at Burson Marsteller, Chris O'Shea, Eliot Kaplan, Elaine Sherman, Jake Chatzky, and Julia Chatzky.

ACKNOWLEDGMENTS

INDEX

INDEX

INDEX

INDEX

repayment plans
  mortgage, 206, 208
  student loan, 216–218
replacement-cost insurance coverage, 268, 271, 273–274
repossession, impact on credit report, 47
Residential Energy Services Network, 142
restaurants
  avoiding arguments about paying, 71
  paying on dates, 71
  separate checks, 70, 71
  splitting checks, 69–71
  tipping, 67, 68–69
RetailMeNot.com, 63–64, 122, 126
retirement, 282–331
  discounts for retirees, 270, 277
  life expectancy, 299–300, 311, 313, 323–326, 330
  location for, 313–314
  paying off mortgage prior to, 172, 177–178
  resources, 326–331
  reverse mortgages, 174–177
  saving for, 307–311, 325–326
  Social Security Disability Coverage (SSDI), 267
  spending during, 311–313
  working during, 310, 318–319
retirement plans
  age and contributions, 287–288
  annuities, 294–296
  beneficiary designation, 84, 87
  college savings versus, 218
  distributions, 297–300, 306–307
  employer stock in, 302–303
  increasing contributions, 304–305
  life insurance versus, 261
  lump-sum retirement distributions, 306–307
  marriage planning, 428–429
  matching funds, 173, 282, 285–286, 303–306
  for self-employed persons, 291–294
  spousal benefits, 288–291

starting a new job, 425
types, 282–290
vesting, 303
See also specific types
reverse mortgages, 174–177, 209
reward programs
  college savings, 220–222
  credit card, 72–73, 151, 220–222
riders, insurance, 272, 273–274
RolloverSystems, 330
Roth 401(k) plans, 286, 429
Roth IRAs, 173, 220, 282, 283, 285–286, 287, 289, 291, 304, 429–430

safe-deposit boxes
  document retention, 60
  insurance for contents, 61–62
safes
  for document retention, 60, 61
  types, 61
Salary.com, 368, 369, 390
salvage title, 45
Salvation Army, 395
Sam's Club, 124
sandwich generation, 325–326
Savingforcollege.com, 228, 236
savings
  on airline fares, 62–63, 64
  on car rentals, 63–64
  of children, 335–337
  college student budgets, 130
  credit card debt versus, 164–165
  goals, 8–9, 49, 54–56, 118–119
  on hotels, 63
  marriage planning, 427
  recent college graduates, 422–423
  retirement, 307–311
  tax refunds and, 345–347
  tips for increasing, 54–55, 58
  utilities, 142–147
  See also emergency funds; shopping
savings accounts
  automatic transfers, 54, 58
  for college, 218–223, 227–229, 284
  emergency funds, 49
  529 plans, 218–219, 227–229, 284, 429